# SWINDOLL'S

## NEW TESTAMENT

# INSIGHTS

INSIGHTS ON

## ROMANS

# CHARLES R. SWINDOLL

# SWINDOLL'S

## NEW TESTAMENT

# INSIGHTS

### INSIGHTS ON
## ROMANS

ZONDERVAN®

ZONDERVAN.com/
AUTHORTRACKER
*follow your favorite authors*

ZONDERVAN

*Insights on Romans*
Copyright © 2010 by Charles R. Swindoll

This title is also available as a Zondervan ebook. Visit www.zondervan.com/ebooks.

Requests for information should be addressed to:
Zondervan, *Grand Rapids, Michigan 49530*

Library of Congress Cataloging-in-Publication Data
   Swindoll, Charles R.
      Insights on Romans / Charles R. Swindoll
         p. cm. (Swindoll's New Testament insights)
         ISBN 978-0-310-28430-7 (hardcover)
         1. Bible. N.T. Romans—Criticism, interpretation, etc. I. Title.
      BS2665.52.S95 2009
      227'.1077—dc22                      2009000846

Published in association with Yates & Yates, www.yates2.com.

*Maps by International Mapping*

*Cover and interior design by Sherri Hoffman*

*Printed in the United States of America*

09 10 11 12 13 14 15 • 15 14 13 12 11 10 9 8 7 6 5 4 3 2 1

# CONTENTS

Author's Preface . . . . . . . . . . . . . . . . . . . . . . . . . . . . . . .7

Introduction to Romans . . . . . . . . . . . . . . . . . . . . . . . . .11

Commentary on Romans . . . . . . . . . . . . . . . . . . . . . . . . .21

    Salutation (1:1–17) . . . . . . . . . . . . . . . . . . . . . . . . . . .21

    The Wrath of God (1:18–3:20) . . . . . . . . . . . . . . . . . .36

    The Grace of God (3:21–5:21) . . . . . . . . . . . . . . . . . .77

    The Faithfulness of God (6:1–8:39) . . . . . . . . . . . . .127

    The Majesty of God (9:1–11:36) . . . . . . . . . . . . . . . .184

    The Righteousness of God (12:1–15:13). . . . . . . . . . .242

    The Community of God (15:14–16:27) . . . . . . . . . . .309

List of Maps, Charts, and Pictures

    Map of Eastern Roman Empire . . . . . . . . . . . . . . . . . .10

    Major Themes of Romans . . . . . . . . . . . . . . . . . . 12–13

    Map of Territory Covered by Paul . . . . . . . . . . . . . . . .14

    The Gospel of Christ and the Pax Romana . . . . . . . . . .18

    Old Testament References in Romans . . . . . . . . . . 26–27

    Ruins of Ancient Corinth. . . . . . . . . . . . . . . . . . . . . 46

    Balance of Justice . . . . . . . . . . . . . . . . . . . . . . . . . . .54

    As It Is Written. . . . . . . . . . . . . . . . . . . . . . . . . . . .70

    Bēma in Corinth . . . . . . . . . . . . . . . . . . . . . . . . . . .82

    "In Christ" in Romans . . . . . . . . . . . . . . . . . . . . . . .145

    The Promised Land in Old Testament Times. . . . . . . .198

    The Remnant. . . . . . . . . . . . . . . . . . . . . . . . . . . . .216

    Grafting. . . . . . . . . . . . . . . . . . . . . . . . . . . . . . . . .228

    Spiritual Gifts Listed in Scripture. . . . . . . . . . . . . . . .251

    Location of Corinth . . . . . . . . . . . . . . . . . . . . . . . .284

    Paul's Missionary Strategy . . . . . . . . . . . . . . . . . . . .318

# AUTHOR'S PREFACE

For almost sixty years I have loved the Bible. It was that love for the Scriptures, mixed with a clear call into the gospel ministry during my tour of duty in the Marine Corps, that resulted in my going to Dallas Theological Seminary to prepare for a lifetime of ministry. During those four great years I had the privilege of studying under outstanding men of God, who also loved God's Word. They not only held the inerrant Word of God in high esteem, they taught it carefully, preached it passionately, and modeled it consistently. A week never passes without my giving thanks to God for the grand heritage that has been mine to claim! I am forever indebted to those fine theologians and mentors, who cultivated in me a strong commitment to the understanding, exposition, and application of God's truth.

For more than forty-five years I have been engaged in doing just that—*and how I love it!* I confess without hesitation that I am addicted to the examination and the proclamation of the Scriptures. Because of this, books have played a major role in my life for as long as I have been in ministry—especially those volumes that explain the truths and enhance my understanding of what God has written. Through these many years I have collected a large personal library, which has proven invaluable as I have sought to remain a faithful student of the Bible. To the end of my days, my major goal in life is to communicate the Word with accuracy, insight, clarity, and practicality. Without resourceful and reliable books to turn to, I would have "run dry" decades ago.

Among my favorite and most well-worn volumes are those that have enabled me to get a better grasp of the biblical text. Like most expositors, I am forever searching for literary tools that I can use to hone my gifts and sharpen my skills. For me, that means finding resources that make the complicated simple and easy to understand, that offer insightful comments and word pictures that enable me to see the relevance of sacred truth in light of my twenty-first-century world, and that drive those truths home to my heart in ways I do not easily forget. When I come across such books, they wind up in my hands as I devour them and then place them in my library for further reference … and, believe me, I often return to them. What a relief it is to have these resourceful works to turn to when I lack fresh insight, or when I need just the right story or illustration, or when I get stuck in the tangled text and cannot find my way out. For the serious expositor, a library is essential. As a mentor of mine once said, *"Where else can you have 10,000 professors at your fingertips?"*

In recent years I have discovered there are not nearly enough resources like those I just described. It was such a discovery that prompted me to consider becoming a part of the answer instead of lamenting the problem. But the solution would result in a huge undertaking. A writing project that covers all of the books and letters of the New Testament seemed overwhelming and intimidating. A rush of relief came when I realized that during the past forty-five-plus years I've taught and preached through most of the New Testament. In my files were folders filled with notes from those messages that were just lying there, waiting to be brought out of hiding, given a fresh and relevant touch in light of today's needs, and applied to fit into the lives of men and women who long for a fresh word from the Lord. *That did it!* I began to pursue the best publisher to turn my dream into reality.

Thanks to the hard work of my literary agents, Sealy and Matt Yates, I located a publisher interested in taking on a project this extensive. I thank the fine people at Zondervan Publishing House for their enthusiastic support of this multivolume venture that will require over ten years to complete. Having met most of them over the years through other written works I've authored, I knew they were qualified to handle such an undertaking and would be good stewards of my material, staying with the task of getting all of it into print. I am grateful for the confidence and encouragement of both Stan Gundry and Paul Engle, who have remained loyal and helpful from the beginning. It is also a pleasure to work alongside Verlyn Verbrugge; I sincerely appreciate his seasoned wisdom and keen-eyed assistance.

It has also been especially delightful to work, again, with my longtime friend and former editor, John Sloan. He has provided invaluable counsel as my general editor. Best of all has been John's enthusiastic support. I must also express my gratitude to both Mark Gaither and Mike Svigel for their tireless and devoted efforts, serving as my hands-on, day-to-day editors. They have done superb work as we have walked our way through the verses and chapters of all twenty-seven New Testament books. It has been a pleasure to see how they have taken my original material and helped me shape it into a style that remains true to the text of the Scriptures, at the same time interestingly and creatively developed, and all the while allowing my voice to come through in a natural and easy-to-read manner.

I need to add sincere words of appreciation to the congregations I have served in various parts of these United States for almost five decades. It has been my good fortune to be the recipient of their love, support, encouragement, patience, and frequent words of affirmation as I have fulfilled my calling to stand and deliver God's message year after year. The sheep from all those flocks have endeared themselves to this shepherd in more ways than I can put into words . . . and none more than those I currently serve with delight at Stonebriar Community Church in Frisco, Texas.

Finally, I must thank my wife, Cynthia, for her understanding of my addiction to studying, to preaching, and to writing. Never has she discouraged me from staying at it. Never has she failed to urge me in the pursuit of doing my very best. On the contrary, her affectionate support personally, and her own commitment to excellence in leading *Insight for Living* for more than three decades, have combined to keep me faithful to my calling "in season and out of season." Without her devotion to me and apart from our mutual partnership throughout our lifetime of ministry together, *Swindoll's New Testament Insights* would never have been undertaken.

I am grateful that it has now found its way into your hands and, ultimately, onto the shelves of your library. My continued hope and prayer is that you will find these volumes helpful in your own study and personal application of the Bible. May they help you come to realize, as I have over these many years, that God's Word is as timeless as it is true.

The grass withers, the flower fades,
but the word of our God stands forever. (Isaiah 40:8)

Chuck Swindoll
Frisco, Texas

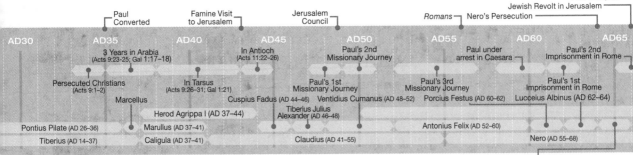

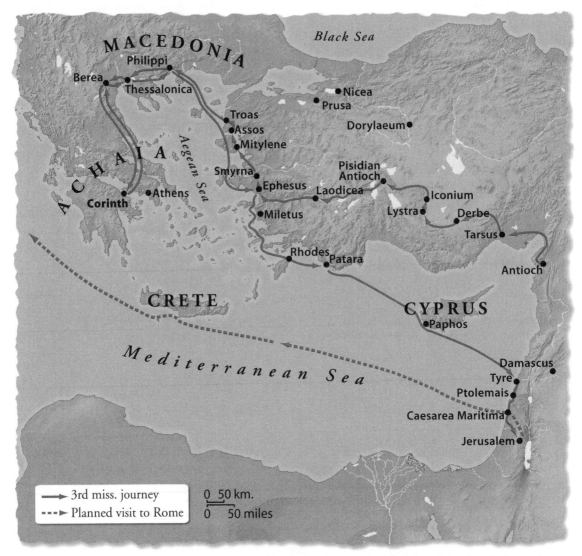

After returning to Israel from his third missionary journey, Paul visited the church leaders in Jerusalem to share the results of his ministry. Then, perhaps after a short visit with his friends in Antioch, Paul planned to sail for Rome, where he would launch his mission to the western frontier of Spain. But, as had been foretold, Paul was arrested (Acts 20:22–23). He would eventually journey to Rome ... in chains.

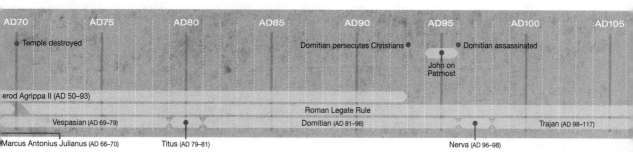

AD70    AD75    AD80    AD85    AD90    AD95    AD100    AD105

● Temple destroyed     Domitian persecutes Christians ●    ● Domitian assassinated

John on Patmost

erod Agrippa II (AD 50–93)

Roman Legate Rule

Vespasian (AD 69–79)     Domitian (AD 81–96)     Trajan (AD 98–117)

Marcus Antonius Julianus (AD 66–70)    Titus (AD 79–81)    Nerva (AD 96–98)

# ROMANS

## Introduction

Travel back in time with me. Let's go back to the winter of AD 57. We're at a narrow land bridge between mainland Greece and the Peloponnese, where a Roman city rakes in fortunes from heavy-laden ships and cash-heavy tourists. Outside the city, in the home of a wealthy and hospitable Christian named Gaius, two men discuss a scroll. One paces the room, pouring out his thoughts to the other, who sits at a large table, taking copious notes.

The speaker walks with a deliberate strength, although his shoulders are rounded and a noticeable hitch interrupts his gait. His arms and face bear the marks of wind, sun, age, and mistreatment. His fingers are knotted and curled and fused in an unnatural angle, the telltale sign of multiple stonings. You would expect that a body such as this would contain a broken, demoralized spirit, but the eyes reveal something different. They flash with energy and sparkle with the optimism of a teenager about to get his driver's license.

The city is Corinth. The one pacing the floor is Paul; his amanuensis at the table, Tertius. The document they are preparing will eventually become the apostle's letter to the church in Rome, the most significant piece of literature the Lord would ever commission His most prolific evangelist to write. Little does Paul or anyone realize the impact it will have through the centuries to come. From [Origen of Alexandria] in the [third century] to Barnhouse of Philadelphia in the twentieth, countless theologians will pen innumerable pages of exposition and meditation from the apostle's magnum opus. Augustine will find the seed plot of his

# Major Themes of Romans

| Section | Salutation | The Wrath of God | The Grace of God |
|---|---|---|---|
| **Themes** | Paul's calling and plans<br><br>The identity of Christ<br><br>The gospel<br><br>Faith<br><br>"Righteousness of God" | "Righteousness of God"<br><br>The moral failure of humanity<br><br>God's judicial abandonment of humanity<br><br>Humanity's hopelessness and eternal peril | "Righteousness of God"<br><br>Powerlessness of Works<br><br>Justification through Faith<br><br>Grace/Free Gift<br><br>Reconciliation |
| **Key Terms** | Apostle<br><br>Gospel<br><br>Faith<br><br>Salvation<br><br>Righteousness | Unrighteousness<br><br>Judge<br><br>Law<br><br>Wrath<br><br>Hand over | Justify<br><br>Works/Law<br><br>Circumcision<br><br>Propitiation<br><br>Grace |
| **Passage** | 1:1–17 | 1:18–3:20 | 3:21–5:21 |

| The Faithfulness of God | The Majesty of God | The Righteousness of God | Conclusion |
|---|---|---|---|
| Righteousness | Righteousness through faith | Love | Gentiles |
| The futility of human effort | Israel in the plan of God | Civic responsibility | The gospel |
| The necessity of the Holy Spirit | The justice of God | Unity | Paul's past |
| Children/heirs of God | The sovereignty of God | Mutual judgment | Paul's future |
| Assurance of future "glory" | The plan of God | Mutual acceptance | |
| | | Joy, peace, and hope | |
| "Flesh" | Mercy | Conform | Obedience |
| Spirit | Harden | Transform | Commend |
| Sanctification | Remnant | Prove | Dissention |
| Predestined | Mystery | Accept | Hindrance |
| Glorified | | | |
| 6:1–8:39 | 9:1–11:36 | 12:1–15:13 | 15:14–16:27 |

faith in this letter. This document will spark a revolution in the heart of Martin Luther, who will reintroduce the truth of justification by grace alone, through faith alone, in Christ alone—a doctrine all but obscured by the dogma of men who stood to profit from a false gospel of works. It will ignite the mind of Jonathan Edwards, strangely warm the heart of John Wesley, and fuel the revival fire of George Whitefield.

## "CALLED AS AN APOSTLE, SET APART FOR THE GOSPEL OF GOD" (1:1)

Paul's journey to this place and time has been a winding one. Though born in the cosmopolitan hubbub of Tarsus, Paul matured in the shadow of the great temple in Jerusalem. Within its enormous, gleaming white walls, he learned at the feet of the famous rabbi Gamaliel (Acts 22:3). Though a Roman citizen (22:25–28), he

In three missionary journeys, spanning no less than fifteen years, Paul labored to evangelize the empire east of Rome—an incredibly dangerous and arduous ministry. Nevertheless, when most would retire, Paul set his sights on the untamed frontier west of Rome: northern Italy, southern France, Spain, and Portugal.

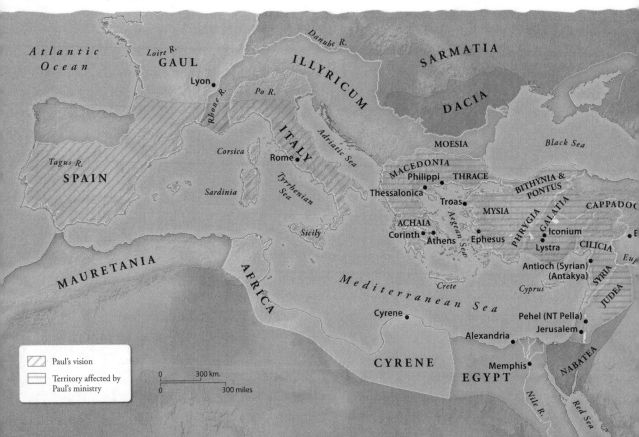

was first and foremost "a son of the covenant." He heard of the great privileges and responsibilities God had given his kindred people. He studied the law of Moses and devoted himself to fulfilling every letter of tradition. And he immersed himself in the inveterate rituals of the Pharisees with a singular goal in mind. He wanted to become like the temple itself: sacred, strong, undefiled, a worthy vessel for the righteousness of God.

But, as often happens in the lives of great men, Paul's zealous pursuit of righteousness took an unexpected turn. While on the road to Damascus in order to silence and persecute Christians, Jesus Christ confronted him, rebuked him, changed him, and then set him on a whole new course (Acts 9:3–22). The righteousness he coveted could not be found in the traditions of the Pharisees, but in the faith of the very people he sought to kill. They would show their former persecutor supernatural grace, first by embracing him, the man who had supervised the stoning of their beloved Stephen (7:58–8:1), and then by showing him the source of their goodness. They were merely passing on the righteousness they had received by grace through faith in Jesus Christ (9:13–19).

Paul's encounter with the risen Christ transformed him. His future lay not in Jerusalem and works of the law, but out among the Gentiles, preaching grace and living by faith. Instead of stamping out Christianity, he would become a tireless apostle, traveling more than twenty thousand miles between Jerusalem and Rome and proclaiming the gospel wherever ears had never heard it. Then, near the end of his third missionary journey, after what many would consider a full life in ministry, the apostle looked westward to the frontier beyond Rome (Rom. 15:24).

## "FULL OF GOODNESS, FILLED WITH ALL KNOWLEDGE AND ABLE ALSO TO ADMONISH" (15:14)

Paul had long admired the congregation in the capital city of the empire. Although he had neither founded the church in Rome nor even visited it, he shared close connections with several leading members (Rom. 16:1–15). Many had been his partners in ministry, some were cell mates in the early days of evangelism, several were the fruit of his labors in other regions. Their obedience to the Word and faithfulness to one another had become legendary among the other churches (16:19). This could not have been easy, given their unique pressures in Rome.

During the reign of Emperor Claudius (AD 41–54), the Roman government—normally tolerant of other religions—began to prohibit proselytizing. Claudius likely expelled the Jews from Rome (Acts 18:2) because Jewish Christians had been evangelizing their neighbors. But within a few years, Claudius was poisoned and his adopted heir, Nero, took his place on the throne, and he allowed Jews and Christians to return. After reclaiming their homes and reestablishing their district, the Jewish community undoubtedly pressured Christians to keep a low profile to avoid more trouble. For the first three years of Nero's reign, all was quiet. The teenaged emperor was too occupied with threats within the palace to notice much going on outside. It was during this time that Paul wrote his brothers and sisters in the capital city. Within a few months, however, Nero eliminated the source of internal danger by poisoning his mother. Then he turned his attention to winning the hearts of Roman citizens with grand festivals and massive gladiatorial spectacles.

At the time of Paul's writing, the population of Rome exceeded one million inhabitants, nearly half of whom were bond-servants and recently freed slaves. And, like modern metropolitan centers, Rome was a wonderful place to live for the elite, but challenging for everyone else. The divide between the rich and poor constantly kept city officials on edge as the lower classes were never far from rioting. Most of them lived amid rampant street crime in squalid, high-rise apartment buildings, as tall as five or six stories, with no sanitation or water available above the first floor.

The great divide between the picturesque villas of the privileged and the crime-ridden slums that comprised most of the city left the residents to fend for themselves, which they did by congregating according to race. In other words, first-century Rome was not unlike New York City during the nineteenth and twentieth centuries. Ethnic neighborhoods became governments unto themselves, vying for dominance while maintaining an uneasy peace with one another to avoid persecution by the government (Acts 18:2).

Life was hard for everyone, but being a Christian in that environment made it even worse. For both Jewish and Gentile Christians, the price of discipleship often meant the loss of family and clan, including the safety they provided. They must have felt like squirrels living among angry giants, any one of whom might decide to crush them on a whim. By AD 64, their feelings proved to be justified. Nero went mad. His persecution of the Christians became so shockingly brutal that citizens actually began to pity them. Some say the crime of the Christians that sent them to their deaths was the burning of Rome, but according to the Roman historian, Tacitus, Christians were punished "not so much for the imputed crime of burning Rome, as for their hate and enmity to human kind."[1]

This general impression of Christians—regardless of how unfair or slanderous it was—would factor heavily into the apostle's practical advice near the end of his letter.

## "MAY THE GOD OF HOPE FILL YOU WITH ALL JOY AND PEACE IN BELIEVING" (15:13)

The believers in Rome desperately needed encouragement, which this divinely inspired letter provided in three ways.

First, *the letter confirmed their understanding of the gospel and clarified what might have been confusing.* Persecution combined with isolation can cause even the most resilient mind to lose its grip on the truth. In fact, pain and seclusion are the principle tools used in the cruel art of mind control. Prisoners of war report that after several hours of torture, the human mind will accept any absurdity as absolute truth in order to end suffering.

In careful detail and with compelling clarity, Paul explained the truth of the gospel. He drew upon his formal training and the best rhetorical style of the day to present the truth of God in logical sequence. He recalled his years of preaching in synagogues and debating in markets to answer every relevant objection. And, of course, the Holy Spirit inspired the content, superintended the process of writing, and safeguarded the document from error. The believers in Rome received a complete, comprehensive, and concise proclamation of Christian truth. And the effect must have been incredibly calming.

Second, *the letter affirmed the authenticity of their faith and commended them for their obedience.* People on a long and arduous journey frequently need confirmation they are on the right course and should continue as they have been; otherwise they will grow discouraged and reduce their efforts or wander off-course. The church in Rome had long been an exemplary model of steadfast faith and authentic community. Paul encouraged them, in effect, "Keep doing what you have been doing. You're right on target!" Furthermore, the congregation in Rome, like every other church in the first century, was susceptible to the influence of false teachers. This letter equipped them to recognize the truth and to leave no room for heresy.

Third, *the letter cast a vision for the future and urged them to become Paul's partners in accomplishing it.* When churches take their eyes off the horizon, the inevitable result is what can be called a "survival mentality." Rather than accomplishing the plans of God to redeem and transform His creation, they forget their reason for being, which begins a long, agonizing slide into irrelevance. Irrelevant churches fret over inconsequential matters, nitpick their leadership, criticize one another, experiment with worldly strategies for growth, and chase vain philosophies. Meanwhile their surrounding communities hear little of Christ, and what they do hear is unattractive. Paul challenged the believers in Rome with an enormous undertaking: evangelization of the newly expanded empire to the west. It was a landmass greater than what the apostle had covered in three missionary journeys, although not nearly as tame.

## THE GOSPEL OF CHRIST AND THE *PAX ROMANA*

Historians call the first two centuries of Roman rule after the birth of Christ, the *Pax Romana* — that is, the "Roman Peace." It was peaceful in that Rome focused less on foreign conquest and more on stabilizing the lands they already ruled, but it was nevertheless a brutal peace. The Empire could quickly mobilize large armies anywhere between Rome and Persia and typi-

cally responded to insurrection with shocking cruelty. Once a revolt had been quelled, it was not uncommon for the survivors to be crucified along the roads leading into the region as a warning to new colonists.

While this "peace" was not without bloodshed, it nevertheless paved the way for Paul's evangelistic ministry … literally. To quickly move troops and commerce around the realm, the Roman government constructed an elaborate highway system, paved with stone and concrete, and regularly patrolled these roads to prevent robbery. This gave the apostle and his entourage unprecedented access to the world as they knew it. And he made the most of his opportunity, circling the Eastern Empire three times in fifteen years and logging more than twenty thousand miles, mostly on government paving and government-controlled shipping lanes.

In the end, the merciless "peace" of Rome became the means of a merciful "peace with God" (5:1) for innumerable Gentiles during Paul's lifetime, and for countless generations thereafter.

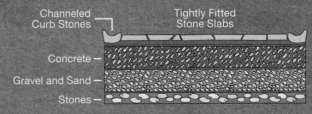

Todd Bolen/www.BiblePlaces.com

## "FOR IN IT THE RIGHTEOUSNESS OF GOD IS REVEALED FROM FAITH TO FAITH" (1:17)

Paul's letter to the believers in Rome can be called many things. Clearly, this became his magnum opus. It is the first systematic theology of the Christian faith. This letter may be considered the believer's constitution—the Christian Magna Carta. We might even call it a manifesto of the new kingdom, for it not only declares our essential beliefs, it establishes our agenda as Christ's disciples. But more than anything, the words Paul and his amanuensis, Tertius, penned twenty centuries ago are no less than the revealed Word of God. Through human agency, the Almighty Creator has breathed out, revealing a grand plan.

"The plan of salvation" outlined in this letter to Christians living in first-century Rome has more than the rescue of individuals in view. The plan of God is more than a mere fire escape through which a few find safety from the flames of eternal punishment. This grand plan—of which all are invited to become a part—is nothing less than the Creator's intention to bring His creation back under divine dominion, to cleanse it of evil, to redeem, reclaim, and renovate the universe so that it, again, reflects His glory. The plan of salvation is good news to each individual, but the greater news is the return of God's righteousness to its rightful place in the world. Some day in the future, Christ will tear the veil between heaven and earth, and the righteousness of God will sweep the "prince of the power of the air" (Eph. 2:2) from his stolen throne, and will again rule over creation. This future is inevitable because God's plan is unstoppable.

In the meantime, the righteousness of God lives in the hearts of those who have received His grace through faith in His Son, Jesus Christ. Therefore, each individual reading Paul's letter to the Romans must answer two questions. First, will you allow God's transformation of the world to begin with you? As Paul will explain, this is not an invitation to try harder, but a plea to submit to His grace before it's too late. Second, if the righteousness of God lives within you now, will you keep it hidden? If you lack knowledge, read on. The book of Romans will explain all you need to know. If you lack courage, this exhortation from an intrepid apostle to a beleaguered church in first-century Rome will revive and reinvigorate your confidence.

Whatever your situation, wherever you happen to be in your spiritual journey, I am convinced that the time you invest in a careful study of this letter will change you forever. This has been true of generations past, and the power of God's Word has not diminished over time. As you read, the Holy Spirit has pledged to provide whatever you lack. You need only believe His promise. If you submit to these truths, then you too will discover, as did Paul, that "the righteous [one] shall live by faith" (1:17).

---

NOTES: Introduction

1. Tacitus, *The Works of Tacitus*, 2nd ed. (London: Woodward and Peele, 1737), 2:698.

# SALUTATION

## Mission: The Gospel (Romans 1:1-17)

[1]Paul, a bond-servant of Christ Jesus, called *as* an apostle, set apart for the gospel of God, [2]which He promised beforehand through His prophets in the holy Scriptures, [3]concerning His Son, who was born of a descendant of David according to the flesh, [4]who was declared the Son of God with power by the resurrection from the dead, according to the Spirit of holiness, Jesus Christ our Lord, [5]through whom we have received grace and apostleship to bring about *the* obedience of faith among all the Gentiles for His name's sake, [6]among whom you also are the called of Jesus Christ; [7]to all who are beloved of God in Rome, called *as* saints: Grace to you and peace from God our Father and the Lord Jesus Christ.

[8]First, I thank my God through Jesus Christ for you all, because your faith is being proclaimed throughout the whole world. [9]For God, whom I serve in my spirit in the *preaching of the* gospel of His Son, is my witness *as to* how unceasingly I make mention of you, [10]always in my prayers making request, if perhaps now at last by the will of God I may succeed in coming to you. [11]For I long to see you so that I may impart some spiritual gift to you, that you may be established; [12]that is, that I may be encouraged together with you *while* among you, each of us by the other's faith, both yours and mine. [13]I do not want you to be unaware, brethren, that often I have planned to come to you (and have been prevented so far) so that I may obtain some fruit among you also, even as among the rest of the Gentiles. [14]I am under obligation both to Greeks and to barbarians, both to the wise and to the foolish. [15]So, for my part, I am eager to preach the gospel to you also who are in Rome.

[16]For I am not ashamed of the gospel, for it is the power of God for salvation to everyone who believes, to the Jew first and also to the Greek. [17]For in it *the* righteousness of God is revealed from faith to faith; as it is written, "But the righteous *man* shall live by faith."

---

Imagine how you would feel if you discovered a 100 percent natural, 100 percent effective, completely free cure for all types of cancer. How much of your own time, energy, and money would you expend to make this wonder cure available to as many people as possible in your lifetime?

Paul is a man on a mission. His assignment? To distribute the most precious commodity the world has ever received: the gospel, a cure formulated by God to be 100 percent effective against the terminal disease of sin. The gospel — the

## KEY TERMS

ἀπόστολος [*apostolos*] (*652*)* "apostle, sent one, official envoy, commissioner"

The New Testament uses this term borrowed from Greek government to describe both the function and the official capacity of certain men during the initial organization of Christianity. To be called an "apostle," one must have personally encountered Jesus Christ after His resurrection and received His commission to bear the good news to others.

εὐαγγέλιον [*euangelion*] (*2098*) "gospel, joyous news, good report"

This English term "gospel" comes from the Middle English compound "good-spell," where "spell" means "tale." The gospel is the "good story." The Greek term described the favorable report of a messenger from the battlefield or the official proclamation that an heir to the king had been born.

σωτηρία [*sōtēria*] (*4991*) "salvation, deliverance protection, preservation"

Most translations render this term "salvation," but the meaning should not be limited to mere rescue from danger. Once the immediate peril has passed, *sōtēria* ensures continued preservation from harm and ongoing opportunity to thrive.

δίκαιος [*dikaios*] (*1342*) "righteous one, morally impeccable, keeper of law"

The secular Greek idea of a "righteous one" is a man or woman who fulfills the requirements of civic duty, someone who is a virtuous citizen. The synagogue teachers generally regarded one as righteous if he or she did more good than bad. In this sense, someone can be more or less righteous than another, depending on how he or she conforms to social and legal norms. Paul, however, deliberately restricted its meaning to a judicial definition in which one either deserves punishment or not. In this sense, there are no degrees of righteousness.

πίστις [*pistis*] (*4102*) "faith, confidence, reliance, trust"

The secular use of this Greek term has almost no connection to religion at all, so Paul's readers would have known the word as it was used in the Septuagint (the Greek translation of the Old Testament.) The Greeks worshiped and feared their gods, but they did not have a relationship with them. For the Jew — and therefore the Christian — *pistis* is the means by which he or she related to God.

*Note: the number refers to Strong's number

*euangelion* ("good news") in his language—became the driving force of his life. And, as he is about to take this magnificent obsession to a completely different level, the apostle enlists the help of his brothers and sisters in Rome. Unfortunately, they have never met.

— **1:1** —

The first seven verses of Paul's letter form one long, complex sentence with several phrases sandwiched between "[From] Paul" (1:1) and "[to the] beloved of God in Rome" (1:7). While the ancient Greeks had no trouble understanding this style of writing, the jumbled phrases can be confusing for us. So, for the sake of simplicity, let me break it down in two ways. First, note the chart "Paul's Greeting," which we will reference later. Second, note that his greeting follows a simple outline:

## Paul's Greeting

¹Paul,
 a bond-servant of Christ Jesus,
 called as an apostle,
 set apart for the gospel of God,
  ²which He promised
    beforehand
    through His prophets
    in the holy Scriptures,
  ³concerning His Son,
    who was born
    of a descendant of David
    according to the flesh,
  ⁴who was declared the Son of God
    with power
    by the resurrection from the dead,
    according to the Spirit of holiness,
 Jesus Christ our Lord,
  ⁵through whom we have received grace and apostleship
  to bring about the obedience of faith among all the Gentiles
   for His name's sake,
    ⁶among whom you also are the called of Jesus Christ
⁷to all who are
  beloved of God in Rome,
  called as saints:
Grace to you and peace from
   God our Father
   and the Lord Jesus Christ.

Author: "Paul ..." (1:1)

Subject: Composed of several phrases foreshadowing the content of his letter (1:2–6)

Recipient: "all who are beloved of God in Rome ..." (1:7a)

Greeting: "Grace to you and peace ..." (1:7b)

The Christians in Rome knew Paul only by reputation. His ministry began a world away in Jerusalem (cf. Rom. 15:19) and stretched across most of the eastern Roman Empire, but he had not yet visited its capital city. So, few had seen the man in person. Nevertheless, his stature as a Christian leader was second to none, especially among Gentiles. So, when identifying himself, Paul could have chosen any number of different titles. He could have called himself a scholar, having been schooled by the renowned Jewish master, Gamaliel (Acts 22:3), and before that, may have attended the highly respected university in Tarsus, which was said to excel those in Athens and Alexandria. He could have called himself a Roman citizen (Acts 22:28), something rare and special among religious teachers and a title of significant influence in the capital city. He could have called attention to his personal encounter with the risen Christ (Acts 22:6–11) or his having seen, first-hand, the splendor of heaven (2 Cor. 12:2–5). Instead, he chooses a designation he considers far loftier, far more impressive than any other: *doulos Christou Iēsou*, "bond-servant of Christ Jesus."

Greeks and Romans despised servitude above all else. They would not have objected to governmental service, as long as it was voluntary, an expression of good virtue by a loyal citizen. Compulsory service, on the other hand, meant the loss of freedom, and to lose one's freedom was to lose one's dignity.[1] Similarly, Jewish culture reserved the term *doulos* for illegal or unreasonable service, such as Israel's slavery in Egypt (Ex. 13:3) and Jacob's servitude after Laban's treachery (Gen. 29:18).[2] Sometimes, *doulos* referred to those who were subject to the rule of another, such as when one ruler had to pay tribute to another, more powerful king.

No one wanted the title *doulos*, unless, of course, he or she served God. In the service of the Creator, no title could have been more prized. "Bond-servants of God" included Abraham, Moses, David, and other noteworthy heroes of faith.

Paul introduces himself by adding two other designations to that of "bond-servant." First, he has been called by God to be His "apostle." In secular Greek culture and in the Septuagint (the Greek translation of the Old Testament), an "apostle" referred to someone sent to accomplish a task on behalf of the sender. An apostle was an envoy. For example, in 1 Samuel 16, God sends Samuel to Bethlehem to anoint one of the sons of Jesse as Israel's new king. Similarly, Paul claims authority, not on the basis of education or personality or even special revela-tion—all of which he could legitimately claim—but on the mandate of the One who had sent him. His authority came from no one other than God, Himself.

Second, Paul wrote that he had been "set apart" to teach and preach the gospel (1:1). The Greek word here is *aphorizō*, which means simply "to separate" or "to reserve." But, for Paul, the term bore a deeply profound meaning, one that stemmed from his personal experience. If I were to transliterate this Greek word into English, it would sound like "off horizon." And if you will allow me some linguistic latitude, I want to use the word picture created by "off horizon."

In 1959, I stood atop the third deck of a massive troopship on its way across the Pacific to Okinawa. As I looked in every direction, the blue-black water stretched as far as the eye could see until it met the sky, forming an imaginary line we call the horizon. It occurred to me that this boundary between earth and sky formed a giant circle that defined my world. I could chase the horizon for eternity and travel to any destination on the sphere of earth, but leaving my circle to enter another was impossible—in the natural, human sense anyway.

Paul says, in effect, "For the better part of my young adult life, I lived within a circle, bounded by a horizon I could not cross. Then, the Lord confronted me on the road to Damascus, where I had intended to persecute and even kill His follow-ers, and He transported me by faith to a world beyond my old horizon. I have been moved—'off-horizoned'—from one circle of existence to another." Moreover, the apostle declared that he had been "set apart" for the purpose of carrying the gospel to the world.

### —1:2–5—

This "gospel" not only fueled the apostle's ministry and message throughout the world, it is the primary subject of his message to the Romans, which he foreshad-ows in a network of phrases between "[From] Paul" (1:1) and "to all who are beloved of God in Rome" (1:7). The chart "Paul's Greeting" shows how the phrases are linked together to establish several truths about the good news and its main character, Jesus Christ.

First, *the origin of the gospel is God.* Paul declared that the gospel was "promised" (1:2). *How?* Look beneath the word "promised" on the chart.

The gospel was promised "beforehand" (1:2). The message Paul carried was not new; it had been the central focus of the Old Testament and the impetus behind the Lord's interaction with humankind since Adam and Eve's tragic disobedience in the Garden of Eden.

# Old Testament References in Romans

| Romans 1:17 | Habakkuk 2:4 | Quote |
|---|---|---|
| Romans 2:6 | Psalm 62:12 | Quote |
| Romans 2:6 | Proverbs 24:12 | Quote |
| Romans 2:24 | Isaiah 52:5 | Allusion |
| Romans 2:24 | Ezekiel 36:20 | Allusion |
| Romans 3:4 | Psalm 51:4 | Quote |
| Romans 3:10-12 | Psalm 14:1-3 (Psalm 53:1-3) | Quote |
| Romans 3:10-12 | Ecclesiastes 7:20 | Allusion |
| Romans 3:13 | Psalm 5:9 | Quote |
| Romans 3:13 | Psalm 140:3 | Quote |
| Romans 3:14 | Psalm 10:7 | Quote |
| Romans 3:15-17 | Isaiah 59:7-8 | Paraphrase |
| Romans 3:18 | Psalm 36:1 | Quote |
| Romans 4:3 | Genesis 15:6 | Quote |
| Romans 4:7-8 | Psalm 32:1-2 | Quote |
| Romans 4:9 | Genesis 15:6 | Paraphrase |
| Romans 4:17 | Genesis 17:5 | Quote |
| Romans 4:18 | Genesis 15:5 | Quote |
| Romans 4:22 | Genesis 15:6 | Quote |
| Romans 7:7 | Exodus 20:17 | Quote |
| Romans 8:36 | Psalm 44:22 | Quote |
| Romans 8:36 | Isaiah 53:7 | Allusion |
| Romans 8:36 | Zechariah 11:4 | Allusion |
| Romans 8:36 | Zechariah 11:7 | Allusion |
| Romans 9:7 | Genesis 21:12 | Quote |
| Romans 9:9 | Genesis 18:10 | Quote |
| Romans 9:9 | Genesis 18:14 | Quote |
| Romans 9:12 | Genesis 25:23 | Quote |
| Romans 9:13 | Malachi 1:2-3 | Quote |
| Romans 9:15 | Exodus 33:19 | Quote |
| Romans 9:17 | Exodus 9:16 | Quote |
| Romans 9:25 | Hosea 2:23 | Paraphrase |
| Romans 9:26 | Hosea 1:10 | Quote |
| Romans 9:27-28 | Isaiah 10:22-23 | Quote |
| Romans 9:27-28 | Isaiah 28:22 | Allusion |
| Romans 9:27-28 | Hosea 1:10 | Allusion |
| Romans 9:29 | Isaiah 1:9 | Quote |
| Romans 9:33 | Isaiah 8:14 | Quote |
| Romans 9:33 | Isaiah 28:16 | Quote |
| Romans 10:5 | Leviticus 18:5 | Allusion |

| | | |
|---|---|---|
| Romans 10:6 | Deuteronomy 30:12 | Allusion |
| Romans 10:7 | Deuteronomy 30:13 | Allusion |
| Romans 10:8 | Deuteronomy 30:14 | Quote |
| Romans 10:11 | Isaiah 28:16 | Quote |
| Romans 10:13 | Joel 2:32 | Quote |
| Romans 10:15 | Isaiah 52:7 | Quote |
| Romans 10:15 | Nahum 1:15 | Allusion |
| Romans 10:16 | Isaiah 53:1 | Quote |
| Romans 10:18 | Psalm 19:4 | Quote |
| Romans 10:19 | Deuteronomy 32:21 | Quote |
| Romans 10:20 | Isaiah 65:1 | Quote |
| Romans 10:21 | Isaiah 65:2 | Quote |
| Romans 11:3 | 1 Kings 19:10 | Paraphrase |
| Romans 11:3 | 1 Kings 19:14 | Paraphrase |
| Romans 11:4 | 1 Kings 19:18 | Paraphrase |
| Romans 11:8 | Deuteronomy 29:4 | Quote |
| Romans 11:8 | Isaiah 29:10 | Allusion |
| Romans 11:9-10 | Psalm 69:22-23 | Quote |
| Romans 11:26-27 | Isaiah 59:20-21 | Quote |
| Romans 11:26-27 | Jeremiah 31:31-34 | Paraphrase |
| Romans 11:34-35 | Isaiah 40:13 | Paraphrase |
| Romans 11:34-35 | Job 41:11 | Quote |
| Romans 11:34-35 | Jeremiah 23:18 | Allusion |
| Romans 12:19 | Deuteronomy 32:35 | Quote |
| Romans 12:20 | Proverbs 25:21-22 | Quote |
| Romans 13:9 | Exodus 20:13-17 | Quote |
| Romans 13:9 | Deuteronomy 5:17-21 | Quote |
| Romans 13:9 | Leviticus 19:18 | Quote |
| Romans 14:11 | Isaiah 45:23 | Paraphrase |
| Romans 15:3 | Psalm 69:9 | Quote |
| Romans 15:9 | 2 Samuel 22:50 | Quote |
| Romans 15:9 | Psalm 18:49 | Allusion |
| Romans 15:10 | Deuteronomy 32:43 | Quote |
| Romans 15:11 | Psalm 117:1 | Quote |
| Romans 15:12 | Isaiah 11:10 | Quote |
| Romans 15:21 | Isaiah 52:15 | Quote |

| | |
|---|---|
| 51 | Direct quotes |
| 10 | Paraphrased quotes |
| 15 | Clear allusions |

The gospel was promised "through His prophets" (1:2). The message Paul carried fulfilled the hope of salvation foreshadowed by every prophet since Moses.

The gospel was promised "in the holy Scriptures" (1:2). The message Paul carried passed the ultimate test of truth; it was born out of God's Word. And the apostle will demonstrate the veracity of the gospel throughout his letter by quoting or paraphrasing Old Testament Scripture no less than sixty times.

Second, *the content of the gospel is Jesus Christ.* Note that the gospel was promised "concerning His Son" (1:3), about whom Paul declares several truths. God's Son "was born of a descendant [literally, 'a seed'] of David according to the flesh"; this means that Jesus is a genuine human male, insofar as His physical nature is concerned (1:3).

Jesus was undeniably proven by His resurrection to be the Son of God (1:4), insofar as His eternal identity is concerned. The phrase "Spirit of holiness" refers to His divine nature; for just as God is spirit, so the Son shares this nature.

God's Son is "Jesus Christ our Lord" (1:4). The "Christ" is none other than the Jewish Messiah, who is our *Kyrios,* the Greek term used throughout the Old Testament to refer to the Lord God.

Because the Roman believers do not know Paul personally, it is important for him to present an unblemished pedigree of truth, to demonstrate a theological kinship with his audience from the outset. And no issue divides true believers from apostates more definitely than the identity of Christ.

Today, we must do the same. The labels "Methodist," "Presbyterian," "Baptist," or even "Evangelical" mean little to the average person on the street. A teacher of authentic Christian truth must have a clear understanding of who Jesus is in relation to the Trinity and as the central figure of the gospel. If any person says that Jesus is anyone other than God in human flesh, then he or she cannot be trusted to teach others. This person might be Mormon or Jehovah's Witness or some undefined strain of skeptic. This person might choose to wear the label "Christian" and carry a Bible; nevertheless, he or she is *not* Christian.

That's not to say we should shun or reject such a person. We must simply recognize that he or she needs to hear the gospel.

Third, *the purpose of the gospel is to produce obedient faith* (1:5). At one time, learning was said to have taken place when an individual's behavior changed as a result of gaining new information. God did not save us merely to deposit a set of theological principles in our heads. We are saved in order to surrender our lives to Christ (Rom. 16:26). When you think of obedience, attach to it the synonym "submission." Paul submitted everything to the will of God, from his encounter with Christ on the road to Damascus to the very end of his life.

Paul reminds the believers in Rome that they too are "the called of Jesus Christ" (1:6). While their calling does not have the official capacity of his apostleship, they share his mission nonetheless. Jesus Christ has called them to faith and obedience, and then charged them with the responsibility to bring Gentiles—that is, their fellow inhabitants of Rome and the Roman Empire at large—to the same faith and obedience.

The responsibility to "make disciples" (Mt. 28:19–20) does not rest entirely on the shoulders of vocational, full-time ministers of the gospel. To be sure, they dedicate their lives to preaching, teaching, and leading, but they are not surrogate servants—hired hands to do work on behalf of others. All of us, every member of Christ's body, are charged with the same mission. We are to seek those who have not heard the good news and become the means by which they come to faith and obedience.

### —1:7—

Paul concludes his greeting by identifying his audience (the "beloved of God in Rome, called as saints") and then blessing them ("grace to you and peace").

He doesn't use the term "saints" to suggest that they are to labor hard in the Christian life in order to attain a lofty spiritual plane. The term "saint" is the noun form of the adjective "holy." Something is kept "holy" when it is set aside for dedicated use, as when a priest reserved certain things in the temple for the rituals of worship. The purpose for "setting aside" something was to keep it pure, undefiled by the world.

The personal application would have been as obvious to them as it is to us. Believers have been called as "set aside ones." While God has done the calling, has set aside His own, and will do the work of purification, Paul appears to suggest there is room for us to participate in the cleansing process.

Moreover, the believers are "beloved," not only by God but by Paul. He doesn't write his brothers and sisters in Rome to give them a neatly outlined notebook of doctrinal truths. He wants them to cultivate lives so abundantly filled with grace that obedience becomes as natural to them as breathing. But this requires balance. The world of fundamentalism teems with people who give little attention to the graciousness of an obedient life. At the other extreme, many emphasize graciousness and love apart from a solid doctrinal foundation. That's worse than building a house on sand. A life submitted to the Father requires both—a genuine understanding of gospel truth that results in an ever-growing obedience.

The double blessing of "grace" and "peace" is a signature greeting for Paul (1 Cor. 1:3; 2 Cor. 1:2; Gal. 1:3; Eph. 1:2; Phil. 1:2; Col. 1:2; 1 Thess. 1:1; 2 Thess. 1:2; 1 Tim. 1:2; 2 Tim. 1:2; Titus 1:4; Philem. 3). "Grace" has a Greek emphasis, while the Jews customarily greeted one another with *shalom*, which had the general meaning of "completion and fulfillment—of entering into a state of wholeness and unity, a restored relationship."[3] It embodies all the blessings of the Promised Land and the fulfillment of God's covenant with Abraham.

"Grace," of course, does not refer to salvation, as his readers are already Christian. The significance of this word will become much clearer as the apostle develops the concept in his letter. It is loaded with theological meaning, which his readers will soon appreciate.

## —1:8–13—

Paul's letter is not written to people living in a small, rural community. In AD 58, the population of Rome exceeded one million inhabitants, nearly half of whom were bond-servants and recently freed slaves. And, like modern metropolitan centers, Rome was a wonderful place to live for the elite, but challenging for everyone else. The lower classes lived in squalid high-rise apartment buildings, with no sanitation or water available above the first floor. They were frequently on the edge of rioting, especially if they could not obtain sufficient food. Crime was rampant. Ethnic neighborhoods became governments unto themselves, maintaining an uneasy peace with one another to avoid persecution by the government (Acts 18:2).

To become a Christian often meant challenging this social order and the safety it provided. For Jewish believers, the price of discipleship often included the loss of family and clan. Life was hard for everyone, but being a Christian in that environment was even worse. They must have felt like squirrels living among angry giants, any one of whom might decide to crush them on a whim.

If the believers in Rome need anything, it is encouragement, and a letter from someone of Paul's stature will help them stand a little taller. Before teaching them anything, Paul chooses four ways to lift the spirits of his Roman brothers and sisters.

*Paul affirms them* (1:8). He expresses his personal admiration and thanks for the reputation of faithfulness the Roman Christians have earned, not only in the capital, but throughout the empire. Most people hear little affirmation—sparse amounts at work, less at home, and almost none at church (to our shame). Words of appreciation or gratitude cost nothing, yet how precious they are to the discouraged. The struggling believers in Rome needed to hear someone say, "Well done! Keep doing what you're doing. It's having a lasting impact on the world."

*Paul prays for them* (1:9). Paul doesn't know most of those people. He has not yet visited Rome. Yet he never fails to include them in his prayers.

For many years, I have had the opportunity to interact with top-level government and military personnel through an organization called "The Christian Embassy." The men and women of this community—generals, admirals, chiefs of staff, members of Congress, White House personnel, and support staff—frequently tell me how much it means to them to know that people are praying for them. Washington, D.C., is a lonely place for the powerful, even more so for believers in high-ranking positions. The knowledge that others are on their knees before God allows them to feel supported and sustained.

*Paul expresses his desire to be with them* (1:10). Paul has been in ministry long enough to understand the value of being physically present with someone who needs encouragement.

I remember my days in the Marine Corps, eight thousand miles from home, desperately lonely, and counting the minutes until mail call. (No computers or cell phones back then!) I don't know a single person stationed overseas who wouldn't skip a few meals if it meant receiving a letter from home or even a postcard from that special "someone." When I received a letter from Cynthia, my heart pounded when I saw her handwriting. I inhaled the aroma of her perfume on the envelope before opening it ... I devoured each word. I read it again, and again, and again, and again. Why? Because she told me what I meant to her. She told me my value. She reminded me of how she was waiting for me and longing to be with me. Surely those believers in Rome felt the same way as they read Paul's words.

We must keep in mind throughout this letter that this is no mere theological treatise. It's a love letter from God to the Romans through His special envoy, Paul. They need to know that they are the "beloved of God," chosen to be His children, set apart as saints (1:7).

*Paul promises to assist them* (1:11–13). While the discouraged need emotional and spiritual comfort, they also need tangible help. Paul gives a couple of reasons for his intended visit, each of which he introduces with the Greek conjunction *hina*, "for the purpose of" or "in order to."

*"So that [in order that] I may impart some spiritual gift to you, [with the result that] you may be established"* (1:11). The Greek phrase *pneumatikon charisma* ("spiritual gift") leads some to suggest that Paul intends to empower the believers in Rome with supernatural abilities from the Holy Spirit. Sometimes he uses the phrase

this way (Rom. 12:6; 1 Cor. 1:7; 12:4, 31) and sometimes he uses it in the more ordinary sense (Rom. 5:15, 16; 6:23). But take note of how he further explains his meaning in verse 12. The "spiritual gift" he intends is something every believer stands to gain by the mutual building of faith.

This is leadership in the Christian sense. Paul is not planning to give them a spiritual gift they lack; he is planning to share with them *his* spiritual gift, the gift of knowledge, the gift of wisdom, the gift of apostleship. He plans to give them a share of the knowledge that God has given him. Paul will be strengthened, in turn, by the spiritual gifts the believers in Rome have to offer.

*"So that [in order that] I may obtain some fruit among you"* (1:13). The "fruit" he hopes to obtain refers to the result of ministry, that is, more converts through belief in Jesus Christ and more Christians living in obedience as a result of their growing faith (Phil. 1:22; Col. 1:6). But he also uses the term "fruit" in reference to money, which, when given generously, is a tangible result of genuine faith and the means of ministering to others (Rom. 15:23–28).

Paul has likely heard of the vibrant Christian community flourishing in Rome despite the many reasons they should not exist. And he must have appreciated their grit. He undoubtedly saw a congregation of kindred spirits who will not only help him in his mission, but embrace it as their own.

— **1:14** —

Jesus explained the good news this way: "For God so loved the world, that He gave His only begotten Son, that whoever believes in Him shall not perish, but have eternal life" (John 3:16). Many have never heard this news. The Son of God entered the world as an embryo, then a fetus, then a newborn infant on the outskirts of a little hamlet called Bethlehem in the hills of Judea. He grew to be a man who, though completely sinless Himself, paid the complete penalty of sin on behalf of the whole world. He paid the price in full, leaving none for us to pay on our own, so that whoever — regardless of age, gender, race, nationality, geographical location, social class, intelligence, education, or even morality — whoever simply trusts God to receive His free gift "shall have eternal life." No strings attached. No hidden fees. No extra work to be done. No additional requirements. Nothing to join. By grace alone through faith alone in Christ alone. That's all. And it's enough!

John preserved these words in his account of Jesus' life written near the end of the first century. Some five decades earlier, around AD 35, shortly after Jesus was raised from the dead and had ascended to the Father, unbelieving Jews began to persecute those among them who chose to believe in Jesus. One man, a Pharisee, pursued and imprisoned Christians with unmatched religious fury (Acts 8:3) and eventually presided over the execution of the first Christian martyr (Acts 7:58). While on his way to the town of Damascus to find and imprison believers, he encountered the risen Savior and believed the good news himself (Acts 9:3–6), which shocked the religious world in and around Jerusalem. The chief persecutor of Christians had joined the ranks of those he had formerly killed.

Twenty-five years later, after studying the Scriptures and growing as a Christian in the predominantly Gentile church in Antioch, Paul has become the chief ambassador of the good news to the world between Jerusalem and Rome. Having accomplished all he hoped in the lands subdued by the empire, the apostle desires to carry the gospel to people living in the newly Romanized, yet still "barbarous," frontier of Spain. But that will come after Rome. As he ministers in each place, he keeps his eyes on the horizon, beyond which lie more people who need to hear the good news.

The apostle pursued his mission of propagating the gospel with more passion and dedication than he had given to snuffing it out. And he expressed that passion using three "I am" statements: "I am under obligation," "I am eager to preach the gospel," and "I am not ashamed."

*I am under obligation* (1:14). His declaration reads, literally, "To both the Greek and the barbarian, to both the learned and the ignorant, I am a debtor."

There is more than one kind of debt. The most familiar is when we borrow a sum of money from the bank. We are indebted to the bank to pay the money back. Paul's debt is of another kind. If someone were to give me money to deliver to someone else, I am indebted to the one who gave me the money and, in a real sense, to the one who should receive it. As the middle man, I am a debtor to both. Paul writes, in effect, "I have been given the good news from the Savior, Himself, and I now have the responsibility—a debt to pay—to give this news to someone else."

It is important for me to point out that this was not a condition of Paul's salvation. Paul did not consider himself a debtor because he owed the Lord anything in return for eternal life. The apostle's debt was a voluntary condition of his calling. It was a deep sense of accountability to the fate of his fellow human beings, most of whom lived in the same spiritual darkness that once made him a persecutor and murderer of those who lived in the light of truth.

"Barbarians" referred not to wild-eyed, brutal, uncivilized savages, but to those not yet cultured in the ways of Rome, those living on the empire's frontier. The Greek word *barbaros* means "stuttering" or "stammering," which the Romans applied to anyone not yet Romanized because they saw them as necessarily crude and ignorant. Paul's use of the term doesn't suggest that he sees non-Romanized people as inferior. He merely uses the language of the Romans to stress that his indebtedness extends to the whole world.

## —1:15—

*"I am eager to preach the gospel"* (1:15). Paul's passion burned with the urgency of someone who had just found the fire escape in a burning high-rise. Desperate to save others, he shouted, "Come this way, come this way! Rush down this stairway! This is how you get out. This is the escape route!" Even after two decades of repeated struggles with hunger, thirst, exposure, shipwreck, robberies, beatings, imprisonment, and several stonings (Acts 14:19; 2 Cor. 11:23–27; 2 Tim. 3:11), even after seeing the success of his labors—seeing the empire dotted with thriving communities of believers—Paul remains eager to fulfill his calling in places yet further from home.

## —1:16–17—

*"For I am not ashamed"* (1:16). The connecting particle "for" means "because." Paul remains undeterred by the fear of what others think for two reasons, both of which rest in the gospel.

The first reason: *"for it is the power of God for salvation."* Let's go back to my earlier illustration. If you had indeed discovered a completely effective, completely free cure for all types of cancer, how little would you care about what people say if your daily joy was to see terminally ill patients leave their hospital beds and enjoy a long, healthy life? Paul remained energized and unconcerned with the opinions of other people because the gospel is too wonderful and too compelling to disregard, especially for the sake of pride.

The second reason: *"for in it the righteousness of God is revealed."* Whereas the disease is sin, good health is righteousness. Sin is nothing less than rebellion against the very nature of God, which is utterly good, and righteousness is right relations with the One who, alone, can judge good from evil. The cure for the terminal disease of sin is the gospel, which allows any who will receive it to enjoy a restored relationship with the Creator.

Paul concludes his greeting with a reminder that, while the good news of Jesus Christ is God's radically different approach to the problem of sin, it is older than creation. He quotes the Old Testament prophet Habakkuk (Hab. 2:4) to show that throughout all time, salvation is a gift provided by grace and received through faith. Thus, in the good news, the righteousness of God is revealed "out of faith into faith" (literally rendered). "The righteous man shall live by faith." One receives right standing before God by *belief,* not deeds.

That's a glimmer of the good news that Paul longs to share and takes great care to explain in this letter. But first, to fully appreciate a cure, one must understand his or her disease and its consequences.

## Application

### *What's Good for Paul Is Good for All*

After greeting the believers in Rome, Paul explains what drives him to preach the gospel with such passion and dedication:

*"I am under obligation"* (1:14). Paul considers himself indebted to all of humanity because he has been entrusted with a priceless gift — the only cure for the deadly disease of sin. Like Paul, those who have received the free gift of eternal life have an obligation to let others know that God has extended the offer of salvation to everyone, whether privileged or poor, sophisticated or simple, religious or rebellious.

*"I am eager"* (1:15). The grace Paul received and his sense of obligation motivate him to act. Anyone who genuinely comprehends the magnitude of the gift he or she has been given will not be able to remain idle. If you are not actively engaged in doing *something* in service of the gospel, something is missing from your spiritual life.

*"I am not ashamed"* (1:16). Let's face it: the gospel appears foolish to those who do not understand. And in the past, ignorance has given way to ridicule and then persecution. Those who have staked their eternal lives on the truth of God's grace must remain steadfast, even if it requires the sacrifice of our earthly lives.

According to Christian tradition, Paul never lost his zeal. He remained energized and shameless in his proclamation of the good news. His lifelong evangelistic journey finally ended with his martyrdom in — of all places — Rome.

---

NOTES: Salutation (Romans 1:1–17)

1. Gerhard Kittel and Gerhard Friedrich, eds., *Theological Dictionary of the New Testament: Abridged in One Volume,* trans. Geoffrey W. Bromiley (Grand Rapids: Eerdmans, 1985), 183.
2. Ibid.
3. Robert Laird Harris, Gleason L. Archer, and Bruce K. Waltke, *Theological Wordbook of the Old Testament,* electronic ed. (Chicago: Moody Press, 1999 [orig.1980]), 930.

# THE WRATH OF GOD (ROMANS 1:18 – 3:20)

If I were to make up my own god, he would be a lot like the one Hollywood depicts in the movies. I would like him to be a cigar-chomping, delightfully witty curmudgeon who keeps me laughing. Or, better yet, he could be a serene, butler-like character who keeps me out of trouble with wisdom greater than my own, yet serves me nonetheless. The god I would make for myself would be kindly and firm, but take a "boys will be boys" stance when I sin. After all, the negative consequences of my poor decisions are punishment enough, right?

What kind of god do you worship? Is he (or she) a designer god? Is he (or she) merely an imaginary "higher power" who possesses all the admirable qualities missing from your close relationships? Or is he (or she) an immensely powerful depiction of the character traits you fear most, like jealousy, rage, petty nitpicking, or passive-aggressive guilt? Do you worship the god of your imagination, or the One who actually exists?

God, as He is revealed in the Bible, doesn't look like the idols we carry around in our imaginations. Yet we too easily see the god of our choosing in the pages of Scripture, like seeing shapes in the clouds. To avoid this unwitting idolatry, we must read the Word in order to know the God who is there (as the great Christian philosopher Francis Schaeffer used to call Him). As we read Paul's letter to the Romans, we confront an unsettling fact about the God who is there. His wrath burns against humanity with fearsome, looming finality. Yes, according to the Bible, this God of love will indeed send people to eternal torment.

If that makes you at least a little uncomfortable, you are perhaps ready to lay aside the idol of your imagination to see the One true God, the God who is there.

The first section of Paul's letter to the Romans is an indictment against humanity. God is angry and we—each and every one of us—are subject to eternal separation from Him in a place of indescribable suffering. The apostle explains humanity's danger this way: Humankind is subject to the wrath of God because, collectively and individually, we have rebelled against Him with our minds and by our deeds (1:18). No one is exempt from judgment; not the Gentile (1:18 – 32), not the moralist (2:1 – 16), not even the Jew (2:17 – 3:8). In fact, we are all subject to God's wrath because we are corrupt, through and through (3:9 – 20).

To prove his case, Paul draws on wisdom gained during his ministry experience, which undoubtedly involved a number of heated debates with Gentile and Jewish philosophers. Some—like today—objected to the notion that people who have not heard of God could be justly condemned for transgressing a law they know nothing about. Paul answers their objections with two indictments, one from nature and the other from conscience. Jews claimed exemption from judgment by virtue of the

## KEY TERMS

ὀργή [orgē] (3709) "wrath, upsurging, indignation, retributive anger"

The Old and New Testaments use two Greek terms for "wrath": *thymos* (to boil up) and *orgē*. In secular Greek literature, *thymos* typically refers to the emotion of anger while *orgē* describes its behavior, but the Bible does not maintain this distinction. *Orgē*, by itself, does not indicate whether the anger is just or sinful. It can be either, depending upon the circumstance and the character of the individual.

ἀδικία [adikia] (93) "unrighteousness, violation of law, legal injustice"

The prefix "a-" negates whatever follows, so *adikia* is the opposite of what is just, right, or legal. The term can have a religious connotation, but its primary use is legal. It describes any behavior that is contrary to an established standard. A person convicted of a crime is guilty of "unrighteousness"; a corrupt ruler is guilty of "injustice."

παραδίδωμι [paradidōmi] (3860) "hand over, surrender, transfer possession"

Based on the verb "to give," this term carries the idea of surrendering possession of something to the control of another. Based on the context, some translators will render the term "betray," but the Greek word does not suggest whether the motivation is good or evil. We see it used extensively in the passion narratives, in which Jesus is "betrayed" or "given over" to the Sanhedrin by Judas (Mark 14:10), to Pilate by the Sanhedrin (Mark 15:1), to the soldiers by Pilate (Mark 15:15), and finally, Jesus "gave up" His spirit to death (John 19:30).

κρίνω [krinō] (2919) "to judge, divide, assess, decide"

The literal meaning is "to sift and separate" in order to isolate the components of a mixture. The primary use is metaphorical in the sense of "sifting through the details to arrive at a conclusion." In terms of a person, the idea is to sift the details of one's life in order to examine them and render a decision about one's character. "Judgment," then, is the result of this sifting.

νόμος [nomos] (3551) "law, that which is assigned, what is proper, standard of right conduct"

*Nomos*, a noun, is closely related to the verb, *nemō*, "to divide and distribute." As opposed to *ethos*, which is unwritten custom, this term refers to written rules of conduct that are defined for the administration of justice. Paul's use of *nomos* almost always refers to the code of conduct Moses received from God, the "Mosaic Law."

covenant they had inherited from father Abraham. Paul answers their objections by correcting their flawed, deeds-oriented theology, and then he levels a stinging indictment from the very Law they claim to cherish.

By the end of this section, Paul has conclusively proved that God is justifiably angry with humanity and that all people stand condemned under His judgment. This isn't a particularly enjoyable portion of Scripture. In fact, if by the end of Paul's indictment of humanity, you feel like running and hiding from God, you are just beginning to see Him as He is, and you are just beginning to understand the gravity of sin.

## God Is Angry (1:18–23)

---

[18]For the wrath of God is revealed from heaven against all ungodliness and unrighteousness of men who suppress the truth in unrighteousness, [19]because that which is known about God is evident within them; for God made it evident to them. [20]For since the creation of the world His invisible attributes, His eternal power and divine nature, have been clearly seen, being understood through what has been made, so that they are without excuse. [21]For even though they knew God, they did not honor Him as God or give thanks, but they became futile in their speculations, and their foolish heart was darkened. [22]Professing to be wise, they became fools, [23]and exchanged the glory of the incorruptible God for an image in the form of corruptible man and of birds and four-footed animals and crawling creatures.

---

People today are more enlightened than their ancestors. They don't fall prey to superstitions; they don't perform incantations to ward off evil spirits; and they don't fear bad omens. Modern people have risen above these primal, animistic beliefs to embrace the world as it really is, a world governed by impersonal forces of nature and laws of physics. Furthermore, the god of their choosing has evolved with them. He is no longer a brutish deity whose anger must be mollified. He is a kinder, gentler god, a grandfatherly god who is grieved when we do bad things, but because he understands how difficult it is to be a human and that wrongdoing isn't really our fault, he doesn't punish sin. Instead, he tenderly tries to correct his children.

The god of today's making looks more like a henpecked, pathetically passive father than the almighty Creator who genuinely cares about his creation. People today don't want a god they fear, supposing that he would be more loving than one who gets upset when people don't please him. But a passive, hand-wringing god who cannot be angered is not one I would characterize as loving. A God of love must hate anything that harms those He loves. A God of love must take action to protect the innocent against the malicious. A God of love must mean business when He declares a certain action "off-limits." After all, a law without consequences is no law at all.

A God of love must also have the capacity for anger. However, the wrath of God is not the kind of bellowing anger we have come to associate with abusive people. Paul describes the Creator's response to sin using the Greek word *orgē*, which means "upsurging." When used to describe wrath, it is a passionate expression of outrage against wrongdoing, and, in this context, it pictures the passionate righteous anger of God cresting the walls of heaven and spilling onto earth. And while it is indeed a passionate, upsurging response, it is completely consistent with God's character, which is also love. His wrath is, without question, fearsome, yet also controlled, deliberate, measured, and utterly just. His wrath is nothing less than a reasonable expression of His righteous character and His unfailing love when confronted with evil.

## —1:18–19—

God is love (1 John 4:8), which is why He will not stand idly by while evil consumes His creation. Note the objects of His wrath. He burns against "ungodliness" and "unrighteousness," two terms that need defining.

"Ungodliness" comes from the Greek word, *asebeia*. The root term is *sebomai*, which originally meant "to fall back before" or "to shrink from," as one would do in the presence of a deity. By the time of Paul, the common understanding was "to show reverence" or "to worship." The Greek prefix *a-* negates whatever it's attached to, so the term refers to attitudes and actions of "not-reverence." This lifestyle of irreverence inevitably leads to contempt.

"Unrighteousness" derives from *adikia*, a term pulled directly from the Septuagint (the Greek translation of the Old Testament), meaning, "violation of divine law." This divine law, of course, refers to the standards of conduct given through Moses, which were to be modeled by the Hebrew nation of Israel.

These standards of conduct, which Paul calls "the Law," are not arbitrary. God didn't sit down one day and decide to list all the ways He could spoil our fun. These rules for living are an expression of His character. His nature as the Supreme Power of the universe defines what is good. In other words, if God were a liar, then lying would be righteous. But God is truth (Rom. 3:4); therefore lying, an action that is contrary to His character, is "sin."

# From My Journal

## Innocence Lost

When you become a grandparent, you cannot help but see things differently. Our first step on the road to maturity is a sudden awakening to the fact that the world is not always a good place. Then, after decades of trying to get a handle on the presence of evil in a universe over which God is sovereign, a grandchild brings you full circle again. As you gather that little one into your arms, suddenly glimmers of something you lost a long time ago flicker in the corner of your mind's eye. And if you don't look too hard, you'll discover it's the precious, fleeting quality of childlike wonder.

Remember childlike wonder? Puppets really talk. The department store Santa travels all the way from the North Pole just to visit *your* town. Uncle Bob truly can pull a quarter from someone's ear and Daddy is, in fact, larger than life. And God really did create the universe, which He continues to watch over with fatherly interest. But something sad, yet necessary happened. We grew up to see the world as it really is. We learned the unhappy truth behind puppets and cheap Santa costumes. Sleight of hand tricks no longer mesmerize and Daddy came down to size all too quickly. And, then … what of God? In the process of growing up, have we abandoned the very quality that Jesus said we must have if we are to embrace His kingdom (Matt. 18:4; Mark 10:15; Luke 18:17)?

In the early 1920s, humanity enjoyed a few fleeting moments of childlike wonder when Edwin Hubble pointed the world's largest telescope toward a dim portion of the sky and made a startling discovery. Until then, everyone thought the universe was limited to our own Milky Way galaxy. Hubble's research proved otherwise. What were once thought to be distant stars turned out to be galaxies, many thousands of them. Suddenly, the universe was a great deal bigger, humankind looked a great deal less knowledgeable, and, for a moment—a precious, fleeting moment—humankind gazed with childlike wonder at the magnificence of God's creation.

Unfortunately, our brush with innocence did not last. As humankind has done for countless millennia, we traded childlike wonder for something easier to manage: the visible for the invisible. And, all at once, our fleeting encounter with truth gave way to a long series of big bang theories and something-from-nothing speculations.

"Ungodliness" and "unrighteousness," then, represent not only a violation of certain rules of conduct, but an utter rejection of God Himself—His deity, His authority, His very nature. Paul declared that God's wrath is revealed against all ungodliness and unrighteousness, that is, sin. When we choose to sin, we express contempt for God's character, calling bad things "good." That's why Paul stated that this ungodliness and unrighteousness are perpetuated by people who "suppress the truth in unrighteousness." God's truth, by which He spoke the universe into existence and which gave it order, is "suppressed" by the evil intent of people.

The word picture painted by "suppressed" depicts a man struggling to keep the lid of a container closed so that whatever is inside cannot escape. The sin of humanity suppresses the will of God; sin keeps the world from working as God originally intended it to. Yes, disease and disasters wreak havoc, but the great majority of the world's evil is instigated and perpetuated by people sinning against one another, such as murder, theft, hostility between nations, and violence in the home. The sin of people prevents the world from being better than it could otherwise be.

Paul then explains the reason for this unbridled rebellion against God and His Law. People suppress their innate knowledge of the Creator, an awareness that is as much a part of their composition as DNA. God created people for the purpose of having a close and meaningful relationship with Him, and this need causes men and women of all races, throughout all time, to instinctively seek their Creator—unless, that is, they willfully push down that desire and purposely ignore this innate knowledge of Him.

## —1:20–21—

Some might object that this innate, instinctive evidence of a Creator is too intangible. But Paul points to the evidence of creation itself. God has enveloped us in the evidence of His handiwork. Gaze into deep space through a telescope and you see evidence of His size and power. Peer through a microscope and you see evidence of His comprehensive intellect. John Calvin wrote, "By saying that God has made it manifest, he means, that man was created to be a spectator of this formed world, and that eyes were given him, that he might, by looking on so beautiful a picture, be led up to the Author himself."[1] Nature itself is the best argument for intelligent design, leaving men and women "without excuse"; yet they wantonly suppress the truth of God—and with tragic results: "Professing to be wise, they became fools."

## —1:22–23—

To us, a fool is someone who is a little mischievous or makes foolish decisions. However, Greek and Hebrew cultures took the term "fool" far more seriously. The Hebrew language uses no less than four terms to quantify the level of foolishness in a person. Each successive term includes and builds upon the qualities of the previous one. According to the Hebrews, the greatest fool of all is the disobedient person who possesses the greatest intelligence!

- *Kesil*: lacking knowledge or practical experience, mentally sluggish
- *Ewil*: callous to the moral implications of foolish choices
- *Nabal*: willfully closed to wisdom and brutishly destructive to self and others
- *Letz*: incorrigibly and willfully rebellious against God

The Greek language also uses four primary terms.

- *aphrōn*: lacking common sense perception of the physical and spiritual world
- *anoētos*: irrational, mindless, incapable of governing lusts
- *asynetos*: void of understanding, unable to reason
- *mōros*: mentally sluggish to the point of being morally worthless in heart and character

Paul chose the term *mōros*, from which we derive the English word "moron." In Greek societies, only someone who was *mōros* deserved censure.

This foolish futility doesn't merely distract humanity from seeking their Creator; it leads them to twist creation into something grotesque. Take note of the downward spiral. Willful ignorance of God (1:21) leads to clever imitation of God (1:21 – 22) and ends with a wholesale replacement of God (1:23 – 25). The creature is worshiped instead of the Creator. The corruptible instead of the incorruptible. The temporal instead of the eternal. The earthly, fleshly animal instead of the heavenly, spiritual Maker.

Humanity has a stubborn habit of looking to the gift rather than the Giver for fulfillment. For example, the ancient Egyptians thrived in the fertile Nile delta region because the river overflowed its banks each year and revitalized the soil. They also understood the vital role of the sun in growing the crops. But rather than thank the Creator of the soil, the river, and the sun, they worshiped the sun and the river. They invented elaborate myths to explain the origins of the river and sun and gave them personalities to account for their cycles. Then they presumed to bribe these objects of creation with sacrifices, supposing they possessed the power to give or take life.

Modern human beings look upon such superstition with amused distain, but they too frequently confuse the gift for the Giver. They look to their paychecks for provision, dutifully serve their own livelihoods, and even sacrifice their marriage and children on the altar of career. They too forget that it is not bread that keeps them alive, but the God who provides it.

It has long been the habit of humankind to trade the one true God for one of their own making. Our fallen nature prefers a creator who does not hold us accountable for wrongdoing and passively waits for us to reinitiate our relationship with him when we've grown tired of our sin. But God is not a passive parent. He will hold us accountable for sin, whether we acknowledge His presence or not. And the consequences of our rejecting Him in favor of sin are far graver than we can imagine.

## Application

### *Faith Is a Choice*

The Enlightenment of the eighteenth century claimed to have ushered humanity out of superstition and into the light of reason. The Enlightenment also placed a wall of separation between philosophy and science, religion and reality, faith and reason. Thus was born the so-called Age of Reason, during which anything supernatural was placed in the category "unreasonable." In short, it was a decision to reject the invisible in favor of the visible, at least until the invisible can be proven through experimentation or made to fit into a workable theory.

People who have adopted this strictly modern manner of thinking prefer to form their beliefs only after objectively analyzing data and performing unbiased evaluations of theories. However, their preference begins with a presupposition. They have either consciously or unconsciously adopted the presupposition of the Enlightenment that anything that cannot be tested or scientifically observed must be placed in the "unreal" category instead of the "real" category. Their preference to form their beliefs in this way reflects that they have already begun to approach the world from the Enlightenment viewpoint.

Accepting the *un*reality of God—presumably because His existence cannot be proven and He will not submit to scientific examination—is not the result of an objective analysis of data and an unbiased evaluation of theories. It is a decision, a choice based upon a presupposition to see the world a certain way. The nature of their presupposition makes their rejection of God's existence a foregone conclusion and, therefore, no less "unreasonable."

The fact is, every person's worldview is a choice. Believers have no trouble admitting this (Ps. 111:10; Prov. 1:7; 9:10) while unbelievers work overtime to prove to everyone that their worldview is an objective choice rather than a presupposition.

The Creator has provided evidence of His existence. The underlying order of the universe, though marred by the fall, points to an intelligent designer. In addition, the mere fact that humankind craves meaning suggests that the universe is not a fortunate accident. On rare occasions in the past this Designer has broken into the natural world with supernatural evidence of His power, and we have the testimony of those who witnessed it. Therefore, belief in God is not unreasonable. In fact, it is no less scientific than the presupposed unbelief of some scientists.

So, if belief or unbelief begins with a choice, it would logically follow that accepting the reality of God is a moral choice rather than an intellectual conclusion. And if belief does not require someone to be unreasonable, those who choose not to accept His reality will have no excuse when they eventually face Him.

Let me challenge you with a few questions. How have you chosen to view the universe? Are you willing to put your decision to a real test? You may have chosen to disbelieve the intelligent design of the world. Or you may have unconsciously decided what God is like. Your beliefs may be correct or they may not. Are you willing to set them aside?

Allow me to suggest a more reasonable approach to your beliefs. We are beginning a journey, guided by the apostle Paul, in which we have the opportunity to discover the character of God, the nature of humanity, the purpose of creation, the truth about good and evil, and the reason why the world is the way it is. Choose today—if only for the sake of examination—to accept two propositions. First, God exists. Second, God is unlike what you imagine Him to be.

## Forsaken, but Not Forgotten (1:24–32)

[24]Therefore God gave them over in the lusts of their hearts to impurity, so that their bodies would be dishonored among them. [25]For they exchanged the truth of God for a lie, and worshiped and served the creature rather than the Creator, who is blessed forever. Amen.
[26]For this reason God gave them over to degrading passions; for their women exchanged the natural function for that which is unnatural, [27]and in the same way also the men abandoned the natural function of the woman and burned in their desire toward one another, men with men committing

indecent acts and receiving in their own persons the due penalty of their error.

²⁸And just as they did not see fit to acknowledge God any longer, God gave them over to a depraved mind, to do those things which are not proper, ²⁹being filled with all unrighteousness, wickedness, greed, evil; full of envy, murder, strife, deceit, malice; *they are* gossips, ³⁰slanderers, haters of God, insolent, arrogant, boastful, inventors of evil, disobedient to parents, ³¹without understanding, untrustworthy, unloving, unmerciful; ³²and although they know the ordinance of God, that those who practice such things are worthy of death, they not only do the same, but also give hearty approval to those who practice them.

Tough love is tough on everybody. Good parents don't enjoy disciplining their children; truth be told, they hate it. And churches must sometimes take a strong stand when a member refuses to stop behavior that is self-destructive, damaging to the family, or clearly dishonoring to God. However, if we genuinely love someone, we cannot remain passive while sin destroys the sinner and everyone affected by his or her evil deeds. While we are not responsible for the choices of another, we can refuse to allow destructive behavior in our presence. This is, in fact, the approach the Creator has taken with sinful creation.

Humanity's complete rejection of God left Him no other choice but to pronounce judgment, which began with His "giving over" humankind to their sin. Theologians call this "judicial abandonment," which some have described in one of two ways. Some see judicial abandonment as a passive forsaking of humanity to the consequences of their evil intentions. In other words, in response to their straining against the leash, God simply releases His grip and allows humanity to run headlong into sin and its consequences, thus allowing them to consummate their lusts. But this is judicial abandonment only in part. There is nothing passive about God's "giving over" humanity to sin.

— 1:24–25 —

To describe this tough-love decision, Paul chooses the same Greek verb used in the Gospels to describe the ordeal Jesus endured. He was given over by Judas to the Sanhedrin (Mark 14:10), by the Sanhedrin to Pilate (Mark 15:1), by Pilate to the blood thirst of His enemies (Luke 23:25), and to the soldiers for scourging and crucifixion (Mark 15:15). Finally, Jesus "gave up" His spirit to death (John 19:30). "Giving over" describes an active decision, not passive neglect. God hands humanity over to their lust, not merely out of frustration or resignation, but to accomplish a specific purpose. Perhaps the most helpful illustration of His judicial abandonment comes from the Old Testament.

When the Israelites wandered in the wilderness forty years as a result of their unbelief, God miraculously sustained them by providing manna (Num. 11:7–9). But they pined for the food of their Egyptian slave masters, complaining, "Who will give us meat to eat?" (11:4–6). The Lord responded,

> "You shall eat, not one day, nor two days, nor five days, nor ten days, nor twenty days, but a whole month, until it comes out of your nostrils and becomes loathsome to you; because you have rejected the LORD who is among you and have wept before Him, saying, 'Why did we ever leave Egypt?'" (Num. 11:19–20)

Similarly, God says to humanity, in effect, "The sin for which you lust, you will have until it comes out of your nostrils and becomes loathsome to you."

**Paul wrote his letter to the Romans from the city of Corinth, in the shadow of the Acrocorinth, shown here at the summit of a monolith overlooking the city. The Acrocorith featured a temple dedicated to Aphrodite, the goddess of love, where temple prostitutes entertained visiting patrons from around the empire.**

As if to illustrate the slippery slope of sin, Paul used the phrase "God gave them over" three times, describing increasingly graver implications. Note the specific sin in each example and how one sin leads to the next.

*"God gave them over ... to impurity"* (1:24). The Greek term translated "impurity" was used primarily in a religious sense to describe the quality that made something or someone useless in the service of a particular god. Today, we might use the words "contaminated" or "infected." An instrument that has been contaminated is no longer sterile and is useless to a surgeon. Therefore, he or she will toss it aside.

God's purpose for turning people over to their impurity is redemptive. Rather than enabling the drug addict by providing a hot shower and a soft bed, the Lord leaves him in the gutter to lie in a pool of his own filth until he decides he wants better. He cannot possibly fulfill his purpose as a human being until he wants to leave the impurity of his addiction behind.

Idolaters contaminate themselves by worshiping "the creature rather than the Creator." Times and cultures have changed, but the heart of humanity has not. Few people in Western culture bow before carved pieces of wood or stone; however, counseling offices are packed with people who derive security or significance from something other than God. And their behavior can become quite bizarre. They trust possessions rather than the Provider. They serve jobs, or relationships, or positions of stature, or bank accounts. They look to drugs, alcohol, sex, work, shopping, pornography, food, and a host of other coping behaviors rather than seek their Creator. They daily exchange the truth for a lie and they make themselves filthy in the process.

— **1:26–27** —

*"God gave them over to degrading passions"* (1:26). Paul is writing this letter from Corinth, a city that lay in the shadow of the temple of Aphrodite, the goddess of love, beauty, and sexual pleasure. Her temple commanded the region from the summit of the Acrocorinth, a plateau nineteen hundred feet overhead, where temple prostitutes enticed worshipers from the farthest reaches of the Roman Empire. So infamous was this city's reputation that Aristophanes coined the word *corinthianize* to mean "to practice immorality."[2] Nevertheless, these "hospitable women"[3] were highly valued as priestesses and were honored guests at public festivals.

This bizarre double standard, taken to extremes in Corinth, merely reflects the general attitude of the Greeks and Romans toward sex. Both cultures valued virtue above all, yet they turned a blind eye to adultery and openly condoned homosexuality. In Greek culture, a high-born male was expected to maintain a same-sex affair with a much younger partner. Or, to put it less delicately, the Greeks and Romans—in their "wisdom"—not only condoned pedophilia, they considered it a necessary part of education.

The *pathos* (intense emotion) of those who pursued impurity is described as "degrading" or dishonoring. In the same way that our leaders and those in authority taint honorable positions when they do something repulsive, so these men and women sullied the dignity of humanity with their lusts. God created the human body with the capacity to enjoy intense sexual pleasure within the context of a life-long covenant between a man and a woman. Far from being something shameful or degrading, sex as God intended honors the gift and the Giver. But humankind has twisted this wonderful gift into something subhuman.

## —1:28—

*"God gave them over to a depraved mind"* (1:28). The Greek term translated "depraved" means "worthless as proven by testing." Unfortunately, the issue of human depravity has been confused by some to mean "as bad as we can possibly be." But this is not how Paul would have understood the term "depraved." The Greek verb at the heart of "depravity" is *dokimazō*, which is based on the root word, "to watch." It means "to prove worthy or genuine by observation or testing." This is the verb chosen by Paul to describe humankind's rejection of God, which the NASB renders well: "they did not see fit." Humanity put God to the test, judged Him, and decided against acknowledging Him. In response, God puts humankind to the test by giving them over to their lust, proving them to be *adokimos,* "*not worthy or genuine.*"

Do you see the irony? In their attempt to put God to the test, humankind proves to be worthless. When allowed to express their full potential, they prove to be the very opposite of God, who is the very definition of "good." The Lord gives them over to their inward desires and the result of the test speaks for itself. In their character, humankind is "filled with all unrighteousness, wickedness, greed, evil; full of envy, murder, strife, deceit, malice" (1:29). By their deeds they have proven to be "gossips, slanderers, haters of God, insolent, arrogant, boastful, inventors of evil, disobedient to parents, without understanding, untrustworthy, unloving, unmerciful" (1:29–31).

The result of this mutual testing is the rejection of God by humankind. They reject Him as Creator, reject His character as the standard of good, reject His authority to determine right from wrong, and reject His judicial right to hold them accountable. Consequently, they have utterly separated themselves from God and, in response, God has formalized the division with a tough-love, severe-mercy decree from heaven called "judicial abandonment."

"Depraved" doesn't mean "as bad as they can possibly be;" it means "as bad *off* as they can possibly be." The Creator and His creatures stand on opposite sides of an infinitely deep, infinitely wide schism called "sin." Humankind is judicially separated from God, helplessly estranged and willfully ignorant of the peril they face.

## —1:29–32—

While the term "depraved" has primarily to do with humanity's position—that is, judicial separation from God—it carries with it grave implications concerning the quality of human nature. Having been "given over" to depravity, their deeds reveal their utter moral worthlessness, which Paul illustrates by listing no less than twenty-one vices. And, as he explained earlier, they are "without excuse" (1:20). They have willingly ignored their Creator, their knowledge of right and wrong, and the penalty for sin, even to the point of praising the wrongdoing of others.

Some suppose that Paul has Gentiles primarily in view when writing this particular section, but this indictment of creation applies to all: to those who lived before the Law was given through Moses, and to those who lived in willful ignorance after it had been handed down. This indictment left God no other choice than to separate Himself from humanity. He said, in effect, "Your willful rejection of Me has left Me no other choice; I must put you out of My presence." And whether we realize it or not, there can be no more dreadful condition than this.

## Application

### Gentiles, Tax Collectors, and Others Who Need Tough Love

"Judicial abandonment" is not the same as rejection. It is, instead, the first step in God's plan of redemption. Jesus taught His disciples about the relentless redeeming love of His Father in the parable of the lost sheep. "If any man has a hundred sheep, and one of them has gone astray, does he not leave the ninety-nine on the mountains and go and search for the one that is straying?" (Matt. 18:12). Then, He taught them how a believer may seek the restoration of a relationship in the aftermath of sin. We are to mimic the Father, whose love is sometimes tough. Note the steps we are to follow.

*First, we must bring an offense to the other person's attention* (Matt. 18:15). Who knows? The matter may have been an unfortunate misunderstanding. How tragic it would be for a relationship to end over something that didn't actually occur.

Other times, the person may have offended another without realizing it, or the offending party may be fearful to address the sin for fear of condemnation. In any case, the rift in the relationship will certainly grow wider without someone taking the risk to talk about the unpleasant division.

*Second, if the person denies the truth or refuses to accept responsibility, enlist support* (Matt. 18:16). Frequently, broken relationships involve differing perspectives. The offended party typically overstates the sin, while the offending person usually tries to minimize it. The help of a companion or two, people both parties trust, may bring enough objectivity to the situation to make it easier to resolve.

*Third, if others are unable to help, appeal to the authority of church leaders* (Matt. 18:17). While the first two steps are recommended with anyone, obviously the third is only appropriate if the offending person is a believer. If private attempts to resolve the sin have failed, the authority of the church may be effective. Truth must be spoken — *in love.* Moreover, these leaders speak with divine authority (assuming they remain qualified); to ignore them is a serious matter.

*Finally, if the person stubbornly refuses to repent, we must hand him or her over to sin* (Matt. 18:17). This is not unlike God's judicial abandonment of humanity. He promised Israel that disobedience would force Him to withdraw His blessing and protection (Deut. 28:15–68). He warned them again through His prophets (Jer. 3:8–10; Hos. 2:5–7), and He followed through with the destruction of Israel and the exile of Judah (2 Kings 17:6; Jer. 39:1–10). Paul tells us that He did the same with humanity so that we would grow sick of our sin and return to Him. Similarly, Paul counseled the church in Corinth to confront the unrepentant sin of a man who had been sexually intimate with his father's wife and to "remove the wicked man from among yourselves" (1 Cor. 5:13). The goal, of course, is repentance followed by restoration (Gal. 6:1–2).

The Lord did not prescribe this final measure to be cruel. His judicial abandonment is merely a tough-love means of redeeming someone from the self-destruction of sin. "Deliver such a one to Satan for the destruction of his flesh, so that his spirit may be saved in the day of the Lord Jesus" (1 Cor. 5:5). The Lord did not command His disciples, "let him be to you as a Gentile and a tax collector" (Matt. 18:17), in order to be unkind. Remember, Jesus came to redeem *all* of humanity, beginning with the most immoral. While He rejected the sin of harlots and tax collectors, He chose to dine with them in order to redeem them. In other words, while He refused to call people who persist in their sin "brother" or "sister," He sought their redemption through kindness.

If someone stubbornly refuses to repent of sin, we may discover that person is not a believer. Upon such discovery, it would be appropriate to make every attempt to lead the individual to Christ. Then, upon repentance and belief in Jesus Christ, embrace him or her as a member of God's household. If, however, we continue to embrace someone who is guilty of unrepentant sin as a fellow believer, we deny the person the opportunity to hear the good news and turn to the Savior for deliverance. And "may [such a thing] never be!" (cf. 3:4, 6, 31).

## The Indictment of Conscience (2:1–16)

---

[1]Therefore you have no excuse, everyone of you who passes judgment, for in that which you judge another, you condemn yourself; for you who judge practice the same things. [2]And we know that the judgment of God rightly falls upon those who practice such things. [3]But do you suppose this, O man, when you pass judgment on those who practice such things and do the same *yourself*, that you will escape the judgment of God? [4]Or do you think lightly of the riches of His kindness and tolerance and patience, not knowing that the kindness of God leads you to repentance? [5]But because of your stubbornness and unrepentant heart you are storing up wrath for yourself in the day of wrath and revelation of the righteous judgment of God, [6]who will render to each person according to his deeds: [7]to those who by perseverance in doing good seek for glory and honor and immortality, eternal life; [8]but to those who are selfishly ambitious and do not obey the truth, but obey unrighteousness, wrath and indignation. [9]*There will be* tribulation and distress for every soul of man who does evil, of the Jew first and also of the Greek, [10]but glory and honor and peace to everyone who does good, to the Jew first and also to the Greek. [11]For there is no partiality with God.

[12]For all who have sinned without the Law will also perish without the Law, and all who have sinned under the Law will be judged by the Law; [13]for *it is* not the hearers of the Law *who* are just before God, but the doers of the Law will be justified. [14]For when Gentiles who do not have the Law do instinctively the things of the Law, these, not having the Law, are a law to themselves, [15]in that they show the work of the Law written in their hearts, their conscience bearing witness and their thoughts alternately accusing or else defending them, [16]on the day when, according to my gospel, God will judge the secrets of men through Christ Jesus.

---

Throughout the first chapter of Romans, Paul consistently referred to sinful humanity as "they" and "them," a nice, safe, third-person pronoun that keeps the accusing finger pointed elsewhere. "*They* are without excuse" (1:20). "Even though *they* knew God, *they* did not honor Him" (1:21)." "*They* became futile" (1:21); "*they* became fools" (1:22); "*they* exchanged the truth of God for a lie" (1:25). "God gave *them* over" (1:24); "God gave *them* over" (1:26); "God gave *them* over" (1:28). Then, having catalogued the depravity of humanity in agonizing detail, Paul suddenly spins the pronoun a full 180 degrees from the outward third person to the inward-pointing second person: *you.*

Some have suggested that Paul here turns his attention from the Gentile to the Jew. The Hebrew Christians in the congregation undoubtedly felt affirmed by their Jewish brother's diagnosis of Gentile depravity. God created all of humanity to worship Him, yet He intentionally and specifically called the offspring of Abraham, Isaac, and Jacob—the Hebrew people—to be His instrument of righteousness in the world. And while God gave the Gentiles over to their degrading passions, He held the Hebrew people accountable and chastised them like his children. Of all the races of humanity, the Hebrews received the blessing of the Law to steward for the sake of all, which gave many Jews not only a sense of high calling, but an exalted sense of superior worth. In fact, many smugly believed that their heritage as "God's chosen people" exempted them from judgment.

While the Jew-Gentile tension that characterized other churches may have plagued the church in Rome, nothing in Paul's language suggests that he specifically had this divide in mind. More likely, the shift from "they" to "you" was not from Gentile to Jew, but from humanity in general to "O man—everyone who passes judgment" (literally translated from the Greek.) Having condemned the world, Paul places the *reader* on trial.

In this segment, three truths become clear: God's judgment is inescapable (2:1–4), God's judgment is impartial (2:5–11), and God's judgment is universal (2:12–16).

— **2:1–4** —

At first, the reader might object to Paul's blanket indictment of his or her character. *Me? Practice the same things? I'm not guilty of Paul's list of crimes!* But let me ask you a question. Take your time and be honest; this is just between you and the Lord right now. How do you determine who is "good" and who is "bad"?

If you're like most people—including me—you have in your unconscious mind at least three moral categories into which you place people. Some are, without question, undeniably "bad." Adolf Hitler. Joseph Stalin. Charles Manson. Judas Iscariot. Nero. Nearly everyone would agree, I think. These people were clearly evil.

Then there are a few undeniably "good" people, like the late Mother Teresa. She's often held up as the modern standard of "good" for most. Another would be

Billy Graham. Someone might say, "Well, I'm no Mother Teresa or Billy Graham, but I'm a pretty decent guy."

Then there's a broad middle category containing the masses of somewhat-good-yet-sometimes-bad and other, yet-to-be-determined people. That's where we usually place ourselves, isn't it? And, within that category, we mentally rank people in order of observable goodness. Some are better than others … clearly. Now, who do you suppose is the measuring rod? (Be honest. Remember, it's just you and the Lord right now.) You guessed correctly: Self.

When driving on the freeway, people who go slower than us are jerks and idiots, and whoever drives faster is clearly a menace to safety! When people are asked whether they are going to heaven or hell, many will answer, "Well, I'm not perfect, but I've never *killed* anyone, so I guess I'm a pretty good person." Alcoholics often look down on "dope-heads," while drug addicts ridicule "drunks." Even in prison, murderers, rapists, and thieves have no tolerance for child molesters and have no compunction about mistreating, even killing them. Such honor among criminals!

With Paul, we all agree that "the judgment of God rightly falls upon those who practice [evil]" (2:2). But he reminds us that the same judgment we call down on others falls on us as well. That's the part that makes us squirm. We all want justice for the world, but we each carry within us a standard of righteousness based on our own perceived goodness. Furthermore, we will tolerate only as much evil in the world as we can accept within ourselves. When we feel resentment toward God for not eradicating evil in the world, we forget that eliminating *all* evil would mean the end of us too! So, from now on we'll have to say what we really mean. "Lord, get rid of all evil *that's worse than what's inside of me.*"

The judgment of God falls on every person because the standard of righteousness is perfection. So why are any of us alive? Why have we not been reduced to a cinder by God's wrath? "The riches of His kindness and tolerance and patience" (2:4). In other words, grace.

— **2:5–11** —

At the end of days, there will be a terrifying courtroom scene involving every human being who ever took a breath on earth. The deeds of each man and woman will be laid on a scale and weighed against the holy character of God—the very definition of righteousness (2:5–6). Wealth, power, position, race, color, nationality, heritage, and philosophy will count for nothing. Religion will count for nothing. The standard will be the same for all—those who have had access to the Law and those who did not. God "will render to each person according to his [or her]

According to Paul, God's holy character is the true standard of righteousness. At the final judgment, our goodness will be compared to the Lord's—not the righteousness of other people or even our own conscience. If the weight of our righteousness fails to tip the balance in our favor, we will be found guilty.

deeds" (2:6), a promise of the Old Testament (Ps. 62:12; Prov. 24:12) repeated by Jesus (Matt. 16:27) and described in detail by John's Revelation. The reward of righteousness is eternal life (Rom. 2:7), but the penalty for unrighteousness is wrath (2:8).

Paul has not contradicted himself. He earlier wrote that the gospel "is the power of God for salvation to everyone who believes" (1:16), and he quoted the Old Testament prophet's declaration that "the righteous will live by his faith" (Hab. 2:4). He merely meant to clarify that each person will be *judged* by his or her deeds, not *saved* by them. At the end of days, each will lay his or her deeds on the scale and they will be found wanting. No amount of good deeds will balance the righteousness of God on the other side — not even close.

The apostle's point is simple: "There is no partiality with God" (2:11). All have equal opportunity to stand before the Judge to present evidence of their own righteousness. And the standard will be the same for all. But, Paul warns, "because of your stubbornness and unrepentant heart you are storing up wrath for yourself"

(2:5). Anyone daring to presume that his or her deeds are sufficiently good for eternal life or that God, who sees all, will overlook sin has chosen a bleak future.

<h2 style="text-align:center">— 2:12–16 —</h2>

The old saying, "The road to hell is paved with good intentions," seems especially appropriate in light of Paul's words. We all intend to do well. The question is, do we act on that knowledge? And when we do act, are our actions righteous?

Some may take issue with the apostle's statement, "All who have sinned without [having heard] the Law will also perish [not having heard] the Law" (2:12). That hardly seems fair. How can someone be justly punished for breaking rules he or she knows nothing about? But that's Paul's point entirely. Gentiles living in places far removed from the Promised Land may have never known a single Hebrew or the Law he kept, but every man and woman bears the image of God—an image smudged by sin, but God's image nonetheless. And part of that image includes an innate sense that some actions are good and some are bad. The details may not be accurate. One's understanding of "good" may be flawed. Nevertheless, even by this imperfect standard, no one lives righteously. No one has ever perfectly obeyed his or her own conscience. Guilt is a universal reaction to doing something one's personal ethic forbids.

At the end of days, when the final verdict is rendered, the deeds of each person will have been weighed and found lacking. And ignorance of the Law is no excuse. Each person will be judged according to his or her knowledge of right and wrong. And by any standard—the Law of Moses or the Gentile's own conscience—each person will be found guilty.

## Application

### *Start Where You Are*

In this segment, Paul turns our accusing finger around to point inward and then makes a bold declaration: "You have no excuse, everyone of you who passes judgment, for in that which you judge another, you condemn yourself" (Rom. 2:1). The Greek verb translated here as "judge" is the same term used by Matthew when recounting the teaching of Jesus, "Do not judge lest you be judged" (Matt. 7:1). But did Paul or Jesus mean that we should "see no evil" or allow the sin of another to go unchecked? Certainly not!

Neither Jesus nor Paul suggests that we should be undiscerning. Paul wrote to the church in Corinth concerning a man who had been intimate with his father's wife, "For I, on my part, though absent in body but present in spirit, have already judged him who has so committed this, as though I were present" (1 Cor. 5:3). He then called for the man to be put out of the congregation in the hope that the chastisement would bring him to repentance (1 Cor. 5:5). Jesus challenged His hearers, "Why do you not even on your own initiative judge what is right?" (Luke 12:57). The Lord gave us a conscience and He expects us to use it to defend the defenseless and to uphold justice. After all, the safety and health of any community are measured by its laws and how well it prosecutes them. Tolerance without limits is unacceptable.

In warning people not to "judge," Jesus and Paul caution against the insidious sin of hypocrisy. When we discern right from wrong and then hold one another accountable, we must be keenly aware of our own motives. Have we adopted an attitude of self-righteousness that cares nothing for the soul of another? Do we name the sins of another and then (like modern-day Pharisees) show no mercy? Have we cultivated a superior attitude that condemns others for the sake of selfish gain? Are we in fact diverting attention away from our own guilt by pointing an accusing finger at the wrongdoing of another? The answers to those questions are gravely important. Jesus warned, "For in the way you judge, you will be judged; and by your standard of measure, it will be measured to you" (Matt. 7:2).

The Lord wants us to care about right and wrong. He wants the righteousness of earth to reflect that of heaven. He wants us to be agents of good and to stand against evil. And the best place to start is not far from where you sit right now. Self-examination is the place to begin. If you genuinely care to eradicate evil from the world, accept Jesus' challenge:

> "Why do you look at the speck that is in your brother's eye, but do not notice the log that is in your own eye?
>
> "Or how can you say to your brother, 'Let me take the speck out of your eye,' and behold, the log is in your own eye?
>
> "You hypocrite, first take the log out of your own eye, and then you will see clearly to take the speck out of your brother's eye." (Matt. 7:3–5)

This brings us back to Paul's purpose for stating, "in that which you judge another, you condemn yourself" (Rom. 2:1). If we genuinely care about the righteousness of God, if we authentically desire to condemn sin and uphold justice, if we truly want to be champions of good, we must begin with an examination of ourselves. Then, if we have any time remaining, we can call the sin of another into account. Being aware of our own flaws, we will more likely "judge" others with a humble attitude in a spirit of grace.

## The Dark Side of Religion (2:17–29)

[17]But if you bear the name "Jew" and rely upon the Law and boast in God, [18]and know *His* will and approve the things that are essential, being instructed out of the Law, [19]and are confident that you yourself are a guide to the blind, a light to those who are in darkness, [20]a corrector of the foolish, a teacher of the immature, having in the Law the embodiment of knowledge and of the truth, [21]you, therefore, who teach another, do you not teach yourself? You who preach that one shall not steal, do you steal? [22]You who say that one should not commit adultery, do you commit adultery? You who abhor idols, do you rob temples? [23]You who boast in the Law, through your breaking the Law, do you dishonor God? [24]For "the name of God is blasphemed among the Gentiles because of you," just as it is written.

[25]For indeed circumcision is of value if you practice the Law; but if you are a transgressor of the Law, your circumcision has become uncircumcision. [26]So if the uncircumcised man keeps the requirements of the Law, will not his uncircumcision be regarded as circumcision? [27]And he who is physically uncircumcised, if he keeps the Law, will he not judge you who though having the letter *of the Law* and circumcision are a transgressor of the Law? [28]For he is not a Jew who is one outwardly, nor is circumcision that which is outward in the flesh. [29]But he is a Jew who is one inwardly; and circumcision is that which is of the heart, by the Spirit, not by the letter; and his praise is not from men, but from God.

Depending on how you look at it, religion can be either good or bad. We generally look on religious people favorably, even when we don't agree with their religion. Mahatma Ghandi undoubtedly changed his part of the world for the better. Martin Luther King Jr. stood on the crest of a great swell of racial resentment and, unlike many of his violent contemporaries, gave it a peaceful, visionary voice. Many who know almost nothing about Christianity revere Billy Graham as a preeminent man of God. Furthermore, statesmen have long understood the crucial role of religion in maintaining a peaceful, orderly society. When people believe in something greater than themselves, they generally behave better.

But religion has a dark side. It has caused dissention, sustained wars, and inspired atrocities. Genocide—the mass destruction of an entire race—is almost always motivated by religious hatred. Consequently, some atheists have declared intellectual and political war on all belief in the supernatural, hoping that this will rid the world of its most prolific evil, religion. Obviously, I don't share their reasoning, but I do appreciate the motive. In fact, if I were given a one-time-only opportunity to preach one message to a group of Christians, it would be, "How to Be a Christian without Being Religious."[4]

That sounds like a contradiction, doesn't it? Isn't being a Christian the same as being religious? As most people understand the term "Christian," yes. But as I read Paul's letter to the Romans, no.

Some people's idea of Christianity reminds me of a treadmill. Every day I see determined Christians climb onto the religious demands of their leaders and peers, and they start running. Faster and faster, working, striving, hoping, pleading, and praying they might please God, or win His favor, or maybe just cause Him to smile on them for a moment or two. With so much distance between the perfection God demands and where we stand, certainly we'll have to work hard to close the gap.

That's religion. All pain, no gain.

Fortunately, genuine Christian practice has nothing to do with religion. For one to become a Christian, he or she must first accept that no amount of effort on the treadmill will put distance between us and our sin, nor will religious effort bring us any closer to God. Only the grace of God will do that. God's grace provides salvation we cannot earn, favor we do not deserve, kindness we cannot repay.

But for the natural mind, grace doesn't make sense. In this world, "there ain't no such thing as a free lunch." "You get what you pay for." Justice demands restitution in exchange for sin. So, finding themselves trapped between the awful vision of damnation and the impossible demands of religion, people delude themselves into thinking that the right "something" will somehow transform them within. They vainly search for the right ritual, the right talisman, the right tradition, the right heritage. However, it's all vain. Religion is all wrong!

By the end of chapter 1, Paul demonstrated that Gentiles have condemned themselves by chasing false gods. And in the first section of chapter 2, he proved that pursuing the one true God on one's own terms is no better. We cannot satisfy our own, self-defined standard of righteousness, to say nothing of God's standard. Now the apostle turns his attention to the most religious people of all, the Jews.

As we read Paul's indictment of God's covenant people, we must keep in mind that it pours from the pen of a Jew. Nevertheless, everything he writes to his kinsmen also applies to present-day Christians. As Donald Grey Barnhouse wrote:

> There are those who are attached to form, ceremony, liturgy, religious precepts and practices, and all the attitudes that go with such attachment, and who are yet alien to the grace of God. They have ritual without redemption, works without worship, form of service without the fear of God in its proper sense, and thus they come under the condemnation of God.

It makes no difference what name they go by, the principle is the same. In the day the New Testament was written the argument was against the religious Jews. Today it would be against zealous Roman Catholics or the fervent Fundamentalist just as much as it was against the Jew in Paul's day. The profession of religion, even though it be divinely revealed religion, is not enough if the one who professes the religion is not in some sense transformed by it.[5]

## — 2:17–20 —

Paul begins by identifying several sources of religious arrogance for Jews:

*Their title*: the very name "Jew" comes from "Judah," meaning "Yahweh be praised." This wonderful reminder of the covenant could also become a source of smugness. Many even claimed the title as a kind of surname, such as "Chuck Swindoll, Jew."

*Their possession of the Law*: God chose the Hebrew people to bear His Word to the rest of the world. Many thought this responsibility exempted them from God's judgment.

*Their unique relationship with God*: To "boast in God" meant to claim superior standing because of someone or something, and to express a high degree of confidence because of it. The secular Greek almost always used the term negatively, as did Paul.

*Their knowledge of God's will*: As recipients of divine instruction, they were capable of discerning His plan for the ages. In addition to the Law, they carefully preserved the writings of the prophets, knowledge of the future that undoubtedly fed their elitist national pride.

*Their responsibility to instruct the nations*: God charged the Jews with the responsibility to teach the rest of the world about Him, a duty that was as old as the covenant with Abraham. They were to be "a guide to the blind, a light to those who are in darkness, a corrector of the foolish, a teacher of the immature" (2:19–20). Many Jews thought mere possession of the truth automatically gave them superior ability to accomplish their task.

The dark side of all these blessings was pride, such arrogance that many Jews referred to Gentiles as "dogs."

Paul's purpose is not to bash his fellow Jews or to suggest that their unique privilege as God's chosen people is bad, but to help his Jewish readers understand that their religion does nothing to transform them. Behaving correctly on the outside will do nothing to cleanse the inside. That's the definition of religion,

## From My Journal

## Shame on the Church

The shrill ring of the telephone broke the silence in my study but the caller's message broke my heart. Another fellow minister had fallen morally. Another soldier of the cross, who once stood tall—who had armed his congregation with truth and encouraged them to stand strong against the adversary—had disgracefully deserted the ranks and given victory to the enemy by his sin. Even before I put the receiver down, tears flooded my eyes.

An ancient scene flashed through my mind, a sickening scene—a battlefield in Israel called Mount Gilboa, littered with the bodies of Hebrew soldiers after a tragic day of combat against the Philistines. Among the dead lay a tall, seasoned warrior-king named Saul. How the pagans of Philistia must have gloated in their victory over the army of God! And while Saul had turned David's life into a nightmare for more than a dozen years, David lamented the king's death with the words, "How have the mighty fallen" in battle (2 Sam. 1:20, 27).

As I sat alone in my study, I thought about David's fall, which began with a stumble on a rooftop overlooking the beautiful Bathsheba. His stumble led to a fall that still causes me to shudder. I wondered if those same words haunted the king after Nathan stuck a boney finger in his face and declared, "You are the man!" (2 Sam. 12:7). God's most valiant warrior—the man who had routed the enemies of his Lord and torn down idols to false deities—had slandered the name of the Most High with his adultery and murderous cover-up. How the enemies of God must have gloated. Even after repentance, nothing was ever the same for David, his household, or his reign.

When anyone in the family of God fails, it affects everyone, but the moral failure of a leader shakes the church all the way to its foundations. And sometimes, a congregation can never quite recover. So there in my study I shuddered to think of my fellow warrior, sitting alone in his own study, perhaps with his face in his hands wondering to himself, *How could I have brought this shame upon myself, my family, my wife, my church, and—more grievous than anything—how could I have so disgraced the name of my Lord?*

Knowing that I am merely a man whose old nature will not die until I am with my Savior in eternity, I pleaded with my Lord, "Protect me from the evil one. Should I stumble, deal harshly with me if You must. Stop me, O God, before I fall! Never let it be said of me, 'How have the mighty fallen' in battle. Not only for my sake, but for the sake of Your name."

after all; doing external things to make the inner person worthy of salvation. Invariably, this disparity between inner and outer righteousness inevitably leads to hypocrisy.

### —2:21-24—

The apostle then dons the robes of a barrister to cross-examine the self-righteous, first by probing his integrity and then by bringing irrefutable evidence of guilt against the source of the Jew's religious pride: his heritage. He asks five pointed questions:

- You ... who teach another, do you not teach yourself? (2:21)
- You who preach that one shall not steal, do you steal? (2:21)
- You who say that one should not commit adultery, do you commit adultery? (2:22)
- You who abhor idols, do you rob temples? (2:22)
- You who boast in the Law, through your breaking the Law, do you dishonor God? (2:23)

If by chance the individual could answer no to the first four or dare deny the fifth, he or she cannot escape the indictment of the prophets Isaiah and Ezekiel (Isa. 52:5; Ezek. 36:20–22). The Jew cannot—any more than the Gentile—claim exemption from God's judgment on the basis of personal holiness or religious heritage. " 'The name of God is blasphemed among the Gentiles because of you,' just as it is written" (2:24).

### —2:25-29—

If, somehow, Paul's Jewish readers remain unconvinced, he addresses the most personal and intimate aspect of the Jew's religious heritage. Circumcision represented a Jewish man's participation in God's covenant with Abraham from their ancestor's earliest days (Gen. 17). This initiation, accomplished on his behalf on the eighth day of life, was a visible reminder that God had claimed the boy as His own, that he should be a "son of the covenant." Many Jews thought participation in God's covenant with Abraham exempted them from divine wrath.

According to Paul, nothing is further from the truth. Drawing on the prophets of the Old Testament, he reminds his kinsmen that circumcision is but an outward symbol of what should be true on the inside. God cares more about "circumcision of the heart" (Deut. 10:16, 30:6; Jer. 4:4), in which followers show honor to His character by being like Him, by obeying His Law.

A classic sign of religion — treadmill religion — is the overemphasis of secondary things and the neglect of primary things. We can accomplish physical circumcision on our own. That's a religious requirement we can do without God's help. But circumcision of the heart requires a kind of surgery beyond our capabilities. That's a supernatural operation. And the outward symbol of this true circumcision is obedience. Paul emphatically states that the Lord prefers a Gentile with a circumcised heart over a disobedient Jew bearing the outward symbol of a broken covenant.

Let me put this in terms that may hit closer to home. Which would you prefer? An unfaithful spouse who proudly wears your wedding band, or a mate who guards your shared intimacy with his or her life but doesn't wear a ring? The wedding band is a circular, gold symbol of eternal fidelity. It's supposed to be an outward symbol of what's true of the wearer's heart. How foolish to think that the ring is the most important element of a marital union. Furthermore, how foolish to think that a ring can keep a person faithful to his or her mate.

Circumcision and a wedding band have a lot in common. They are supposed to be outward symbols of one's inner conviction. Unfortunately, religion places undue emphasis on the symbol while ignoring what God considers most important.

In my experience, religion reveals itself in at least three ways.

First, *religion emphasizes the physical over the spiritual.* It underscores pious activities and the *appearance* of sacrificial labor. Religion keeps a person busy to the point of exhaustion and emphasizes doing good in order to be seen and admired.

Second, *religion emphasizes secondary matters while ignoring matters of primary importance.* Symbols, traditions, and rituals become more important than the actual mission of the church or the true maturity of its people. Outward appearances become the focus of attention rather than sincere belief and genuine obedience.

Third, *religion promotes self-interest above all else.* Make no mistake. The religious zealot is thinking about himself. Whatever is done, his motivation remains a desire to be seen and known. Remaining obscure and refusing to seek the limelight is foreign to his or her way of thinking. Religion prompts pride to reach ever more prominent positions of power and notoriety.

If all of that were not bad enough, religion also blinds the devotee to his or her need for God's grace. How ironic, how tragic that religion should lead so directly to damnation.

## Application

## *A Question of Privilege*

As Paul reviewed the five sources of Jewish arrogance (2:17–21), I am prompted to take a close look at my own attitudes, as well as the general spirit of the church I serve. The privileges enjoyed by the Hebrew nation are now the privileges of the Christian—at least for this season in God's redemptive plan. Each of these privileges begs a self-examining question. If you are a Christian leader—pastor, elder, deacon, teacher, small-group leader, volunteer coordinator, or the head of a household—let me challenge you to read each privilege and contemplate your response to each question carefully.

- *Our title*: We should wear the label "Christian" with honor. To declare yourself a Christian is to publicly affirm a code of conduct that others can trust and invites your peers to hold you accountable to it. *When we don the title "Christian," who receives the glory, God or self?*

- *Possession of divine truth*: The responsibility to protect and steward God's written Word—the sixty-six books that comprise the Bible—belongs not to any one official institution, but to all believers and communities of believers. We have been chosen by God to bear His message to the rest of the world. This enormous privilege comes with immense responsibility. *Do we behave as though God's truth doesn't apply to us or that we have somehow risen above the need for grace?*

- *Our unique relationship with God*: As believers, we now have "peace with God" (5:1) by grace, through faith in Jesus Christ. Furthermore, we have the Spirit of the almighty Creator living within us, a privilege more wonderful than the Old Testament saints could have imagined. *In what do we "boast"—that is, "assign credit"—the grace of God or our own merit?*

- *Our knowledge of God's will*: Scripture has revealed that God's will is to reclaim His creation from evil and then fill it with His righteousness. Scripture has also declared how He will do this and what specific events will signal His coming. *Are we simply biding our time until end-time events usher in the next age, or are we actively taking part in God's plan to reach our world with the good news and fill it with His righteousness?*

- *Our responsibility to instruct the nations*: Jesus commanded His followers to "go and make disciples of all the nations" (Matt. 28:19–20), a continuation of God's command to Israel (Rom. 2:19–20). Printing, distributing, and carrying copies of the Scriptures is an honorable undertaking, but it cannot be a substitute for allowing the Word of God to be seen in our actions. *As we teach, memorize, and quote Scripture, do we practice the truth we preach so that the world might be won, virtually without a word?*

Current church growth models in our culture place a great deal of emphasis on vision statements. As you reflect on these five privileges and their associated responsibilities, how would you change the vision statement of your church? If you were asked to write a personal vision statement for your own life in one sentence, could you? Give it a try.

## "Objection Overruled" (3:1–8)

---

[1]Then what advantage has the Jew? Or what is the benefit of circumcision? [2]Great in every respect. First of all, that they were entrusted with the oracles of God. [3]What then? If some did not believe, their unbelief will not nullify the faithfulness of God, will it? [4]May it never be! Rather, let God be found true, though every man *be found* a liar, as it is written,

> "That You may be justified in Your words,
> And prevail when You are judged."

[5]But if our unrighteousness demonstrates the righteousness of God, what shall we say? The God who inflicts wrath is not unrighteous, is He? (I am speaking in human terms.) [6]May it never be! For otherwise, how will God judge the world? [7]But if through my lie the truth of God abounded to His glory, why am I also still being judged as a sinner? [8]And why not *say* (as we are slanderously reported and as some claim that we say), "Let us do evil that good may come"? Their condemnation is just.

---

In 1886, Scottish author Robert Louis Stevenson wrote a novella that reflected a disturbing truth about everyone. He titled it *The Strange Case of Dr Jekyll and Mr Hyde*. It's the story of a respected physician and medical researcher, who embodied the very best Victorian ideals of morality and decency. However, experiments on himself released a murderous savage that had been lurking in the shadows of his gentle public demeanor.

At the heart of great literature, you will often find good theology. Stevenson's bizarre tale continues to captivate and fascinate audiences more than a century later because — at some level — we see ourselves in Dr. Jekyll and we fear the Mr. Hyde we deftly keep hidden. Mark Twain, perhaps influenced by Stevenson's tale, noted, "Everyone is a moon and has a dark side which he never shows to anybody."

The central theme of Paul's letter to the Romans is the gospel, the good news. He begins, however, with the bad news, the dark side of the moon, the universal problem of human depravity. For how can anyone understand the need for a Savior who does not first acknowledge the evil lurking in the shadows of his or her public self?

Now, don't misunderstand. As we learned earlier, the term "depraved" doesn't mean that we are as bad as we can possibly be. People with a Mr. Hyde nature often accomplish good things, including great deeds of kindness to others. Furthermore, we could always be much worse than we are. However, we deserve none of the credit for whatever good we may have accomplished. We have a nature that is enslaved to evil and, were it not for the fear of being caught and the inevitable consequences of wrongdoing, nothing would prevent any one of us from falling headlong into abject corruption. You've probably heard the expression, "Power corrupts and absolute power corrupts absolutely." It's true. Absolute power means the absence of restraint. Someone with absolute power can do anything he or she pleases without consequence. And in the absence of external restraint, the depraved human nature lurking within each of us will express itself with astonishing acts of selfishness, cruelty, lust, and murder.

The term "depravity" has more to do with the vertical plane of existence — our relationship with God — than our horizontal dealings on earth. We are not as bad as we can possibly be; however, our sinful deeds prove that we are as bad *off* as we can possibly be. Our good deeds do nothing to overcome our separation from God, legally or relationally. We stand condemned, not only because of what we have done, but because of what we *are*.

To prove that the rule applies to everyone, Paul systematically turned from one person to the next, peeling off whatever mask he or she might be wearing. He has stripped the upright intellectual Gentile of his disguise to reveal a simpering fool, who merely professes to be wise, worships creation over the Creator, and exchanges the natural for the unnatural (1:18–32). Consequently, God has given such people over to "impurity," and to "degrading passions," and to a "depraved mind" — that is, a mind proven to be worthless by its deeds.

He then sliced through the armor of the self-satisfied crusader, the self-righteous moralist, who presumes to be above judgment by virtue of his or her rituals and traditions. To no one's surprise, we find beneath the gleaming breastplate of religion a corrupt heart, quivering under the condemnation of his own conscience, unable to satisfy her own moral code, to say nothing of God's (2:1–16).

Lastly, the apostle defrocked his fellow sons of the covenant. Clearly, God chose the Hebrew people to receive His Word and to share it with the world, yet despite their unique relationship with the Creator, they were not exempt from divine judgment. In fact, they deserve a greater portion. Gentiles sin in ignorance and must reap the wages of sin, but Jews rebel against God with a greater knowledge of what they have rejected, knowing fully whom they are offending and the consequences their sin will reap.

By this point in his letter, Paul has sufficiently demonstrated that everyone is guilty: the willfully ignorant (1:18–32), the self-righteous (2:1–16), and the super-religious (2:17–19). They all deserve the wrath of God. As Paul taught this truth in the synagogues, he undoubtedly encountered a number of objections. To anticipate rebuttals among his readers, the apostle restates each of the four most common objections in the form of a question:

- the question of *racial advantage*
- the question of *divine faithfulness*
- the question of *confused righteousness*
- the question of *twisted logic*

## —3:1–2—

The question of *racial advantage*: "Then what advantage has the Jew? Or what is the benefit of circumcision?" (3:1). In other words, If God's covenant with the descendants of Abraham (and those Gentiles who entered the same covenant by choice [Gen. 17:12–13; Ex. 12:48–49]), doesn't make them righteous, what was the point?

Paul explains that God's covenant does not exempt anyone from judgment; however it is an unequalled privilege. The descendants of Abraham, Isaac, and Jacob received more truth than any other group of people on earth. To them the Scriptures were given. Through them the Scriptures were shared. From them the whole world would receive God's invitation to receive grace.

## —3:3–4—

The question of *divine faithfulness*: "What then? If some did not believe, their unbelief will not nullify the faithfulness of God, will it?" (3:3). In other words, Does the failure of the Hebrew people to keep their end of the bargain prevent God from accomplishing His plan to save the world?

The answer is obvious. The unbelief of the entire Jewish race will never in any way prevent God from accomplishing His will. He keeps His promises and He will remain faithful despite the failure of humanity. In fact, His light only shines brighter against the inky-black backdrop of humanity's darkness. To illustrate, Paul draws on King David's prayer of repentance in Psalm 51:

> Against You, You only, I have sinned
> And done what is evil in Your sight,
> So that You are justified when You speak
> And blameless when You judge. (Psalm 51:4)

## —3:5–6—

The question of *confused righteousness*: "But if our unrighteousness demonstrates the righteousness of God, what shall we say? The God who inflicts wrath is not unrighteous, is He?" (3:5). In other words, Because God made these moral demands knowing humanity would fail, does that make His wrath unjustified? After all, weren't we doomed to failure from the beginning?

As Paul will explain later, the giving of the Law did not suddenly make humankind guilty of wrongdoing. He didn't arbitrarily paint a target somewhere other than where we had already shot the arrow and then call it a miss. The target has always been present. God's utterly righteous character is—and always has been—the standard. The Law merely illuminates and magnifies the target, leaving humankind with even less excuse for missing it. Paul will explain this in greater detail in the next major section of his letter (4:15; 5:13).

The Lord did not give the Law to humanity in order to justify His wrath. On the contrary, He established clear lines between right and wrong as a means of grace, to confront humankind with our offences. The giving of the Law was a first step in His plan to redeem us.

## —3:7–8—

The question of *twisted logic*: "But if through my lie the truth of God abounded to His glory, why am I also still being judged as a sinner? And why not say ... 'Let us do evil that good may come'?" (3:7–8). In other words, If God's light shines brighter because of our darkness, haven't we glorified God all the more by our wrongdoing? Let's sin like crazy so we'll know grace like never before!

What bizarre thinking! It fails to comprehend the destructive nature of sin. That kind of logic is no better than saying, "If fires and disasters give rescue workers an opportunity to display their skills and bravery, why not set far more fires and cause more disasters so they will have greater opportunity to show their courage?" Sounds great until you consider the victims.

But there are no victimless sins. Every choice to do wrong harms someone; if not right away, inevitably, and if not directly, indirectly. At some level, all of humanity suffers. And far from glorifying God, sin grieves Him—as an affront to His character, all that He is and everything He desires. Sin separates the Creator from the creation He loves so dearly.

Note Paul's final remark. Referring to those who would justify their willful sin with such twisted logic, he declares simply, "Their condemnation is just."

## Application

### *Religion versus Grace*

Paul's Jewish readers objected to the doctrine of justification by grace through faith for the same reasons that are protested by all human-empowered religions. First, God's unmerited favor releases the individual from religious control. Second, grace removes religion as the means by which a person maintains a relationship with God. And third, grace completely changes the purpose of good deeds in the life of the believer. Consequently, grace renders religion obsolete and ineffective, which is bad news for those who derive their power, purpose, or livelihood from religious followers.

Because grace profoundly affects how we relate to God, grace also changes how we think and live. Specifically, receiving God's grace determines how we handle our possessions, how we conduct our lives, and how we regard ourselves (to name only a few specifics). Religion and grace send these conflicting messages:

*Our possessions*
> Religion says: "Keep it, be proud of it, it is your reward for good behavior."
> Grace says: "Share it, be grateful for it, it is God's to steward wisely."

*Our actions*
> Religion says: "Continually strive to earn God's favor, because enough is never quite enough."
> Grace says: "You already have God's favor, because His grace is sufficient."

*Our self-regard*
> Religion says: "I am a good person because of what I have accomplished. Look at me!"

Grace says: "I am a sinner who has been given the righteousness of God. Look at Christ!"

As you examine your life—how you handle your possessions, what drives your activity, how you regard yourself—which voice do you hear and heed? Do you answer the daily call of religion and then strive for acceptance, or do you accept the invitation of God and then daily rest in that relationship?

Receiving God's grace begins with a most unnatural choice for natural humanity: we must admit our helplessness and accept His supernatural intervention. Daily.

## An Autopsy of Depravity (3:9–20)

---

⁹What then? Are we better than they? Not at all; for we have already charged that both Jews and Greeks are all under sin; ¹⁰as it is written,

> "There is none righteous, not even one;
> ¹¹ There is none who understands,
> There is none who seeks for God;
> ¹² All have turned aside, together they have become useless;
> There is none who does good,
> There is not even one."
> ¹³ "Their throat is an open grave,
> With their tongues they keep deceiving,"
> "The poison of asps is under their lips";
> ¹⁴ "Whose mouth is full of cursing and bitterness";
> ¹⁵ "Their feet are swift to shed blood,
> ¹⁶ Destruction and misery are in their paths,
> ¹⁷ And the path of peace they have not known."
> ¹⁸ "There is no fear of God before their eyes."

¹⁹Now we know that whatever the Law says, it speaks to those who are under the Law, so that every mouth may be closed and all the world may become accountable to God; ²⁰because by the works of the Law no flesh will be justified in His sight; for through the Law *comes* the knowledge of sin.

---

The rhetorical question translated "Are we better than they?" in the NASB is actually one Greek word, the form of which could mean either "Are we making ourselves excel?" or "Are we being excelled?" Most translators opt for the former because it

## As it is written ...

| | | | |
|---|---|---|---|
| 3:10–12 | "There is none righteous, not even one; There is none who understands, There is none who seeks for God; All have turned aside, together they have become useless; There is none who does good, There is not even one." | Ps. 14:1–3 (Ps. 53:1–3) | The fool has said in his heart, "There is no God." They are corrupt, they have committed abominable deeds; There is no one who does good. The LORD has looked down from heaven upon the sons of men To see if there are any who understand, Who seek after God. They have all turned aside, together they have become corrupt; There is no one who does good, not even one. |
| 3:10–12 | | Eccl.7:20 | Indeed, there is not a righteous man on earth who continually does good and who never sins. |
| 3:13 | "Their throat is an open grave, With their tongues they keep deceiving," "The poison of asps is under their lips" | Ps. 5:9 | There is nothing reliable in what they say; Their inward part is destruction itself. Their throat is an open grave; They flatter with their tongue. |
| 3:13 | | Ps. 140:3 | They sharpen their tongues as a serpent; Poison of a viper is under their lips. Selah. |
| 3:14 | "Whose mouth is full of cursing and bitterness"; | Ps. 10:7 | His mouth is full of curses and deceit and oppression; Under his tongue is mischief and wickedness. |
| 3:15–17 | "Their feet are swift to shed blood, Destruction and misery are in their paths, And the path of peace they have not known." | Isa. 59:7–8 | Their feet run to evil, And they hasten to shed innocent blood; Their thoughts are thoughts of iniquity, Devastation and destruction are in their highways. They do not know the way of peace, And there is no justice in their tracks; They have made their paths crooked, Whoever treads on them does not know peace. |
| 3:18 | "There is no fear of God before their eyes." | Ps. 36:1 | Transgression speaks to the ungodly within his heart; There is no fear of God before his eyes. |

parallels the question Paul posed in 3:1. To link the two questions as synonymous, he introduces each with the Greek expression, "*Ti oun*," or "what then?" But he then proceeds to answer the same question differently:

"What advantage has the Jew?" "Great in every respect." (3:1–2)

Are we [Jews] advantaged? "Not at all." (3:9)

### —3:9—

So, which is it? Did the Jews have an advantage over Gentiles? The answer is yes ... and no—depending upon how you look at it.

Suppose a multibillionaire were to visit your home with a proposition: "I want to give my money to the most needy people in the world and I want to funnel those funds through your personal bank account. As I make the deposits, you write the checks." Now imagine ten years have gone by and no one was any better off than before. None of the recipients cashed their checks; even you failed to make a withdrawal for yourself. Did you have an advantage? Certainly! You enjoyed complete access to the billionaire's wealth. Yet, in a practical sense, you gained nothing. Because you failed to withdraw funds for yourself, you're no better off than the people who mindlessly tore up their checks.

The Hebrew people were given direct access to the truth of God as the agent of His Word, the means by which He would bless the world (Gen. 12:3; 22:18). Yet, just as the Gentiles "exchanged the truth of God for a lie, and worshiped and served the creature rather than the Creator" (1:25), so the descendents of Abraham, Isaac, and Jacob turned from God, causing His name to be "blasphemed among the Gentiles" (2:24). The Jew and the pagan are no different. Within each beats the same sin-sick heart.

### —3:10–18—

A good friend of mine has been in the funeral business for more than thirty-five years. One particularly vivid conversation with him made a lasting impression on me. He said in a pensive tone, "I have seen what most people will never see. In my career, I've had just about every age, race, nationality, size, and religion represented on my coroner's table. When you cut them open and look inside, they all look the same. And, let me assure you, it's never pretty."

In a final, dramatic flourish, Paul settles the issue of universal human depravity, leaving no room for argument or objection. And, in the time-honored tradition of a rabbi, he strings together the indisputable words of God like pearls. Note the apostle's direct quotations and clear allusions from the Old Testament:

Paul lays humanity on the examining table and cuts through all outward appearance to expose what lies within.

> Their throat is an open grave.
> With their tongues they keep deceiving.
> The poison of asps is under their lips.
> Their mouth is full of cursing and bitterness.
> There is no fear before their eyes.
> Their feet are swift to shed blood.

These are not my words or the words of any other human being. These are the charges of the Ultimate Judge against all of humanity—including you, including me. Does this sound too extreme? To raw? Perhaps you're thinking, *That may be true of the worst elements of humanity, but I'm not* that *bad.* Let's examine each charge in detail.

*"There is none righteous, not even one"* (3:10). We must, of course, remember that the standard by which our righteousness is measured is not merely the goodness of a very good person, but the unblemished, perfect character of God. God has placed the goodness of each person on a scale opposite His own perfection and no one—not even the best among us—has been, or can be, good enough.

*"There is none who understands, there is none who seeks for God"* (3:11). The verb for "understands" means "to bring together," not unlike what someone might do with puzzle pieces. "No one has put the puzzle together correctly so no one can see the picture." Moreover, no one "seeks out" God by his or her own initiative. Only when people have no other choice do they turn toward Him. Francis Thompson captured this idea well in his poem, "The Hound of Heaven":

> I fled Him, down the nights and down the days;
> I fled Him, down the arches of the years;
> I fled Him, down the labyrinthine ways
> Of my own mind; and in the mist of tears
> I hid from Him, and under running laughter.
> Up vistaed hopes I sped;
> And shot, precipitated,
> Adown Titanic glooms of chasmed fears,
> From those strong Feet that followed, followed after.
> But with unhurrying chase,
> And unperturbed pace,

Deliberate speed, majestic instancy,
They beat—and a Voice beat
More instant than the Feet—
"All things betray thee, who betrayest Me."

Some flee faster and longer than others—some to their grave—but none seeks Him apart from His pursuit.

*"All have turned aside, together they have become useless"* (3:12). "Turned aside" comes from a Greek term that combines *ek*, "out of," and *klinō*, "to bend." The meaning is to bend aside. Peter calls for believers to "turn away from evil and do good" (1 Peter 3:11). Instead, people "bend away" from God. The Lord designed us with certain needs that only He can fulfill, and rather than come to Him to satisfy those longings, we pursue fleeting, temporal, even destructive substitutes. Invariably, these substitutes not only fail to fill our longings, they leave us more empty than before.

*"Their throat is an open grave, with their tongues they keep deceiving, the poison of asps is under their lips"* (3:13). Paul draws on the laments of David, who petitioned God to judge his enemies. To say that one's throat is an open grave is to accuse him or her of giving destructive advice. Poisonous lips deliver a kiss of death. Perhaps, enemies disguised as friends offered counsel that nearly killed him.

Paul recasts David's specific laments to draw a more general principle concerning false religions. Note: ". . . they keep deceiving." Faith healers prey upon the pain of those willing to do anything, go anywhere, pay any amount to end their suffering. Mediums and channelers convince the distraught that a modest fee will help them communicate with their deceased loved ones. Religions of all sorts promise salvation in exchange for deeds of service or sacrifice. Preaching a false religion is no better than convincing cancer patients that aspirin will substitute for their prescribed treatments.

*"Whose mouth is full of cursing and bitterness"* (3:14). Paul draws on another psalm, this time concerning the powerful and prosperous who live completely unaware of their coming judgment.

For the wicked boasts of his heart's desire,
And the greedy man curses and spurns the LORD.
The wicked, in the haughtiness of his countenance, does not seek Him.
All his thoughts are, "There is no God."
His ways prosper at all times;
Your judgments are on high, out of his sight;
As for all his adversaries, he snorts at them. (Psalm 10:3–5)

Let's face it; we tend to think of God only when things stop working well. When the wheels of prosperity whirl and our creature comforts feel cozy, the Lord is the last thing on our minds. We may fire up a quick prayer of thanks, but no one seeks God or searches for spiritual insight during times of prosperity — not like we do when enduring harsh suffering.

*"Their feet are swift to shed blood, destruction and misery are in their paths, and the path of peace they have not known"* (3:15 – 17). In 1954, William Golding published his Nobel prize-winning novel *Lord of the Flies*, which tells the story of British school boys shipwrecked and stranded on a small island. They began well, creating an ad hoc society that provided food, shelter, and safety for all, and even maintained a signal fire to attract passing ships. Before long, however, most of the boys abandoned their society for savagery, even to the point of killing some of the weaker boys to get what they wanted. A small minority chose to remain civilized. One crucial factor divided the savage boys from the civil: hope of rescue. Those who expected to be found and subsequently held accountable for their actions

## FAITH OF OUR FATHERS

Paul taught and quoted from the Old Testament to demonstrate clearly that the righteous have always received their justification by grace through faith and not by obedience to God's standard of goodness. Naturally, this raises the good faith question, "How were people saved by grace through faith before Jesus The answer has been and always will be, "Faith in God as He has revealed Himself." If one genuinely believes, his or her belief will naturally result in obedience to God's instructions. Nevertheless it is God's grace that saves, and this grace can only be received through faith.

While God remains the same and never changes, He has nevertheless revealed Himself to humanity differently in times past, and His instructions have changed over time. The Lord revealed Himself to the people of Israel in the form of a glowing cloud above the ark of the covenant. He then instructed them to build a sacred structure, to obey certain rules of conduct, and to sacrifice animals when they inevitably failed. The genuine belief of those who had placed their faith in God could be seen in their obedience to His instructions. God's grace, His revelation of Himself to Israel, saved those who believed. Meanwhile, their obedient response was a tangible expression of their genuine trust in Him.

We don't go to a sacred temple or sacrifice animals anymore. In a dispensation "suitable to the fullness of the times" (Eph. 1:10), God perfectly revealed Himself in the form of a man, the Son of God, Jesus Christ. And, moved only by grace, He instructed, "Come to Me, all who are weary and heavy-laden, and I will give you rest. Take My yoke upon you and learn from Me, for I am gentle and humble in heart, and you will find rest for your souls" (Matt. 11:28 – 29). Those who respond to God as He revealed Himself in these latter days — that is, in the person of Jesus Christ — will be declared righteous by grace through faith, just like our Old Testament forefathers.

behaved well. Those who abandoned that hope saw no reason to keep their natures in check, and their depravity found complete expression.

That's human nature. The veil between savagery and civility — Dr. Jekyll and Mr. Hyde — is only as thick as our sincere belief that our actions have consequences. And history has shown that the veil is extremely thin.

*"There is no fear of God before eyes"* (3:18). This "fear" can take two forms, both of them proper in the right context. Those who oppose the goodness of God should tremble in terror because of His power. At some point in our lives, everyone should experience such fear. The right kind of fear leads to repentance and a restored relationship with Him. Unfortunately, many will not acknowledge their Creator and will continue to ignore the anger stored up against them (Rom. 2:4–5; 2 Cor. 5:10; Rev. 16:1–21).

## —3:19–20—

Paul concludes the first major section of his letter with a clarification of the Law and why God gave it, a point he will develop in the following section. The Lord never gave the Law with the expectation that anyone could keep it. He knew the outcome from the beginning because He recognized what we ourselves refuse to see, that humanity — Jew and Gentile alike — is lost to sin. Not *sins*, the things we have done. *Sin*, what we have become, inside and out, through and through. As one scholar has noted, if sin were blue, we'd be blue all over.

The grace of God's Law cannot be found in the healing it brings, for it can only bring death to the guilty. As Martin Luther wrote, "The principle point of the

### NO SECRETS WITH GOD

While every man, woman, and child conceived by a human father has a dark side that he or she never shows to anybody, nothing can be hidden from God. Humanity may sing our praises, but our Maker and Judge sees all.

- God sees not as man sees, for man looks at the outward appearance, but the LORD looks at the heart. (1 Sam. 16:7)
- Then hear in heaven Your dwelling place, and forgive and act and render to each according to all his ways, whose heart You know, for You alone know the hearts of all the sons of men. (1 Kings 8:39)
- Know the God of your father, and serve Him with a whole heart and a willing mind; for the LORD searches all hearts, and understands every intent of the thoughts. (1 Chron. 28:9)
- You scrutinize my path and my lying down, and are intimately acquainted with all my ways. (Ps. 139:3)
- "I, the LORD, search the heart, I test the mind, even to give to each man according to his ways, according to the results of his deeds." (Jer. 17:10)
- And [Jesus] said to them, "You are those who justify yourselves in the sight of men, but God knows your hearts; for that which is highly esteemed among men is detestable in the sight of God." (Luke 16:15)
- And there is no creature hidden from His sight, but all things are open and laid bare to the eyes of Him with whom we have to do. (Heb. 4:13)

law in true Christian theology is to make people not better but worse; that is to say, it shows them their sin, so that they may be humbled, terrified, bruised, and broken, and by this means be driven to seek comfort and so to come to that blessed [Christ]."[6] But thank God for His Law! Thank God for His relentless, loving confrontation of our problem!

There are preachers today who don't want to focus on the negative side of Christian truth; that is, the terminal disease of sin. They prefer to remain focused only on the positive, which sounds wonderful on the surface. But that's like a doctor who only likes to talk about pleasant things. I can't speak for you, but I don't go to my doctor for smiles and compliments. I want the truth; the plain, ugly, unvarnished truth about my body. If he or she finds a tumor, I expect to know about it — right away. And if I have cancer, I want to know that I have cancer. Especially if it's treatable!

God gave us the Law because He knows that the bad news of our terminal condition leads us to the good news: It's treatable; there's a cure. Best of all, the cure is 100 percent effective and 100 percent free! Small wonder it's called "good news."

---

NOTES: The Wrath of God (Romans 1:18–3:20)

1. John Calvin, *Commentaries on the Epistle of Paul the Apostle to the Romans*, trans. and ed. John Owen (Whitefish, MT: Kessinger, 2006), 70.
2. Geoffrey W. Bromiley, *The International Standard Bible Encyclopedia*, rev. ed. (Grand Rapids: Eerdmans, 1988), 1:773.
3. So called by Pindar, the fifth-century BC Greek poet.
4. My title is inspired by Fritz Ridenour's commentary on Romans, *How to be a Christian without Being Religious* (Glendale, CA: Regal, 2002).
5. Donald Grey Barnhouse, *God's Wrath: Exposition of Bible Doctrines, Taking the Epistle to the Romans as a Point of Departure* (Grand Rapids: Eerdmans, 1964), 2:110–11.
6. Martin Luther, *Galatians* (Wheaton, Ill.: Crossway, 1998), 176.

# THE GRACE OF GOD
# (ROMANS 3:21–5:21)

Not long after the Hebrew descendants of Abraham left captivity in Egypt to claim their Promised Land, they found themselves alone in the wilderness and unable to find water or food. The initial flush of excitement of being free had barely worn off when many began to grumble against Moses, "Why didn't God let us die in comfort in Egypt where we had lamb stew and all the bread we could eat? You've brought us out into this wilderness to starve us to death, the whole company of Israel!" (Ex. 16:3 MSG). At that point, several hatched a plan to go back to their painful, yet predictable, bondage in Egypt.

Of course, the Lord had led His people to a place in the wilderness where no water and no food could be found, not to be cruel but to start them on the first leg of their spiritual journey. Ultimately, He wanted them to say with absolute certainty, "Man does not live by bread alone, but man lives by everything that proceeds out of the mouth of the LORD" (Deut. 8:3; Matt. 4:4). But this ability does not come naturally to humanity in their natural state. The sons and daughters of Adam would need to be taught. To give tangible expression to this truth about life and dependence on God, He gave them a fine, white, flaky substance that tasted like wafers and honey. Each morning, His beloved people woke to find it lying on the ground just outside their tents. They were to gather just enough for that day and trust that the Lord God would provide for tomorrow. This gift of life lasted only a brief time, so they could not delay their gathering, and it turned foul if not eaten before the next sunrise.

Eventually, they called it "bread from heaven," but they initially gave it the name "Manna," which is Hebrew for "What is it?"

Indeed, what is this life-sustaining substance that cannot be hunted, cultivated, manufactured, bought, or sold? What is this other-worldly, utterly free, absolutely indispensable substance that cannot be earned but only received? What shall we call it? For the Hebrew in the wilderness, it took physical form and they called it "bread of heaven." Before another gathering of Hebrew people in a barren place, this spiritual substance took physical form again and He called himself "the bread of life" (John 6:35).

Paul calls this supernatural substance "grace." Manna illustrated the principle; Jesus came to reveal it perfectly. Nevertheless, not all will see. So, then, if you do, "blessed are your eyes, because they see" (Matt. 13:16).

# KEY TERMS

δικαιόω [*dikaioō*] (*1344*) "to justify, to declare righteous, to prove innocent, to vindicate"

In the New Testament, this verb almost always bears a legal connotation in which a person is granted the legal status of "not guilty." This official pronouncement may or may not reflect the actual guilt or innocence of the subject. An innocent person may be vindicated, such that the governing authority officially affirms his or her righteousness, or one may be declared righteous despite actual guilt, so that he or she receives the same rights and privileges as a genuinely innocent person.

ἱλαστήριον [*hilastērion*] (*2435*) "means of forgiveness, means of restoration"

Based on the adjective *hileōs*, which means "happy, friendly, gracious," *hilastērion* is the means by which one achieves these good relations with another, especially if the relationship has been broken. *Hilastērion* appeases one's anger, satisfies the requirements of justice, and seeks continued fellowship. The term does not suggest that the offended person is not already willing to forgive or to extend grace; instead, it describes the action of a genuinely repentant person seeking to receive forgiveness and restoration.

ἔργον [*ergon*] (*2041*) "work, deed, completion of a task or duty"

This Greek term, like the English noun "work," describes both the act of labor and its result. For example, if a person were to build a house, the structure is said to be his or her "work." That is, the house represents both the effort and the result of the builder's activity. In Romans, Paul assigns this common term a more specific, almost technical meaning. For the apostle, "works" or "deeds" describe one's striving to obey the Law of Moses and the results of his or her effort. Therefore, Paul often uses the term "law" and "works" interchangeably.

περιτομή [*peritomē*] (*4061*) "circumcision, a circumcised one, one among the circumcised"

The Greek noun derives from the verb "to cut around" and describes the Hebrew rite in which the foreskin of a male is cut away. As instituted by God, the ritual identifies the male as a participant in God's covenant with Abraham. In time, this distinguishing feature became symbolic of the people, the covenant, and the culture. Eventually, many thought the circumcised state entitled the man to blessings from God and exemption from divine judgment.

χάρις [*charis*] (*5485*) "grace, undeserved or unmerited favor, cause of delight"

In secular literature, this term is closely associated with the word for "joy"; therefore, *charis* is what brings good will, favor, pleasure, or delight. Much of the New Testament uses the word in the straightforward, secular sense. Paul, however, saw in *charis* a new covenant (Jer 31:31–33) expression of the Old Testament term *chesed*, which describes God's spontaneous goodness toward His chosen people. So for Paul, "grace" is a rich technical term for the entire process of salvation.

# Unwrapping the Gift of Grace (Romans 3:21-31)

<sup>21</sup>But now apart from the Law *the* righteousness of God has been manifested, being witnessed by the Law and the Prophets, <sup>22</sup>even *the* righteousness of God through faith in Jesus Christ for all those who believe; for there is no distinction; <sup>23</sup>for all have sinned and fall short of the glory of God, <sup>24</sup>being justified as a gift by His grace through the redemption which is in Christ Jesus; <sup>25</sup>whom God displayed publicly as a propitiation in His blood through faith. *This was* to demonstrate His righteousness, because in the forbearance of God He passed over the sins previously committed; <sup>26</sup>for the demonstration, *I say,* of His righteousness at the present time, so that He would be just and the justifier of the one who has faith in Jesus.

<sup>27</sup>Where then is boasting? It is excluded. By what kind of law? Of works? No, but by a law of faith. <sup>28</sup>For we maintain that a man is justified by faith apart from works of the Law. <sup>29</sup>Or is God *the God* of Jews only? Is He not *the God* of Gentiles also? Yes, of Gentiles also, <sup>30</sup>since indeed God who will justify the circumcised by faith and the uncircumcised through faith is one. <sup>31</sup>Do we then nullify the Law through faith? May it never be! On the contrary, we establish the Law.

---

If there's one kind of person I admire least, it's the "self-made man."

I've been around a lot of those in my ministry—men and women who start with nothing and, through grit, sweat, and sacrifice, become amazingly significant (at least as the world judges significance). They invariably rise to the top of any organization or must run their own. While I'm not overly impressed by people the world calls "successful," I do admire many of their qualities. I appreciate their charisma. I marvel at their uncanny ability to motivate people and coordinate their efforts. I respect their dogged determination, their maverick spirit, their refusal to allow the majority opinion to deter them from doing what they know is right. And I rejoice with them when their honest efforts are rewarded handsomely. But I don't admire *self*-made people because they too often worship their maker.

Of course, you don't have to be rich to be a self-made person. Churches are full of them—people who daily labor in sweatshops of religion, desperately trying to crank out more good deeds than their neighbors, hoping to impress the gatekeepers of heaven. And, ironically, at the end of their labors, just before lowering them into the ground, a congregation of their closest family and friends join in singing their favorite hymn:

Amazing grace! How sweet the sound—
That saved a wretch like me!

I once was lost but now am found,
Was blind but now I see.

'Twas grace that taught my heart to fear,
And grace my fears relieved;
How precious did that grace appear
The hour I first believed.[1]

John Newton did not write a hymn in honor of self-made righteousness. His stanzas resound from an empty soul that longs to be filled from above. Those who presume to work for their place in heaven should sing instead:

Excessive works! How sweaty the sound
That came from the god in me!
I once was bad but now I'm good
Thanks to my sincerity.

'Twas works that earned my place with God
And deeds that made Him smile.
How long I toiled and proved my worth
And trudged that second mile.

When we've been there ten thousand years
Being paid our hard-earned fun,
We've no less days to sing our praise
And boast of all we'd done!

This is *not* the gospel that Paul received from Jesus Christ and then dedicated his life to teaching! The good news is not a "find the good in you and make it grow" kind of message. The gospel does not suggest in the least that "God helps those who help themselves." In fact, the good news begins with a clear understanding of the truth of our sin-sick condition: it's terminal! Fortunately, it's also curable. However, the deadly disease of sin cannot be treated with good nutrition and vigorous exercise—as good as those are. We need radical surgery. We are spiritually dead and we need nothing less than a transplant.

Paul's words in Romans 3:21, "But now apart from the Law the righteousness of God has been manifested," mark a crucial transition in his presentation of the gospel. Having delivered the awful truth of our soul-decayed depravity, our willful rebellion against God, our pitiful attempts at self-improvement, our skewed moral compass, and our pathetic pride, the apostle turns us toward a hopeful truth. The following verses outline no less than four significant truths about the gospel:

- Salvation is a transfer of righteousness.
- Salvation is a gift of grace.
- Salvation is a display of love.
- Salvation is a declaration of faith.

## —3:21–22—

Paul describes the "righteousness of God" in very poetic terms. The Greek word *phaneroō*, rendered "manifested" or "made known," was often used figuratively in Greek literature to mean "shine, light up, appear," much like someone would describe the rising of the sun. In the darkest gloom of human history in which people vainly labored to obtain the righteousness of God, grace dawned with the rising of the gospel. And it produces genuine righteousness, which Paul distinguishes from self-made righteousness in three ways.

First, genuine righteousness cannot be obtained through obedience to the Law—at least not for those who have been infected with sin. No one can purge his or her body of cancer by eating healthful food. Shunning cancer-generating toxins is a good way to avoid contracting the disease, but once someone has it, a cure demands radical action. Unfortunately, we were born with the disease of sin.

Second, genuine righteousness is not a new concept. It has been witnessed, declared, and made available to humankind from the beginning of time. The Law and the prophets describe this righteousness and demonstrate it to be a part of God's redemptive plan throughout the ages.

Third, genuine righteousness does not come from somewhere within us; it comes solely through faith in Jesus Christ.

## —3:23—

Humanity and God do not measure righteousness by the same standard. Whereas the Lord demands perfection, we prefer to think in terms of competition. In other words, instead of asking "What does God require?" we judge our own goodness based on the relative goodness of other people. And, comparatively speaking, some people *do* lead impressively moral lives. Nevertheless, Paul states that gaining entrance to heaven isn't a high jump contest.

As of this writing, the world record for the high jump stands just a little more than eight feet above the ground. *Eight feet!* Without shame, I freely confess that on a good day, I might be able to clear about half that height. If the standard of righteousness were measured by one's vertical leap, professional athletes would put most of us to shame. While we're barely able to push away from the table long enough to spend thirty minutes on a treadmill, they're beating their bodies into peak performing condition. While the ability to leap over a bar some eight feet from the ground is an amazing feat, the standard of heaven is far higher. More than eight feet ... or ten ... or one hundred.

Religions have long celebrated the dedication of men and women who leap higher than any of us can imagine. And Christianity is no exception. Churches celebrate perfect attendance, revere those who carry well-worn Bibles, and admire significant donors to worthy causes. Seminary training somehow suggests a higher level of spiritual worth. Ordination must certainly usher one onto another spiritual plane. And missionaries? Why, they must have earned the most moral credit of all!

As a Roman colony of immense strategic importance, Corinth became a miniature version of the capital city, complete with a *bēma*, or "judgment seat," shown here. This image of justice would have been particularly vivid for the Christians living in Rome.

But imagine watching a high jump contest from an airplane circling 32,000 feet above the field and you'll have a good idea of God's perspective on human righteousness. How absurd to think that any one of those top athletes could leap his or her way into heaven! How much more absurd to suggest that anyone could obtain God's righteousness through human effort. God's character is the moral standard, which sets the bar thousands of light years above the surface of the earth, and all have fallen absurdly short of His *doxa* ("opinion, repute, image, reflection").

— 3:24 —

So how does one obtain a righteousness worthy of God and His heaven? It can only be received as a gift.

Paul's term "justified" needs some explanation, for it describes a key spiritual principle. "Justified" describes the legal status of a defendant before a judge, and this legal standing ultimately determines his or her future. If a person is considered "just," he or she will not receive punishment. If, however, a person is considered "unjust," he or she faces fines, imprisonment, or worse. In human courts, one must establish his or her innocence against a charge of guilt in order to be declared just by the judge.

This imagery would have been especially vivid for both Paul and his readers, who lived under the iron rule of Rome. The imperial governor of the region typically sat on a large, elevated, blue and white marble platform, called the *bēma* or "seat of judgment," from which he ruled on judicial cases brought before him. A few years earlier, on his first visit to Corinth, Paul stood before the *bēma* to face charges brought against him by Jewish leaders, but the Roman proconsul dismissed the case, declaring it not reasonable to hear.

According to Paul's earlier argument (1:18–3:20) no one stands irrefutably innocent before our Creator and Judge. All of humanity has fallen absurdly short of God's standard of righteousness. Therefore, we must be justified by some other means. We are justified — declared just:

"as a gift"
"by His grace"
"through the redemption which is in Christ Jesus"

Though we stand guilty, completely devoid of righteousness before God, we are *declared* just by means of a transfer of righteousness to our account from that of Jesus Christ.

# From My Journal

## Celebrating with My Fellow Felon

As I drove to my friends' house, I recall thinking aloud to my family that it was a most unusual party we were to attend. My friends, a wonderful couple, were celebrating the homecoming of their son, who had been paroled after seven long years in prison. While he was guilty of the charges against him, the sentence he received was extraordinarily harsh when compared to the crimes of other inmates. No matter. He was home. And his exuberance for life energized everyone around him. The experience that so often hardens men and turns them bitter had refined and softened this young man. What emerged from the crucible of prison was a serenely repentant, mellow, and humbly grateful child of God.

He spoke freely of his experiences, beginning with the moment the judge accepted the jury's verdict and slammed the gavel down. As everyone else gathered their belongings and headed for the parking lot, he was led through a side door and placed inside a cage. Next, he was stripped, searched, photographed, printed, shackled, and then put aboard a tan prison bus. For the next seven years, he bore the title "convict," and for rest of his life, he will be called "ex-con" or "felon."

As I reflect on this young man's experience, I must ask myself, "How are he and I different?" There are several differences. His record of wrongdoing is a matter of public record; mine is locked away in heaven. He suffered punishment most can scarcely imagine; I will not endure a single moment of retribution for my wrongs. The world will forever count him the least among its citizens; I am unjustly celebrated. "Where then is boasting? It is excluded" (3:27)! For the felon and I are more alike than different. My heart is no less depraved than his … or yours. Earthly courts saw fit to place him behind bars, but you and I are no less guilty before our almighty Judge. Truth be told, you and I deserve far worse.

Therefore, if we dare boast in the presence of my paroled friend, let us boast *with* him. Let us join him in bragging about Jesus Christ and His inexplicable gift of grace. Let us see ourselves as his equals, paroled felons enjoying undeserved freedom. For "where then is boasting?" Not with us. Not in *our* goodness. And may I remind you once again? Salvation is *a gift*, and this gift demonstrates the goodness of the Giver, not of those who receive it.

Consider this modern-day illustration. On June 23, 2000, a deaf couple stood before Judge Donald McDonough in a Fairfax, Virginia, court and offered no rebuttal to their landlord's complaint that they were behind on the rent. Their recent marriage unfortunately resulted in the loss of disability benefits, most of which kept a leased roof over their heads. Now they were $250 behind and had no hope of making up the deficit.

Judge McDonough couldn't disagree. The landlord was due his rent, the couple was indeed guilty of nonpayment, and justice could not be set aside. Nevertheless, the judge's compassion would not allow him to drop the gavel. Not just yet. Once the attorney for the plaintiff had closed his case, the judge suddenly left the courtroom. A few moments later, he returned from his chambers with $250 in cash, handed it to the landlord's attorney, and said, "Consider it paid." With a transfer of funds from the just to the unjust, the debt was paid and the case dismissed. The law had been satisfied. The defendants were then "just" or "righteous" in the eyes of the court.

In a similar way, we have a transfer of righteousness from the account of another to cover our moral deficit so that we might stand justified before the court of heaven. How did this happen? "By His grace." A free gift given, not because *we* are good, but because *He* is good.

By what means did we receive this transfer of righteousness? "Through the redemption which is in Christ Jesus." Redemption. That's another key term we must understand. This ancient illustration will help.

Long before governments offered poverty assistance programs, a person could fall into debt, lose his or her land, and become completely destitute—hopelessly impoverished with no family to whom he or she could turn. The only possible means of avoiding debtor's prison or starvation was to become indentured to someone wealthy; that is, ask someone with lots of money to pay off one's creditors in exchange for slavery. Normally, the years of service would be determined by the amount of the debt paid. However, a greedy or cruel master could keep a slave perpetually indebted and hopelessly indentured forever. He also had the right to sell his slaves at auction if he ever needed cash.

If someone were unimaginably kind, he could bid on a slave, purchase him or her for himself, and then set the slave free. The slave would thus be "redeemed" from debt and slavery.

All of humankind has been enslaved to sin by virtue of our moral debt. The Law of God demands payment in order for us to be considered "righteous" or "just," but we are hopelessly unable to pay enough out of our own goodness. We need a redeemer. We need someone to pay our debt for us. And according to the gospel, we have such a Redeemer in Jesus Christ, who paid it *in full*.

## —3:25—

The key term in Paul's explanation of how Christ redeemed humanity is rendered "propitiation" in the NASB and "sacrifice of atonement" in the NIV. The Greek term is *hilastērion*, for which we have no direct English translation. The Hebrew related word in the Old Testament is *kippur*, as in the holiday, Yom Kippur (Lev. 16:1–34; 23:26–32).

On Yom Kippur, the "Day of Atonement," the high priest was to take two male goats before the congregation of Israel and cast lots (the ancient equivalent of flipping a coin) to determine the fate of each goat. Of course, the Hebrews didn't believe in chance. Casting lots was their way of releasing control into the sovereign hand of God. The priest was then to "offer the goat on which the lot for the LORD fell, and make it a sin offering" (Lev. 16:9).

Having sacrificed a bull on behalf of himself and his family, the high priest entered the Most Holy Place of the tabernacle, where the Ark of the Covenant rested. The Old Testament tells us that the special presence of God could be seen in the form of an other-worldly light (the "Shekinah") above the cover of the Ark, which the Hebrew called "the mercy seat" (Lev. 16:2). The high priest—and only the high priest—could enter the Most Holy Place once each year on Yom Kippur, and any violation of this restriction would bring about the immediate death of the guilty intruder.

The priest was to sprinkle the blood of the sacrificed goat on the *kapporet* (a Hebrew noun derived from the verb *kopher*, meaning "to ransom, to secure favor through a gift"). *Kapporet* means "mercy seat; cover of atonement; place of propitiation, satisfaction, appeasement." The Greek translation of this particular passage in the Old Testament uses the term *hilastērion*. This sacrificial rite symbolized the satisfaction of God's holy wrath against sin by means of death.

The high priest then laid his hands on the head of the other goat in the sight of the congregation, symbolically transferring the sins of the community to the "scapegoat." The more fortunate goat was then allowed to run free into the wilderness, bearing "on itself all their iniquities to a solitary land" (Lev. 16:22).

When Adam sinned, he reaped the consequences of sin, which is death (Rom. 6:23). He instantly died spiritually and his body began its decaying march toward the grave. And the same is true of us. The penalty of our sin has become our overwhelming debt in the court of heaven. We stand before a Judge whose wrath against sin must be satisfied. As we discovered in our study of 1:18–23, God is love (1 John 4:8), but His is not a pathetic love that stands idly by while evil consumes His creation. His holy nature burns against "all ungodliness and unrighteousness"

(Rom. 1:18). It demands justice. And the only just penalty for sin is death—not only the physical end of life on earth, but separation from God in eternity—a far more fearsome destiny.

Paul declares the crucifixion of Jesus to be a public sprinkling of blood—a Day of Atonement rite of propitiation—that fulfilled two important requirements. First, the atonement of Christ has satisfied the wrath of God, which demanded justice for humanity's sin. Second, this atonement has silenced the slander against God. Throughout the Old Testament, God delayed judgment, which caused some to suggest that He was not entirely good. For how can a holy God allow violence and cruelty against the innocent to go unpunished? "[Christ's public atonement] *was* to demonstrate His righteousness, because in the forbearance of God He passed over the sins previously committed" (3:25).

To summarize Romans 3:21–25: The standard of righteousness has never been anything less than moral perfection, which no mere mortal can ever achieve. Therefore, our only hope is to be declared righteous by the gracious gift of God. We receive this gift through faith in Jesus Christ, who took our punishment on our behalf, thus satisfying the heavenly court's requirement that justice be served.

## —3:26—

The wrath of God calls for the just penalty of sin to be paid and His wrath has been satisfied in the atoning death of His Son. Therefore, God is "just," because sin does not go unpunished, and He is the "justifier," because the death of His Son clears the way for Him to declare believers righteous without contradicting His own nature. However, in order for you and me to benefit from this offer of eternal life, we must *receive* it. We accept this gift through faith.

What if the couple in Judge McDonough's courtroom refused to accept the $250 needed to cover their debt? What if their pride prevented their willingness to accept his charity? A gift does the recipient no good until it is received!

There is a name for what the compassionate judge offered. It's called "grace." Unmerited favor. Mercy that is neither earned nor deserved. It cannot be demanded; only offered. It cannot be reciprocated; only received.

This bold declaration of truth prompts Paul to pause and ask three questions of those who suggest that they somehow deserve salvation:

"Where then is boasting?" (3:27)
"Is God the God of Jews only? Is He not the God of Gentiles also?" (3:29)
"Do we then nullify the Law through faith?" (3:31)

—**3:27–28**—

"Where then is boasting?" Will heaven be filled with people singing their own praises?

> When we've been there ten thousand years
> Being paid our hard-earned fun,
> We've no less days to sing our praise
> And boast of all we'd done!

No! The grace of God cancels everyone's right to boast.

In 1959, I stood in the semicircular atrium of a church in San Francisco gazing up at enormous oil portraits of such great men as Mahatma Gandhi, Martin Luther King Jr., Abraham Lincoln, and George Washington. I felt surrounded and—I will admit—somewhat dwarfed by them. If greatness is measured by one's impact on the world, these were undeniably great men. All of them had become champions of freedom in their age. Bronze lettering at the foot of the portraits read:

> "You are all the children of God ..."

I knew this church encouraged the highest ideals of Christian love and conduct, but it had long ago cast off the moorings of scriptural truth. I gave them credit for recognizing that all people, however great or small, are subject to the sovereignty of God, and I admired their genuine desire to do what was right at a time when the struggle for racial equality was unpopular. But I resented the implication that good deeds qualified these men for "greatness" in the kingdom of God.

I sat in the congregation for nearly an hour, listening to someone eloquently say nothing. If the name of Jesus Christ was uttered, it—like the paintings in the foyer—stood alongside those of other noteworthy examples of charity and kindness. No one heard the story of His atoning sacrifice or His triumph over death. No one heard that we have been invited to share the spoils of His victory.

After the service, I stood in the atrium with my friends, who were members of the church. I pointed to the bronze lettering and asked, "By the way, do you see the ellipsis? Do you know what the rest of that verse says?"

"No," one replied. "Do you?"

"It's from Paul's letter to the Galatians. 'You are all the children of God *by faith, which is in Christ Jesus.*' Have you placed your faith in Jesus Christ?" I sensed by his cold indifference that this marked the end of our conversation.

The truth of the gospel is offensive to our pride. Pride suggests that enough goodness can substitute for belief in the Son of God. Faith requires a humble admission that we are helpless to redeem ourselves.

Paul's next statement is pivotal. Up to this point, his letter has demonstrated the insufficiency of good deeds to save us. Now he begins to prove the absolute necessity of faith: "A [person] is justified by faith apart from works of the Law."

## —3:29–30—

Paul's second hypothetical question examines the notion that God is somehow partial. If justification comes by obedience to the Law of God and He gave the Law exclusively to Israel, this would suggest that God only wants Hebrews to be saved. The apostle answers the question simply and directly, saying in effect: "No, because one is justified through faith and not by obedience to the Law, and because everyone is invited to believe, God is the God of all." Some trust in His grace and demonstrate their belief through the right of circumcision; some trust in His grace apart from Hebrew custom. The common denominator is faith.

## —3:31—

Does this suggest that the Law given to Israel through Moses is irrelevant? Paul uses the Greek term *katargeō*, which means "to nullify, render useless, reduce to nothing." His hypothetical question bears two implications. First, that this "law of faith" is a new principle that wasn't a factor before Christ; and, second, that the supposedly new truth about faith renders obsolete the old truth concerning the Law.

Anyone familiar with the rules of logic knows that two contradictory statements cannot both be true. God is one and He does not change. And in 4:1–13, Paul will use the example of Abraham and the Hebrew rite of circumcision to illustrate that this "law of faith" is as old as time. The code of conduct given to the Israelites through Moses was an expression of God's grace, but not as the means of justification. On the contrary, He gave the Law to expose our sin and to prove our guilt. Because the Law reflects the character of God, we can never say that the Law is bad. However, it did contribute to our ruin because it objectively proves that we have rebelled against Him.

Far from undermining or contradicting the truth of God's Law, faith "causes to stand" or "establishes" the Law. This "law of faith" or "faith principle" predates the Law of Moses and, more importantly, it provides the foundation on which the Law rests. Disobedience is nothing less than objective proof of disbelief in the goodness and power of God. One then receives the grace of God apart from good deeds through faith.

Salvation—being declared righteous before our Creator and Judge—is a gift to be received, not a wage to be earned.

## Application

### *The Gift and the Glory*

In Romans 3:21–31, Paul sums up his indictment of humanity as having fallen far short of God's righteousness and then makes his case for faith. Salvation is not a reward for good behavior. Instead, salvation is:

- a transfer of righteousness from Jesus Christ's account to ours (3:21–23)
- a gift of grace motivated by God's goodness, not ours (3:24)
- a display of God's love for us, not ours for Him (3:25–26)

Therefore, salvation is a gift that glorifies the Giver. In other words, while salvation is *for* us, it is not *about* us; the central focus of salvation is God.

Paul then turns from humankind's need to God's provision of grace, which is received through faith—a doctrine many religious authorities rejected. He anticipates their objections by repeating the questions he often encountered in his travels.

*Question:*     "Where then is boasting?" (Who deserves credit for salvation?)
*Implied Answer:* God! (3:27–28)

*Question:*     "Is God the God of the Jews only?" (Is salvation restricted?)
*Implied Answer:* No, anyone may receive salvation! (3:28–30)

*Question:*     "Do we then nullify the Law?" (What role does the Law play?)
*Implied Answer:* The Law is God's means of confronting and diagnosing our problem. Turn to Him! (3:31)

While Paul's emphasis on the role of faith in salvation is an essential part of proclaiming the good news to unbelievers, it is no less crucial to the daily conduct of believers. The Puritans have often been vilified for their strict manner of life—unjustly for the most part—but I have found their writings to be just what I need when pride begins to lace my speech or influence my decisions. They remind me that we never rise above our need for grace and that trusting God's power to save us from evil is a daily decision.

I highly recommend adding Puritan writings to your daily time with God. I have in my library a well-worn collection titled *The Valley of Vision*, from which the following is taken:

O Lord God, Who inhabitest eternity,
The heavens declare thy glory,

The earth thy riches,
The universe is thy temple;
Thy presence fills immensity,
Yet thou hast of thy pleasure created life, and communicated happiness;
Thou hast made me what I am, and given me what I have;
In thee I live and move and have my being;
Thy providence has set the bounds of my habitation, and wisely administers all
    my affairs.
I thank thee for thy riches to me in Jesus, for the unclouded revelation of him
    in thy Word, where I behold his Person, character, grace, glory, humiliation,
    sufferings, death, and resurrection;
Give me to feel the need of his continual saviourhood, and cry with Job, "I am
    vile," with Peter, "I perish," with the publican, "Be merciful to me, a sinner."
Subdue in me the love of sin,
Let me know the need of renovation as well as of forgiveness, in order to serve
    and enjoy thee for ever.
I come to thee in the all-prevailing name of Jesus, with nothing of my own to
    plead, no works, no worthiness, no promises.
I am often straying, often knowingly opposing thy authority, often abusing thy
    goodness;
Much of my guilt arises from my religious privileges, my low estimation of them,
    my failure to use them to my advantage,
But I am not careless of thy favour or regardless of thy glory;
Impress me deeply with a sense of thine omnipresence, that thou art about my
    path, my ways, my lying down, my end.[2]

Whenever any one of us begins to believe our own goodness is sufficient for even a single day, reading this prayer helps to bring us down to size. And that's a good thing!

To *God* be all glory!

## Righteousness Is a Five-Letter Word (Romans 4:1–15)

[1]What then shall we say that Abraham, our forefather according to the flesh, has found? [2]For if Abraham was justified by works, he has something to boast about, but not before God. [3]For what does the Scripture say? "Abraham believed God, and it was credited to him as righteousness." [4]Now to the one who works, his wage is not credited as a favor, but as what is due. [5]But to the one who does not work, but believes in Him who justifies the ungodly, his

faith is credited as righteousness, [6]just as David also speaks of the blessing on the man to whom God credits righteousness apart from works:

> [7] "Blessed are those whose lawless deeds have been forgiven,
> And whose sins have been covered.
> [8] "Blessed is the man whose sin the Lord will not take into account."

[9]Is this blessing then on the circumcised, or on the uncircumcised also? For we say, "Faith was credited to Abraham as righteousness." [10]How then was it credited? While he was circumcised, or uncircumcised? Not while circumcised, but while uncircumcised; [11]and he received the sign of circumcision, a seal of the righteousness of the faith which he had while uncircumcised, so that he might be the father of all who believe without being circumcised, that righteousness might be credited to them, [12]and the father of circumcision to those who not only are of the circumcision, but who also follow in the steps of the faith of our father Abraham which he had while uncircumcised.

[13]For the promise to Abraham or to his descendants that he would be heir of the world was not through the Law, but through the righteousness of faith. [14]For if those who are of the Law are heirs, faith is made void and the promise is nullified; [15]for the Law brings about wrath, but where there is no law, there also is no violation.

---

John Milton Gregory penned one of the finest volumes on teaching I have ever read. I keep my tattered, well-worn copy of *The Seven Laws of Teaching* close at hand, and it helps to keep my communication on target. His fourth law declares that new knowledge builds upon old knowledge. Perhaps that's why illustrations are so helpful. Good illustrations use the familiar to explain new concepts. The great British preacher Charles Spurgeon described a sermon as a house in which the windows of illustration allow light to fill the darkness.

Paul understood the need for illustration. For centuries, the truth of God's grace had been obscured by the clutter of Greek philosophy and Jewish traditions, both of which taught, essentially, "God helps those who help themselves." Every good Jew spent his or her life trying to achieve the "righteousness of God" by carefully obeying His laws and meticulously observing His rituals. Many taught that Christianity was merely a continuation of that pursuit—a new life made possible by the atonement of Christ, which one joined by following Him in obedience to the Father. So Paul's declaration, "A [person] is justified by faith apart from works of the Law" (3:28), sounded like a radically new doctrine, especially to Jewish believers. To demonstrate that the doctrine of justification by grace through faith is not new at all, Paul draws on two familiar icons of Jewish faith and practice: Abraham (4:1–8) and the rite of circumcision (4:9–12).

## —4:1–2—

When Americans discuss what makes them quintessentially American, they usually point to men commonly referred to as "the founding fathers," men who held certain principles and decided to form a nation around them. We debate the answers to several questions. What did they believe? What timeless, universal ideals guided their actions? Are we remaining true to those principles in the policies we adopt today? To make our case, we might draw upon the examples of George Washington, Benjamin Franklin, Thomas Jefferson, and James Madison.

Similarly, Jews looked beyond all their prophets, the long line of kings, the judges, and even Moses—all the way back to father Abraham, the physical progenitor of the Hebrew race through his son Isaac and his grandson Jacob. If an honest examination of his life revealed a man justified by obedience to the laws and rituals handed down by God, then all who desire the righteousness of God should take note and follow his example. After all, Abraham was the physical and spiritual father of God's specially chosen nation.

Paul then poses a hypothetical condition he knows to be false but assumes to be true for the sake of examination: "If Abraham was justified by works"—that is, if Abraham could be considered righteous because of what he did—then Abraham would have the right to praise his own accomplishments. Even so, Paul recoils from the idea. He can barely tolerate the suggestion that anyone can earn his own righteousness through deeds.

## —4:3—

Rather than dwell on the preposterous notion that anyone—even the venerated father of the Hebrew people—can earn his or her own righteousness, Paul quotes Genesis 15:6 as the foundation of his argument. "Then [Abraham] believed in the LORD; and He reckoned it to him as righteousness" (Gen. 15:6). Early in the patriarch's adult life, the Lord chose him to play a crucial role in a great plan to redeem the world from evil. He did this by establishing an unconditional covenant with the man and his descendants.

> ¹Now the LORD said to Abram,
>
> "Go forth from your country,
> And from your relatives
> And from your father's house,
> To the land which I will show you;

²And I will make you a great nation,
And I will bless you,
And make your name great;
And so you shall be a blessing;
³And I will bless those who bless you,
And the one who curses you I will curse.
And in you all the families of the earth will be blessed." (Gen. 12:1–3)

Note that the man's parents had given him the name Abram, which means "exalted father." But in an ironic twist, he married a woman who could not conceive a child. Nevertheless, Abram obeyed God's instructions to leave his family relatives and settle in the land God promised to give him and his descendents (Gen. 12:7; 13:15; 15:18; 17:7–8).

If I were writing this story, I would have rewarded Abram's obedience right away. I would have allowed him to settle down in a fertile and beautiful valley in the Promised Land and then given him a gaggle of little Abrams, who would call him "exalted." I would have taken his obedience as an opportunity to show everyone that I am a god worth obeying. Fortunately, the one true God is wiser than I am. He waited. The Lord wanted something more than an obedience-in-exchange-for-blessing business arrangement. He wanted a relationship, and relationships require intimacy and trust in equal portions.

As Abram and Sarai, his wife, faced several dangers, they frequently faltered. They bravely defeated enemies, but lied when the enemy appeared too strong (Gen. 12:11–13). They rejected idol worship, but survived famine by seeking refuge in the prosperity of Egypt. They believed God's promises, but saw no way to claim them except through human customs (15:2–3). And through all this they aged considerably.

As Abram approached his eighty-fifth birthday, long after Sarai had gone through menopause, he wondered about the promises of God. In response, the Lord reassured him. "He took him outside and said, 'Now look toward the heavens, and count the stars, if you are able to count them.' And He said to him, 'So shall your descendants be'" (Gen. 15:5).

Abram's response was to believe. Not in himself. Not in the promise. Not as an attempt to impress God and certainly not as an act of righteousness. Abram "believed *in the* LORD" (Gen. 15:6). In other words, the old man trusted God. He trusted His character. He believed that God was willing and able to fulfill His promises despite the obvious natural difficulties. And the Lord responded to Abram's trust by declaring him just. He "reckoned it to him as righteousness."

"Reckon" is an accounting term that describes the process of analyzing and squaring accounts. You have a credit card. Each month the credit card company sends you a statement with a detailed list of transactions: expenditures, accrued interest, fees, and payments you have made. Your balance — the total amount you owe — is then reckoned to reflect all of this activity; charges are debited against your account while payments are credited.

The Lord entered a credit, as it were, to Abram's account because of his belief and then stamped his account "paid." Abram was declared righteous, not because he earned or deserved the designation, but because the One to whom he owed everything — God — decided to extend him grace.

— **4:4–8** —

Paul extends his accounting analogy to underscore the unconditional nature of grace and to demonstrate how this grace principle applies to all.

If you have a job in which you provide service to an employer, you receive a paycheck based on an agreed salary, or the number hours you worked, or what you produced. It's not a gift; you earned that money. You worked for it and you have a right to expect whatever you have coming. And your employer is indebted to you until it is paid. While you are wise to be grateful for your job, the wages you receive are just compensation, not grace.

On the other hand, Paul declares that the grace Abraham received through faith is available to us as well. In the same way as God reckoned it as righteousness for the father of the Hebrews, He will reckon it to us. However, Paul does not mean to suggest that faith is just another form of payment. Faith is not a virtue that simply has more power than other noble qualities, such as honesty, kindness, humility, or selflessness. Believing God is good — even necessary — but it is not a good deed that makes one worthy of grace. Paul continues to call those who receive God's grace "ungodly" because faith has done nothing to remove the depravity that is ours because of sin.

Through faith, *God* addresses the problem of sin and depravity. However, our transformation is not instantaneous. We will continue to struggle with sin and failure until we die. That's why we must carefully distinguish between one's *position* and his or her *condition*. When one receives God's grace through faith, he or she is considered righteous and treated as such despite his or her current behavior. Imagine a prisoner locked in a cell whose sentence has been commuted by a judge. Judicially and legally (position), he is free; however, experientially (condition), he remains confined. Eventually, his experience will match his judicial standing.

By the sovereign act of God, the unjust person who receives God's grace through belief is declared "just." King David, another significant person in Hebrew history, celebrated this truth in Psalm 32. He had fallen from the heights of success to commit adultery with the wife of his loyal follower Uriah, whom he subsequently had killed in order to conceal the sin (2 Sam. 11:2–25). After being confronted with his guilt, David admitted, "I have sinned against the LORD" (12:13). He then repented and received God's pardon. In response, David wrote:

> How blessed is he whose transgression is forgiven,
> Whose sin is covered!
> How blessed is the man to whom the LORD does not impute iniquity,
> And in whose spirit there is no deceit!
> When I kept silent *about my sin*, my body wasted away
> Through my groaning all day long.
> For day and night Your hand was heavy upon me;
> My vitality was drained away *as* with the fever heat of summer.
>
> Selah.
>
> I acknowledged my sin to You,
> And my iniquity I did not hide;
> I said, "I will confess my transgressions to the LORD";
> And You forgave the guilt of my sin. (Ps. 32:1–5)

## —4:9–12—

Having demonstrated that Abraham—the father of God's chosen race—was declared righteous by grace, through faith, and not as a result of obedience, Paul then turns his attention to a second icon of Jewish faith and practice, the rite of circumcision. He asks, in effect, "Is this faith principle intended only for those who are identified with God's covenant with Abraham?"

The apostle responds to his own rhetorical question with a question for his reader: At the time Abram believed God and received His grace, was he in a circumcised state or was he in an uncircumcised state?

The answer about Abram and his state of uncircumcision would have been obvious to Jews, who knew better than anyone the story of Abraham's covenant and its association with circumcision. The Lord confirmed His covenant with Abraham no less than three times throughout the patriarch's life. The first occurred when He instructed the man to leave his homeland (Gen. 12:1–3). The encounter referenced by Paul earlier was the second (15:1–21). God did not connect the rite of circumcision with this covenant until many years had passed (17:9–14). In fact, it was more than a dozen years later (16:16–17:1).

Through the centuries after Abraham, God's covenant people placed greater and greater emphasis on the outward symbol of circumcision and virtually forgot the internal spiritual significance of their relationship with God. Unfortunately, that's a common occurrence in religion, even today. I shudder to think of countless thousands submitting to baptism and observing communion without a personal knowledge of Jesus Christ. These rites are meaningless apart from a relationship between God and the individual. So, Paul needs to clarify the original purpose for circumcision to demonstrate that participation in God's covenant with Abraham had always been a matter of the heart.

The rite of circumcision did nothing to save a man from sin or credit him with righteousness. Paul calls it a "seal." An older translation renders the Greek term as "signet." The *Theological Dictionary of the New Testament* describes the legal significance of this term:

> The seal serves as a legal protection and guarantee. It is thus placed on property, on wills, etc. Laws prohibit the misuse of seals, which owners often break just before death. Seals serve as proof of identity. They also protect houses, graves, etc. against violation. Both testator and witnesses seal wills. In Roman law all six witnesses must break their own seals to open the will, and in South Babylonia beneficiaries signify or seal when the inheritance is divided. Seals also serve as

## CIRCUMCISION: A RIGHT OR A RITE?

When the Lord confirmed His covenant with Abraham for the third and final time (Gen. 17), He commanded that all men living in the covenant community were to be circumcised as a symbol of his participation. Refusing circumcision was tantamount to divorcing the community and rejecting God. Therefore, the rebel was to be removed from Hebrew society and regarded as an outsider. Furthermore, his rejection of God and His covenant clearly marked him as a condemned man. Submitting to circumcision, by contrast, allowed a young man access to all the rights and privileges of Hebrew society once he came of age.

With such emphasis placed on this intimate rite of participation in God's covenant, it is easy to see why many Jews enlarged its significance. Many reasoned that if refusing circumcision condemned a man, then circumcision must save him. Participation in the covenant and obedience to the Law came to be seen as the exclusive path to salvation, an attitude that some Jewish Christians attempted to carry over to the church (Acts 15:1; Gal. 2:3–4). For many Jews, to be uncircumcised was to be unsaved and submitting to circumcision began a man's arduous journey toward justification.

accreditation, e.g. of weights and measures. The seal plays an important public role in government. All authorities have seals. The king's seal confers authorization. In both private and public life holding a seal expresses an element of power.[3]

Perhaps the most common present-day example of this would be a notary stamp, which distinguishes official copies of a document from unofficial ones. Another good example would be a diploma. An official seal sets it apart from forgeries. The Lord intended the rite of circumcision to be a seal of authenticity on the covenant between a man and his God. While this covenant with Abraham was unilateral and unconditional—God gave an oath to do what He promised regardless of the people's response—the Lord intended Hebrew participation in the agreement to include more than a mere outward sign. A plainly visible godly character was to accompany the very private symbol of circumcision.

Similarly, baptism follows one's decision to trust in Jesus Christ. It's a public declaration of his or her turning from sin to lifelong pursuit of Christlikeness. One cannot be saved through the rite of baptism, nor must one be baptized in order to be saved. It's intended as the Lord's "notary seal" on a new believer's participation in the new covenant. Ideally, the Christian's conduct will make his or her relationship with Christ plainly evident to a watching world. After all, the very term "Christian" means "little Christ."

Because Abraham believed and received the "righteousness of God" years before he was circumcised, Paul calls him "the father of all who believe," both circumcised and uncircumcised. Many non-Hebrew men and women have received God's grace through faith, and many circumcised Hebrews have trusted in the outward symbols of a faith not centered in Christ. Therefore, Abraham's faith gives him the role of patriarch over the family of genuine believers.

—4:13–15—

Paul comes full circle to conclude his argument: "Now to the one who works, his wage is not credited as a favor, but as what is due. But to the one who does not work, but believes in Him who justifies the ungodly, his faith is credited as righteousness" (Rom. 4:4–5). What Paul said in these verses he now says again in 4:13–15. Contrary to the most common misunderstanding of God's expectation of humankind, we cannot be declared righteous through obedience to His Law. (Please reread that sentence!) If it were possible to be declared righteous through perfect obedience, there would be no need for God's grace. In reality, though, we have no hope apart from the grace of God because no one can earn the title "righteous" through good deeds. Even if we were to obey perfectly from this moment on, future righteousness cannot erase past sin.

Why, then, did God give us His Law? Not to suggest we can be saved by it. Far from it! He gave us the Law to make our disobedience obvious, to demonstrate how our fallen, sinful nature runs contrary to His. Anyone who believes the Law was given as a means for one to prove his or her worth will soon be frustrated and ultimately fall into despair. Anyone who expects to be declared righteous through obedience to the Law will experience repeated failure. Our only hope is to receive the righteousness of God as a gift by believing God's promise. Righteousness is really a five-letter word. You spell it F-A-I-T-H.

## Application

### *God's Don't-Do-It-Yourself Kit*

Paul drew upon the example of Abraham, the undisputed model of Hebrew belief and practice, to illustrate the principle that justification (being declared righteous by God) has always been a matter of faith. Because of Abraham's faith, God adjusted the man's account to reflect a surplus of righteousness (4:1–3). The patriarch's salvation had nothing to do with good behavior. On the contrary, Paul used Abraham's faith to demonstrate a key spiritual principle: Working earns a wage (4:4), while trusting in God's grace brings a gift (4:5–8).

To further illustrate the role of faith in salvation, Paul examined the rite of circumcision and noted the following:

1. Abraham's salvation occurred before God instituted the ritual of circumcision (4:9–10).
2. God never implied that this rite (or any other activity) did anything to change the person within. Instead, circumcision was intended to be an outward indicator of the boy's inward belief in God's grace (4:11).
3. The rite was given in trust. That is, the outward symbol of inward faith was to be performed on an infant boy with the expectation that he would one day place his trust in God's grace.
4. The rite of circumcision and the covenant it symbolized was given with the expectation that Abraham's example (and that of his offspring) would bring the rest of the world to faith in God's grace (4:12).

The principles behind these characteristics also apply to the roles of activity, ritual, and tradition in the church. Nothing can substitute for God's grace, which can be received only by faith in Jesus Christ. Jesus commanded His followers to be baptized as an external symbol of their inner transformation. Like circumcision for the Jew, baptism is a seal of authenticity that marks the individual as a recipient of God's grace. It does not guarantee salvation, nor does it do anything to change the heart of the person submitting to the rite.

Jesus also commanded His followers to take communion as a way to remember the grace they received through His own sacrificial death on their behalf. The bread is merely bread; the wine is merely wine. These elements are natural symbols of a supernatural reality. An unbeliever remains unchanged if he or she participates in this ordinance of the church, and a believer is no more or no less a child of God after the ceremony is complete.

This is, of course, no new information to the mature believer. However, on a less conscious level mature Christians can become guilty of placing unhealthy significance on other rituals and traditions. Without daily reminders of God's grace, we unconsciously suppose that attending church, giving money, studying or memorizing Scripture, working in the community, and performing other worthy activities adds to our righteousness. This inevitably causes us to judge those who do not do these things.

I wholeheartedly encourage activities and rituals that deepen our intimacy with the Almighty, but these healthy expressions of faith must never become the tools of do-it-yourself righteousness. We cannot make ourselves cleaner on the inside. God alone must do that for us. So why should we devote ourselves to spiritual disciplines? For one reason: they are a means by which we come to know the Son of God intimately and experientially.

As you take part in the rituals or customs of the church, as you take up the spiritual disciplines, as you put your energies into doing good work, refocus your expectations by offering the following prayer:

> *Father, help me to understand more about Your Son and to become more sensitive to the teaching of Your Holy Spirit as a result of what I am doing. Amen.*

God's gift of righteousness is based on the principles He has established. Think of them as the tools of His Don't-Do-It-Yourself kit. And the label on that kit? *Grace.*

## Hoping Against Hope (Romans 4:16–25)

---

¹⁶For this reason *it is* by faith, in order that *it may be* in accordance with grace, so that the promise will be guaranteed to all the descendants, not only to those who are of the Law, but also to those who are

of the faith of Abraham, who is the father of us all, [17](as it is written, "A father of many nations have I made you") in the presence of Him whom he believed, *even* God, who gives life to the dead and calls into being that which does not exist. [18]In hope against hope he believed, so that he might become a father of many nations according to that which had been spoken, "So shall your descendants be." [19]Without becoming weak in faith he contemplated his own body, now as good as dead since he was about a hundred years old, and the deadness of Sarah's womb; [20]yet, with respect to the promise of God, he did not waver in unbelief but grew strong in faith, giving glory to God, [21]and being fully assured that what God had promised, He was able also to perform. [22]Therefore it was also credited to him as righteousness. [23]Now not for his sake only was it written that it was credited to him, [24]but for our sake also, to whom it will be credited, as those who believe in Him who raised Jesus our Lord from the dead, [25]*He* who was delivered over because of our transgressions, and was raised because of our justification.

---

Having nailed down the truth that human beings cannot earn the righteousness of God by works in the first half of the fourth chapter (4:1–15), Paul then illustrates how God can credit his righteousness to us. It is by our "faith," a term that has gone through many changes of meaning through history.

Mark Twain placed the following words on the lips of his character, Pudd'nhead Wilson, an amateur detective with an uncommon love for facts that can be proved: "Faith is believing what you know ain't so."[4] Unfortunately, this has become the primary definition of faith in our time. Or, more precisely, faith is the "firm belief in something for which there is no proof."[5] But it was not always so. This particular definition of faith is the result of a philosophical shift, a fundamental change in the way people think about the universe that began as far back as the thirteenth century and the teachings of Thomas Aquinas. His writings set the spiritual and physical realms into distinct categories and suggested ways to prove that they were connected. This is profoundly important because, until then, nearly everyone perceived the universe as the result of simultaneous natural *and* supernatural causes.[6] In other words, people generally presumed that all events were the result of both physics and the actions of God (or gods, in pagan cultures.)

Tragically, what began with Aquinas's conceptual division of the spiritual and physical realms has become an ugly divorce. Most every philosophical system since his time has tried to explain the relationship between the seen and unseen as though the two cannot live in the same intellectual house. Eventually, a twentieth-century philosophy called existentialism suggested that the gap between the two realms cannot be bridged intellectually, that neither science nor logic can lead one to experience spiritual realities. According to existentialists, the spiritual realm is so completely "other" that one must defy all logic and leap across the gap; one must take a blind "leap of faith" and trust that something rather than nothing is there. Today, therefore, the most common understanding of faith is nonrational belief, or "believing what you know ain't so."

Faith, as the Bible presents it, is anything but nonrational. Faith often transcends proof, but that's not to say that faith calls us to shut off our brains, ignore logic, and blindly believe what we *hope* to be true. To help make this clearer, substitute the word "trust" for "faith." Exercising the kind of faith described in the Bible is a choice to trust something or someone. You exercise faith each time you board an airplane or allow a physician to perform a procedure on your body while you are anesthetized. Having reasonable expectation that the aircraft is designed and built correctly and that the crew is competent to operate it, you climb aboard with every expectation to land safely at your destination. Having reasonable assurances that your doctor is both knowledgeable and experienced, you submit your unconscious body to his or her care, expecting to be better off than before. No one can prove that your travel will end safely or that you will be healed. However, what you have seen allows you to trust what you cannot yet see. In time, experience reinforces the decision to trust. Eventually, repeated experience allows faith in air travel or medicine to grow strong.

Faith — or trust — allows us to move beyond what we see in order to experience what cannot yet be seen. Nevertheless, faith is not a leap ... and faith is never blind. Paul illustrates this truth in Abraham's relationship with God.

### — 4:16–17 —

Paul's expression "for this reason" establishes a logical connection between what he has just written and what he will declare next. Just as wages are obtained through work and failure to obey the Law reaps God's wrath, grace is received through faith. Grace and faith must go together because grace is utterly alien to our world. It's a miraculous act of God — not unlike parting seas (Ex. 14:13–31) and raining bread from heaven (16:1–7) — in which divine power supersedes all other forces. To illustrate the supernatural dynamic of God's grace and genuine faith, the apostle again points to the experience of father Abraham. In the same way Abraham is the father of the Hebrews and their covenant with God, he is the father of all who would be joined to God through trust in Him.

Abraham's life was a journey in faith. It started relatively small when God chose him from among the Chaldeans, an idolatrous civilization nestled in the cradle of humanity. No one knows why God selected this particular Chaldean; all we know is that it was *not* due to any particular merit in the man. The Lord promised to give this man a large parcel of land, a burgeoning progeny, and an everlasting blessing. So, the future patriarch traveled up the Tigris-Euphrates basin, over the crest of the "Fertile Crescent," and down the Jordan Valley.

Decades later, the aging Chaldean despaired. Nearing the age of one hundred, having seen his Promised Land sick with famine (Gen. 12:10 – 20), his family divided by greed (13:4 – 12), and his shalom shattered by intruders (14:5 – 24), Abram — "exalted father" — still had no children. To encourage Abram, the Lord appeared to him in a dream and confirmed that he would indeed become "the father of a multitude of nations" (17:4). To seal His promise, the Lord changed Abram's name to Abraham, "father of a multitude," and his wife's name from Sarai, "contentious," to Sarah, "princess." The old man responded the way most of us would: He *laughed*!

> Then Abraham fell on his face and laughed, and said in his heart, "Will a child be born to a man one hundred years old? And will Sarah, who is ninety years old, bear *a child*?" And Abraham said to God, "Oh that Ishmael might live before You!" (Gen. 17:17 – 18)

Who is Ishmael? The product of Abraham's lapse in faith. Thirteen years earlier, Abram and Sarai decided the divine plan needed a little human intervention. (We're all good at that.) After all, a careful study of God's promise didn't say anything about Sarai being the mother of Abram's covenant children. Maybe God intended a surrogate. Childbearing had become physically impossible for Sarai, but not for Abram. Perhaps they weren't thinking creatively enough. So. . .

> Sarai said to Abram, "Now behold, the LORD has prevented me from bearing *children*. Please go in to my maid; perhaps I will obtain children through her." And Abram listened to the voice of Sarai. After Abram had lived ten years in the land of Canaan, Abram's wife Sarai took Hagar the Egyptian, her maid, and gave her to her husband Abram as his wife. (Gen. 16:2 – 3)

But the plan backfired. It always does when we decide to help God fulfill His promises. Hagar and Ishmael became a source of bitter contention in the patriarch's household, far from the blessing he thought to grasp through his own efforts. So when the Lord clarified that Sarai's withered womb would indeed be the source of his "multitude," Abram could not suppress an incredulous laugh (Gen. 17:17).

As you would expect, when Sarah later heard the news from the lips of angels, she laughed as well (18:12).

We can't be too hard on Abram and Sarai. Because we have the Bible, we already know God to be the all-powerful Creator of the universe. But they knew almost nothing about Him at the beginning. Then, as the Lord revealed more and more of His character and power, their faith grew in response. Far from a blind leap, theirs was a journey of faith led by the Lord in which trust was required in small measures at first. Each choice to trust was rewarded with blessing and a greater understanding of God. As He proved faithful, their faith matured.

Note the angel's response to the incredulous laughter of the aging couple: "Is anything too difficult for the LORD?" (Gen. 18:14). Our limited, nature-bound perspective would have us focus on the fact that ninety-year-old women cannot have babies. But God is not bound by the limitations of the natural world. He is supernatural — above nature — both able and willing to accomplish what no one else can.

A few chapters later in the story of Abraham and Sarah, we read the words, "And the LORD attended to Sarah like He said He would and did for her what He said He would" (Gen. 21:1, my translation). The aged woman then conceived, carried her child nine months (that must have been a sight!), and gave birth to a son, whom they named *Yitschaq*, "he laughed." We know him as Isaac. Sarah commented on the irony of Isaac's name when she declared:

> "God has made laughter for me; everyone who hears will laugh with me." And she said, "Who would have said to Abraham that Sarah would nurse children? Yet I have borne him a son in his old age." (Gen. 21:6–7)

How wonderful to see her laughter transformed from scoffing to joy . . . from cynicism to celebration!

So what does this have to do with Romans 4:16–25? Everything! Especially for all Jewish readers. Paul had earlier declared, "For we maintain that a man is justified by faith apart from works of the Law" (3:28). He then demonstrated that Abraham's righteousness came through faith (4:1–15). And faith was required because Abraham could no more obtain righteousness through natural means than a ninety-year-old woman could conceive a child. God's covenant with Abraham promised a multitude of descendants. The patriarch tried to claim the promise through natural means (Sarah's handmaid, Hagar), but to no avail. The only thing he had to offer was his belief in the character and power of God to do as was promised. And in time, God sovereignly, supernaturally fulfilled His promise without any help from Abraham or Sarah.

## —4:18—

The wording "in hope against hope" is a paradoxical turn of phrase that some use to support their "leap of faith" approach to Christian belief. Paul means by this expression to separate natural hope from supernatural hope. In other words, Abraham placed his hope in the supernatural power of God to accomplish what is hopeless by any natural means. However, his hope was not a blind leap. It was quite reasonable for him to believe in God's supernatural power because he had seen it in action before. Furthermore, God's faithfulness allowed Abraham to trust Him without having to know specifically how the future would unfold.

Paul uses Abraham's "hope against hope" as a pattern for the kind of faith we are to have. Becoming good enough for heaven is not something we can achieve by any human, natural means. It is something we can only receive through faith. However, this faith is neither a blind leap nor a choice to trust against all reason or proof. God has proven Himself trustworthy.

Abraham and Sarah experienced a long period of waiting, which might seem cruel from a human point of view. But the Lord used the delay to accomplish two important objectives. First, He wanted Abraham and all of his descendants to understand that His covenant was divine in its origin and supernatural in its fulfillment. Second, He wanted — through their personal experience — to cultivate Abraham and Sarah's faith as they gained greater knowledge of His holy character and limitless power.

## —4:19–21—

I am encouraged to see Paul's divinely inspired comment on the faith of Abraham and Sarah. As I read their story, I see multiple examples of wobbly-legged faith. Yet God looked not so much at their faltering growth but at their ultimate destination. From our perspective they wavered a lot along the way; the Lord looks instead upon the fact that they arrived despite the presence of natural hindrances. They may have laughed, but that laughter did not nullify their trust. The aging couple took full account of their decaying bodies and waning sexual potency as they, together, chose to believe God. Despite the occasional setbacks, Abraham's mind remained undivided — weak in human understanding but always trained on God and no other.

Gradually, Abraham's experience with God gave him greater ability to trust Him despite the apparent contradictions that surrounded him. His trust was empowered to the point that he was able to believe without reservation that God would fulfill all that He promised. And one last trial, not mentioned in this passage but fully in view to all who know his story of faith, proved the mettle of Abraham's trust. Think of it as the man's final exam.

Several years after the birth of Isaac, Abraham's only child and the very embodiment of God's covenant promise, the Lord commanded him to do something humanly unthinkable. "Take now your son, your only son, whom you love, Isaac, and go to the land of Moriah, and offer him there as a burnt offering on one of the mountains of which I will tell you" (Gen. 22:2). Without hesitation (although with great anguish, I have no doubt), the faithful father obeyed.

As the two approached the appointed place of sacrifice, Isaac, who was no fool, asked the obvious question, "Behold, the fire and the wood, but where is the lamb for the burnt offering?" (Gen. 22:7). His father's answer could be construed as coy, but I see in his words a choice to trust in the goodness of God without having to understand when or how He would fulfill His promise: "God will provide for Himself the lamb for the burnt offering, my son" (22:8).

If this had been Abraham's first experience with God, his faith could be considered a giant leap. Instead, it is the culmination of a journey, initiated by God, led by God, sustained by God, cultivated by God, and completed by God—with, of course, Abraham's willing participation. The patriarch's fully developed faith yielded the fruit of obedience, to which the Lord responded, "In your seed all the nations of the earth shall be blessed, because you have obeyed My voice" (Gen. 22:18).

## —4:22–25—

From a natural, human perspective, one might think that Abraham's obedience to the command of God earned him the covenant blessing. Paul's illustration from Mount Moriah proves that Abraham's obedience was simply a visible manifestation of his faith, and that it was his faith that allowed him to receive God's gift of righteousness.

Paul belabors the point in order to make an important connection. Abraham is the father of the Hebrews, but not of them only. He is the father of all who receive God's grace through faith and are declared righteous through no merit of their own. The only difference between Abraham and us is what, specifically, we are to believe. Abraham was called to obey the command of God to sacrifice his only son, Isaac, with the understanding that "God will provide" (Gen. 22:8). We are called to "believe in Him who raised Jesus our Lord from the dead, *He* who was delivered over because of our transgressions, and was raised because of our justification" (Rom. 4:24–25).

This is the gospel in its most straightforward terms. Christ died for our sins according to the Scriptures and He was buried. Then Christ was raised from the dead and was seen by His disciples, including one meeting in which He interacted with a gathering of more than five hundred followers (1 Cor. 15:6). And by trusting in God's provision despite the apparent finality of death, we "hope against hope" and receive the gift of eternal life.

## Application

### *Becoming a "Big-Godder"*

Paul freely admitted that the justification of a sinful person was impossible ... at least in human terms. He then used Abraham and Sarah's inability to have children to illustrate another key principle in salvation — the promise of God and the principle of grace make all things possible, even the impossible. Therefore, God has the ability to give life to the dead and create something out of nothing (4:16–17).

God promised Abraham that he would be the progenitor of multitudes, nations in fact. But many years passed, as did Sarah's ability to bear children. Long after it became physically impossible for her to conceive, God reaffirmed His promise and "in hope against hope" Abraham trusted Him. This wasn't a blind faith. The old man acknowledged the impossibility of the circumstance, yet trusted in the greatness of his God (4:18–21).

Abraham worshiped and served a big God. He understood his Maker to be immensely more powerful than any human impossibility. And from him we learn two important lessons about faith.

- *Genuine faith is strengthened when we must wait on God's promises to be fulfilled.* When we must wait to receive something the Lord has promised, we gradually turn our eyes away from circumstances to look instead on the greatness and faithfulness of God.
- *Genuine faith is directly proportional to our knowledge of God.* As we fully comprehend His nature, our faith cannot help but grow.

Robert Dick Wilson is mostly remembered for his outstanding achievements in linguistics at Princeton Theological Seminary. He learned more than forty-five ancient languages in his quest to understand the Scriptures more accurately. But his students remember him more for his unique approach to evaluating their preaching.

He did not critique their ability to parse verbs or dissect ancient turns of a phrase, and he did not analyze their scholarship or pay attention to their charisma. Instead, he listened for another, more crucial quality. After hearing one particular student preach the professor remarked, "I am glad that you are a big-godder. When my boys come back, I come to see if they are big-godders or little-godders, and then I know what their ministry will be."[7]

How big is your God? Are you tossed about by the waves of circumstance in a sea of chaos? Or do you understand that God has every matter under His divine control and that He has a purpose for every event you encounter?

Do you accept the finality of impossibilities, or do you allow God to have the final say in those matters?

When you pray, do you shy away from asking God to accomplish big things, or do you trust that He is not only able, but likely willing to dramatically and supernaturally act on your behalf?

The size of your God has everything to do with your answers. Who is directing your future, no matter what your age? Is it a puny god with no imagination and little power? Or do you serve an infinitely creative, immensely powerful, immeasurably gigantic God?

Let me challenge you to become a "big-godder." Begin by committing yourself to knowing Him as He is.

## Peace with God (Romans 5:1–11)

¹Therefore, having been justified by faith, we have peace with God through our Lord Jesus Christ, ²through whom also we have obtained our introduction by faith into this grace in which we stand; and we exult in hope of the glory of God. ³And not only this, but we also exult in our tribulations, knowing that tribulation brings about perseverance; ⁴and perseverance, proven character; and proven character, hope; ⁵and hope does not disappoint, because the love of God has been poured out within our hearts through the Holy Spirit who was given to us.

⁶For while we were still helpless, at the right time Christ died for the ungodly. ⁷For one will hardly die for a righteous man; though perhaps for the good man someone would dare even to die. ⁸But God demonstrates His own love toward us, in that while we were yet sinners, Christ died for us. ⁹Much more then, having now been justified by His blood, we shall be saved from the wrath *of God* through Him. ¹⁰For if while we were enemies we were reconciled to God through the death of His Son, much more, having been reconciled, we shall be saved by His life. ¹¹And not only this, but we also

exult in God through our Lord Jesus Christ, through whom we have now received the reconciliation.

---

I once asked my sister, Luci, "What, in your opinion, is the very best emotion a person can experience?" I expected her to say something like love, delight, contentment, accomplishment, or joy, but her answer surprised me. She said immediately and with confidence, "Relief."

After thinking a short time, I had to agree. And experience has confirmed for me that relief is indeed the best and most enjoyable of all life's emotions. Consequently, relief is a key ingredient in art and entertainment. Great stories, symphonies, speeches, and even roller coasters gradually build tension to a climax and then resolve the crisis. It's a formula that never fails to satisfy audiences.

Paul's crafting of his letter to the Christians in Rome not only utilizes the very best literary style, it epitomizes our experience with God. The opening chapters find readers complacent in their relationship with Him. Some trust that their Hebrew heritage qualifies them for special treatment. Others trust that their good deeds and clean rap sheet will sufficiently impress the Judge of heaven. But Paul quickly introduced the crisis and built it to a crescendo: "There is none righteous, not even one" (3:10); "all have sinned and fall short of the glory of God" (3:23).

Having agitated the soul with the dreadful news that no one can possibly escape the wrath of God through any natural means, the apostle resolved the crisis with the good news. The righteousness required for one to gain eternal life with God and all the joys of heaven is a free gift received through faith (3:28). And to settle the matter conclusively for Jew and Gentile alike, he pointed to the example of God's grace to Abraham, which was received through faith (ch. 4).

But there's a problem. It would seem that Paul has cut the story of God's grace too short. Four chapters into a sixteen-chapter novel is not the right time to bring the narrative to a climax and resolve the crisis! That tends to leave audiences wondering, *Okay . . . What now?*

In Paul's letter to the Romans, this is where the story actually begins. With the crisis of God's wrath resolved through the death and resurrection of Jesus Christ and the righteousness of God received through faith, the believer must then come to terms with the relief that salvation brings. Now, before you dismiss that thought, let me assure you that this is no easy task. If it were, Paul would not have dedicated three quarters of his letter to the subject!

The apostle's message in chapter 5 is essentially, "Now that you have peace with God, you've only just begun to live . . . and it only gets better from here." The first eleven verses begin with a glance at the past (5:1), continue with an appreciation of the present (5:2–8), and then escort us into the future with anticipation (5:9–11).

## —5:1–2—

To prepare his readers for the rest of the journey, Paul directs us to stop for a moment to consider where we are. We have now believed! This step is monumental in the life of a believer, and if we don't pause to appreciate its significance, the rest of our journey will remain a mystery. He takes us by the shoulders, as it were, turns us around to look back down the road we traveled, and says, "Having been justified by faith, we have peace with God through our Lord Jesus Christ."

Stop!

Don't go any further!

Read that again slowly.

"Peace with God." There's more relief in those three words than any other. More than the words "You are cured" to a cancer patient. More than "You are free" to a death row inmate. And it seems the more one comprehends the danger of God's fearsome wrath, the more he or she experiences the incredible relief (there's that best of all emotions) of having peace with Him. Jesus illustrated this truth with a parable in Luke 7:41–43:

> "A moneylender had two debtors: one owed five hundred denarii, and the other fifty. When they were unable to repay, he graciously forgave them both. So which of them will love him more?" [43]Simon answered and said, "I suppose the one whom he forgave more." And He said to him, "You have judged correctly."

"Peace" does not refer to inner tranquility, although that's part of the relief we feel. "Peace" refers to our no longer being subject to God's wrath because of sin. The death of Jesus Christ satisfied our debt of sin and set aside the resulting hostility so that God and people are no longer divided by rebellion but reconciled in peace. And the resulting relief is indescribable. Anyone who has spent his or her life trying to earn God's pleasure or trying to accumulate enough good deeds to escape hell understands this parable better than most.

Martin Luther spent much of his early life trying to appease the wrath of God through the litany of good deeds prescribed by the Roman Catholic Church. But he found no relief. In fact, the more he worked, the more aware of its futility he became.

Though I lived as a monk without reproach, I felt that I was a sinner before God with an extremely disturbed conscience. I could not believe that he was placated by my satisfaction. I did not love, yes, I hated the righteous God who punishes sinners, and secretly, if not blasphemously, certainly murmuring greatly, I was angry with God, and said, "As if, indeed, it is not enough, that miserable sinners, eternally lost through original sin, are crushed by every kind of calamity by the law of the [ten commandments], without having God add pain to pain by the gospel and also by the gospel threatening us with his righteousness and wrath!" Thus I raged with a fierce and troubled conscience. Nevertheless, I beat importunately upon Paul at that place, most ardently desiring to know what St. Paul wanted [in his letter to the Romans].[8]

The problem with trying to earn one's way out of debt to God is that we can never know how much is enough. Ask most people, "Are you going to heaven after you die?" and most will answer, "I hope so." Those who trust religion to save them, if they take it seriously, must remain in a constant state of terror, knowing that only death will solve the mystery of their eternal destiny and that their fate might be eternal suffering.

At long last, Luther found relief.

By the mercy of God, meditating day and night, I gave heed to the context of the words, namely, "In it the righteousness of God is revealed, as it is written, 'He who through faith is righteous shall live'" [Romans 1:17]. There I began to understand that the righteousness of God is that by which the righteous lives by a gift of God, namely by faith. And this is the meaning: the righteousness of God is revealed by the gospel, namely, the passive righteousness with which merciful God justifies us by faith, as it is written, "He who through faith is righteous shall live." Here I felt that I was altogether born again and had entered paradise itself through open gates. There a totally other face of the entire Scripture showed itself to me. Thereupon I ran through the Scripture from memory. I also found in other terms an analogy, as, the work of God, that is what God does in us, the power of God, with which he makes us wise, the strength of God, the salvation of God, the glory of God.

And I extolled my sweetest word with a love as great as the hatred with which I had before hated the word "righteousness of God." Thus that place in Paul was for me truly the gate to paradise.[9]

Paul calls the experience of receiving God's grace through faith and the resulting peace an "introduction." The Greek word is *prosagōgē*, which is variously rendered "access" or "introduction," but these fail to capture the cultural word picture it contains. *Prosagōgē* describes the process of being ushered into the court of a king and then being announced, which thereupon implies the right or opportunity to address the ruler. Paul used the same term to describe prayer for the Christians in Ephesus: This was "in accordance with the eternal purpose which He carried out in Christ Jesus our Lord, in whom we have boldness and confident *access* through faith in Him" (Ephesians 3:11 – 12, italics mine).

Paul's use of *prosagōgē* declares that Jesus Christ has ushered us into a completely new territory called "grace," in which we have the right or opportunity to live according to a completely different perspective. This new land operates according to an utterly different standard, one that is in many ways the opposite of where we came from. Note also the phrase "in which we stand." The Greek term for "stand" implies the establishment of something permanent. Like immigrants, we have come to take up permanent residence in the land of grace. Of course, this will require a major adjustment on our part. We must learn the culture and adapt to its ways.

Paul concludes this introductory sentence with the phrase, "and we exult in hope of the glory of God," which uses three important terms worth studying. They will become increasingly significant as Paul describes the Christian life.

"Exult" is probably the best English word to render the Greek term used by Paul, which literally means "to boast." We typically think of boasting as a negative behavior, but one respected lexicon defines the Greek use of the verb as "to express an unusually high degree of confidence in someone or something being exceptionally noteworthy."[10] Whereas some live by an uneasy expectation that their good deeds will be good enough for heaven, those who take up residence in the land of grace can live with complete confidence. Ironically, the "boasting" of believers is inherently humble because they do not have any confidence in their own goodness; instead, they express complete confidence in the free gift of grace. For our purposes, let's render the verb this way: "to live with joyful confidence."

"Hope" in the biblical sense does not have the element of wishful thinking that we give it in English. A child might say, "I hope I get a red bicycle for Christmas," and he might be surprised to find it next to the tree. Or he might not. The word used by Paul is a noun meaning "an assured expectation." When someone purchases a ticket to a concert, she has in her hand the hope—the assured expectation—of a seat on the given day. Paul uses this term in a specific way to describe the future day when Jesus returns to rule the world and renovate it to His liking.

"Glory" refers to the state of things as God desires them. Good triumphs over evil, justice prevails, sin has no place, and everything exists in harmony with His holy character.

## —5:3-5—

Paul describes "exultation" (living with joyful confidence) as having three levels. First, we "exult in hope" (5:2). That is, we live with joyful confidence in the assured expectation that Christ will one day set all things right. It's the joy of knowing we have been renewed and that we are in the process of becoming more like Jesus. It's the kind of joy we experience when things are going well and we can anticipate His coming again without unpleasant circumstances to distract us.

Unfortunately, life this side of heaven will include suffering. This is true for everyone; perhaps more so for the believer (John 15:18–19), which leads to the second level of joy: "we also exult [live with joyful confidence] in our tribulations" (Rom. 5:3). The first level comes quite naturally. When we think of the wonderful future that awaits us, how can we not be joyful? The second, however, must be cultivated under the careful guidance of heaven.

The word for "tribulation" in Greek is *thlipsis*. The literal meaning is "pressure," which of course is used figuratively to describe "distress, hostility, affliction, or oppression." In this context, "pressure" fits best. "Tribulation" suggests the challenges to joy are always grand or dramatic, when in reality, they come in all shapes and sizes. Furthermore, we all face them. The pressures of deadlines, the economy, people's expectations, work-place politics and demands, home and auto repairs, relationships. And these pressures can become intense with failing health, job loss, grief, divorce, persecution, and other major life events. Nevertheless, because we have been ushered into a completely new manner of life, we can live with joyful confidence in *thlipsis*, under pressure, through tribulation.

How do we come by this supernatural ability? Obviously not from other people, or our jobs, or internal fortitude. We gain the ability to rejoice under pressure through a carefully monitored training program directed by the Lord Himself. Paul describes this program as a chain reaction in which one phase leads to another, eventually giving us the ability to experience joy despite our circumstances. This chain reaction involves several key terms. Think of them as dominoes, standing on end, one toppling the next.

"Tribulation brings about perseverance." *Thlipsis* cultivates *hypomonē*, which means "remaining under" in the literal sense and "patiently enduring" in the figurative. Naturally, when the pressure builds we should take reasonable measures to relieve the discomfort. No one is suggesting we volunteer for pain or ignore the opportunity to eliminate it. But sometimes there is no solution, no remedy, no relief. Sometimes we cannot avoid or escape the pressure. When that happens, we deliberately choose to "remain under" and to do so with graceful and calm dignity.

The chain of truths spans the gap between verses 3 and 4 with the phrase, "perseverance [brings about] proven character." *Hypomonē* cultivates *dokimē*, or "tested worth." *Dokimē* derives its meaning from the verb "to watch" and pictures a metallurgist placing a sample of gold or silver under intense heat to observe how it responds. It came to be used of soldiers and athletes, whose mettle was proven by their endurance in combat or competition. We might also render *dokimē* as "triumphant fortitude."

This isn't pretending, or denial, or the power of positive thinking. This triumphant fortitude isn't even something we can choose to develop. It comes as the trials of life in a fallen world become instruments in the hands of the Holy Spirit, who crafts deep within us "proven character."

"Proven character [brings about] hope." *Dokimē* cultivates *elpis*, "assured expectation," the certainty of a promised outcome. We experience this kind of hope when we watch a nail-biting, come-from-behind victory over a superior team against insurmountable odds … after having learned the final score. Knowing the outcome of a competition profoundly changes how we experience it. We observe without anxiety. We endure setbacks without panic. This is a kind of hope that cannot disappoint because we have an assured outcome.

Looking at Paul's logic in reverse: God's character-building program for believers rests entirely on this assured expectation (vv. 4–5). Our guaranteed victory provides a foundation for our "proven character" (v. 4), which displays "perseverance" (v. 4), which in turn allows us to endure "tribulation" with dignity and grace (v. 3). To provide the assurance we need, Paul introduces two great truths for the first time in his letter to the Romans: the great love of God and the indwelling of His Holy Spirit (v. 5).

We learned of God's wrath in 1:18–32; now we discover that those who now have peace with God can experience His love. His Spirit fills, transforms, and empowers us. He provides strength in our weakness, wisdom in our foolishness, love in our doubt, and evidence in our despair. The Holy Spirit living within us is our ever-present guarantee of future victory.

—**5:6–9**—

Many Christians make the mistake of thinking that once we are saved by grace, we're on our own to do the rest. Some like to think they can behave anyway they please once they have a ticket to heaven in their pockets. Many others work themselves to exhaustion trying to become worthy of the grace they have received. Neither perspective recognizes the fact that after the moment when our eternal life after death has been sealed, we still need our Savior. We are still helpless without the grace of God. We never rise above our need for God to bend down and lift us up.

To illustrate our continuing need for grace and God's faithfulness in providing it, Paul retraces the steps of the gospel. In doing so, he stresses the fact that nothing in us deserved saving, yet Christ died for us. How remarkable it is when one good person sacrifices his or her own life to save that of another good person. Most of us can identify with that kind of selflessness and hope to have similar courage if called upon to do the same. But who would volunteer to take the place of a serial killer on death row? Who would give his or her own life to save that of a Hitler or a Stalin?

Jesus Christ did.

You might be saying to yourself, *Well, I'm certainly no mass murderer!* But let's not forget the lesson Paul taught us in chapter 2. The same sin-corrupted heart that beats in the chest of the worst criminal beats in ours as well. Heaven doesn't rate sin on a scale as we are prone to do. Our sin renders us no less helpless than that of humanity's most depraved examples. Nevertheless, I urge you to memorize Paul's declaration: "God demonstrates His own love toward us, in that while we were yet sinners, Christ died for us" (5:8).

Take note of the verbs "demonstrates" and "died." The first is present tense, which is curious. Normally, we would expect to see, "God *demonstrated* His love toward us, in that while we were yet sinners, Christ died for us." Paul uses this unexpected turn of tenses to make an important point. We weren't what we should have been *before* we were saved, and we aren't what we should be *now*. Nevertheless, God, who faithfully provided undeserved favor to save us from sin, continues to offer undeserved favor now.

Because of Christ's death, we (by grace, through faith) have been declared "just" by the Judge of heaven. We no longer have to fear His wrath. We are no longer subject to punishment. His sacrifice paid our debt for sin. Not only those in the past, but those we will certainly commit in the future. We have not only escaped God's wrath at the final judgment after death, we are not subject to His wrath during our lifetime.

Paul wrote all of this to support his opening statement in 5:1. The death and resurrection of Jesus Christ have ushered us into a completely new territory called "Grace," in which we have the opportunity to thrive according to a completely different perspective.

— **5:10–11** —

But that's not all. As if peace with God—freedom from His wrath—were not enough, there's more. *Much more.* The death of God's Son on behalf of humankind

## From My Journal

### Absurd Teaching

Many years ago I taught a home Bible class, which soon grew to more than seventy people. Because so many of them had not heard the gospel and were obviously eager to understand it, I decided to make the good news our focus. After nine weeks I thought, *Let's see how many are getting the message.* So, I handed each person an index card and asked them to write a brief explanation of the gospel in no more than a sentence or two—nothing complicated. Out of approximately seventy students, how many turned in a correct response?

*Five!*

At first I was confused and disillusioned. How could my teaching have been so ineffective? But then as I continued to work with the class, I discovered that people find it very difficult to connect the dots and to accept the concept of grace. It is humanly illogical, and even seems irresponsible, to think that anything in life is free. Because the world is a "you only get what you pay for" kind of place, we naturally expect salvation to be the same. Before long, we're earning Brownie points toward heaven, attending church, feeding the hungry, giving money to worthy causes, memorizing Scripture, turning the other cheek, nursing wounded sparrows back to health ... Eventually, we arrive at a logical conclusion: *All this work is surely getting God's attention. Hopefully, He will reward me ... maybe even let me into heaven.*

But God's economy doesn't work like that. Grace is the currency of heaven, which makes grace an utterly absurd concept to the world. Grace is free to the receiver and costly to the giver. Grace transfers blessing from the storehouse of the deserving to the need of the unworthy. Grace is given with no expectations, no conditions, no constraints, and no record. In fact, grace is not genuine if it cannot be abused by the person receiving it—and many do abuse grace.

When someone continually lavishes grace on undeserving people, who for the most part abuse it, we call that someone a sucker, a patsy, a dupe. Certainly God would never set aside His dignity or stoop so low ... would He?

He would. And He did. Read this slowly ... preferably *aloud*:

[Jesus], although He existed in the form of God, did not regard equality with God a thing to be grasped, but emptied Himself, taking the form of a bond-servant, and being made in the likeness of men. Being found in appearance as a man, He humbled Himself by becoming obedient to the point of death, even death on a cross. (Phil 2:6–8)

God stooping to become a man? And then stooping to suffer the punishment we deserve? After four years of seminary and well over four decades in pastoral ministry, I can scarcely take this in. No wonder new believers struggle to connect the dots.

is only part of the story. He not only died, He rose again! His death stripped away the condemnation of death; His resurrection gives us abundant, eternal life.

Take note of the verb tenses again. "Were reconciled" is in the past tense. The work of reconciliation is complete. The gaping chasm that stood between God and us has been permanently bridged. The death of Christ became the means of our *prosagōgē*—our access, our introduction (remember 5:2?)—to living in harmony with God. And "having been reconciled" (perfect tense),[11] we "shall be saved" (future tense).

Paul's use of the term "saved" includes far more than preservation from the torments of hell. He means preservation from all things that are opposed to God, including any future sin that threatens to keep us from enjoying our new life in the territory called "Grace." And this assurance, Paul declares, allows us access to the third level of joy: "we also exult in God" (5:11).

Mature believers experience a kind of joy that transcends all other considerations because it is anchored in their "peace with God," their reconciled relationship with the Almighty. They live with joyful confidence despite the afflictions of a fallen world, despite the physical consequences of past sin, even despite their failure to live as they ought. They live by the words of an old hymn I learned as a young man and still love to sing:

> Then we shall be where we would be,
> Then we shall be what we should be;
> Things that are not now, nor could be,
> Soon shall be our own.[12]

Things are not yet as they should be. The world does not operate according to God's way, and we still have too much of the old nature within us. Nevertheless, having been declared "just" by faith, we have peace with God through our Lord Jesus Christ, through whom we have been ushered into a whole, new realm of existence, in which we have the opportunity to thrive with assured confidence in the day when all things will be made right—a day in which good triumphs over evil, justice prevails, sin is removed, and everything exists in harmony with God's holy character.

This third level of joy, which I call "triumphant joy," rises above present circumstances to celebrate the Lord's victory over sin, affliction, sorrow, and death. This joy, which cannot be obtained by any natural means, is the work of the Holy Spirit within the believer. His is a voice of assurance that continually whispers into the souls of His beloved Christians, "Now that you have peace with God, you've only just begun to live . . . and it only gets better from here."

## Application

### *Peace with God, Joy in Tribulation*

Once believers receive God's grace through faith in Jesus Christ, we have "peace with God" (5:1–2). Therefore, we may rest in the knowledge that no circumstance is the result of punishment. Bad things do not happen because we have been bad. No event is an expression of God's ill will against us. On the contrary, He has promised to use every circumstance, whether pleasant or painful, to guide His own toward maturity (5:3–5).

To demonstrate the truth that God is *for* us, Paul points out that God's grace reached down to save us while we were still hostile to Him, long before we began walking with Him in a faith-based relationship (5:6–8). How foolish to think that after having "peace with God" He would send harmful circumstances to punish our wrongdoing! Far from it. Now that we have been justified, saved from wrath, and reconciled, we may forever rejoice, even as painful events cause heartache (5:9–11). Those harsh events are never punitive.

The plain, unfortunate fact of life is that we live in a fallen world that is not yet redeemed. One day, it will be redeemed and transformed (Rev. 21–22). But until then, our "peace with God" comes at the expense of hostility with the corrupted world system. Jesus promised that we would be hated by the world because of our unity with God (John 15:18–21). Nevertheless, what the world intends for our evil, God commandeers for our good! Therefore, even in tribulation we can rejoice. To fully rest in this truth, we must apply three principles:

1. *The secret of rejoicing is having the right focus.* My focus can no longer be myself or my circumstances. My focus must now be my Savior and His purposes. He has taken up residence in my life and longs to have first place on the throne of my will. He is carrying out a great plan for the world, of which I am a vital part. In every circumstance, I must deliberately ask: "What is God accomplishing in me and through me to carry out His plan for the world?"

2. *Choosing the right focus leads to having the right attitude.* Once I have shifted my focus away from myself and my pain to concentrate on God's plan to accomplish something good in me and through me, I no longer wander in doubt or wallow in self-pity. I no longer wonder about God's goodness or His faithfulness, I no longer fear that my misfortune is somehow the fallout of some sin, I no longer wile away hours wondering when it will end. When my focus is right, I learn submission, humility, and gratitude.

3. *The fruit of a right attitude is triumphant joy.* As the Lord makes me teachable, humble, and grateful, I find growing within me a joy that carries me above my circumstance. This is a joy that comes from sensing the presence of God and perceiving His purpose. Such joy is downright contagious! I may not know His specific purpose, but I know it is for my good and His glory. And that makes even the worst of times serenely good.

My mentor and friend Howie Hendricks once asked a pastor, "How you doin'?" The guy replied, "Oh man, under these circumstances it is terrible."
Hendricks said, "So, what are you doing under there?"
Don't allow yourself to live *under* the circumstances of your life. Learn to rise above them, not through your own power or ability, but by trusting in the goodness of God and His unbounded love for you. You have peace with God. So, REJOICE!

## Guilt versus Grace (Romans 5:12–21)

¹²Therefore, just as through one man sin entered into the world, and death through sin, and so death spread to all men, because all sinned — ¹³for until the Law sin was in the world, but sin is not imputed when there is no law. ¹⁴Nevertheless death reigned from Adam until Moses, even over those who had not sinned in the likeness of the offense of Adam, who is a type of Him who was to come.

¹⁵But the free gift is not like the transgression. For if by the transgression of the one the many died, much more did the grace of God and the gift by the grace of the one Man, Jesus Christ, abound to the many. ¹⁶The gift is not like *that which came* through the one who sinned; for on the one hand the judgment arose from one *transgression* resulting in condemnation, but on the other hand the free gift *arose* from many transgressions resulting in justification. ¹⁷For if by the transgression of the one, death reigned through the one, much more those who receive the abundance of grace and of the gift of righteousness will reign in life through the One, Jesus Christ.

¹⁸So then as through one transgression there resulted condemnation to all men, even so through one act of righteousness there resulted justification of life to all men. ¹⁹For as through the one man's disobedience the many were made sinners, even so through the obedience of the One the many will be made righteous. ²⁰The Law came in so that the transgression would increase; but where sin increased, grace abounded all the more, ²¹so that, as sin reigned in death, even so grace would reign through righteousness to eternal life through Jesus Christ our Lord.

As you read these words, a great cosmic battle rages around you and within you. And you cannot remain neutral; you must choose a side. I'm not talking about the ongoing war between good and evil. I'm referring the conflict between grace and guilt. Which will have your allegiance? Which will guide your choices? Which will characterize your relationships? Which cause will you advance? Which will shape your perspective on that *other* great conflict (the one between good and evil)?

The struggle between these two great forces began in the Garden of Eden, not long after the creation of humanity. The Creator fashioned the first people and placed them in a pristine environment, which He created specifically with their physical needs in mind. Surrounded by such plenty, all the man and woman had to do was tend the garden, savor its delights, love one another, and enjoy intimate fellowship with God forever. Furthermore, the Lord delegated authority to the couple, empowering them and charging them to be His vice-regents over the earth (Gen. 1:26–27; 2:15). Having been cradled in this lavish abundance of good, they were to avoid one solitary tree.

Adam, with a nature unpolluted by sin, had the freedom to choose between obedience and disobedience, good and evil. And we all know which he chose. His decision to rebel against God's single prohibition changed everything. Whereas "the man and his wife were both naked and were not ashamed" (Gen. 2:25) before his disobedience, they "hid themselves from the presence of the LORD God among the trees of the garden" (3:8) when He came to confront them. This was Adam's second tragic choice. He covered himself in

## SHAME ON YOUR GUILT!

The term "guilt" can be confusing. On the one hand, it can refer to "objective guilt," which has nothing to do with feelings but describes the moral state of a person who has done something wrong. Whether or not a person experiences negative emotion after doing an evil deed is irrelevant; he is objectively guilty no matter how he or she feels. On the other hand, "subjective guilt" can produce feelings of sorrow or remorse and usually causes a person to struggle with self-condemning thoughts.

I prefer to call this subjective feeling "shame." When a person is guilty — that is, objectively blameworthy for wrongdoing — feelings of shame *should* follow! Parents used to say to their misbehaving children, "Shame on you for doing that!" In other words, "The fact that you are guilty should make you feel shameful." Shame is a God-given emotion, and its purpose is to bring us to repentance.

Unfortunately, people are reluctant to repent, even when overwhelmed with shame. If the shame becomes intense and repentance doesn't follow, they invariably make irrational and destructive choices. Adam and Eve sewed fig leaf underwear rather than repent, and shame-induced behavior has only grown more and more bizarre.

God has provided the means to remove shame: He sent His Son to remove guilt!

guilt and ran from grace. Certainly he must have known that God's love fueled His wrath.

After the Lord flushed the trembling couple from their place of hiding, He pronounced a series of curses. That is, He set forth the inescapable consequences of their sin. He had earlier stated, "In the day that you eat from it you will surely die" (Gen. 2:17). Adam soon discovered that this death involved far more than just the end of his physical existence. His tending the garden would become drudgery, because the very soil of earth would rebel against his dominion. Eve's joy in childbirth would become mingled with agony. The couple's intimacy would become a bitter struggle of their wills as each would seek to dominate the other. And death—the end of physical life—would lead to a second, more dreadful death, eternal separation from the Creator.

This is the first man's legacy. He chose evil over good, and in so doing, doomed us to follow in his sinful steps. In the same sense that a monarch, a president, or a prime minister acts on behalf of his people, who then reap the consequences of his or her policies, Adam chose this path for all of humanity—indeed, for all of creation. That includes you and me. Moreover, we have inherited his mutated nature so that we are incapable of choosing only good and avoiding all evil.

This doesn't seem fair, does it? Adam chose my fate? I am doomed because *he* disobeyed? But wait! Don't forget that we ratify our representative's inaugural sin by adding sins of our own. Our sinful choices place us squarely behind Adam in the rebellion against God's goodness. Let's face it; we are utterly "without excuse" (1:20). Like Adam, our head, we must come out of hiding and admit, "I ate" (Gen. 3:12). Like Adam, our head, we must come out of hiding and face our Creator. We will never find grace hiding in the bushes.

Paul began this portion of his letter with the conjunctive adverb, "therefore," which says, in effect, "Because the preceding information is true, the following is also true." Believers receive the righteousness God requires as a gift through faith, a truth that is confirmed by Abraham's example (4:1–25). *Therefore*, believers have peace with God and have the right or opportunity to live with assured confidence that when Christ eventually sets all things right, we will share that triumph (5:1–11). *Therefore* (5:12)...

Paul's "therefore" behaves like a comma rather than a period. One revealed truth naturally leads to another that we must consider. This intriguing passage compares and contrasts the significance of two pivotal men in human history: Adam and Jesus. Furthermore, it summarizes everything the apostle has written to this point and prepares us for the next monumental Christian truth. This section can be outlined:

| 5:12–14 | Humanity's Ruin (summarizing 1:18–3:20) |
| 5:15–19 | Humanity's Rescue (summarizing 3:21–5:11) |
| 5:20–21 | Humanity's Reign (introducing 6:1–8:39) |

## —5:12–14—

Sin brings death. It's a fundamental law of the universe no less predictable and pervasive than the law of gravity. Like king and queen, sin and death rule together. In the earliest days after creation, the sinful decision of one man became the conduit of death. (Paul omits his name, but we all know which man.) "Death," remember, is not limited to the inevitable end of physical existence; "death" includes the curses God pronounced in Genesis and eternal separation from Him in eternity. And like a virus, sin infected all of humanity, dooming us all to a death-like existence.

God did not specify and codify His standard for human conduct until the time of Moses, several thousand years after creation. Thus, Paul declared, sin was not "imputed" until then, which is not to suggest that humankind was any less guilty of sin or any less deserving of punishment. Death—the natural consequence of sin—reigned over humankind nonetheless. Paul's point is a judicial one.

The "Law" is nothing less than a particular expression of God's holy character preserved for us in written form. Before the Law was given to Moses, who gave it to Israel to preserve and distribute, men and women lived in contention with their Creator. Nonetheless, they were "without excuse," even without the written Law, as Paul has already proved (1:18–2:16). The word "imputed" is yet another accounting term in Greek, which means "to charge against one's account" (see Philem. 18).

Think of it this way. A young couple comes home from their honeymoon, settles into an apartment, and begins life together. He works; she works; they spend their earnings and all seems well. Three years later, mortgage rates drop and they have a golden opportunity to buy a house. Unfortunately, they have no money for a down payment. In fact, they have accumulated a few thousand dollars in credit card debt. To get their finances in order, they consult a financial expert, who helps them establish a budget. He places their income on one side of a ledger and then lists their monthly expenses on the other. Lo and behold, they have been slowly digging a financial hole for many months and they must adjust their habits.

What changed as a result of seeing the ledger? Certainly not their financial situation. Only their *awareness* of it. The ledger sheet brought the truth of their fiscal irresponsibility to light, which gave them an opportunity to do something about it.

The Law is a moral ledger sheet that brings to our attention the truth about our moral debt. With or without the ledger, we remain indebted. Consequently, before the ledger of the Law was given to humanity, "death reigned from Adam until Moses." Even those who did not sin against an explicit command as Adam did are nevertheless guilty of sin and deserving of death.

## — 5:15–17 —

The last phrase of 5:14 establishes a parallel between Adam and Jesus, who are similar in two important ways. First, both men when tempted by evil were morally unpolluted—Adam before the Fall and Jesus by virtue of His divine nature and virgin conception. Second, both men represented all of humanity—Adam as the physical progenitor of all humankind and Jesus as our divinely delegated representative. But the similarity ends there. Paul then draws an imaginary line down the page and placed the names "Adam" and "Jesus" on opposite sides in order to contrast their impact on humanity:

| Adam | Jesus |
| --- | --- |
| forbidden tree | the cross |
| "transgression" | "free gift" |
| many died | grace abounded to many |
| condemnation | justification |
| death reigned | gift of righteousness will reign |

Note the contrasted effect of each man's moral choice. Adam sinned; Christ obeyed (Matt. 26:39; Mark 14:36; Luke 22:42). Whereas all of humankind suffered the consequence of death as a result of Adam's sin, grace was offered to all human beings by Christ's obedience. Adam's sin brought condemnation down upon all, but the provision of Christ's death offers justification to all. Adam's sin placed death on the throne of creation, while Christ's gift of righteousness will one day rule the world.

It's also important to note one other crucial difference in how the action of each man impacts humanity. The deadly fallout of Adam's sin is a universal, historical fact, while the life-generating gift of Christ's obedience is a potential future for some, but not all. The gift of grace "abounds to the many" (that is, the same "many" who were affected by Adam's transgression: everyone). However, not everyone will choose to receive the gift of God's grace.

Now compare the two clauses "death reigned" and "those who receive ... will reign." The first verb is past tense, describing something that has already occurred. The second verb is future tense, describing an event yet to take place. The subject of the first clause is "death"; death reigned over creation. The subject of the second clause is "those who receive [grace and the gift]"; believers will one day unseat "death" from the throne of creation and rule in its place.

## —5:18–19—

To clearly establish the contrasting impact of the two men on humanity, Paul reduces everything to two pairs of parallel statements, which I will arrange this way for the sake of clarity:

Adam:    Through one transgression there resulted condemnation to all men.

Jesus:   Through one act of righteousness there resulted justification of life to all men.

Adam:    Through the one man's disobedience the many were made sinners.

Jesus:   Through the obedience of the One the many will be made righteous.

The Greek verb translated "made" (5:19) is a judicial term used to appoint someone to an official post. One man's disobedience appointed the many to be sinners; and one man's obedience appointed the many to be righteous. Our newly appointed position as "righteous people" comes with certain rights and responsibilities, which a person receives when appointed (see Titus 1:5). This is another way Paul describes justification by faith, in which the believer is declared righteous—having right standing before the Law and therefore exempt from punishment.

## —5:20–21—

To say that the transgression "increased" as a result of the Law can be interpreted in two ways. First, sins "abounded" in the sense that we now see what had been invisible before the Law clearly defined what was right and wrong. Second, the presence of the Law stimulates the rebellious heart to do the very opposite of what it commands. Both interpretations are valid. Paul's comment accurately reflects the judicial role of the Law of indicting the evil in humanity, but it also accurately describes our rebellious human nature. Being told "Do not ..." actually prompts our old nature to rebel.

Paul brings this particular section of his letter to a close by summarizing his primary point: Salvation cannot be gained through obedience to the Law; salvation is a gift of grace (5:20). The final sentence in this section then foreshadows the topic of the next one: the rise of grace over sin in the life of the believer and its eventual conquest of the world.

As you read these words, a great cosmic battle rages within you. As we have learned, the battle is not between good and evil. Evil has already claimed your heart. No, the forces vying for your soul are guilt and grace. You have sinned, so guilt is an appropriate response, whether you feel it or not. Like many, you may have coped with the guilt of wrongdoing by any number of means; denial, minimization, distraction, blame-shifting, or even religion. Unfortunately, those means cannot cover guilt any better than Adam's fig leaf covered his disobedience.

God's answer to Adam's sin could have been swift and severe. He could have spoken the universe out of existence as easily as He created it, and He would have been no less holy to do so. In fact, many philosophers question how a good, all-powerful God can tolerate the presence of evil. The answer, again, is grace. Undeserved favor. Inexplicable mercy. Rather than execute justice and reduce creation to a cinder, the Lord, moved by love, confronted Adam with his sin.

Many English translations depict the coming of God to the Garden as an evening stroll accompanied by a gentle sundown breeze. But a more accurate rendering suggests the wrath of God blew into the Garden with a violent windstorm. His first question, "Where are you?" is rhetorical. It was a bold invitation to come out of hiding.

At the right time, the Lord confronted humanity with our sin by giving us the Law. While the Law is dangerous and deadly because it convicts and condemns those who sin, it is also God's means of grace. Through the Law, His wrath blows into our garden and boldly urges us to come out of hiding. We are right to fear His wrath but foolish to distrust His grace. After all, if His chief desire were to execute the just penalty of sin, He would have done that already.

So, you have a choice. Guilt or grace? You may have either. You can remain in hiding, cling to your guilt, and suffer the inevitable judgment for your sin — eternal, agonizing separation from God. Or you can stop hiding, stand before Him, acknowledge your sin, admit you are helpless to please Him on your own, and receive His free gift of grace.

God sent His Son, Jesus Christ, to live the guiltless life we cannot live, to die the atoning death we deserve, to rise again and claim new life on our behalf, and to usher (*prosagōgē*) those who believe in Him into a completely new kind of existence. His gift is free, extended by grace and received through faith. So, the choice is yours. Guilt or grace?

NOTES: The Grace of God (Romans 3:21–5:21)

1. John Newton, "Amazing Grace," 1779.

2. Arthur Bennett, ed., *The Valley of Vision: A Collection of Puritan Prayers & Devotions* (Carlisle, Penn.: The Banner of Truth Trust, repr. 2006), 6–7.

3. Gerhard Kittel and Gerhard Friedrich, eds., *Theological Dictionary of the New Testament: Abridged in One Volume*, trans. Geoffrey W. Bromiley (Grand Rapids: Eerdmans, 1985), 1127.

4. Mark Twain, *Following the Equator and Anti-Imperialist Essays* (New York: Oxford Univ. Press, 1996), 132.

5. *Merriam-Webster's Collegiate Dictionary*, 11th ed., s.v. "faith."

6. Many would correctly argue that this change occurred with the ancient Greek philosophers, Herodotus, Socrates, and Aristotle; however, Western thought not only stopped moving forward, it regressed during the so-called "Dark Ages." Thomas Aquinas picked up where the ancient Greeks left off and, more or less, gave their cosmology a Christian veneer.

7. John Huffman Jr., *Who's in Charge Here?* (Chappaqua, N.Y.: Christian Herald Books, 1981), 63.

8. Martin Luther, *Luther's Works*, vol. 34, Career of the Reformer IV (St. Louis: Concordia, 1960), 336.

9. Ibid., 336–37.

10. Johannes P. Louw and Eugene Albert Nida, *Greek-English Lexicon of the New Testament: Based on Semantic Domains*, electronic ed. of the 2nd ed. (New York: United Bible Societies, 1996 [orig. 1989]), 1:430.

11. Both of these are aorist tense in the Greek. The context helps us establish what tense these verbs should be in English.

12. Thomas Kelly, "Praise the Savior, Ye Who Know Him," 1806.

# THE FAITHFULNESS OF GOD (ROMANS 6:1 – 8:39)

On September 22, 1862, President Abraham Lincoln issued a proclamation, which began:

> On the first day of January, in the year of our Lord one thousand eight hundred and sixty-three, all persons held as slaves within any State or designated part of a State, the people whereof shall then be in rebellion against the United States, shall be then, thenceforward, and forever free.

The Union would have to fight for many months before slaves in the South could claim their precious freedom. Booker T. Washington was nine when emancipation reached his plantation in southwest Virginia, a day he recalled in his autobiography, *Up from Slavery*:

> The most distinct thing that I now recall in connection with the scene was that some man who seemed to be a stranger (a United States officer, I presume) made a little speech and then read a rather long paper — the Emancipation Proclamation, I think. After the reading we were told that we were all free, and could go when and where we pleased. My mother, who was standing by my side, leaned over and kissed her children, while tears of joy ran down her cheeks. She explained to us what it all meant, that this was the day for which she had been so long praying, but fearing that she would never live to see.[1]

In time, after the final surrender of the Confederacy, the assassination of a president, and a difficult political fight, the States ratified the Thirteenth Amendment, which officially abolished slavery in America. On December 18, 1865, the news swept across Capitol Hill, and down the Shenandoah, over the Appalachians, along the back roads of the Carolinas, deep into the plantations of Georgia, Alabama, Mississippi, and Louisiana, and into the cotton fields of Texas and Arkansas. The word was out: Slaves are free ... at least officially. The practicality of freedom was another matter.

> The wild rejoicing on the part of the emancipated coloured people lasted but for a brief period, for I noticed that by the time they returned to their cabins there was a change in their feelings. The great responsibility of being free, of having charge of themselves, of having to think and plan for themselves and their children, seemed to take possession of them. It was very much like suddenly turning a youth of ten or twelve years out into the world to provide for himself. In a few hours the

great questions with which the Anglo-Saxon race had been grappling for centuries had been thrown upon these people to be solved. These were the questions of a home, a living, the rearing of children, education, citizenship, and the establishment and support of churches. Was it any wonder that within a few hours the wild rejoicing ceased and a feeling of deep gloom seemed to pervade the slave quarters? To some it seemed that, now that they were in actual possession of it, freedom was a more serious thing than they had expected to find it. Some of the slaves were seventy or eighty years old; their best days were gone. They had no strength with which to earn a living in a strange place and among strange people, even if they had been sure where to find a new place of abode. To this class the problem seemed especially hard. Besides, deep down in their hearts there was a strange and peculiar attachment to "old Marster" and "old Missus," and to their children, which they found it hard to think of breaking off. With these they had spent in some cases nearly a half-century, and it was no light thing to think of parting. Gradually, one by one, stealthily at first, the older slaves began to wander from the slave quarters back to the "big house" to have a whispered conversation with their former owners as to the future.[2]

After a brief celebration, many former slaves returned to the fields to continue their servitude as "sharecroppers." Though officially free to go anywhere, little changed for them in a practical sense. Legal emancipation merely presented slaves with the opportunity to live as free men and women. Turning their legal status into actual experience would require an internal transformation. Those who found this challenge too daunting chose the uncomfortable familiarity of slavery instead.

How foolish this appears from the perspective of people who have never known slavery. Yet, Christians—I would say the majority of them—choose slavery over freedom every day. Having been set free, for them to live as free men and women comes neither easily nor naturally. It's a process and, like salvation, it must be accomplished supernaturally. Theologians have given a name to the gradual, internal transformation of a newly freed slave of sin into a fully mature and completely free individual. That term is "sanctification." That is the subject of this section of Paul's letter to the Romans.

## Dying to Live (Romans 6:1–14)

---

¹What shall we say then? Are we to continue in sin so that grace may increase? ²May it never be! How shall we who died to sin still live in it? ³Or do you not know that all of us who have been baptized into Christ Jesus have been baptized into His death? ⁴Therefore we have been buried with

# KEY TERMS

ἁγιασμός [*hagiasmos*] (*38*) "sanctification, consecration, holiness"

This was a common word in pagan worship, describing anything that was cleansed, set aside for specific use in the worship of a particular god, and therefore ceremonially pure. The Jews used the term in reference to anything reserved for God's use, including the Hebrew race. Paul gave the term an even greater personal application. Because the Holy Spirit dwells within the believer, the believer is a temple and, therefore, no less consecrated than "the Most Holy Place" (Ex. 26:33–34; Lev. 16:2).

σάρξ [*sarx*] (*4561*) "flesh, the physical aspect of humanity"

It was not uncommon for Paul to adopt a secular Greek term and add to its usual meaning to describe a complex spiritual truth. For the apostle, *sarx* was not merely the material aspect of humanity; it stood for our sinful, rebellious manner of thought and deed that permeates the perverted world system after the Fall (Gen. 3:14–19). *Sarx* is that part of our preconversion nature that opposes God's new kingdom manner of thought and deed.

πνεῦμα [*pneuma*] (*4151*) "spirit, the immaterial aspect of humanity, Holy Spirit"

*Pneuma* literally means "wind" or "breath," but was more commonly used in secular Greek literature to speak of a person's immaterial aspect — that which ceased to exist after death, or continued to live apart from the body. Paul used *pneuma* similarly, but also used the term in reference to God's Holy Spirit. Furthermore, the "Spirit" was not only the third person of the Trinity; the term also represented the mindset of God as opposed to the fallen manner of life in the world. "Spirit" is the opposite of *sarx*.

προορίζω [*proorizō*] (4309) "to determine beforehand, to decide in advance, preordain"

While Paul was not opposed to giving common Greek words a specialized or technical meaning, he more often used their normal, lexical definition. This word simply means "to determine beforehand." While the verb assumes foreknowledge, it does not suggest how knowledge of the future impacts decision-making, if it does at all.

δοξάζω [*doxazō*] (*1392*) "to glorify, to make glorious, to render excellent, to reveal the worth of something"

In the Greek translation of the Old Testament, God's *doxa* is usually a physical manifestation of His holy, righteous nature, which humanity may observe at great risk of death (Ex. 33:18–23). In the New Testament, "the emphasis shifts to participation"[3] whereby the believer shares the glory of Christ (Rom. 8:17; Col. 1:27; 3:4) and eventually receives a resurrected body like His (Phil. 3:21). In the vocabulary of heaven, *doxa* is righteousness made visible.

Him through baptism into death, so that as Christ was raised from the dead through the glory of the Father, so we too might walk in newness of life. [5]For if we have become united with *Him* in the likeness of His death, certainly we shall also be *in the likeness* of His resurrection, [6]knowing this, that our old self was crucified with *Him*, in order that our body of sin might be done away with, so that we would no longer be slaves to sin; [7]for he who has died is freed from sin.

[8]Now if we have died with Christ, we believe that we shall also live with Him, [9]knowing that Christ, having been raised from the dead, is never to die again; death no longer is master over Him. [10]For the death that He died, He died to sin once for all; but the life that He lives, He lives to God. [11]Even so consider yourselves to be dead to sin, but alive to God in Christ Jesus.

[12]Therefore do not let sin reign in your mortal body so that you obey its lusts, [13]and do not go on presenting the members of your body to sin *as* instruments of unrighteousness; but present yourselves to God as those alive from the dead, and your members *as* instruments of righteousness to God. [14]For sin shall not be master over you, for you are not under law but under grace.

## DO YOU REALLY EXPECT AN ANSWER?

A rhetorical question is really a statement in the form of a query, so it doesn't expect an actual response. That makes it a particularly effective tool in the art of debate. In addition to making a strong point, the rhetorical question appears to put the opponent in the position of having no answer and therefore no response. For example, someone might seal an argument by asking, "You don't expect me to betray my principles, do you?"

Paul undoubtedly faced a number of such situations in his travels across the Roman Empire, and he includes some of them in his letter to the Romans as if to anticipate common objections. These questions do not reflect his teaching on the matter; they merely give him an opportunity to respond. He frequently introduces a rhetorical question with the phrase, "What then?" before responding with an explanation of sound doctrine.

Here are several examples (emphasis added):

**Then what** advantage has the Jew? Or what is the benefit of circumcision? (3:1)

**What then**? If some did not believe, their unbelief will not nullify the faithfulness of God, will it? (3:3)

**What then**? Are we better than they? (3:9)

**Where then** is boasting? It is excluded. By what kind of law? Of works? (3:27)

**What then** shall we say that Abraham, our forefather according to the flesh, has found? (4:1)

**What** shall we say **then**? Are we to continue in sin so that grace may increase? (6:1)

**What then**? Shall we sin because we are not under law but under grace? May it never be! (6:15)

**What** shall we say **then**? Is the Law sin? (7:7)

**What** shall we say **then**? There is no injustice with God, is there? (9:14)

"There ain't no such thing as a free lunch."
"Eat, drink, and be merry, for tomorrow we die."
"Keep your friends close and your enemies closer."
"Let the buyer beware."
"You get what you pay for."
"God helps those who help themselves."

What passes for worldly wisdom is usually bad theology. That's because the world stopped working the way God intended soon after Adam's disobedience dragged the rest of creation into rebellion with him. Consequently, the order and beauty that once graced God's creation, while not completely obliterated, has become twisted and grotesque. Now, the world operates according to a different system, one that leaves little or no room for such heavenly qualities as humility, selflessness, faith, or, the most alien of all, grace.

As Paul concluded the last section, he boldly declared that whereas sin reigned over the earth and death through sin, Jesus Christ had initiated a takeover. To use his words: "Grace multiplied … so that just as sin reigned in death, so also grace will reign through righteousness to eternal life through Jesus Christ our Lord" (5:20–21 NET). This summarizes what he will explain in chapters 6–8.

To begin his explanation, the apostle asks two questions that illustrate how alien grace is to a world dominated by death and to minds given over to depravity. These are two questions for which he already has answers:

"Are we to continue in sin so that grace may increase?" (6:1)
"Shall we sin because we are not under law but under grace?" (6:15)

He undoubtedly encountered these challenges to grace in every synagogue between Jerusalem and Rome.

## —6:1—

A rhetorical question is actually a statement merely disguised as a query and, therefore, does not expect an outright answer. But it is effective in debate because it makes a seemingly irrefutable statement and puts the opponent on the spot. Paul takes his opponents' rhetorical question, a challenge to the doctrine of grace, and puts it on display: "If sin brings grace, and lots of sin brings a lot more grace, shouldn't we sin as much as possible in order to keep grace flowing from heaven?" The opponents' response would naturally follow: "We know that can't be true; so the doctrine of grace must be false."

Paul's opponents have made a valid point. A depraved mind will certainly see grace from a twisted perspective. But Paul turns the attack to his advantage. His opponents have demonstrated all too clearly by their distorted point of view that God cannot allow those who receive His grace to remain in their depraved state of mind or they will mangle grace as Paul's detractors did. Therefore, believers must receive a new nature, a new mind.

— 6:2-3 —

Paul responds to the faulty notion with a strong rebuke: "May it never be!" That is, "May such a thing never occur!" He then put two more rhetorical questions before his readers, each containing a monumental Christian truth. The first question, "How shall we who died to sin still live in it?" highlights the fact that believers no longer serve their old master. We had been enslaved to sin because our old nature found it irresistible. But death has freed us from that bondage. How tragic it would be if an emancipated slave continued to suffer the pain of mistreatment and the degradation of servitude when he or she could run free!

Naturally, this begs the question, "How is it we died to sin when we are obviously very much alive?" Paul answers with a second rhetorical question: "Do you not know that all of us who have been baptized into Christ Jesus have been baptized into His death?" And this second question introduces a complex truth called "identification." According to this truth, all those who have placed their faith in Jesus Christ have been "baptized into" Him. The context makes it clear that this is not water baptism. This is a strong word picture that would have been familiar to the Roman believers, especially the Jews.

The word "baptize" is a transliteration of the Greek term *baptizō*, which means "to immerse, submerge." To be baptized into something is to be completely enveloped by it. Furthermore, the primary significance of baptism was identity. New converts to Judaism were baptized into the God's covenant with Abraham, so that they became identified with natural-born Jews and became heirs to all that God promised Abraham's Hebrew descendents.

When we place our trust in Jesus Christ for salvation from sin, we are said to be enveloped by Him in a spiritual sense. In a very real way, our identity becomes united with His, such that His experience becomes ours. He died and we died with Him. He rose from the dead to a new kind of life, and so shall we. By virtue of our identification with Jesus Christ, His death, and His resurrection, we have been emancipated from bondage to sin. Identity with Christ began with belief, but it has ongoing consequences.

This is a difficult concept because it's so abstract. But it's really not that much different from the truth we learned in Romans 3:21–5:21. We were identified with Jesus Christ when He suffered punishment on our behalf and He paid the legal penalty for sin in our place. God then credited His Son's righteousness to our moral accounts and we receive this grace through faith. But grace doesn't stop there.

Warren Weirsbe has created a chart that beautifully illustrates the continuing benefits of the grace we receive through faith in Jesus Christ.[4]

| Romans 3:21–5:21 | Romans 6–8 |
| --- | --- |
| Substitution: He died for me | Identification: I died with Him |
| He died for my sins | He died unto sin |
| He paid sin's penalty | He broke sin's power |
| Justification: righteousness imputed (put to my account) | Sanctification: righteousness imparted (made a part of my life) |
| Saved by His death | Saved by His life |

Identification allows the believer to partake of everything the Son of God enjoys. To help believers make the most of this gift, Paul first explains the intricacies of this vital Christian truth (6:4–10), outlines the significance of identification (6:11–12), and then concludes with an explanation of how to apply it (6:12). Three key terms to watch:

Know
Consider
Present

## —6:4 (Know Truth)—

Emancipation legally releases a person from involuntary bondage, but it doesn't guarantee that he or she will experience freedom. The person must first *know* that he or she has been released.

Paul's explanation of identification uses three conditional terms: "Therefore ... so that ... so [that] ..." The conjunction "therefore" (*oun*) is important because it indicates that the apostle's next statement is a logical continuation of what he has just written. In other words, the next sentence doesn't stand alone; it further explains the truth, "All of us who have been baptized into Christ Jesus have been baptized into death" (6:3). Therefore, "[because we have been baptized into death], we have been buried with Him through [the same] baptism [just mentioned] into death." The baptism of 6:4 is the same as that in 6:3—spiritual, not water.

I want to make this clear because some claim that grace and the promises of salvation are received through a pool of water and not through faith alone. Paul labored to establish the truth that circumcision—an important symbol of Jewish participation in God's covenant with Abraham—does not have the power to save anyone. Circumcision is a "notary seal" intended to verify the authenticity of one's faith. Remember that it was Abraham's faith that was credited to him as righteousness. Similarly, water baptism—an important symbol of Christian participation in God's new covenant through Christ—does not have the power to save anyone. Water baptism is a "notary seal" that verifies the authenticity of one's spiritual baptism into Christ.

The words and phrases of 6:4 are densely packed with meaning, so let me break the verse down this way:

| "Therefore ..." | As a logical consequence ... |
|---|---|
| "we have been buried with Him ..." | our experience is His experience ... |
| "through baptism ..." | through our identification with Him ... |
| "into death ..." | in that He was enveloped by death ... |
| "so that as Christ was raised ..." | so that, in the very same manner in which Christ was resurrected ... |
| "through the glory of the Father ..." | by the power of God the Father ... |
| "so we too might ..." | we would, potentially, ... |
| "walk in newness of life." | experience the new kind of life Christ experienced and then conduct ourselves accordingly. |

## —6:5–7—

As a logical consequence of our identification with Christ in His death (His dying in our place), we will be identified with Him in His resurrection. This is true whether we know it or not. In eternity, we will be like Him. Our bodies will be like His; we will not be subject to pain, suffering, weakness, or temptation. However, in the meantime, while we live in these bodies in a fallen creation, this new kind of life is potentially ours. To experience it here and now, we must claim it (see 1 John 3:2–3).

"Body of sin" is an expression that Paul will explain in greater detail later. For now, we need only recognize that while the body is not inherently evil (as some claim), it is nonetheless the vehicle of our old sinful nature. It is not inherently sinful; however, it is a part of this fallen world and, therefore, subject to temptation and corruption. In a spiritual sense, we have died. Dead bodies don't respond to temptation. Dead bodies don't choose to do wrong. Temptation and sin have no power over corpses. And someday we will experience this truth in a physical sense. In the meantime, before we die physically and are raised to a new kind of life physically, we have the opportunity to experience this truth.

The first step toward experiencing this new, abundant Christ-life is "knowing this" (6:6). Knowing what? That "our old self was crucified with Him, in order that our body of sin might be done away with." In other words, we are under new management. We are subject to God's authority rather than that of sin, or the world, or any other ruler. We are no longer obligated to choose sin.

When I first began my years in the Marine Corps, I was subject to the authority of a drill instructor, perhaps the most intimidating, overpowering authority I have ever encountered. His objective: to break the wills of simple country boys and street-wise city slickers, to turn strong-willed boys into strong-hearted warriors. Drill instructors aren't known for their compassion. They tell you every move to make; when to eat, when to drink, when to sleep, when to wake up, and even when to relieve yourself. And the consequences for disobedience are extreme.

After basic training, I was told where to live and what job to do. And the Marine Corps didn't ask me if it was okay to ship me to the other side of the globe from my wife and to keep me there for sixteen months. The relationship was simple. They told me what to do and that I was obliged to do it. Then, I was honorably discharged, leaving me no longer under their authority.

Many years later, I waited to board a flight in Dallas-Fort Worth Airport and I heard a familiar sound echoing from my distant past. "YOU PEOPLE GET IN LINE. A STAIGHT LINE! DO YOU KNOW WHAT A STRAIGHT LINE IS? YOU STAND HERE. YOU THERE!" I'd know that sound anywhere! A pair of drill instructors prepared a bunch of raw recruits to board a plane for boot camp.

I watched all of this while standing to one side. After a few moments, one looked my way and I said, "How's it going, Gunny? Got all these wet-nosed kids in line?" He looked at me, flashed a grin, and said, "Yes, Sir." I had a great time with him. Why? Because he had no authority over me. He even said "Sir" to me! If he had tried to order me into line, I would have laughed out loud, done a quick about-face, and marched myself into a coffee shop! I don't have to obey Marine Corps drill instructors, or even generals for that matter. They no longer have control over me.

When we died with Christ, our bodies were relieved from submission to sin. We've been honorably discharged.

## — 6:8 – 11 (Consider Truth) —

Once we know that God's gift is available, we must claim it. Paul continues his reasoning with another logical conjunction, "if" (*ei*). In this case, the "if" is conditional because what follows is only true for those who have believed and have therefore "died with Christ." If we have died with Christ, we believe we will also live with Him; that is, have the same kind of life He has. And this new kind of life can never end in death.

Jesus raised His friend Lazarus from the dead … temporarily (John 11). Sometime later, Lazarus succumbed to disease or old age or disaster, and he died again. This is not the kind of resurrection Jesus experienced. He was raised to a new kind of life. His physical body not only awakened from death, it was transformed into a kind of body that was no longer subject to disease, disaster, or aging. It was no longer a body that the world could abuse. This will be true of us when our bodies have died and we are raised to this new kind of life.

That's a marvelous future we can anticipate with confident assurance. However, we don't have to wait. We can begin enjoying the benefits of this truth now. The death Christ died, He died on behalf of all (3:21 – 5:21); and the new kind of life He now lives, He lives "to God" (chs. 6 – 8). The resurrected life has God as both its source and its purpose. And to claim this gift, we must "consider" or "reckon" it to be true and then act on it. Paul, based on his authority as an agent of the good news, commands believers, "Consider yourselves to be dead to sin." Reckon it as true. Claim this truth as a reality. Count on it and live it out.

## — 6:12 – 13 (Present Truth) —

Once we *know* about our emancipation from slavery and have *considered* ourselves to be freed from that old bondage, we must *present* ourselves to our new Master to enjoy the benefits of new life.

Slaves do the bidding of their master. They are the master's instruments, utilized by him to accomplish his desires. Before emancipation, we could not refuse sin's authority; but now we do not have to obey its commands. Rather than allowing our physical bodies to be instruments of sin's desire, "unrighteousness," we must now present our bodies to our new Master, God, to accomplish His desire, "righteousness."

The Greek word translated "instrument" frequently refers to weapons of war. We are no longer to present our bodies as weapons to be used by sin to accomplish evil ends, but to become foot soldiers in the interest of righteousness.

—6:14—

Paul concludes his point with a summary statement: "Sin shall not be master over you." Then he introduces his next point: "You are not under law but under grace." Because we have been freed from the bondage of sin, laws have no application. The purpose of the Law is to point out transgression; therefore, those who have no involvement in sin are not subject to laws.

I am certainly far from perfect; however, I have never been tempted to use illicit drugs. They have nothing to offer me, and if they suddenly ceased to exist, nothing about my life would be any different. So, if the laws concerning the sale and possession of heroin suddenly changed, I would not be affected in the least. Heroin has no place in my life, so laws restricting me from selling or using it are irrelevant. As far as I'm concerned, those statues may as well not exist. They have no meaning for me. In other words, I am not "under" those laws.

Imagine someone whose nature had been so completely transformed that he or she lost all desire for anything sinful. He or she would no longer be subject to laws—not only those concerning heroin, but all laws. That person could live the rest of his or her days as though laws, policemen, courts, and prisons didn't exist. Furthermore, that transformed spirit could live as though God had never defined which actions are sinful and which are not. Rules restricting his or her behavior would be irrelevant. This, according to Paul, is the potential of someone who is subject to the transforming power of grace.

Grace is not of this world. It is supernatural in origin and unfathomable to a depraved mind. So it should be no surprise that a newly emancipated spirit struggles to understand and apply something so foreign to its old nature.

I am told by those who studied under Lewis Sperry Chafer, the founder and first president of Dallas Theological Seminary, that he spent the last of his eighty-one years teaching systematic theology from a wheelchair. His favorite topic was grace. A mentor of mine who studied under Chafer told me that after a particularly moving lecture, the aged professor closed his Bible, rolled over to the door, and turned off the lights. The students never moved. Then he said, "I have spent all my life studying the grace of God and I am just now beginning to understand a little of it. And, gentlemen, it is magnificent."

The men who studied under Dr. Chafer and who later became mentors of mine were all models of grace. Every one. The winsome charm of grace has powerful, lasting influence on others. Tragically, the same can be said of legalism.

## Application

### *The Best Life Now*

Because grace is so foreign to the depraved mind, it is not easy for a newly restored mind to adjust. Nevertheless, the Holy Spirit will be faithful to use every circumstance and all experiences to transform the new believer from within. Eventually, when this physical life gives way to eternal life, we believers will be like Christ (1 John 3:2). Until then, we are works in progress.

While the Holy Spirit is able to do the work of transformation and will be faithful to complete the task (Phil. 1:6), we are invited to participate in that process. We have a genuine stake in determining the quality of life we enjoy here and now. Of course, the quality of life I am referring to has little to do with our physical circumstances. I am referring to authentic joy, intimacy with the Almighty, liberty from the compulsions of sin, and becoming like Christ. God will be faithful to accomplish in us what He wills, but the degree to which we participate either helps or hinders our progress.

Growing in grace begins with three specific changes in how we operate. This pattern will be repeated each time we encounter a new spiritual truth.

*Know the truth* (6:3–10). In this case, the truth of our new spiritual condition is that we are dead to sin. Before we believed in Christ, we were enslaved to evil. We did not possess the power to stop our own wrongdoing. Now, sin has only one weapon: deception. Satan wants you to think that compulsions to sin cannot be broken. But the truth stands. We are free!

*Consider the truth* (6:11). Once we encounter a new truth, we must discard our old manner of thinking and replace it with this new understanding. Often, that's not easy. We have been conditioned by the old pattern of thinking unconsciously to behave a certain way. Furthermore, we have become emotionally attached to our old manner of living—even when it's unpleasant. Habits are tough to break. Therefore, we must repeatedly and continually "consider" divine truth; that is, we must *decide* it is true.

*Present our bodies to truth* (6:12–13). Having decided something is true, we must change our behavior accordingly. Paul expresses this command in its most basic terms. Your mind controls your body, so take command and make your body operate in agreement with what you have accepted as true.

Imagine what it would be like if a billionaire were to inform you that for no other reason than kindness, he or she deposited one hundred million dollars into your checking account. Completely free. No strings attached. After taxes. I don't know how you would respond, but here's what I would do.

*Know the truth.* I would contact the president of my bank and verify that the funds are indeed credited to my account.

*Consider the truth.* I would take out my checkbook (yes, I still carry one!), make an entry in the register to reflect the deposit, and adjust my balance.

*Present my body to the truth.* After a substantial donation to my church and several favorite ministries, I would start writin' checks! I might struggle to accept the truth of my super-wealth, but I would make every effort to apply the necessary adjustments.

If you presently struggle with a particular repetitive or compulsive sin, you likely suffer from the delusion that you will never loosen its grip on you. I won't insult you by saying that transformation will be easy. It isn't. However, the truth is uncomplicated. If you are a believer, if you have accepted God's free gift of eternal life though faith in Jesus Christ, you have within you spiritual riches beyond your imagination. The power to overcome any evil lives within you. He is none other than God in the person of the Holy Spirit. Call on Him to help!

Knowing, considering, and presenting is not the entire solution to our problems, and I don't mean to oversimplify the process of spiritual growth. Deeply entrenched patterns of sin require much more attention than a simple accounting procedure. However, it is a necessary beginning.

So, don't wait. Begin now. It's never too late to start doing what is right.

## Whose Slave Are You? (Romans 6:15–23)

<sup>15</sup>What then? Shall we sin because we are not under law but under grace? May it never be! <sup>16</sup>Do you not know that when you present yourselves to someone *as* slaves for obedience, you are slaves of the one whom you obey, either of sin resulting in death, or of obedience resulting in righteousness? <sup>17</sup>But thanks be to God that though you were slaves of sin, you became obedient from the heart to that form of teaching to which you were committed, <sup>18</sup>and having been freed from sin, you became slaves of righteousness. <sup>19</sup>I am speaking in human terms because of the weakness of your flesh. For just as you presented your members as slaves to impurity

and to lawlessness, resulting in *further* lawlessness, so now present your members as slaves to righteousness, resulting in sanctification.

[20]For when you were slaves of sin, you were free in regard to righteousness. [21]Therefore what benefit were you then deriving from the things of which you are now ashamed? For the outcome of those things is death. [22]But now having been freed from sin and enslaved to God, you derive your benefit, resulting in sanctification, and the outcome, eternal life. [23]For the wages of sin is death, but the free gift of God is eternal life in Christ Jesus our Lord.

---

One of my mentors, Ray Stedman, ministered in the San Francisco area of California, which has always been an interesting place. This was especially true during the sixties and seventies. One year, J. Vernon McGee invited him to preach a series of messages at the Church of the Open Door in Los Angeles, which Ray gladly did. During a break one evening, he strolled down Hope Street, which reminded him a lot of his own mission field up north. He didn't go very far before encountering one of the area's more colorful residents; an eccentric man with long, tangled hair, a scraggly beard, and filthy clothes walked toward him wearing a sandwich board. Written on the front in bold letters — no doubt by the man himself — were the words, "I am a slave for Jesus Christ." The scruffy prophet held Ray's eyes in a steady gaze until he passed by, and as he continued up the sidewalk, Ray turned to read the backside of the sandwich board. It read, "Whose slave are you?"

A good question asked by a strange example! We all serve something; it's just a matter of what.

Some are slaves of their work. These servants of busyness and achievement can't shut down their laptops for more than a couple of hours at a time and their electronic devices are all but surgically implanted in their hands. They take working vacations to appease neglected loved ones and miserly hoard days off they never intend to take. A balanced life always lies just beyond the current project deadline.

Some are slaves to things, possessions, temporal stuff. Driven by the fantasy that contentment can be found in the having of things, they cannot stop acquiring long enough to enjoy what they already own, which prompts the question, "How much is enough?" H. L. Hunt, the billionaire oil tycoon, is credited with the most honest reply I've heard to date: "Money is just a way of keeping score."

Perhaps more than ever, people are enslaved to relationships. They magically mutate into whatever pleasing shape will gain them the approval of another. They cycle between self-acceptance and self-loathing, depending upon the affirmation or criticism they receive. They eagerly sacrifice themselves and, ironically, those they love to avoid the most dreadful condition of all: aloneness.

Perhaps the most pathetic and increasingly common slaves are those who are enslaved to the god of self. Psychologists call them narcissists. The name comes from a figure in Roman mythology named Narcissus, who fell in love with his own reflection in a stream. When he tried to kiss the object of his love, his lips disturbed the water and his image ran away, which left him heartbroken. He dared not drink from the stream for fear of losing his lover forever. Eventually, the slave of self-love died of thirst.

Narcissists serve themselves, even when they appear to be selfless, and they relentlessly demand the time, attention, admiration, devotion, and nurturing of others. But this, like the other forms of slavery, only leads to greater emptiness.

We all serve something; it's just a matter of what.

— **6:15–16** —

Paul concluded his response to the question, "Are we to continue in sin so that grace may increase?" (6:1), with the statement, "Sin shall not be master over you, for you are not under law but under grace" (6:14). In other words, because believers can now choose not to sin, they have the freedom to rise above the law. This prompts a second rhetorical question — again, one Paul likely heard often in response to the gospel: "Shall we sin because we are not under law but under grace?"

Paul again responds emotionally, saying in effect: "May such a thing never occur!" He then demonstrates the absurdity of the question, beginning with a rhetorical question of his own. (Remember, a rhetorical question is really a statement in the form of a query.) "Do you not know that when you present yourselves to someone as slaves for obedience, you are slaves of the one whom you obey, either of sin resulting in death, or of obedience resulting in righteousness?" The apostle reminds his readers that a man is a slave to the one he commits himself to obey. And to be a slave of something is to become an instrument in serving its interests (6:12–13). Because grace has freed us, we now have a choice between two masters. The old master, "sin," is dedicated to the destruction of those who serve it. The new master, "obedience," seeks righteousness, those things that please God and give life to those who serve Him.

The ancient Romans were well known for their slavery, which took two forms. The more familiar kind of slavery involved capturing an enemy, destroying anything that might tempt him to return home, and then transporting him to Rome for sale on the auction block. But an older, more common type of slavery was "voluntary indenture." Impoverished people could offer themselves as slaves to someone in order to have food to eat and a place to live. In other words, people willingly accepted slavery in order to meet their basic needs.

In the American South after the Civil War, many freed slaves had no other choice but to become "sharecroppers," which gave them land and livelihood, but required them to "share" most of their produce with the landowner. Of course, this was merely servitude with a gentler, kinder name. Nevertheless, no one chose a cruel master except as a last resort.

Paul asks, in effect, "Why would you choose a master whose dedicated purpose is to keep you enslaved and ultimately kill you? That's like an emancipated slave choosing to help his old master reinforce his chains and build a gallows! Why would anyone willingly serve such a cruel master?"

We have basic needs we must have met. And we have a choice between two masters. To whom will we go? Whose interests will we serve? One promises life; the other, death.

Serve sin? What an absurd thought!

## —6:17–18—

This prompts Paul to break out into a spontaneous doxology: "Thanks be to God!" The gospel has present, ongoing, and eternal implications. Eternal life begins sometime in our future, after this life has ended. But something happens immediately when a person receives the grace of God through faith. He or she is instantly given a new heart, a new nature that hates sin and desires to obey its new master: righteousness.

## —6:19—

As a pastor, I can appreciate Paul's parenthetical comment. A good illustration has the power to simplify and clarify difficult concepts. Charles Spurgeon likened a great sermon to a cathedral, which would be dark inside were it not for the windows of illustration. Illustrations allow light to fill the space so everyone can see clearly. However, a particularly good illustration can take on a life of its own and become a distraction. Preachers have to be careful not to turn an analogy into an allegory. While the illustration of slavery is powerful, it is flawed in one important respect. The truth Paul labors to teach is really a paradox. Slavery to God is the greatest freedom a human can ever know.

When God created Adam and Eve, they perfectly bore their Creator's image. They lived in perfect harmony with their created purpose, which was to live in limitless communion with Him, to enjoy uninhibited intimacy with one another, and to rule over the rest of creation as His vice-regents. Never was humankind so free as when they lived in harmony with their created purpose, or as Paul chooses to put it, "as slaves to righteousness."

When we "serve righteousness," we not only please God, we do what is best for ourselves. That's how the Lord created the universe to work before it was corrupted through disobedience. But humanity exchanged truth for a lie and looked to sin rather than their Creator to meet their basic needs. That decision only perpetuated sin and intensified the accompanying bondage. This is the downward cycle of sin.

The grace of God changed all of that. Christ's sacrificial death creates the potential for us to recapture some of the innocence and freedom of Eden. Just as service to sin binds us closer to sin, service to righteousness frees us to live in harmony with our created purpose, which is to live in limitless communion with God, enjoy uninhibited intimacy with one another, and rule over the rest of creation as His vice-regents. Paul called this *hagiasmos*, which is commonly translated "sanctification, holiness, consecration, or purity." For Paul, sanctification is both a state of being and a process. While it appears only twice in his letter (6:19, 22), it is nevertheless the central theme of this larger section (Romans 6–8).

### —6:20-22—

Again, Paul clarifies the believer's choice. Sin and righteousness are mutually exclusive. In the words of Jesus, "No one can serve two masters; for either he will hate the one and love the other, or he will be devoted to one and despise the other" (Matt. 6:24). Moreover, human nature abhors a vacuum. God created humanity with certain needs. In the beginning, those physical, emotional, and spiritual needs were filled as humankind enjoyed peace with God. After the Fall, we looked to sin instead.

This leads the apostle to ask another rhetorical question, not as a clever strategy of debate, but to prompt the reader to look within. He asks, in effect, "When you were trying to meet those God-given needs by pursuing sin, what did you gain?"

For centuries, people have turned to mind-altering drugs for a variety of reasons, but the most basic desire is to feel good rather than bad. They usually find that the payoff is immediate and immensely satisfying ... in the short term. Medical experts tell us that these drugs have a double impact in the long term: they increase the user's need for the drug while decreasing his or her body's response. In other words, the drug gradually creates a greater need for more, and it takes larger and larger doses to achieve the same satisfying effect.

The same is true of sin. Sin is usually the result of someone trying to fill a legitimate, God-given need in an illegitimate way. Paul reminds his readers that once we have been freed from bondage to sin, we still have needs that must be filled. And we will look to something to fill them. As I stated before, we all serve something; it's just a matter of what.

The believer, having been freed from bondage to sin—released from his or her addiction to sin, as it were—may now look to the Creator for fulfillment. While the pull of sin is down, the cycle of sanctification draws the believer closer to God. Increasing dependence on the Lord provides meaningful satisfaction and, ironically, greater freedom. And rather than leading to death, slavery to God ultimately leads to eternal life.

Who wouldn't want that?

## —6:23—

Paul masterfully concludes his answer to the charge that grace encourages sin with a succinct couplet. Take note of the contrast:

| The wages | | The free gift |
|-----------|-----|---------------|
| of sin | BUT | of God |
| is death, | | is eternal life |

This verse is commonly used to explain the gospel to those who have yet to believe, but Paul writes it to encourage believers in sanctification. And in this concluding statement, he introduces a new concept, one that he will take great care to explain in the next chapter.

In chapter 6, Paul has stated that those who place their trust in Jesus Christ and receive God's grace through faith are "baptized into" Him. Believers are therefore identified with Him so that His experiences become our experiences, His blessings become our blessings, and His power becomes our power. We have none of the above on our own. We have everything by virtue of our being "in Christ." We are "dead to sin, but alive to God *in Christ*" (6:11). Moreover, we receive eternal life by being "in Christ" (6:23).

This "in Christ" concept becomes the key to understanding everything Paul tells his readers in the following chapters. The believer's life derives from being in Christ, his or her joy must be found in Christ, his or her success depends on resting in Christ, and we have fellowship with others who are in Christ.

As we will see, our being "in Christ" provides the opportunity to escape the downward drag of sin and to enjoy freedom as we never thought possible. However, it's no guarantee that we will experience that kind of joy in this lifetime. Like emancipation, we must "know" (understand its truth), "consider" (claim its truth), and "present" (apply its truth). Unfortunately, our old master refuses to release its grip. The emancipation proclamation has gone out; nevertheless a war rages around us and within us. If you are a believer in the Lord Jesus Christ, you have a daily question to answer, and your response will lead either to life or death. Whose slave are you?

## Application

### *Choose Your Master*

Paul boldly declares that we are no longer compelled to serve sin or accomplish the purposes of unrighteousness (6:15–21). We may freely choose to obey sin and then reap its sorrowful consequences, or we may freely choose to obey Christ and then share in His joy (6:20–23).

As I reflect on Paul's words and review my years in pastoral ministry, I find that much of my time is spent combating one of two problems.

First, *it is possible to be a slave to something and think you are free.* This is the

---

**"IN CHRIST" IN ROMANS**

The phrase, "in Christ," is deeply meaningful for Paul and appears no less than eighty-four times in his letters, thirteen times in his letter to the Romans.

| | |
|---|---|
| Rom 3:24 | … being justified as a gift by His grace through the redemption which is in Christ Jesus; |
| Rom 6:11 | Even so consider yourselves to be dead to sin, but alive to God in Christ Jesus. |
| Rom 6:23 | For the wages of sin is death, but the free gift of God is eternal life in Christ Jesus our Lord. |
| Rom 8:1 | Therefore there is now no condemnation for those who are in Christ Jesus. |
| Rom 8:2 | For the law of the Spirit of life in Christ Jesus has set you free from the law of sin and of death. |
| Rom 8:39 | … nor height, nor depth, nor any other created thing, will be able to separate us from the love of God, which is in Christ Jesus our Lord. |
| Rom 9:1 | I am telling the truth in Christ, I am not lying, my conscience testifies with me in the Holy Spirit, |
| Rom 12:5 | … so we, who are many, are one body in Christ, and individually members one of another. |
| Rom 15:17 | Therefore in Christ Jesus I have found reason for boasting in things pertaining to God. |
| Rom 16:3 | Greet Prisca and Aquila, my fellow workers in Christ Jesus, |
| Rom 16:7 | Greet Andronicus and Junias, my kinsmen and my fellow prisoners, who are outstanding among the apostles, who also were in Christ before me. |
| Rom 16:9 | Greet Urbanus, our fellow worker in Christ, and Stachys my beloved. |
| Rom 16:10 | Greet Apelles, the approved in Christ. Greet those who are of the household of Aristobulus. |

predicament of the lost. They slavishly serve something they think will bring them fulfillment or eliminate their problems. Money, career, sex, relationships, adventure, power, notoriety, education, achievement, even addictions ... the idols of this world are legion. I see people sacrifice to keep their god alive and fear what life will be if — or when — the object of their hope passes away. And I stand amazed at their inability to comprehend the extent of their slavery, all the while trying to convince themselves and others that life is good just the way it is. Moreover, they refuse to heed the good news for fear that submission to Christ will take away their freedom!

Second, *it is possible to be free and think you are enslaved*. This second problem is almost as tragic as the first. Counseling offices around the world are filled with Christians who struggle to accept the fact that they no longer must serve imaginary gods. They remain shackled to compulsions, hiding in shame, unaware that they now worship a God who doesn't demand but empowers. They have peace with God, who does not condemn His children but who longs to see them victorious over sin.

The remedy for both problems is the same: *truth*.

On the one hand, unbelievers need to know that "the wages of sin is death, but the free gift of God is eternal life in Christ Jesus our Lord" (6:23). The "freedom" they experience is an illusion designed to draw their attention away from the fact that sin is robbing them of everything they value and will eventually drag them into eternal torment.

Believers, on the other hand, must learn to embrace their freedom and recognize temptation for what it is. Each opportunity to sin is an invitation to submit our bodies to something. Temptation asks the following question: "To which master will you submit your body for the next few moments: your compulsion, which always leaves you feeling emptier than before, or Christ, who always affirms your value as a child of God?"

Frankly, I have found that simply *not* doing something wrong when tempted is not enough. I need something else to which I can submit my body. Here is a four-step process that I find helpful when tempted to do wrong:

1. *Flee temptation*; that is, change your circumstances. Physically move from where you are and quickly go somewhere different, even if it's just for a few minutes.
2. *Do something that brings honor to God as an alternative*. Prayer is good, but I suggest adding something more tangible. Systematically answer the urge to sin with a godly activity.
3. Thank God for providing the freedom to choose Him over wrongdoing and ask Him for encouragement. Spiritual warfare is exhausting!

4. Try to discern what triggered the temptation and take practical steps to steer clear of the same situation.

## Portrait of a Struggling Christian (Romans 7:1-25)

---

¹Or do you not know, brethren (for I am speaking to those who know the law), that the law has jurisdiction over a person as long as he lives? ²For the married woman is bound by law to her husband while he is living; but if her husband dies, she is released from the law concerning the husband. ³So then, if while her husband is living she is joined to another man, she shall be called an adulteress; but if her husband dies, she is free from the law, so that she is not an adulteress though she is joined to another man.

⁴Therefore, my brethren, you also were made to die to the Law through the body of Christ, so that you might be joined to another, to Him who was raised from the dead, in order that we might bear fruit for God. ⁵For while we were in the flesh, the sinful passions, which were *aroused* by the Law, were at work in the members of our body to bear fruit for death. ⁶But now we have been released from the Law, having died to that by which we were bound, so that we serve in newness of the Spirit and not in oldness of the letter.

⁷What shall we say then? Is the Law sin? May it never be! On the contrary, I would not have come to know sin except through the Law; for I would not have known about coveting if the Law had not said, "You shall not covet." ⁸But sin, taking opportunity through the commandment, produced in me coveting of every kind; for apart from the Law sin is dead. ⁹I was once alive apart from the Law; but when the commandment came, sin became alive and I died; ¹⁰and this commandment, which was to result in life, proved to result in death for me; ¹¹for sin, taking an opportunity through the commandment, deceived me and through it killed me. ¹²So then, the Law is holy, and the commandment is holy and righteous and good.

¹³Therefore did that which is good become *a cause of* death for me? May it never be! Rather it was sin, in order that it might be shown to be sin by effecting my death through that which is good, so that through the commandment sin would become utterly sinful.

¹⁴For we know that the Law is spiritual, but I am of flesh, sold into bondage to sin. ¹⁵For what I am doing, I do not understand; for I am not practicing what I *would* like to *do*, but I am doing the very thing I hate. ¹⁶But if I do the very thing I do not want *to do*, I agree with the Law, *confessing* that the Law is good. ¹⁷So now, no longer am I the one doing it, but sin which dwells in me. ¹⁸For I know that nothing good dwells in me, that is, in my flesh; for the willing is present in me, but the doing of the good is not. ¹⁹For the good

that I want, I do not do, but I practice the very evil that I do not want. [20]But if I am doing the very thing I do not want, I am no longer the one doing it, but sin which dwells in me.

[21]I find then the principle that evil is present in me, the one who wants to do good. [22]For I joyfully concur with the law of God in the inner man, [23]but I see a different law in the members of my body, waging war against the law of my mind and making me a prisoner of the law of sin which is in my members. [24]Wretched man that I am! Who will set me free from the body of this death? [25]Thanks be to God through Jesus Christ our Lord! So then, on the one hand I myself with my mind am serving the law of God, but on the other, with my flesh the law of sin.

---

As portrait painters go, few can match the realism of Dimitri Vail. His choice of colors and shading, his attention to minute details, even the texture of his brush strokes gave his paintings such a literal quality you weren't quite sure it wasn't a photograph. I visited his gallery more than once, many years ago. It was in an old part of Dallas. Walking down the long, narrow corridor where the portraits hung was like stepping back in time for a visit with Hollywood's luminaries. Each frame was labeled with a small brass engraving of the subject's name, as if anyone needed them.

Bill Cosby grinned at me with that characteristic tight-lipped smile of his. I saw comedians, Rowan and Martin hanging right next to Martin and Lewis. There was Benny Goodman with his clarinet, which he played with such ease, alongside Jack Benny with his violin, which made the most torturous sounds imaginable. John Wayne, James Dean, Red Buttons, Ed Sullivan, Frank Sinatra, and Sophie Tucker. They were all there along with a few presidents, astronauts, and world-class athletes. At the end of the long row of the world's brightest, boldest, and most beautiful people hung a dimly lit portrait of a somber, almost sad figure. The frame was smaller and more rugged than the others, and it didn't bear the name of the subject. So I asked the attendant to come over and tell me about the painting.

"Who is this?" I asked.

She smiled knowingly and said, "I'm asked that question a lot. This is a self-portrait of the artist. He painted it rather recently, during a period of intense personal struggle. He chose to put it here. It isn't for sale."

I admit to being surprised. I supposed I expected that someone who ran with people of this caliber—celebrities, popular heroes, and politicians—would have been a perpetual-motion machine of joy and excitement. Instead, he was a man like many I've known, struggling with life.

As far as we know, the apostle Paul never held an artist's brush. Nevertheless, his portrait of humanity, done in pen and ink, hangs in the gallery of his letter to the

Romans. The first frame bears the name "Lost Person," and it's bluntly accurate. His is a picture of depravity, emptiness, and pride. The second frame holds the image of a grateful figure named "Justified Sinner." Newly freed from the death grip of sin, this person can barely contain his joy. The next frame is encouraging because it captures the exuberance of one "Victorious Believer." He has discovered that, in reality, eternal life doesn't begin after death; it begins the moment one believes in Christ.

At the end of the corridor, a dark picture hangs. The subject is a sad, exhausted, defeated man. Who is this, you ask? It's a self-portrait of the artist. It's Paul. If you dust off the brass nameplate, you'll see the name, written in his own hand: "Wretched Man."

Romans 7 is Paul's self-portrait, in which he uses the first person singular pronoun, "I," almost thirty times. Near the end of his verbal self-portrait, he exclaims, "Wretched man that I am!" The term "wretched" is translated from a Greek word that means "suffering, afflicted, miserable."

In Texas, we have a slang term for squeezing water out of wet clothing. You "wrench" the water out of something when you roll the article up, hold it at either end, and twist in opposite directions. That's the idea behind "wretched." Paul described himself as feeling like something had "wrenched" the life out of him. But why? How could this be? Obviously the portraits form a progression, beginning with "Lost" and rising to "Victorious." Why, after escaping the tyranny of sin, does the next portrait depict a suffering, afflicted, miserable man?

To find the answer, we must first understand the relationship between the believer and rules governing conduct, or "law."

## — 7:1–4 —

Paul had earlier made the provocative statement that the believer is "not under law but under grace" (6:14). He now returns to explain how this could be true, first by way of a familiar illustration using civil law.

Paul proposes a hypothetical scenario for his readers to consider. In that scenario, a marriage between a man and a woman is apparently strained by her desire to be with another. But the law of marriage forbids her to leave her first husband to be married to someone else; this law would label her guilty of adultery. However, should her mate die, she will be released from her obligation to the law and can freely marry someone else. "Therefore" — that is, by the same reasoning — the believer's obligation to the Law of Moses has been terminated by death.

Paul's illustration involves three elements: A husband, a wife, and the law that regulates their behavior. Many make the mistake of casting the Law in the role of the husband, suggesting that the Law of Moses is like an autocratic, abusing mate who finally dies to the great relief of the surviving partner! But take note of who dies in Paul's application. He didn't state that the Law dies. It's still very much alive and active, fulfilling its purpose in God's redemptive plan. The *believer* dies, and with him, his marital obligations to sin (6:2, 18, 22). This becomes clear as Paul concludes his point in 7:6: "But now we have been released from the Law, having died to that by which we were bound." We were formerly bound to sin.

A relationship between the believer and the Law exists after his or her death "in Christ," but it's a very different relationship.

— 7:5–6 —

God gave the Law to accomplish two objectives. First, the Law exposes our *sins*. God gave His Law to confront us with our sin so that we might repent and come to Him in faith. (We learned this truth during our study of 5:12–13.) Second, the Law exposes our *sinfulness*. The Law rouses our rebellious nature into action, which demonstrates our inability to help ourselves and proves our need for God to change our hearts.

Years ago, one of the first high-rise hotels to open in Galveston, Texas, sat directly above the Gulf; it was so close to the water, in fact, that the owners worried that people would want to drop their fishing lines into the water from the guest room balconies. The high winds, the large lead sinkers, and the first story glass windows were certain to be a bad combination. Thus, the management placed a sign in each room facing the ocean:

ABSOLUTELY NO FISHING FROM THE BALCONY

What happened? You guessed it. Guests in the first story restaurant dined to the frequent smack of lead weights against the plate glass windows. Sometimes the glass literally cracked. Finally, the people managing the hotel realized their error and made a wise decision: they removed all the signs in the guest rooms.

Problem solved! No one ever fished from their balconies again.

Paul gives this rebellious nature a name. He calls it "the flesh," and his use of the term is unlike any other writer in the Bible. Throughout the New Testament, "flesh" is often used figuratively of humanity's material aspect, as opposed to our souls or spirits. Jesus once said that the flesh is weak (Matt. 26:41), but no one before Paul called it sinful or evil.[5]

Paul uses the term "flesh" symbolically to represent humanity it its fallen state. The flesh is programmed to think like the world system, which is a perverted version of God's original created order, and it continues to oppose His will. As the fallen world is opposed to grace, so the flesh is opposed to the Holy Spirit. And to be "in the flesh" is to be thinking and acting in concert with the fallen, depraved world as Paul described it in 1:18–32.

"But now," Paul declares, we have been released from our legal obligation to carry out the objectives of sin. Furthermore, our relationship with the Law has changed because we have a new nature that isn't opposed to the Law. Paul called this new nature "Spirit," with a capital "S," because it is God's Spirit whom we have received. Instead of living in harmony with the Law by studying it and following every letter (which we were powerless to do anyway), we allow the Spirit of God to live through us, who cannot disobey.

One poet has expressed the change this way:

A rigid master was the Law,
Demanding brick, denying straw;
But when with gospel-tongue it sings,
It bids me fly, and gives me wings.[6]

## THE WORLD ACCORDING TO PLATO

Around 400 BC, a student of Socrates named Plato described the universe in terms that have influenced Western philosophy, science, and religion for millennia. In fact, much of Christian theology has been unwittingly influenced by the teaching of Plato, usually with dreadful consequences.

Plato divided the universe into two realms. The realm of "idea" (or "forms") consisted of all things theoretical. This intangible realm is perfect, orderly, morally pure, and eternal. It is the dwelling of *theos* ("god"), which is not a person as much as impersonal, the origin of reason and order. The realm of "materials" (or "substance"), by contrast, is the physical, material world we inhabit. It is a flawed, inferior representation of the far superior realm of idea.

In the realm of idea, for example, the concept "chair" is expressed in the material realm in various ways. There are dining room chairs, desk chairs, rocking chairs, and even reclining chairs. They are different, yet they all embody an intangible quality, or idea, that defines each of these items as a chair. However, these material representations are flawed. Unlike the incorruptible, eternal chair idea, they can be destroyed or altered or contaminated. Therefore, they are inferior; each material chair is a mere shadow of the real chair, which resides in the realm of idea.

This model of the universe became the source of endless religious and philosophical systems. Most of them saw people as fragments of pure idea, "spirits," trapped in corrupt material bodies of flesh. While the spirit of a person is pure and incorruptibly good, the body is a defiled prison, which is inherently bad.

Paul was familiar with Greek philosophy, but he rejected Plato's universe in favor of the Old Testament. Therefore, we must be careful to interpret "Spirit" and "flesh" as Paul intended, not as our culture, influenced by Greek philosophy, subtly suggests.

## —7:7–13—

Paul probably feels his Jewish readers might misunderstand him at this point. His passionate tone might lead some to think he considers the Law evil or that grace opposes the Law. Others may have misinterpreted his illustrations to mean that sin and the Law are synonymous. So, he addresses the question directly: "Is the Law sinful?"

Again, the apostle responds emotionally: "May it never be!" Then, as always, he offers a thorough clarification. The Law is good for its intended purpose, which is to call us into account for sin and to expose the sinfulness of our "flesh." A modern-day illustration of Paul's clarification may help.

Not long ago, most people didn't find out about their cancer until it was too late. The first symptoms usually led to bad news from the doctor. Then someone invented the MRI, a marvelous machine that quickly and accurately probes the patient's flesh and yields a detailed image of his or her body. A trained eye can then examine the image and locate cancerous tumors long before the patient presents any symptoms. If the MRI leads to a diagnosis of cancer, the patient would be foolish to blame the machine for his illness. If anything, he should be thankful that his problem was discovered early enough to be treated.

In essence, Paul said, "I did not know that I was dying from the disease of sin until the Law revealed my terminal condition. Furthermore, the Law showed me that I loved my disease and that I would do anything to keep it. I was like a living dead man! By pointing out my problem, the Law demonstrated that I was living under a death sentence."

The Law is God's diagnostic tool. Its purpose is to expose the disease of sin and to confront us with the prognosis: the disease is deadly if not treated, but it's completely curable. Does the Law cause death? No more than the MRI causes cancer.

## —7:14–16—

Paul introduced the concept of "the flesh" earlier, declaring it to be the opposite of Spirit. But he needs to explain how it continues to impact a believer, especially as the interactions become more complex. Before someone believes, the flesh serves sin and feels the condemnation of Law. Even if he or she wanted to obey the law consistently, any endeavor would soon end in failure. Once someone has received God's grace though faith, the Holy Spirit takes up residence in that believer. And so begins the internal struggle. The flesh continues to serve sin, while the Spirit serves righteousness. "For what I am doing, I do not understand; for I am not practicing what I would like to do, but I am doing the very thing I hate. But if I do the very thing I do not want to do, I agree with the Law, confessing that the Law is good" (7:15–16).

## —7:17–23—

Paul describes the fleshly pull toward sin as the "dwelling-within-me sin." While he received a new nature when he believed in Jesus Christ, his body seems to have a mind of its own. It's as though he were conjoined to a person who loves the very things he hates most. And the same is true for every believer. Every Christian receives a new nature, one that wants nothing more than to behave as Jesus Christ behaves. Meanwhile the flesh, the old human nature, wants life to continue as it was. Here's part of the battle's description:

> So now, no longer am I the one doing it [what I don't want to do], but sin which dwells in me ... nothing good dwells in me ... for the willing is present in me, but the doing of the good is not. For the good that I want, I do not do, but I practice the very evil that I do not want ... I joyfully concur with the law of God in the inner man, but I see a different law in the members of my body, waging war against the law of my mind and making me a prisoner of the law of sin which is in my members. (7:17–23)

Let me draw again upon the heroin analogy. Most experts agree that cold-turkey withdrawal from heroin addiction is one of the most excruciating ordeals a person can endure. Bone and muscle pain, insomnia, diarrhea, vomiting, and shock-like symptoms usually peak two or three days after the last dose, and it usually takes more than a week to subside. The physical anguish would be enough without the psychological trauma the addict suffers. Yet, even after enduring the torment of withdrawal and moving beyond physical dependence on the drug, many return to using it. The problems that encouraged the addict to escape into heroin are still present, and the craving for relief becomes too much to bear alone.

Anyone who has experienced physical dependence on anything will affirm that the craving is never far away. Even chronic smokers who have kicked the habit tell me that, years later, they sometimes long to enjoy a cigarette after a good meal. That's why drug treatment experts are unanimous in their opinion. Treating the body to overcome physical dependence is only a beginning. The key to lifelong sobriety lies in treating the mind, which is itself a lifelong endeavor. The addict is never really "cured." The addiction will always be a part of their lives. However, addicts can remain "in recovery" forever.

All of us are chronically addicted to sin. Long after we are saved, our bodies crave that which gave us short-term pleasure and caused long-term anguish. And the pull to indulge the craving for sin will always be a part of our lives … at least until we are freed from "the body of this death" (v. 24). As for the present? "Wretched man that I am!"

— 7:24–25 —

Paul's description of his personal struggle with the old nature paints a bleak picture of the future for the average Christian, doesn't it? I readily admit that I am no Paul, so if he felt defeated, what hope is there for me?

Paul used the word "wretched" to describe himself. We don't use that word much in modern language, but I can think of no one word to replace it. So let me draw a word picture. Imagine a boxer after a fifteen-round pummeling. With months of training, hype, and dreams of championship glory down the drain, he stands exhausted, demoralized, barely able to see through the swelling around his eyes, and barely able to breathe with a couple of ribs fractured. And to make matters worse, he must take his place in the middle of the ring to hear his defeat announced to the crowd.

The fight Paul has described has left him wretched. Unable to defeat his flesh by means of his flesh—that is, by his own ability—he cries out for help. What, other than death, can free him from a body that craves sin more powerfully than his mind craves righteousness? Who will rescue him from his misery?

The answer comes quickly: "God—through Jesus Christ our Lord."

Just before I left Dimitri Vail's gallery in Dallas, the attendant said, "Our hope is that Mr. Vail will paint another portrait of himself on a better day." I don't know if he ever did. Fortunately, Paul didn't stop painting with chapter 7. His best work was yet to come. And because his hope is our hope, we can anticipate the same glorious future with confident assurance. Just wait and see.

## Application

### *Chasing Rainbows, Self-Improvement, and Other Futile Pursuits*

Once a believer has died to sin, "in Christ" his or her relationship with the Law is forever changed. The new covenant (Jer. 31:31–33) gives us a new rule of life: the Holy Spirit (7:1–6). God gave the Law to humanity to confront our unrighteousness and to demonstrate our need for salvation. Once a person abandons his or her futile attempt to keep the Law and receives God's grace through faith in Jesus Christ, the Law has served its purpose (7:7–13). The believer's relationship with the Law is then severed.

So, what is our goal in life now that we are saved? Is it not to please God by keeping the Law? Are we not to become like Christ, who is morally perfect? Shouldn't we repay God's kindness by pursuing good deeds and eradicating sin from our lives? Now that we are saved from condemnation by the grace of God, are we to sanctify ourselves through fasting, praying, studying Scripture, tithing, and the other spiritual disciplines?

If Paul's self-portrait teaches us anything, it's that self-improvement carried out in the energy of the flesh is a vain pursuit (7:14–25). You can push yourself to fatigue trying hard to be like Christ, but you will have an easier time catching rainbows. Some teachers and preachers acknowledge the impossibility of achieving the perfection of God, but nonetheless find value in aiming high. Others lower the standard of perfection to bring it within easier reach and then claim victory over sin. Most people simply work themselves into a wretched exhaustion and then collapse — sometimes with destructive force.

But God never demands perfection. (Read that again — aloud!) Untainted morality vanished with Eden. No, we are not saved by grace and then sanctified by our own labors. The work of grace is not half done. The point of Paul's miserable self-portrait in 7:13–25 is to demonstrate that humanity can no more purify itself of sin after salvation than before. Only God can purify a soul.

So, what is our duty now as believers saved by grace? Our primary purpose is to know Jesus Christ personally with ever-deepening intimacy (Phil. 3:8–11). If we read Scripture, pray, meditate, journal, or fast, let us do it for the sole purpose of knowing His mind. If we worship, serve, partake of communion, or spend time in the company of believers, let us learn about Him through His transforming work in others. If we feed the poor, defend the weak, comfort the lonely, or proclaim the gospel to a broken and needy world, let our walking in His sandals give us firsthand knowledge of His character. Let every trial or triumph bring us closer to knowing Christ's nature and to understanding His purposes.

The spiritual disciplines are not a means to holiness; they are a means of knowing Christ. As we engage in personal piety, have fellowship with other believers, and engage the world at large in the name of Christ — as we come to know Him more intimately — the Holy Spirit will do what only He can do: make us more like our Savior. As the moon reflects the light of the sun, yet has no light of its own, so we will shine with God's radiance as we live in proximity to His Son.

Now, *that* is a worthy pursuit.

## Let's Talk About Our Walk (Romans 8:1–17)

[1]Therefore there is now no condemnation for those who are in Christ Jesus. [2]For the law of the Spirit of life in Christ Jesus has set you free from the law of sin and of death. [3]For what the Law could not do, weak as it was through the flesh, God *did*: sending His own Son in the likeness of sinful flesh and *as an offering* for sin, He condemned sin in the flesh, [4]so that the requirement of the Law might be fulfilled in us, who do not walk according to the flesh but according to the Spirit. [5]For those who are according to the flesh set their minds on the things of the flesh, but those who are according to the Spirit, the things of the Spirit. [6]For the mind set on the flesh is death, but the mind set on the Spirit is life and peace, [7]because the mind set on the flesh is hostile toward God; for it does not subject itself to the law of God, for it is not even able *to do so*, [8]and those who are in the flesh cannot please God.

[9]However, you are not in the flesh but in the Spirit, if indeed the Spirit of God dwells in you. But if anyone does not have the Spirit of Christ, he does not belong to Him. [10]If Christ is in you, though the body is dead because of sin, yet the spirit is alive because of righteousness. [11]But if the Spirit of Him who raised Jesus from the dead dwells in you, He who raised Christ Jesus from the dead will also give life to your mortal bodies through His Spirit who dwells in you.

[12]So then, brethren, we are under obligation, not to the flesh, to live according to the flesh — [13]for if you are living according to the flesh, you must die; but if by the Spirit you are putting to death the deeds of the body, you will live. [14]For all who are being led by the Spirit of God, these are sons of God. [15]For you have not received a spirit of slavery leading to fear again, but you have received a spirit of adoption as sons by which we cry out, "Abba! Father!" [16]The Spirit Himself testifies with our spirit that we are children of God, [17]and if children, heirs also, heirs of God and fellow heirs with Christ, if indeed we suffer with *Him* so that we may also be glorified with *Him*.

The drive from West Texas to Colorado is one of extremes, especially in the heat of summer. I've done it without air conditioning and I can only imagine what it would have been like on horseback. The journey starts in barren, dusty flatland that seems to go on forever. Endless hot miles pass beneath you as you travel up the Panhandle and, after monotonous hours, you begin to wonder if you'll ever cross the State line. Eventually, you do pass through the cleverly named town of Texline, Texas, into New Mexico to join the old Santa Fe Trail, now Interstate 25. Much of that terrain remains flat, dusty, and *hot*. Did I mention how oppressively hot it can be in the desert?

Eventually, though, you cross Raton Pass, which rises more than seven thousand feet above sea level. The air conditioner goes off, the windows come down, green replaces brown, and you get your first glimpse of snow-capped mountains in the distance. You know before long you'll be breathing cooler air during the day and listening to rainfall through the night. Sometimes, I'm tempted to think God must live in the mountains of Colorado. When you hear thunder rolling over the peaks and through the canyons, it's as if He is clearing His throat.

Paul's letter has taken us through some difficult terrain. It started in the dusty flats of spiritual wasteland and has taken us many miles through endless arid prairies. And the desert of Romans 7 was particularly disheartening because it looked so much like the place we were grateful to leave.[7] Fortunately, Paul's letter is a lot like life, particularly for the Christian. Just as hopefulness begins to fade, we enter his Raton Pass.

What the apostle described in his bleak self-portrait is the futility of trying to live the Christian life without the Spirit of God. It's no less futile than trying to earn righteousness apart from faith. We were helpless to overcome the deadly disease of sin without His unmerited favor, and we are equally powerless to please God without His Spirit providing grace. As Paul puts it, "Nothing good dwells in me, that is, in my flesh; for the willing is present in me, but the doing of the good is not" (7:18).

In my own Christian journey, I have discovered that "wretchedness" seems to be a necessary waypoint. Like Paul, I came to a place of utter hopelessness. I felt trapped by my inability to live in a manner that God would find pleasing, a mode of life I genuinely desired. I labored under the weight of condemnation, which is perhaps the most demoralizing feeling a Christian can endure. Nothing will drag you more quickly to a halt and pull you toward sin than shame.

To make matters worse, I was guided by well-meaning people with bad theology. Many churches today preach a gospel that goes strangely silent after one believes in Jesus Christ and only promises to speak again after death. According to this version of the good news, Christians are left to wrestle the flesh on their own until Judgment Day, at which time a tape of their miserable pummeling will be played for all to see just as the pearly gates open to receive them. Strange teaching.

Saved by grace, but sanctified by works? That's not good news.

After reaching my own wretched state, I surrendered to the fact that I am not able to live the Christian life. Only then—having come to the end of myself and not a day sooner—only *then* was I ready to accept the truth of Paul's stunning declaration at the beginning of Romans 8. Like a flash in the darkness, like Raton Pass on the journey to God's dwelling, the truth comes into view: "Therefore there is now no condemnation for those who are in Christ Jesus" (8:1). This is the cardinal truth of every believer's new life "in Christ." This is the truth on which we stand, by which we live, and through which we ultimately achieve victory.

We have reached a significant turning point. From this place forward, the journey will be frequently challenging and sometimes confusing, but never exasperating. From this vantage point, the good news only gets better.

## —8:1–4—

We must not rush by the first word. The connecting adverb, "therefore," is too important to ignore. It tells us that the statement in verse 1, "There is now no more condemnation for those who are in Christ Jesus," is a continuation of a prior thought.

In the dark desperation of Paul's lonely and futile struggle against the flesh, he cried out, "Who will set me free from the body of this death?" Note the future tense, "*will* set me free." The issue of eternal destiny had already been decided (3:28; 5:1–2; 6:23). The question on Paul's mind was his present struggle. And the answer came: "God through Jesus Christ our Lord [will set me free from the body of this death]." "Therefore, there is *now* no more condemnation …"

Let me point out three crucial truths derived from 8:1–4:

First, we are eternally secure, *now* as well as when we face judgment (8:1). God has officially declared our justification and He never rescinds His Word.

Second, we are internally free from the control of sin, *now* as well as when we get to heaven (8:2). The Spirit of life has set us free (past tense with ongoing results.)

Third, we are positionally righteous, *now* as well as when we stand before our heavenly Judge (8:3–4). What the Law could not accomplish, God has accomplished on our behalf through His Son.

I appreciate Paul's putting this reassurance up front. It not only consoles the wretched, it frees us to hear and absorb what he has to teach us next. More than once, I've gotten a call from someone about one of our children and I deeply appreciated their saying immediately, "Chuck, let me tell you first that your son/daughter is okay." With my worst fears immediately put to rest, I can hear what needs to be said more clearly.

## —8:5–8—

When Paul painted his dark self-portrait in chapter 7, we learned about the two natures struggling for control: "the flesh," our old sin nature, and "the Spirit," the gift of God's presence within us. Having been put at ease by the truths in 8:1–4, this struggle looks much different. Even though the old nature never gives up, never backs off, and never concedes defeat, we can live with confident assurance that the Holy Spirit is stronger. Now, the question is, "To whom will we yield control?" Paul's explanation implies a choice on the part of the believer. For simplicity, here is a more literal rendering of the Greek:

"Those existing according to the flesh set their minds on things of the flesh, but,
those [existing][8] according to Spirit [set their minds on] things of the Spirit."

The next couplet predicts the implications of each choice. Fleshly thinking is death; Spirit thinking is life and peace.

So what is fleshly thinking? What does it mean to "exist according to the flesh?" As always, we allow Scripture to interpret Scripture. Paul's self-portrait describes in painful detail what existing according to the flesh looks like. Existing in the flesh can involve a headlong pursuit of sin. After all, the flesh is hostile to God. Before we received His grace and before His Spirit took up residence within us, the flesh craved only evil. Consequently, Christians have been known to abandon themselves to wrongdoing for a variety of reasons. Some spectators would suggest they were not genuine believers at the time, but we can only speculate. I have been close to one or two people I am reasonably certain were genuine believers but, for a season, behaved like pagans.

In this passage, however, Paul appears to describe something far more common in Christian experience. A believer exists according to the flesh when he or she tries to become righteous by simply trying harder. Remember our study of 3:23 and the illustration of the high jump contest? Those who train hard, expecting to leap into heaven under their own power, will "fall short." That's the old-nature way of thinking. The world system says, "God helps those who help themselves." Grace declares, "A [person] is justified by faith apart from works of the Law" (3:28).

Fleshly thinking can have noble ideals and admirable desires; however, it is also proud to the bone. Fleshly thinking presumes to achieve godly objectives without God. It rejects the grace of God in favor of its own will, its own way, its own ability to do good on its own terms. Fleshly thinking buys into the "self-made man or woman" philosophy and aligns itself remarkably well with the entrepreneurial spirit. While rugged individualism and a "can do" attitude may be good for business, it's death to the spiritual life. It will leave you downright wretched.

However well-intentioned the flesh may appear, we must never forget that it was hostile to God before we received salvation; therefore, we are foolish to think the flesh will cooperate now. The flesh cannot change; it can only be left behind.

## —8:9–11—

Paul reminds his readers that they are no longer deluded by fleshly thinking, but have gained the capacity to think and choose as a result of their freedom "in Christ." The Spirit of God has given them this freedom. Interestingly, Paul qualifies his assurance, limiting it to those who have received God's grace through faith. Therefore, everything the apostle teaches concerning the believer does not apply to everyone in general. In fact, much of his instruction will appear as nonsense to those who are not "in the Spirit."

Donald Gray Barnhouse has provided a wonderful illustration of the need for the Spirit to give us access to spiritual truths:

> Two men, each accompanied by a dog, meet along a road in the country. The men start to talk and the dogs touch noses and begin to communicate, dog-fashion, with each other. Perhaps they have some way of telling each other that there is a rabbit trail over in the bushes and they romp off together. They come back to their masters and their dog ears hear the sounds of the conversation that is taking place between the two men, but they have not the slightest knowledge of the meaning, whether the men are talking about atomic physics or the price of corn by the bushel. Now what dog knoweth the things of a dog except by the nature of the dog that is within him? Even so the things of a man knoweth no dog, but only the spirit of a man can understand them ... For just as a dog may understand a dog but cannot understand a man, so a man may understand a man but can never understand God, unaided by the Spirit.[9]

## —8:12–13—

Because the Spirit lives within us and because we have access to the mind of God, we have an obligation. Sounds like work, doesn't it? Some respected, popular theologians teach that the sacrifice of Jesus Christ on our behalf puts us in His debt. They proclaim that while His gift is priceless and we can never repay the cost, we owe Him a debt of gratitude, nonetheless. And this debt demands our complete devotion to do good works until we die ... and perhaps longer.

The Greek word for such teaching is *hogwash*!

We do indeed have an obligation, but it is not to do good things for God. The obligation is to allow the Spirit to do good deeds on our behalf, through us, so that we will become more like Jesus and share the blessings that are due Him. (How great is that?) Paul taught this in Ephesus, Philippi, Colossae, Thessalonica, and perhaps a hundred other places between Jerusalem and Rome. To the Ephesians, he wrote:

> For by grace you have been saved through faith; and that not of yourselves, *it is* the gift of God; not as a result of works, so that no one may boast. For we are His workmanship, created in Christ Jesus for good works, which God prepared beforehand so that we would walk in them. (Eph. 2:8–10)

To the Philippians, he wrote:

> For I am confident of this very thing, that He who began a good work in you will perfect it until the day of Christ Jesus. (Phil. 1:6)

The Lord has good works prepared for us beforehand. He has the desire and the ability to prepare us for those good works. Best of all, He has promised to bring it all together to accomplish what He has determined. Our only responsibility is to let Him. If we do, we live. If we don't, if we give ourselves over to the flesh, then a deathlike, miserable existence is our inevitable end.

## —8:14–17—

Paul has focused on the negative (telling what *not* to do) long enough. He quickly turns to the positive. In each of the next four verses, we find a practical benefit of living in the Spirit.

*The first benefit: practical everyday leading from God (8:14).* This is frequently used as a proof text to support the notion that believers receive either verbal or nonverbal messages from the Holy Spirit telling them what decisions to make or what to do next. This is *not* Paul's teaching here. This actually shortchanges the promises of the new covenant. As we will learn by the end of this chapter, the Lord will do something far more profound, far more useful than merely whispering commands in our spirit's ear. In fact, Paul's next statement assures us that the Holy Spirit is a gift, not a dictator.

Note how Paul phrases the sentence: "For all who are being led by the Spirit of God, these are sons of God." Many turn it around to support their predetermined conclusion: "The sons of God are led by the Spirit." But this would not be a true statement. While the Lord is certainly faithful to lead genuine believers, most are either too distracted or too stubborn to follow, so they aren't really going anywhere. Paul's teaching in other portions of Scripture makes it clear that the Spirit does lead, but the believer may elect to go his or her own way, thus "grieving" Him (Eph. 4:30).

This verse is both a promise and a practical means of assurance. Those who are actively following the Spirit will bear the unmistakable evidence of that leading (see Gal. 5:18–25). When that evidence—or "fruit," as Paul likes to call it—is visible, it assures the believer that he or she is indeed a "son of God."

By the way, we shouldn't replace the word "son" with "child," even for women.

Paul could have chosen the neutral Greek term for child, but he deliberately chose "son" to indicate that believers stand to inherit something. Women are "sons of God" because they, no less than men, are a part of God's estate.

*The second benefit: fearless intimacy with God (8:15).* Paul again reinforces the good news that believers have been emancipated. They no longer serve a master who tells them what to do, when to do it, how long, how often, and where. We have been freed and therefore we are free indeed. God has purchased us. The payment was His Son's death. While He had every right to own us as slaves, He tore the bill of sale into shreds and drafted a new document: adoption papers! He is not merely a kinder, gentler Master; He is our "Abba." That's the Aramaic term of endearment for one's father. It's the closest word we have to the name "Daddy."

Intimacy with the Almighty Creator of the universe! What an awesome thought.

We have an obligation, not as slaves repaying a debt, but as sons, who have a genuine stake in our Daddy's estate. The obligation doesn't come as orders from the Big House, whispered secretly from Spirit to spirit, but as an invitation to become a contributing member of a family. If we do good, it is not for His sake alone, but for ours and for everyone else's in God's household.

*The third benefit: assurance of belonging to God (8:16).* If the Holy Spirit speaks into the souls of His beloved sons, it's only to say this: "You are my precious child."

This is the only place the New Testament we are told that the Holy Spirit speaks in a prophetic way *as a general practice.* After Jesus inaugurated the new covenant (which we will examine later), the Lord spoke through designated people. He spoke prophetically through apostles and prophets until the last of the New Testament books, the book of Revelation, was written by the last remaining apostle, John.

Some critics object to this, pointing to the fact that the Bible is replete with stories of God speaking to, and through, people, and that He still has the power to do so. This is true. The Lord specifically chose some to be His spokespeople for a given time and for a defined purpose. But, as one insightful commentator states, what is *narrative* is not necessarily *normative.* Just because someone in the Bible has experienced something doesn't mean we should expect it will become a common occurrence.

Balaam's donkey, for instance, under the supernatural direction of God, rebuked his master (Num. 22:28–30). The event took place in the Bible, the Lord still has the ability to speak through anything He chooses, and there's nothing to prevent Him from doing it again. Nevertheless, I recommend we keep to our Bibles instead of visiting barnyards to hear the voice of God.

We need no other prophetic utterance until the end-time events begin to unfold. We have all the information we need. Truth be told, we have more than we can handle in a lifetime as it is! This is not to say that we're on our own or that the Spirit does not lead. He is with us and He leads us. (We will soon learn from the apostle how the Spirit leads.) However, at this stage in the timeline of redemption, God does not speak prophetically to, or through, people. That is one of the major tenants of the Reformation (*sola scriptura*) and something that, in part, defines us as Protestant. We have no need of popes, neither in Rome nor next door, nor do we need night visions. We have God's Word in black print on white paper, accessible in multiple languages, and understandable to all. I suggest we keep our focus there.

*The fourth benefit: a continual reminder of our value before God (8:17).* Adoption was a common practice in Roman law. Much of Roman society depended on a system called "patronage," in which one person became a "godfather" to less powerful people. This person, in turn, owed allegiance to his patron. Frequently, a patron would adopt a favorite unrelated client to inherit his estate. When Paul spoke of "adoption as sons," his Roman readers would have immediately recalled that Caesar Augustus received much of his power through adoption by his patron, Julius Caesar, the founding father of the Roman Empire.

Through adoption, believers have become coheirs with God's one and only Son. And through our identification with Him, we stand to inherit everything that is due Him. Fast forward to Revelation 5:12 to see what that entails. He will share everything with His adopted brothers and sisters ... all, that is, except worship. That is His alone.

Paul took great pains to convince believers that only unbelieving people exist according to the flesh and that only sons and daughters of God exist according to the Spirit. A natural reaction to that truth is to say, "Then I want to live by the Spirit! How do I do that?" And I will admit that my first inclination was to comb that passage for applications. But I found no imperatives; no commands, no "should" or "should nots," not even a helpful suggestion. The apostle didn't describe what kind of behavior will help us "exist according to the Spirit" or prescribe a seven-step plan to becoming more spiritual.

To be honest, I found that frustrating. I confess that, in my flesh, I tried to turn this Spirit-led life into a self-made holiness. Suddenly, I found myself back in chapter 7 and I began to feel that telltale, wretched ache all over again. Then I was reminded that the flesh is ever with us and, oh, how it wants to be in control!

Instead of citing a list of deeds that result in holiness, Paul assures us that the Spirit of God decides on His own to start living in and through believers. Then he describes what the Spirit will do for us and the blessings we will receive as a result! Existing in the Spirit is not about what we do for Him; remember ... we can do nothing. The Spirit life is about what He will do on our behalf, because the indwelling presence of God's Spirit is a gift of grace. The same gift that redeems us from slavery to sin also rescues us from it. The free gift of salvation from sin begins now, not after we've gone to the grave.

So, what must we do? What is our obligation? The answer is uncomplicated. Difficult to do because the flesh will not surrender control easily, but the answer is straightforward enough: *Nothing.*

Nothing?! You don't have to pray? You don't have to get up at 4 a.m. for a "quiet time"? You don't have to have family devotions? You don't have to give away all your money, or shower every day, or obey the Ten Commandments, or wear dark clothing, or eat low-fat foods, or do a pile of good deeds to become more spiritual?

No. Nothing. If you have the Spirit within you, you are as spiritual as you're ever going to be.

If there is an imperative to be found in Paul's description of the Spirit life, it is to quit *trying so hard* to be spiritual. Stop all of that. Instead, let the Spirit be spiritual. When that makes sense to you, you can be sure you're setting your mind on the things of the Spirit … and you're starting to understand grace. Until then, you will not be ready to accept Paul's teaching in the latter half of his letter to the Romans.

## Glorying and Groaning (Romans 8:18 – 27)

[18]For I consider that the sufferings of this present time are not worthy to be compared with the glory that is to be revealed to us. [19]For the anxious longing of the creation waits eagerly for the revealing of the sons of God. [20]For the creation was subjected to futility, not willingly, but because of Him who subjected it, in hope [21]that the creation itself also will be set free from its slavery to corruption into the freedom of the glory of the children of God. [22]For we know that the whole creation groans and suffers the pains of childbirth together until now. [23]And not only this, but also we ourselves, having the first fruits of the Spirit, even we ourselves groan within ourselves, waiting eagerly for *our* adoption as sons, the redemption of our body. [24]For in hope we have been saved, but hope that is seen is not hope; for who hopes for what he *already* sees? [25]But if we hope for what we do not see, with perseverance we wait eagerly for it.

[26]In the same way the Spirit also helps our weakness; for we do not know how to pray as we should, but the Spirit Himself intercedes for *us* with groanings too deep for words; [27]and He who searches the hearts knows what the mind of the Spirit is, because He intercedes for the saints according to *the will of* God.

In 1957, I was eight thousand miles away from home in Southeast Asia, bunked up with forty-seven other Marines in a Quonset hut, and lonely for my wife. We had been married only two and a half years—practically newlyweds—so, Okinawa was *not* where I wanted to be, and I very much resented God for putting me there. Fortunately, another man had chosen to be there and served his Master through an organization called The Navigators. One particularly lonely evening, he placed a gift in my hands that would change everything for me ... starting with me.

I sat on my bunk and slid an attractively bound volume out of its protective covering to read the front: *The Amplified New Testament.* Until that time, the only versions available were the old King James and the J. B. Phillips translation, but this was brand new and unique. I broke it open that Christmas night and sat perusing familiar passages in the solitude of the empty barracks, for how long, I don't know. When I came across Philippians 3:10, the amplified verse impacted me so profoundly, I decided it would be my focus for the new year.

As Paul shared his enthusiasm for ministry and the gospel with his brothers and sisters in Philippi, his passion reached a climax with a statement of his purpose in life:

> [For my determined purpose is] that I may know Him [that I may progressively become more deeply and intimately acquainted with Him, perceiving and recognizing and understanding the wonders of His Person more strongly and more clearly], and that I may in that same way come to know the power outflowing from His resurrection [which it exerts over believers], and that I may so share His sufferings as to be continually transformed [in spirit into His likeness even] to His death. (Phil. 3:10 Amplified)

In January, I focused on the first few phrases. "[For my determined purpose is] that I may know Him [that I may progressively become more deeply and intimately acquainted with Him]." For the entire month of January, I would focus my time and attention on knowing Him deeply, intimately, and progressively. I spent extended time with Him, I talked with Him through the day by prayer, and I tried to think like I imagined He would. I would turn in at night, mentally focused on Him.

In February, I concentrated on the next portion: " ... that I may in that same way come to know the power outflowing from His resurrection [which it exerts over believers]." I thought, *Lord, if You could give me that kind of dynamic. Who knows? I might be able to speak to one of my buddies here about Jesus. So I give you this part of the verse for my February of 1958.* Before the year ended, seven came to know Christ. While that might not seem significant, a lot of people would consider seven out of forty-eight in a Marine Corps Quonset hut a revival! So, the eight of us formed a small Bible study group and committed ourselves to a Scripture memory program. We attended a GI fellowship on Friday nights and worked our way through the little InterVarsity hymnal. I committed to memory a lot of those great hymns. It was one incredible year.

In March, I concentrated on the phrase "that I may so share His sufferings." I don't mind telling you that the phrase didn't go down well. The resentment I felt toward the Lord for landing me on an island had diminished some, mostly because of my missionary friend, but it had not been completely resolved.

Many people come to Christ in the hope that all their troubles will evaporate once they believe and begin following Him. A lot of popular preachers proclaim that false gospel, a doctrine they call the "Word of Faith." I had been a Christian for many years by that time, but I still expected the Lord to make things easy for those He redeems and calls "sons." Placing the entire globe between a newlywed couple felt cruel to me, and I struggled to find His goodness in my circumstances.

Few people have enjoyed a more intimate relationship with God than Paul. Few have experienced the joy that he reported in his letters throughout his ministry. Yet few have suffered more than he. His unguarded words to the believers in Corinth summarize just some of his hardships.

> Are they servants of Christ?—I speak as if insane—I more so; in far more labors, in far more imprisonments, beaten times without number, often in danger of death. Five times I received from the Jews thirty-nine *lashes*. Three times I was beaten with rods, once I was stoned, three times I was shipwrecked, a night and a day I have spent in the deep. *I have been* on frequent journeys, in dangers from rivers, dangers from robbers, dangers from *my* countrymen, dangers from the Gentiles, dangers in the city, dangers in the wilderness, dangers on the sea, dangers among false brethren; *I have been* in labor and hardship, through many sleepless nights, in hunger and thirst, often without food, in cold and exposure. Apart from *such* external things, there is the daily pressure on me *of* concern for all the churches. (2 Cor. 11:23–28)

Experience is sometimes the most convincing authority a teacher can have. Paul's body bore the scars of suffering for the sake of Christ and each mark commemorated a victory to Him. Perhaps no other person on earth could have encouraged the Romans so effectively. Having assured his readers that the Lord will be faithful to complete in them what He started, Paul needs to address an obvious question. "If there is now no more condemnation, and if I am now a son of God, why do I feel as if I'm being punished?"

## —8:18—

Paul has just declared that the Holy Spirit continually affirms the believer's place in God's family as one of His children (8:16). Furthermore, we stand to share

Christ's inheritance, which includes both blessing and suffering, glorying and groaning (8:17). While the apostle does not minimize the intensity of our present distress—including his own, which was more severe than most—he considers it a mere fraction of the future splendor we will enjoy forever.

Alan Redpath wrote in his book *The Making of a Man of God*, "There is no victory without a fight, and there is no battle without wounds."[10] I'm not suggesting that we must pay for our glory with groaning or that sanctification can be purchased with suffering. Throughout Christian history, well-meaning men and women have literally beaten themselves with rods and whips in the hope of overcoming the flesh and gaining for themselves more Spirit. Some of these "flagellants" discovered later that sanctification didn't hurt as much if they wore a thick leather jacket under their clothing, which is, of course, absurd. Neither senseless pain nor going through the motions of self-deprecation puts someone on the fast track to spiritual maturity.

We don't need to go looking for suffering. Just living authentically in the Spirit under the tyranny of a fallen world, as He did, will bring enough suffering on its own. And that affliction allows us to share some measure of His experience. After all, He warned us that the world would afflict us as it did Him, for no other reason than our breaking ranks with evil (John 15:18–20). So, in a practical sense, suffering tells us we're on the right path. As F. B. Meyer stated in his book *Christ in Isaiah*, "If in an unknown country, I am informed that I must pass a valley where the sun is hidden, or over a stony bit of road, to reach my abiding-place—when I come to it, each moment of shadow or jolt of the carriage tells me I am on the right road."[11]

"Although He was a Son, [Jesus] learned obedience from the things which He suffered" (Heb. 5:8), and obedience led Him to die a torturous death. Paul followed Christ down the path of suffering and it led to martyrdom. In this section of his letter, the apostle bids us to follow him as he follows Christ.

— 8:19–22 —

Our suffering after adoption as sons is not the result of senseless beating by God either. While the Creator remains sovereign over His creation, the bad things that happen to us are *not* His original desire. He did not create these bodies to endure pain, or to wither under disease, or to crave evil. God created us to worship and enjoy Him forever; therefore, death is the ultimate affront to His creative act. Death is the result of sin, a perversion of His original design ... an enemy (see 1 Cor. 15:26).

The story of Creation concludes with a pristine world in which every blade of grass is jade green, every stream is crystal clear, every tree laden with fruit. God pronounces it all "good" and then gives it to His first children, Adam and Eve, as an inheritance to steward (Gen. 1:27–30). But then the children of God exchange the truth for a lie, they sell their inheritance as sons for bondage as slaves, and they open the door for disease, disaster, death, and decay to enter God's once-idyllic world. Paul personifies here creation as moaning in desperate, anguished anticipation of a future event: "the revealing of the sons of God" (8:19).

Note how he chooses to describe this future event. Not, "the revealing of God's plan," which, of course, it will be. Not even "the revealing of God's Son," as will certainly occur. But the revealing of the *sons of God*, which bears the subtle suggestion that the identity of the sons remains a mystery. We will undoubtedly be surprised to discover some among the saints we thought to be pagan, and others, who were admired as spiritual giants, missing! Furthermore, it's no coincidence that Paul chooses the Greek word *apokalypsis*—from which we derive our word "apocalypse"—to describe this event. It is the time when Jesus returns to set all things right again.

When humankind fell, creation fell. When God restores the believing remnant of humanity, creation will be restored. The Lord Himself will rule as King, the desert will blossom like a rose, the lamb and the lion will lie down together, and sin will have no place. Until then, we live in the meantime. Until that day, creation groans in anguished expectation like a mother in labor. Verses 19–22 reveals four important facts about the groaning of creation:

> The groaning of creation is temporary. (8:19)
> The groaning of creation is a consequence of sin. (8:20)
> The groaning of creation is a means to an end. (8:20–21)
> The groaning of creation is universal. (8:22)

## —8:23–25—

Because we are an integral part of creation, we too groan. We groan through the inescapable hardships of life in fallen creation: tragedies of financial ruin, broken relationships, nature's disasters, terminal illness, and inevitable death. Moreover, we groan as the drag of the flesh keeps us from enjoying complete and uninterrupted intimacy with our Creator. We are like children in an orphanage, waiting with bags packed and completed adoption papers in hand for the coming of our Father ... whom we can call "Daddy" (8:15).

Paul again used the Greek term *elpis* ("hope") to describe the "assured expectation" (5:2–5) of our inevitable future. While we have been adopted and redeemed, there is an aspect of those gifts that remains to be fulfilled. In this "assured expectation" we have been saved, but we are citizens of another King though living in hostile territory, living behind enemy lines, as it were. We have only received the "first fruits" of our salvation.

People who derive their living from the land understand the concept of "first fruits." They toil against weeds, drought, pests, and the weather's extremes to grow a crop. They drop their seeds into the ground or tend their trees and vines with no guarantees. So, the first sign of yield is cause for celebration. Furthermore, the quality of that first fruit is an indication of how the rest of the season will go. If the first ear of corn, bushel of apples, bunch of grapes, or bundle of wheat is of excellent quality, the people who labored over it breathe a sigh of relief. All they need to do is protect the crop and wait for it to ripen. They persevere and eagerly wait for it (cf. 8:23).

In addition to groaning through the turmoil of life and its inevitable heartaches, we also groan because of the flesh and its continual drag on the life we long to enjoy. Our bodies and our natural way of thinking are a part of creation, which is no less twisted now as when Adam and Eve brought death and decay into the world through sin. So, we groan inwardly as the civil war between the old nature and new nature drags on.

## — 8:26-27 —

"In the same way . . ." In the same way as what? The answer is found in the progression of Paul's teaching from 8:19 to this point. Creation groans (8:19–22) and we groan within ourselves (8:23–25); in the same way, the Spirit also groans (8:26). He groans on our behalf because, like the Son, the Spirit has taken the problem of evil upon Himself, voluntarily, by dwelling within His children. Jesus promised His followers that another being would come to be with them in their struggles — a comforter, a teacher, an advocate. He promised His Holy Spirit. Not only does the Spirit convict us of sin and teach truth, He endures our suffering with us. He has been "called alongside" (a literal translation of the Greek term *paraklētos*, or Paraclete in English) to help us endure.

When I am tempted to think that God is cruel to leave us in our suffering, I remember that He, too, moans with "groanings too deep for words." When I see a mother sobbing over the dead body of her child, I know the Holy Spirit suffers her anguish too. When I see a man kiss the cold cheek of his bride and give her body to the care of a mortician, I know the Holy Spirit feels his desperate ache. He is the Spirit of the Creator, who made these bodies to reflect His glory, not suffer

## From My Journal

## Praying without Words

I can remember one particular struggle that kept me on my knees for weeks. My prayers started out with my outlining a reasonable plan of action for the Lord to follow. But as the difficulty continued, I realized He could see issues that were hidden to me and He could account for infinite variables that I could not (Isa. 55:8–9). So, I decided it was best to leave the "how" in His hands and concentrate on requesting my desired outcome. As the difficulty dragged on, I began to accept that my desired outcome might not be the right resolution, so I surrendered that to the Lord as well. This particular burden eventually brought me to the end of my own strength and left me in a listless heap, too exhausted for prayer. My suffering overwhelmed my capacity for speech, so all I could express to God as the turmoil intensified were pleading moans—emotions too intense for words.

I admit that I often don't understand the Lord. I cannot fathom why He would allow me to suffer so much for so long when, in an instant, with a mere word, He could resolve the issue and end my sorrow. He seemed distant and uncaring at that particular time, so I made it a discipline to remind myself of His wisdom and goodness.

> The ways of the LORD are right,
> And the righteous will walk in them,
> But transgressors will stumble in them. (Hos. 14:9)

At the end of all reason, after my strength had been drained and my words fell silent, when anguished emotions seeped through every pore of my body and left me dry, I lay submitted to His will and His way. And I rested in the assurance that while I had no words and did not know what to pray, the Spirit of God had been interceding on my behalf. He was doing what I could not.

When my difficulty ended, the Lord resolved many issues far more effectively than I could have imagined. He left some matters unresolved, of course, but I trust His judgment. More importantly, I was changed, and undoubtedly for the better. I emerged from my trial serenely submitted to God's will, a posture I find much easier after my ordeal. For that, I am grateful.

I have the distinct feeling I am not alone in the struggle I have just described.

disease, disaster, death, and decay. He loves us even more than we love ourselves, and therefore He groans with us.

Fortunately, the Holy Spirit possesses power we do not. At the end of our strength, we groan and that's it. There's nothing more. The Spirit groans with a purpose. He intercedes on our behalf, praying with wisdom we do not possess, requesting for us what we are too shortsighted to perceive. And—most important of all—He groans His intercessions in heaven so that our minds and the mind of the Father will unite to accomplish His will.

Sixteen months in Okinawa was not my will. Stationed in San Francisco, I had a beautiful young bride, a wonderful little apartment, an enviable post with the Marine Corps, and a delightful opportunity to cultivate our marriage. I had it made! Then came the telegram that ruined all of that. Sitting on my bunk all alone that Christmas night in a cold Quonset hut, I felt abandoned by the Lord. That is, until He confronted me with a life-changing question I would never have heard in the commotion of my happiness back in the States: "Do you want to know Me?"

Because of Paul's letter, I know the Holy Spirit groaned through my loneliness and disappointment with me. But where I would have given up all hope of joy, He interceded for me, praying the Father's will into my life on my behalf. The Spirit tugged me in the direction of God's plan for my future, a ministry I could never have imagined and would have certainly missed if I had selfishly pursued my own agenda. A. W. Tozer wrote, "It is doubtful whether God can bless a man greatly until He has hurt him deeply."[12] I wish there was an easier, more pleasant way to prepare a heart to receive joy—some means other than crushing. If there were, our God of love would certainly use it.

Looking back, sixteen months was a short time compared to the hardship of others. Those sixteen months of groaning prepared me to receive more than forty-five years of joy in ministry. The return has far exceeded the suffering. Today I can barely imagine what my short seventy-plus years on earth will yield in eternity!

## Application

### Groaning... then Glory!

The problem of evil is difficult for everyone. Unbelievers struggle to comprehend how a good, all-powerful God can allow evil to continue. Believers begin to question everything when the intensity of sorrow or suffering becomes unbearable. Even creation itself groans in anguished anticipation for disease, disaster, death, and decay to end. Nevertheless, Paul considers this present suffering to be minor when compared to the glory of eternity (8:17–25).

As I have taught and lived this portion of Scripture for the better part of half a century, I observe two principles at work.

First, *the greater the groan, the greater the glory.* God is not the source of pain and He did not promise to prevent our suffering. Instead, He promises that no pain will go to waste. What the world intends for harm, God will use for our good. Not only will He make us more like His Son, He will use afflictions to give us a greater capacity for future blessing.

When you find yourself afflicted and suffering, rest assured that however deeply you hurt, your joy will be greater when the trial ends. Therefore, endure with hope—confident assurance.

Second, *the weaker our spirit, the stronger His support.* I recall many times when I barely had the strength to stand in the pulpit on Sunday. One Friday afternoon, our daughter fell to the pavement from a cheerleading pyramid and broke her back. For the next thirty-six hours—Friday night, Saturday, and Saturday night—we sat by her hospital bed praying that her paralysis wouldn't be permanent. With her long-term condition still uncertain, I preached as scheduled on Sunday. I blinked through tears and somehow made my way through the sermon, which surely flopped. Or so I thought. The recording of that particular sermon ultimately became the most requested of any I had delivered in that church. Why? I am convinced that it was because I preached it in utter weakness.

When affliction and suffering bring you to your knees, that is when the power of God has the greatest effect in your ministry (2 Cor. 12:10). I don't mean to suggest that taking a step back from work isn't sometimes necessary. You should be fit to serve. However, when you do continue ministering to others in the midst of suffering, God multiplies His power in your weakness.

Let me boil this down to several practical dos and don'ts:

**Don't** assume your suffering is the result of God's punishment.

**Do** expect that when the suffering ends, He will give you even greater joy.

**Don't** assume the Lord has abandoned you.

**Do** confess your fear and doubt and ask Him for strength to press on.

**Don't** assume you have been rejected or forsaken by God.

**Do** remain faithful to your duties, even if you must reduce your load for the time being.

**Don't** assume your prayers are not heard.

**Do** continue praying, even when you don't know what to say.

**Don't** assume that your suffering gives you permission to give up.

**Do** trust that the Lord will magnify His strength through your weakness.

Jesus warned His followers that the world will hate them on His account and mistreatment will mark their days as certainly as it did His. Nevertheless, His experience established the pattern for us. "In the days of His flesh, [Jesus] offered up both prayers and supplications with loud crying and tears to the One able to save Him from death, and He was heard because of His piety. Although He was a Son, He learned obedience from the things which He suffered" (Heb. 5:7–8). He shared in our suffering; soon we shall share in His glory! How great is *that*!

## We Overwhelmingly Conquer (Romans 8:28–39)

[28]And we know that God causes all things to work together for good to those who love God, to those who are called according to *His* purpose. [29]For those whom He foreknew, He also predestined *to become* conformed to the image of His Son, so that He would be the firstborn among many brethren; [30]and these whom He predestined, He also called; and these whom He called, He also justified; and these whom He justified, He also glorified.

[31]What then shall we say to these things? If God *is* for us, who *is* against us? [32]He who did not spare His own Son, but delivered Him over for us all, how will He not also with Him freely give us all things? [33]Who will bring a charge against God's elect? God is the one who justifies; [34]who is the one who condemns? Christ Jesus is He who died, yes, rather who was raised, who is at the right hand of God, who also intercedes for us. [35]Who will separate us from the love of Christ? Will tribulation, or distress, or persecution, or famine, or nakedness, or peril, or sword? [36]Just as it is written,

"For Your sake we are being put to death all day long;
We were considered as sheep to be slaughtered."

[37]But in all these things we overwhelmingly conquer through Him who loved us. [38]For I am convinced that neither death, nor life, nor angels, nor principalities, nor things present, nor things to come, nor powers, [39]nor height, nor depth, nor any other created thing, will be able to separate us from the love of God, which is in Christ Jesus our Lord.

Many years ago, Rod Serling penned an episode of *The Twilight Zone* in which a kindly antique dealer happened to release a genie from an otherwise worthless bottle. In keeping with tradition, the man was granted wishes—a generous four wishes—but warned by the genie to choose wisely. After wasting one wish on something insignificant and then consulting his wife, the man called for money, one million dollars to be exact, which the genie granted immediately. After giving away nearly $60,000 to their needy friends, the man and his wife eagerly totaled the balance of their nest egg. Unfortunately, before they could finish, the IRS auditor handed them a bill for all but five dollars of what remained.

He should have wished for one million tax-free dollars. He failed to consider the consequences of his wish and to wish accordingly.

Next, he wished for power, to be the leader of a modern, powerful country in which he could not be voted out of office. The genie immediately granted his request and, in a flash, he found himself in a bunker, surrounded by Nazi attendants and sporting a style of mustache that will never come back.

He should have considered the genie's fondness for irony and been more specific.

The poor man had no alternative but to use his final wish to restore life as it was. The temporarily rich and powerful shopkeeper gained only wisdom from the experience. He learned, firsthand, that the power to wish without complete foreknowledge could be the making of his own hell. If only he had found a genie who genuinely cared about him.

In describing the problem of evil that continues to afflict the world as a result of sin, Paul has highlighted two human limitations that tend to make matters worse. First, "we do not see" (8:25). Our perspective is limited. We see nothing of the future and can never predict what will occur only a few minutes ahead. Second, "we do not know how to pray as we should" (8:26). We may do our very best to pray in harmony with God's will, but we frequently wish for the very opposite of what is good for us. Fortunately, we do not have an evil genie for a god. And I cannot count the number of times I have thanked my Lord for *not* granting an earlier, short-sighted request!

## —8:28—

We do not see and we do not know how to pray as we ought; however, we do know one all-important fact. The verse doesn't begin, "We hope," "We suppose," or "We wish," but rather "We know." We have a promise founded upon the character of our Creator: "To those who love God, He works together all things into good, to the ones who are called according to His purpose" (my literal translation). Paul cautiously chooses his words and arranges them carefully to state this foundational promise. Each phrase warrants closer examination.

*To those who love God.* The Greek language places great importance on word order. Paul places this phrase at the beginning of the clause to stress that the promise is intended for believers. While the Lord acts in the best interest of everyone, He makes this particular promise exclusively to His very own "sons."

*He works together.* The term Paul uses is a compound of "with" and "work." It conveys the idea of a weaver carefully interlacing strands of colored cloth into a preplanned pattern.

*All things.* Greek writers frequently used this term to refer to the universe, all things both seen and unseen, good and bad, real and even imagined. God utilizes everything—including the evil deeds of evil people.

*Into good.* The preposition "into" carries the idea of space, as though all things are being corralled by His sovereign will. A good rendering might use "unto," which reflects His accomplishing a specific purpose, but I prefer "into." He not only has a purpose in mind as He weaves all things, He will achieve a result. And it will be good.

Our flesh would have us believe that the "good" God causes *our* good, that is, what will give us happiness, contentment, or joy. But this is only partially true. Throughout Romans, Paul uses the term "good" almost exclusively in a moral sense. "Good" is that which pleases God because it reflects His nature and conforms to His original created order. In the beginning, He created the world good, and at the end of days, the world will be recreated good.

God's "good" is not completely focused on humanity; however, people are happy, content, and joyful when they live in His goodness and with Him in proper perspective.

*To the ones who are called according to His purpose.* These people are identical to "those who love God." Jesus said, "If you love Me, you will keep My commandments" (John 14:15), and "So that the world may know that I love the Father, I do exactly as the Father commanded Me" (14:31). Love for God and following His commands are inexorably linked.

Putting it all back together, we have: "For those who love God, the Lord sovereignly weaves the strands of every circumstance, every influence, every atom or idea they encounter for the purpose of creating moral good within them—those whom He has called to join His redemptive plan for the world."

When the Lord restores His universe, it will be even better than His original design. And His restoration begins with His people. To accomplish His plan in each of us, He orchestrates all things, including disease, disaster, death, and decay. The world's destructive designs then become tools in the hand of the Almighty, who will turn them to accomplish His good.

Does this mean that all things in the world are good? Clearly, they are not. The world is unfair, brutal, shocking, and demoralizing, and it includes people who relentlessly oppose God's created order. Nevertheless, as evil tries to destroy, the Lord turns the world's destruction into our gain.

If God uses evil for His purposes, does this mean He brings evil on His people? Never! God is not the author of sin. Only good things come from God. He does not bring evil into the world; we do that through sin and, as a race, we perpetuate suffering through continued sin. The Lord merely allows humanity and the world to continue living as they choose, but never beyond His sovereign control over creation.

## —8:29–30—

Nothing will subvert or alter the plans of God. The destiny of each believer is what Paul earlier called "good," which he further defined as "conformed to the image of His Son." This gives the apostle an opportunity to reveal another confidence-building truth. Having shown the Christians in Rome the destination of their spiritual path, he turns them to look in the direction from which they came.

Foreknew ▸ Predestined to be like Christ ▸ Called ▸ Justified ▸ 🗣 ▸ Glorified

*God foreknew them*, which is to say, He knew them intimately through active involvement in their lives. The Greek verb *ginōskō* (which is the equivalent of the Hebrew verb, *yada*) describes a scrutinizing knowledge that goes beyond mere awareness. The verb was a common euphemism for sexual intimacy shared between a married couple.

Those whom God foreknew in this active sense do not include everyone. This has led some to suggest that God deliberately passed over some, electing them to damnation. That may be a logical inference, but we must be careful not to take Scripture beyond what it actually says. This is Paul's teaching about believers; he isn't commenting on nonbelievers at this point.

Those God foreknew, *He predestined*. This Greek term is based on the same word we studied in 1:1, in which Paul wrote that he had been "set apart" (*aphorizō*), or as I had playfully suggested, "off-horizoned." The root word *horizō* means "to limit, appoint, determine." The prefix *pro*, of course, indicates that the action was done ahead of time, as when someone is "*pro*active." Those the Lord knew intimately and actively, He appointed in advance to become like Jesus in their character. Thus, the one and only Son of God will become, as it were, the eldest brother of all those the Father has adopted.

Those God predestined are *called to believe*, and those who believe *are justified* (3:21 – 5:21). Eventually, all believers *will be glorified*, which does not involve exaltation like a hero; it is to be like Christ. To be glorified is to have both pure character and a body that cannot be harmed by the world any longer.

## — 8:31–36 —

Paul continues his encouragement by asking the rhetorical question, "What shall we say to these things?" I understand "these things" to be the summation of Paul's teaching to this point: the depravity of humankind (1:19 – 3:20), justification by grace through faith (3:21 – 5:21), and sanctification by the Holy Spirit (6:1 – 8:30). As the believer considers the course of salvation, he cannot miss the proactive role of God in bringing him or her along the path.

Foreknew ▸ Predestined to be like Christ ▸ Called ▸ Justified ▸ Glorified

Paul's use of the provisional term "if" assumes the condition to be true for the sake of argument. Therefore, the term "because" can be inserted to render the verse: "Because God is for us, who can be against us?"

He asks, in effect, "Because God proactively foreknew and predestined believers to be like His Son, and then faithfully called and justified us, will He not be faithful to complete the final step?" This leads Paul to reassure his readers by asking and answering four rhetorical questions, much like an orator stirring a crowd into a frenzy. Each question takes clear aim at Satan and his minions, but demands the same response: "No one!" for evil is powerless before Almighty God.

Who is against us? (8:31)
Who will bring a charge against God's elect? (8:33)
Who is the one who condemns? (8:34)
Who will separate us from the love of Christ? (8:35)

*Who shall oppose us? (8:31).* Make no mistake about it; there is plenty to oppose us in life. Hardships and tragedies relentlessly batter away at the hope of all believers. Persecutors and naysayers oppose us. Indwelling sin opposes us. Fear of loss opposes us. The evil one and those who serve him oppose us. And, eventually, death opposes us. But what are they compared to the power of God?

If anyone doubts the Lord's faithfulness, Paul cites the fact that He has already sacrificed His Son to redeem us, to emancipate us from slavery. With the price paid, it makes no sense for Him to refuse to take delivery on what He has purchased. And having completely committed His greatest object of love, why would

He then hold back what He values far less than His Son? Let me illustrate the absurdity this way:

Let's say the manager of a local jewelry store called one afternoon to let you know your name had been entered in a drawing and that you are the winner of a very expensive diamond necklace. "All you need to do is come to the store at ten o'clock tomorrow and receive your prize!"

So, you arrive the following morning shortly before ten to find a small crowd gathered around a presentation platform. After a few comments, the manager places the necklace around your neck for a few photographs, everyone applauds, and the ceremony ends. You have your gift, but you don't want to wear it home, so you kindly ask the manager, "May I have a box for this beautiful necklace? I want to keep it safe for the trip home."

No manager on earth would respond, "No! We gave you the necklace, the box is your responsibility!" The cost of a box is nothing compared to the necklace.

We have everything we need in Christ, and the Father will withhold nothing to protect His children and to bring them safely to Himself.

*Who will bring a charge against God's elect? (8:33).* This is a legal question. The Greek term translated "bring a charge against" means simply "to call in." It's an official summons to appear in court to face an accusation.

I remember standing in the front row of the church I was pastoring years ago, singing along with the congregation shortly before I was to preach. A grim-looking man in a suit entered the back of the sanctuary and slowly walked toward the front. I thought he would slip into one of the rows, take a hymnal, and join the singing, but he kept walking. He came all the way to the front, faced me, and slapped an envelope against my chest. It was a summons!

I read it over and quickly determined it was another nut with a frivolous case, but it still unnerved me. Something about being called before a judge puts a knot in my stomach, even if I know I'm legally faultless. I have this nagging worry that a particularly slick lawyer might be able to fool the court.

Now suppose the only judge with any jurisdiction happened to be my father. The nut's frivolous charge would stand no chance of even getting a hearing.

Any charge brought against us will not stand up in court. Because our debt for sin has been paid in full, we are unimpeachable. We are and forever will be considered just before the Judge of heaven.

*Who is the one who condemns? (8:34).* When I received the summons, I knew the charge was frivolous. I trusted that a judge would take one look and throw the case out, and that would be the end of it. (That's exactly what happened.) A false accusation is difficult to bear, but at least I had justice on my side. I can face an unjust accuser without fear as long as a just judge will hear the case. But what if the judge is against you? What hope do you have?

Paul's answer highlights four great Christian doctrines:

*"Christ Jesus is He who died."* That's the doctrine of *substitution*. The Son of God paid the debt of sin on our behalf.

*"Who was raised . . ."* That's the doctrine of *resurrection*. The Son of God was raised to new life and, by our identification with Him, we too have new life.

*"Who is at the right hand of God . . ."* That's the doctrine of *accession*. The Son of God has received title to the entire universe and now rules as its king and ultimate judge.

*"Who also intercedes for us."* That's the doctrine of *intercession*. The Son of God is our advocate, our representative in heaven, faithfully looking out for our welfare.

So, we have the Father, who sacrificed His one and only Son to free us from bondage to sin. We have the Son, who paid the price to set us free and now holds title to everything. And we have the Holy Spirit, who lives within us to share our suffering and to be the spiritual driving force we cannot. With the triune God working for us on all sides, what possible chance does any form of evil stand?

*Who will separate us from the love of Christ? (8:35–36).* Paul suggests no less than seven possibilities, all of which he has personally endured (2 Cor. 11:23–28). And let's be honest. When we suffer the afflictions of pressure, prejudice, persecution, or poverty, we naturally begin to wonder if the Lord still cares about us or even remembers we're alive. Our flesh feels nurtured when it's most comfortable, and it feels abandoned during hardship. To reassure his readers of God's love, Paul quotes Psalm 44:22 to remind his readers that hardship has always been the experience of God's faithful followers.

After having a medical procedure, I always appreciate the physician telling me what I can expect to feel in the days to follow. "You may experience sharp pains around the affected area. Don't worry. That's normal." Then, when the pain comes, I know not to call the doctor or run to the hospital. I just need to ride out the painful episodes, knowing they will eventually subside and then disappear completely.

Paul reassures the believers in Rome, in effect, "You may experience hardship from the world or even persecution from nonbelievers. Don't worry. That's normal."

## — 8:37–39 —

Believing and accepting grace does not come naturally to the flesh; therefore we must do now what we did in the beginning: Know the truth, reckon the truth, and apply the truth as we depend on the Holy Spirit to keep us connected to the Father.

"In all these things …" (8:37). What things? Everything the Christian experiences. From the initial elation of emancipation, to the sobering reality of freedom, to the realization that our old slave master will not let us go so easily, to the struggle with the flesh, to the persecution of the world. The joys, the sorrows, the setbacks, and triumphs—all of it. In all these things we, the sheep, conquer.

The image of sheep overcoming and conquering an enemy is laughable! Fighting sheep? Not really. We conquer because we have a champion, Jesus—who is the "Lamb of God" but is also the "Lion of Judah." The Suffering Servant in the book of Isaiah the prophet is also the conquering king of the Psalms and the book of Revelation. We will be victorious because He will win the victory on our behalf.

Writing with full apostolic authority, Paul declares, "I am persuaded …" His words in Greek mean "I stand convinced" (8:38). The verb is a Greek perfect tense, indicating that something occurred in the past with ongoing results to the present time. He was convinced that nothing in life, or even our archenemy, death, can keep the love of Christ from us. His own death and resurrection reveal His power over anything and everything that threatens us in the natural realm. Furthermore, nothing in the supernatural realm—including angels (elect or fallen) and spiritual forces—can harm us. God created all things, including everything in the supernatural realm, and He continues to rule over His universe.

Because God rules over everything in time and space, nothing can subvert His will, which is to bring His people to Himself, cleanse us of sin inside and out, shape us into the image of Christ, restore us to life, and allow us to enjoy "peace with God" forever.

---

Paul began this major section with a penetrating question. "Are we to continue in sin?" (6:1). In other words, now that we have been emancipated from slavery to sin, shall we continue to serve sin as before? The obvious answer is a resounding "No!" However, sin will not give up its slaves easily. The battle persists.

On August 26, 1863, several months after the Emancipation Proclamation had taken effect, President Lincoln reassured the nation with a word picture from Herman Melville's *Moby Dick*. "We are like whalers who have been on a long chase: we have at last got the harpoon into the monster, but we must now look how we steer, or with one 'flop' of his tail he will send us all into eternity."[13]

I'm ready for eternity. I have nothing to fear in the life to come. But learning to live in the freedom of God's grace will come neither naturally nor easily. Fortunately, my God has His harpoon in the monster. Slaying him is only a matter of time.

## Application

### *Mark These Words*

I have no idea what challenge you are facing today or what sorrow weighs heavily on your heart. Chances are good that few, if any, know about your struggle. And if they do, no one can appreciate the complexity, the absurdity, the hopelessness of that burden—a difficulty words cannot adequately describe. In many ways we are not free to share it with others because, in truth, no one can fully enter our sorrow, despite their best efforts to understand. We welcome whatever fleeting moments of empathy we encounter, but they fail to satisfy.

You would expect me to say this; nevertheless I must because it is true: *God knows.*

It is a great truth of Scripture that God knows everything. He is omniscient. God is not discovering, God is not learning, God is not watching and then adapting His plan to fit what might help make us comfortable. His plan is set. His knowledge is thorough. He gives purpose to every chaotic circumstance of this fallen, corrupted world. Moreover, He loves us completely—more than any one can love us, even ourselves. Therefore, we can rest in His plan. As musician Michael W. Smith said in a recent concert, "God is still God and I'm still not."

In my experience, submitting my trials to the sovereign plan of God and embracing His providence over all earthly matters are a process.

*Rejection.* Initially, we refuse to accept the injustice or the absurdity or the finality of our difficulty, and we throw our whole selves against it. To beat it down, we will exhaust every financial, emotional, intellectual, and relational resource. We search every crevice of life for an honorable escape ... and then we consider the ones that are not so honorable. The notion that this affliction might, in fact, be the sovereign plan of God is a detestable, unthinkable thought.

*Toleration.* Progressively, as circumstances either drag on or grow worse, we begin to entertain the possibility that God may not miraculously intervene, that He might leave the affliction in place. Frustration, outrage, pleading, negotiating, seeking purpose, and further attempts to escape our pain eventually dissolve into a despairing sadness. We struggle less under the crushing weight of God's sovereign plan, resigned to make the best of a future that cannot be avoided.

*Epiphany.* Gradually, we begin to see glimmers of God's purpose, a silver lining as some have called it. Having long ago surrendered our will to His sovereign plan—though with sulking hopelessness—we accept His providence, little by little. We gather scraps of joy from here and there, and before we know it, life becomes enriching. Our affliction has changed from an unwanted enemy to an indispensable part of who we have become. A sorrowful but vital addition. Then, one day, we see it. The purpose. We perceive with sweet sadness how the affliction was necessary for us to receive the blessings we now enjoy and how the plan of God could have taken no other path.

You might recognize a familiar pattern in the process of submission to God's plan. Elisabeth Kübler-Ross called this process "the stages of grief" in her book *On Death and Dying*: denial, anger, bargaining, depression, and acceptance. But don't mistake this natural ability to recover from tragedy for the supernatural working of the Holy Spirit. Yes, sooner or later, we will reach the final stage of "acceptance," but only God can transform us and only God will give us spiritual insight. Many unbelievers come to terms with the calamities they face, but they rarely emerge whole. Believers, however, become like the Son of God: "Although He was a Son, He learned obedience from the things which He suffered" (Heb. 5:8).

I want to encourage you to do something unusual. Open your Bible to Romans 8:28–39. Think of a word (or two) that best encapsulates the one struggle you face now, the affliction that makes your life miserable, which you would do almost anything to remove. Draw a bracket in the margin of your Bible alongside 8:28–39 and then note your affliction along the bracket.

For the next few days, place your Bible somewhere close to where you will be during the day and keep it open to this passage. Read it periodically and, each time, pray. Pray that the promises of this passage will penetrate your mind. Pray that the Holy Spirit will heal your wounds and teach you both trust and submission. Pray that your affliction will end, but then quickly surrender control to God's way.

I would not presume to tell you how things will unfold for you, nor do I dare suggest the path to obedience will be short or easy. On the contrary! But I can promise you this: This page from your Bible with the words you write next to Romans 8:28–39 will one day become a treasure for you. You will reflect back on this time and you will realize how far you have come ... and you will not want to trade anything for the richness of God's blessing you will have received.

---

NOTES: The Faithfulness of God (Romans 6:1–8:39)

1. Booker T. Washington, *Up from Slavery* (New York: Doubleday, 1901), 19–20.
2. Ibid., 20.
3. Gerhard Kittel and Gerhard Friedrich, eds., *Theological Dictionary of the New Testament: Abridged in One Volume*, trans. Geoffrey W. Bromiley (Grand Rapids: Eerdmans, 1985), 180.
4. Warren W. Wiersbe, *The Bible Exposition Commentary* (Wheaton, IL: Victor Books, 1989), comment on Rom. 6:1.
5. Jesus came close when He contrasted humanity's standard of judgment and God's (see John 8:15).

6. Ralph Erskine, *Sermons and Other Practical Works* (Falkirk: Peter Muirhead, Rev. John Stewart, and Hugh Mitchell, Publishers, 1796), 7:275.

7. Please, no letters from West Texas. I am a Texan and I love *all* of Texas. My illustration is not intended to suggest that my friends out there are lost and living in misery! It's hot, but it isn't Hell!

8. Greek syntax frequently drops verbs in a couplet with the understanding that they are the same as the first line.

9. Donald Grey Barnhouse, *Exposition of Bible Doctrines, Taking the Epistle to the Romans As a Point of Departure* (Grand Rapids: Eerdmans, 1955), 3:34.

10. Alan Redpath, *The Making of a Man of God: Studies in the Life of David* (Westwood, NJ: Revell, 1962), 93.

11. F. B. Meyer, *Christ in Isaiah* (London: Morgan and Scott, 1917), 9.

12. A. W. Tozer, *The Root of the Righteous* (Camp Hill, PA: Christian Publications, 1986), 137.

13. Abraham Lincoln, quoted by Doris Kearns Godwin in *Team of Rivals* (New York: Simon and Schuster, 2005), 688.

# THE MAJESTY OF GOD
# (ROMANS 9:1–11:36)

The Almighty Creator of the universe has not hidden Himself from His creatures. His handiwork offers compelling evidence that the world was crafted by an intelligent mind. Unfortunately, sin has dulled the senses of humanity so that despite our instinct to look heavenward for a Creator, it takes more than a minor miracle for us to see Him.

A more powerful instinct is to replace Him with things of our own making. In ancient days, we replaced Him with things we dug out of the ground and whittled into one grotesque shape or another. Now we prefer idols of a more theoretical kind, like something-from-nothing scientific myths and vain philosophies that celebrate the unlimited potential of human evolution. No matter. They are, like their predecessors, substitute gods inspiring a false hope.

Knowing that revealing Himself through nature does not suffice, the Lord has also revealed Himself to humanity in dramatic, miraculous ways. He spoke audibly to some and visited others in dreams and visions. He appeared in various physical forms throughout early history and then manifested His special presence among the Israelites in the other-worldly glow of the *shekinah* above the Ark of the Covenant. He revealed His holy character through the Law of Moses and spoke to all of humanity through prophets and apostles, who dutifully and inerrantly recorded His message for all to read and apply. Ultimately, He revealed Himself perfectly in the person of His Son, Jesus Christ.

The Almighty has revealed Himself in every conceivable manner humans would find meaningful, and He did it accurately and sufficiently. Still, He remains a mystery. And the same can be said of His ways. Though we see Him accurately, we cannot comprehend Him fully.

A good example of God's inscrutable nature is His tri-unity. The Bible speaks of Him as Father, Son, and Holy Spirit, three persons who affirm unity yet distinctly refer to—and even speak to—one another. Many are not satisfied simply to accept this paradox as God's incomprehensible nature. Consequently, history is replete with well-meaning men and women who have tried in vain to explain or illustrate His tri-unity, and each pathetic attempt has resulted in one dangerous heresy after another. Better that we should accept what we cannot possibly understand and sing with the poet Walter Chalmers Smith:

> Immortal, invisible, God only wise,
> In light inaccessible hid from our eyes,
> Most blessed, most glorious, the Ancient of Days,
> Almighty, victorious—Thy great name we praise.[1]

In the same way I cannot comprehend how God can be one and three, yet One, I do not understand His inscrutable ways. Therefore, I will admit without shame that this section of Paul's letter to the Romans contains mysteries I have no ability to unravel. Like the enigma of God's nature, I accept that God's sovereign plan as Scripture has revealed it and then I faithfully teach it as the Holy Spirit enables me.

Unfortunately, this will not satisfy everyone. Some will think I have not been bold enough because I don't develop doctrine from what Scripture merely infers. Others will chafe because I don't round off the edges Paul intentionally left jagged. But, at the end of the day, I want to base my teaching on sound biblical exegesis, even if it leaves gaps in my theology or appears to undermine another truth clearly taught elsewhere in Scripture. I don't want to repeat history, which is littered with the efforts of men and women who must have every secret in heaven codified, classified, cataloged, correlated, and connected. Their legacies would be laughable if they had not led so many believers to embrace one bizarre doctrine or another.

In the first eight chapters of this letter to the Romans, Paul was marvelously sequential and logical in his presentation. And for the final five chapters (chs. 12–16), he is equally straightforward. Not so for this section! In fact, most commentators begin their exposition with a warning, either acknowledging the "problems" raised by this passage or denying that any difficulties exist. I will state, unambiguously, that both positions are correct.

The section is clearly difficult because it defies what we would consider logic. It is here that we learn about predestination and election. We encounter the disbelief of the Jews and the fate of God's promises to them. And we are forced to consider how Gentiles factor into God's master plan for the world. But when we allow Paul's treatise on the sovereignty of God to stand on its own, it's quite simple to understand. Therefore, we must accept Romans 9–11 as we do the will of God, which often appears contrary to common sense. In those difficult times, we must learn to trust Him and then, sooner or later, we must surrender to His way. Then, as our perspective aligns with His and we're no longer pushed or pulled by circumstances, we inevitably discover that He was right ... as always. So let it be with Romans 9:1–11:36. As one of my beloved and much-respected theology professors often warned, let's not try to make these truths "walk on all fours."

In our study of this section, we will examine three facets of God's nature. Without too much explanation, we will encounter *the sovereignty of God* in chapter 9, wrestle with the implications, and ultimately learn to rest in its truth. Then we will consider *the justice of God* in chapter 10. We will learn to accept that He does not submit to our notion of fair play; He has all the power, so He is the Judge. And then we will find comfort in *the faithfulness of God* in chapter 11. Where answers fail, we can trust in the unfailing goodness of our Creator and His unsurpassed love for His creatures ... and leave it at that.

## KEY TERMS

σκληρύνω [sklērunō] (4645) "to harden, to cause to be stubborn"

Sklērunō is the origin of our medical term sclerosis, as in "sclerosis of the liver," in which the hardening of tissue prevents the organ from performing its normal function. Biblical writers used the term figuratively, suggesting that one's conscience or will is like an organ of the body and that repeated abuse steadily decreases its ability to function as God originally intended.

ἔλεος [eleos] (1656) "mercy, gracious faithfulness"

The Greek translation of the Old Testament typically chose eleos to translate the profoundly significant Hebrew term chesed. Chesed describes the act of a superior blessing an inferior in keeping with their relationship, such as when a monarch protects or rewards a subject, or when a parent provides for a child. Chesed is a freely chosen deed of grace, motivated by love. In the New Testament, eleos is the attitude in believers that mimics God's disposition toward sinners. For Paul, the eleos of God is the opposite of His wrath.

ὑπόλειμμα [hypoleimma] (5275) "remnant, remains, what is left over"

In secular Greek, the term referred to food scraps after a meal or the remains of burned wood. When Old Testament prophecy predicted a period of divine judgment, the hypoleimma were the Hebrew survivors who would carry on tradition and become the recipients of Abraham's covenant blessing. Whereas the rabbis of Jesus' time optimistically saw the Jewish remnant as a majority, Paul realistically thought of the remnant as residue.

μυστήριον [mystērion] (3466) "mystery, previously unrevealed secret"

The noun derives from a Greek verb myō, "to mute," and generally refers to a secret. In pagan worship, "mysteries" are secret knowledge reserved for the few who are willing to sacrifice, perform complex rituals, or even suffer in devotion to a particular god. In Hebrew and Christian literature, however, a "mystery" is a divine truth that has been revealed to all of humanity for the first time. What was a secret is now common knowledge to all who choose to acknowledge it.

## Straight Talk about Predestination (Romans 9:1–33)

¹I am telling the truth in Christ, I am not lying, my conscience testifies with me in the Holy Spirit, ²that I have great sorrow and unceasing grief in my heart. ³For I could wish that I myself were accursed, *separated* from Christ for the sake of my brethren, my kinsmen according to the flesh, ⁴who

are Israelites, to whom belongs the adoption as sons, and the glory and the covenants and the giving of the Law and the *temple* service and the promises, [5]whose are the fathers, and from whom is the Christ according to the flesh, who is over all, God blessed forever. Amen.

[6]But *it is* not as though the word of God has failed. For they are not all Israel who are *descended* from Israel; [7]nor are they all children because they are Abraham's descendants, but: "through Isaac your descendants will be named." [8]That is, it is not the children of the flesh who are children of God, but the children of the promise are regarded as descendants. [9]For this is the word of promise: "At this time I will come, and Sarah shall have a son." [10]And not only this, but there was Rebekah also, when she had conceived twins by one man, our father Isaac; [11]for though *the twins* were not yet born and had not done anything good or bad, so that God's purpose according to *His* choice would stand, not because of works but because of Him who calls, [12]it was said to her, "The older will serve the younger." [13]Just as it is written, "Jacob I loved, but Esau I hated."

[14]What shall we say then? There is no injustice with God, is there? May it never be! [15]For He says to Moses, "I will have mercy on whom I have mercy, and I will have compassion on whom I have compassion." [16]So then it *does* not *depend* on the man who wills or the man who runs, but on God who has mercy. [17]For the Scripture says to Pharaoh, "For this very purpose I raised you up, to demonstrate My power in you, and that My name might be proclaimed throughout the whole earth." [18]So then He has mercy on whom He desires, and He hardens whom He desires.

[19]You will say to me then, "Why does He still find fault? For who resists His will?" [20]On the contrary, who are you, O man, who answers back to God? The thing molded will not say to the molder, "Why did you make me like this," will it? [21]Or does not the potter have a right over the clay, to make from the same lump one vessel for honorable use and another for common use? [22]What if God, although willing to demonstrate His wrath and to make His power known, endured with much patience vessels of wrath prepared for destruction? [23]And *He did* so to make known the riches of His glory upon vessels of mercy, which He prepared beforehand for glory, [24]*even* us, whom He also called, not from among Jews only, but also from among Gentiles. [25]As He says also in Hosea,

> "I will call those who were not My people, 'My people,'
> And her who was not beloved, 'beloved.' "
> [26] "And it shall be that in the place where it was said to them, 'you are not My people,'
> There they shall be called sons of the living God."

[27]Isaiah cries out concerning Israel, "Though the number of the sons of Israel be like the sand of the sea, it is the remnant that will be saved; [28]for

the Lord will execute His word on the earth, thoroughly and quickly." [29]And just as Isaiah foretold,

> "Unless the Lord of Sabaoth had left to us a posterity,
> We would have become like Sodom, and would have resembled Gomorrah."

[30]What shall we say then? That Gentiles, who did not pursue righteousness, attained righteousness, even the righteousness which is by faith; [31]but Israel, pursuing a law of righteousness, did not arrive at *that* law. [32]Why? Because *they did* not *pursue it* by faith, but as though *it were* by works. They stumbled over the stumbling stone, [33]just as it is written,

> "Behold, I lay in Zion a stone of stumbling and a rock of offense,
> And he who believes in Him will not be disappointed."

*Predestination.* Just the word appears intimidating. It is perhaps one of the most difficult concepts in all of Christian doctrine because it appears on the surface to rob humans of their most precious treasure: their autonomy. While the doctrine challenges our notions of self-determination, it is ultimately what separates Christians from humanists, who proclaim that the fate of the world is *ours* to decide. The past, they say, has been fired in the kiln of history and cannot be altered, but tomorrow is still soft and pliable clay, ready to be shaped by the hands of humanity. Individually and collectively, we—not an almighty figment of wishful thinking—will determine our own future. Put in today's terms, "It's all about us."

Today, I stand in the company of great theologians, preachers, teachers, missionaries, and evangelists to proclaim exactly the opposite. I join the ranks of reformers like William Tyndale, John Wycliffe, John Calvin, Huldrych Zwingli, John Huss, John Knox, and Martin Luther. I sing with the poets Isaac Watts and John Newton and preach with George Whitefield, Jonathan Edwards, and Charles Spurgeon. I respond to the call of pioneer missionary William Carey, who stirred his slumbering Calvinist generation to follow the command of Christ and make disciples of all nations. I place my theology alongside those of John Owen, A. H. Strong, William Shedd, Charles Hodge, B. B. Warfield, Lewis Sperry Chafer, John F. Walvoord, Donald Grey Barnhouse, and Ray Stedman. And I am numbered alongside my contemporaries, John Stott, R. C. Sproul, John Piper, John MacArthur, and J. I. Packer. Today I stand in a great company of sound biblical scholars to declare that God not only created humanity and directed our past, He has already shaped our future. In doing so, I also stand against what has come to be known as "open theism." "Our God is in the heavens; He does whatever He pleases" (Ps. 115:3).

Coming to terms with the doctrine of predestination requires a dramatic shift in our perspective. We emerge from the womb and progress through childhood viewing the universe with ourselves at the center. Then something wondrous happens at some point in the process of maturing—for most healthy adults, anyway. We suddenly realize that the world extends beyond the circle of our own horizon and that others see the same world from a different viewpoint. Soon, the universe no longer revolves around us and we accept that our little circle is but a very small part of a much greater reality.

The same is true of salvation!

We faithfully share God's "plan of salvation" with individuals—as we should—but we too often fail to appreciate that Christianity is not "all about us"; it's about *Him*. If we are to proclaim the complete gospel of Jesus Christ, we must recognize and embrace God's *master plan* of salvation. The Almighty Creator is fulfilling His own agenda for His universe, a plan that cannot be altered; therefore, those who have heard and accepted the "plan of salvation" have become a part of something much greater than themselves, even if they don't realize it.

Take a few moments now and reread Romans 8:28–39 in light of God's master plan of salvation.

---

We tend to claim those promises as individuals. While God does indeed love us personally and individually, note that Paul used the first-person *plural*, "we" and "us," throughout the passage. This does not promise that God will alter the universe to ensure the highest good of each individual. On the contrary, God's "plan of salvation" is a mighty river of destiny into which a believer plunges. This river of righteousness will eventually flood the world, washing away the old order to make room for the new. And when Jesus returns to set all things right, our belief in Him allows us to become a part of that new order.

Make no mistake; Paul's letter to the Romans is *not* about our salvation. His primary subject is the righteousness of God, of which our salvation is a part. The Lord is pursuing His own agenda, remember. It is to remove death from the throne of creation and give it to His Son so that the righteousness of God will rule all things. And He will do this whether anyone decides to join Him or not.

God's promises at the conclusion of chapter 8 raise some important questions, though. By the time of Paul's writing the church in Rome, the majority of Jews had rejected Jesus as their Messiah and, in growing numbers, were rejecting God's master plan of salvation. So, what about their destiny as a people? Were they not part of God's master plan centuries ago? Didn't God's promises to [Abraham,

Moses, Israel,] and David assure that the Jewish people would be saved? If He is not faithful to save His covenant people, what kind of assurance do we have as Gentile believers?

Paul takes this opportunity to address the thorny question of the Jews and their rejection of the gospel. But this is no mere parenthetical aside before resuming his main topic in chapter 12. In many ways, this is the apex of the gospel. While Romans 8:28–39 describes God's ultimate victory over evil, Romans 9:1–11:36 allows us a deeper glimpse into His nature. And the first attribute we see is His sovereignty.

## —9:1–5—

No one more than Paul wanted the Jews to accept Jesus as the Messiah and to receive the blessings of their covenant. He no doubt prayed for this often and with complete confidence that he prayed according to God's will. After all, it was certainly God's plan to fulfill His covenant with Abraham. The Hebrew people were to become God's prototypical nation, ruled by Him and blessed by Him as a living invitation to submit to Him and receive His grace through faith. But they failed. Even under the rule of David and Solomon, they never came close to claiming all the land that had been promised (Gen. 15:18–21). Paul longed for his Jewish brothers and sisters to be saved. If only the children of the old covenant could be *compelled* to embrace the new covenant.

But this is how *Paul* would run the world. He even went so far as to say he would instantly take their place in torment to see them saved (9:3).

Do you see the irony? It is intentional. Someone had already taken their place in torment. Yet they rejected their Messiah. And if they rejected the Son of God, why would they accept the same gift from a little evangelist from Tarsus? This led Paul to list seven advantages enjoyed by the Hebrew children of Abraham, none of which compelled the majority of Jews to see the truth.

*Israelites*—When God established His covenant with Abraham, He promised to bless generations of people without regard for merit. In other words, the descendants of Abraham would receive blessing and privileges simply because they were born of Hebrew parents—a privilege no one could possibly earn or even choose.

*Adoption as sons*—When God interceded for Israel and freed them from slavery in Egypt, He claimed them as His children (Ex. 4:22).

*The glory*—When God led Israel out of Egypt, He gave them a visible manifestation of His presence and protection to follow (Ex. 13:21–22; 14:19–20), and the other-worldly light of the *shekinah* remained above the Ark of the Covenant in the tabernacle and, later, the temple (Ex. 40:34–38).

*The covenants*—When God brought Israel to the border of Canaan, it was to fulfill His unconditional covenant with Abraham (Gen. 12:1–3; 15:1–21; 17:1–22). At the time, a remnant urged the majority to trust God, but the majority balked at the size and strength of the inhabitants. Consequently, the entire company had to wander in the wilderness until the unbelieving generation had passed away (Num. 13:25–33; 14:33–38). Forty years later, Israel claimed the first portion of their Promised Land in faith, at which time God established another covenant—this one conditioned upon their obedience (Deut. 28).

Later still, God established another unconditional covenant with King David, promising that only his descendants would hold legitimate claim to the throne of Israel (2 Sam. 7:12–16). And during one of Israel's darkest periods, the Lord promised to establish a "new covenant" (Jer. 31:31–34). Whether the covenant depended on human obedience (as in Sinai) or whether God acted unilaterally (as with Abraham), the blessing came to God's people, the Jews.

*The giving of the Law*—When God established Israel as a nation, He gave them a perpetual code of conduct that reflected His holy character (Deut. 5:1–22). The laws of other nations came and went with the whims of selfish kings. No other nation or race could claim the privilege of absolute truth as the basis for justice.

*The temple service*—When God gave His people a code of conduct, He also provided a means of restoring them when they inevitably failed to keep it (Ex. 25–30). He established the temple as a means for men and women to approach Him, and He entrusted its care to His covenant people.

*The promises*—When God chastised Israel, He also gave them hope: the promise of a Messiah, who would be the mediator of a new covenant (Jer. 31:31–34).

These seven advantages illustrate God's perpetual faithfulness compared to Israel's long history of stubborn rebellion. Were it not for a faithful minority within the nation at key moments in their history, Israel would have been lost entirely. Furthermore, this quick inventory of Israel's blessing and privilege underscores their lack of excuse for failing to believe. The unbelieving majority ignored the mountain of evidence before them and *chose* not to trust God, proving that their unbelief was a moral issue, not an intellectual one. Ironically, they turned their unique relationship with God into an idol—again mistaking the gift for the Giver—supposing their heritage would save them apart from faith.

Paul affirms that the promises given to the "fathers" are still available through Jesus Christ, who is their descendant in the physical sense. In other words, He is the true *Bar Mitzvah*, the true "Son of the Covenant." Whereas all others failed, He succeeded. He has claimed the covenant blessings due Israel and has made those blessings available to all who believe.

Having declared the will of *Paul*, the apostle sets out to declare the will of *God*. In this portion of his letter, which runs from verse 6 through the end of the chapter, there are four great truths regarding the doctrine of predestination:

Predestination begins with the sovereign choice of God (9:6–13).
Predestination upholds the perfect character of God (9:14–18).
Predestination shows us the mercy of God (9:19–22).
Predestination defends the fairness of God (9:23–33).

This is Paul's defense against the notion that God's redemptive plan has failed as a result of Israel's rejecting their Messiah and the new covenant. He begins by illustrating how God's perspective differs from that of humanity.

— 9:6–13 —

*Predestination begins with the sovereign choice of God.*

We are democratic by nature in that we contend that the majority rules. Most modern forms of government give power to the person who represents the majority opinion, who then sets policies and acts on their behalf to carry out "the will of the people." In a real sense, this representative defines his or her entire nation, including its dissenting minority. Not so with God. The true nation is defined by His sovereign choice, which may cut against the grain of human customs. To illustrate his point, Paul points to two pivotal moments in Israel's history.

You may have noticed that I have been careful to limit the covenants of God to the Hebrew descendants of Abraham. They do not apply to all of his descendants. First, Abraham had sons other than Isaac. He fathered Ishmael through Sarah's handmaid, Hagar (Gen 16), and after Sarah's death, took another wife, who bore him no less than six male children (Gen. 25:1–2). But God limited His covenant with Abraham to his offspring through Sarah alone (Gen. 17:18–21; 21:12). Why? Put bluntly, because God decided it would be this way. We can speculate as to why and point to several good reasons for His choice being the best course of action, but it really comes down to this: God sovereignly chose Isaac to be the bearer of the covenant.

Second, Isaac fathered more than one son; twins, in fact. The custom of the day was for the firstborn male to receive a double portion of the inheritance and to succeed his father as the patriarchal leader of the clan. In the case of Isaac's twins, Esau should have received the covenant blessing as the firstborn. Yet, before the twins were born, the Lord told their mother, "The older shall serve the younger"

(Gen. 25:23). This was no mere prediction. This was the sovereign choice of God that, contrary to custom, the younger boy would carry the covenant of Abraham.

Paul's illustration corrects two misconceptions about God's covenant with Abraham. First, one cannot claim its promises merely because he or she carries his DNA. Of the patriarch's many sons—no less than eight—only one could claim legitimate right to the blessing. Second, only one received the blessing by virtue of God's choice, not on the basis of merit and not by right of custom (which is the choice of men.)

Eventually, Jacob received the blessing instead of his older brother, Esau. Why? Again, because that's the way God chose it to be. Before either man had the capacity to choose right or wrong, the Lord elected Jacob, who was, by the way, an incredibly undeserving man. The very name Jacob means "one who displaces" or "one who usurps." He was a shameless schemer and deceiver, who left a number of angry enemies in his wake. Eventually, though, the Lord broke him of his old way and gave him a new name: Israel, "strives with God."

Adding a final validation to his point, Paul quotes in 9:13 the prophet Malachi:

> "I have loved you," says the LORD. But you say, "How have You loved us?" "*Was* not Esau Jacob's brother?" declares the LORD. "Yet I have loved Jacob; but I have hated Esau, and I have made his mountains a desolation and *appointed* his inheritance for the jackals of the wilderness." (Mal. 1:2–3)

## Does God Hate?

"Hate" is a powerful word. We are taught from childhood to avoid hatred at all costs and to obey the command of Christ to love everyone, including our enemies. So it's shocking to read the words of Malachi, who declared that God loved Jacob but hated Esau (Mal. 1:2–3). How can a God of love hate?

Let's begin by examining the Hebrew terms. The Old Testament uses two words that can be translated "hate": *sane* (sah-NAY) and *ma'as* (ma-AS); they differ only slightly in meaning. In fact, Old Testament writers sometimes used them interchangeably. For example, the prophet Amos placed them side-by-side to express God's disgust with Israelite worship, saying, "I *hate*, I *despise* your religious feasts; I cannot stand your assemblies" (Amos 5:21 NIV, emphasis mine).

While *sane* and *ma'as* can express intense emotional displeasure toward something, "hating" in ancient Near East cultures has more to do with one's priorities than with his or her emotions. For example, Esau "despised" his birthright when he made a freewill choice for a bowl of soup over his covenant blessing (Gen. 25:29–34). Esau didn't have intense negative emotions about his birthright—he certainly didn't "hate" it as we would use the term; in fact, he fought hard to regain what he had lost and was inconsolable when he failed.

In another example, Genesis 29 tells the story of Jacob's two wives and how he "loved" Rachel and "hated" her sister, Leah. Again, the term indicates Jacob's choice to favor one over the other. He wasn't repulsed by Leah. After all, he did conceive at least seven children with her!

Furthermore, in the New Testament, Jesus required His followers to "hate" their money, their families, and even their own lives (Matt. 6:24; Luke 14:26; John 12:25). Obviously, He wasn't instructing His disciples to treat others cruelly. The issue at hand was *priority*, choosing discipleship over all other things and choosing Christ over all other relationships.

It would be convenient to stop here and pretend the uglier side of "hate" didn't exist; however, we cannot ignore the only other significant use of "hate" in the Old Testament. In Genesis 37, "hate" describes the obsessive loathing of Joseph's older brothers. They plotted to kill him, but when a caravan of slave traders happened to pass by, they decided to sell him off instead. Clearly the term "hate" can describe either meaning, dispassionate choice or passionate loathing. So where does that leave us with Malachi 1:2–3?

The book of Malachi was a warning to that nation of Judah, who profaned the temple by offering substandard sacrifices and keeping the best livestock for themselves. He accused the priests of "despising" their covenant blessing, much like Esau "despised" his birthright. By recalling the story of Jacob (whose name was changed to Israel) and Esau (whose descendants formed the nation of Edom), the prophet drew a clear parallel:

| Jacob *prized* the covenant. | Esau *despised* the covenant. |
|---|---|
| God promised to rescue Israel (Deut. 4:29–31; 30:1–10). | God vowed to condemn Edom (Jer. 49:7–22; Ezek. 35). |

By the time of Malachi, both prophecies had been fulfilled. God had restored a faithful remnant of Israel to the Promised Land; however, they could not afford to become smug. By despising their covenant blessing, the Israelites ran the risk of suffering Esau's fate. In other words, "Take heed, Israel. Esau despised his birthright and Edom incurred the judicial abandonment of God. What do you think will happen if you despise your birthright?"

God's "hatred" is a double-edged sword. While it is indeed filled with emotion, it is not motivated by it. Like His wrath, His act of choosing one over another ("hating") is absolutely righteous and utterly just.

— **9:14–18** —

*Predestination upholds the perfect character of God.*

There are certain jobs for which I'm not suited. For instance, I would not make a good surgeon. First, I hate the sight of blood. Second, I too easily empathize with someone else's pain, so I would not have the necessary objectivity. Third, I did not pursue training in that field. So, however much I love my wife, I must entrust her to the care of a qualified surgeon if she ever needs surgery. I cannot do the job.

If the job of "Supreme Judge of the Universe" ever opened, here are the qualifications necessary. The right applicant must be omnipotent (all-powerful), omniscient (all-knowing), omnipresent (present everywhere at once), immutable (unchanging), eternal (above and beyond the bounds of time), self-existent (needing nothing), holy (the very definition of "good"), and just (absolutely right in all decisions). Not only is all humanity woefully unqualified for the position, we have no basis to second-guess the One who is.

Furthermore, we have no right to govern that which does not belong to us. For example, I cannot walk into the home of another man or woman and change the rules of that household. I don't own the place. Similarly, we do not own this world. We have been given the privilege of living in God's world and we can leave it anytime we choose, but only He has the right to govern His creation. Nevertheless, because of His qualifications, we can trust God's judgment.

Paul illustrates the Lord's right to rule over creation with the story of Moses and his confrontation with the sovereign ruler of Egypt. God's statement to Moses establishes a universal principle: Because grace is a gift, the giver has the right to offer it or withhold it at will. Therefore, mercy does not depend upon:

"the man who wills." Mercy can only be the choice of the giver, never the receiver.

or,

"the man who runs." Mercy is a gift; therefore it cannot be earned through effort.

The case of Moses and Pharaoh is a study in contrasts. The men began their lives the same. Both were reared in the pagan household of the Egyptian sovereign. Both received an education in the pagan schools of idolatrous priests. Both enjoyed a standard of living that far exceeded the mud pit existence of slaves. Both were heir to royal privileges. However, their paths diverged when God intervened in the life of one. Though Moses was guilty of murder, the Lord hid him on the other side of nowhere and devoted the next forty years to transforming his character.

Pharaoh, on the other hand, continued his privileged existence in the palace of Egypt and eventually became its sovereign. He did not endure the humiliation of becoming a fugitive; he did not endure the hardscrabble existence of an itinerant shepherd in a wilderness. He spent forty years living as he had before, as a pagan.

When the proper time arrived for the next stage in God's redemptive plan, He brought the two men face to face. Moses demanded the release of the Israelites, but Pharaoh refused, claiming the right of sovereignty over them. At that moment, the Lord could have batted an eyelash and reduced Egypt to a piece of lint on the page of history. Instead, He responded with a series of afflictions, which gradually increased in severity. His stated purpose: "To show you My power and in order to proclaim My name through all the earth" (Ex. 9:16).

Pharaoh dedicated *himself* to evil in direct opposition to God's redemptive plan. This was Pharaoh's personal choice. He chose evil; God did not choose it for him. However, the Lord did "harden" him — that is, solidified his resolve to pursue the evil deeply embedded in his heart. And the Lord was completely righteous in doing so. He does not owe grace to anyone. Therefore, He was no less just to allow Pharaoh to remain in his chosen evil and to suffer the consequences of it. Moreover, the Lord turned Pharaoh's evil into an opportunity to assert His own sovereign claim over the Israelites and to demonstrate His power to triumph over evil.

Paul recounts the divergent paths taken by Moses and Pharaoh to vindicate the righteous character of God. Their story does this in two ways. First, it demonstrates God's grace in that he intervened in the life of both men, giving both ample opportunity to humble themselves and accept His right of sovereignty. Second, it demonstrates God's justice, in that He responded to each man according to his own choice. The bottom line: God alone deserves credit for salvation; the condemned person is solely culpable for his or her punishment.

## —9:19–22—

*Predestination shows us the mercy of God.*

Paul anticipated a common objection to the doctrine of predestination. If God "hardens" someone as He hardened Pharaoh, how can that person be justly condemned? The apostle responds with a common Old Testament illustration (Isa. 29:16; 45:9; 64:8; Jer. 18:6) to clarify two points.

First, *because God is the sovereign Creator, He has the right to do with His creation whatever He chooses* (9:19–21). Again, God does not answer to humanity any more than He must answer to flowers. The very fact that we were given life is grace. That we were given a limited amount of autonomy to choose our own fate is grace upon grace. And having rebelled, both as a race and as individuals, to be given hope of redemption is overwhelming, super-abundant grace!

Having confirmed God's sovereign right to do with His creation as He pleases, Paul continues his line of reasoning with an "if . . . then" statement (9:22–23) — where the "if" is assumed to be true. And it supports his second point: *We lost our right to complain about poor treatment when we chose to rebel; therefore, anything we receive other than immediate death is mercy.*

People in need of mercy don't have "rights." In the case of Pharaoh, the sovereign of Egypt was given time to enjoy privileges that the vast majority of his peers could barely dream of having. Grace. He was given no less than ten opportunities to repent of his sin. Grace upon grace. If he was extended no more grace than that, he was still much better off than he deserved.

Don't be confused or misled by the phrase "vessels of wrath prepared for destruction" (9:22). Many grammarians understand the Greek verb translated "prepared" as being in "the middle voice," which indicates that the subject of the verb acts upon itself (reflexive action). So, it should be translated "vessels of wrath fitted *by themselves* for destruction" (italics mine). Although God has the right to mold clay into anything He chooses, He allowed Pharaoh to choose his own shape; the Lord merely hardened him. And, out of grace, He did it gradually instead of immediately.

All of humanity deserves immediate termination, so the fact that we live proves that God has *not* exercised justice. He has acted upon His sovereign right to withhold justice for a time. Rather than complaining that some will not be saved, we should see the glass more than half full and thank God that *anyone* will be saved! Rather than complaining that He exercised His sovereign right to harden some in the sinful shapes *they* have chosen, we should be thankful that He exercised his sovereign right to grant mercy to anyone ... including *us* of all people!

At this point, let me add another clarification. Paul doesn't state this point here, but it's clearly implied. God does not compel anyone to sin (see James 1:13–16). Furthermore, God does not entice or encourage anyone's sin. In the case of Pharaoh, which is probably typical of everyone God hardens, a rebellious heart was "given over" or judicially abandoned to the sin it lusted for.

— **9:23–33** —

*Predestination defends the fairness of God.*

Verses 23–24 answer the question implied by verse 22: Why does the Lord "endure with much patience the vessels who had fitted themselves for destruction"? In other words, what is the point of allowing those who are destined for destruction to continue living? Two reasons.

First, God exists outside of time while we must progress through it. Those who are elected to receive mercy and are destined for glory will emerge from the womb lost and enslaved to sin. They will exist for some time that way before receiving grace and becoming transformed by the Holy Spirit. The Lord has determined to allow that process to unfold through time for our sake. All creation is allowed to

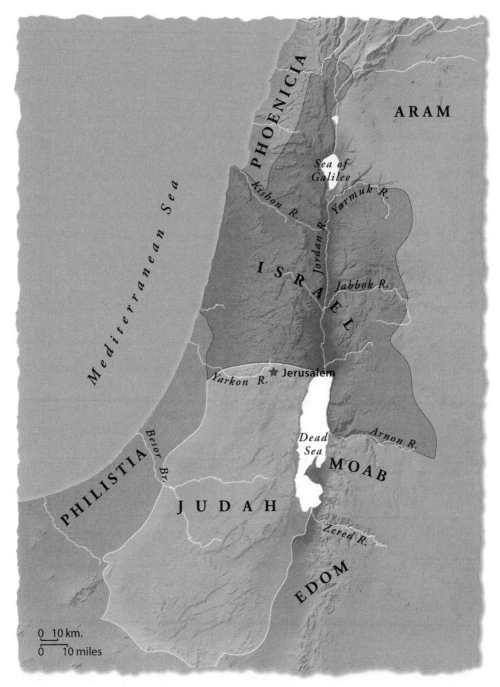

After Solomon died, civil war divided the Promised Land between two continuously warring nations: the northern kingdom of Israel and the southern kingdom of Judah. David's descendants ruled over Judah, while Israel saw the rise and fall of several illegitimate dynasties.

see the process of mercy given to unworthy vessels, and their transformation glorifies God.

Second, the Lord allows the progress of time within creation to separate the elect from the nonelect. God knows who has been elected to receive mercy and who has not, but we don't. He sees and judges the inner hearts of men and women, while we see and judge only the exterior. Someone who appears evil to us may in fact be a "vessel of mercy" yet to be transformed. For example, Paul was a murderer and a persecutor of Christians before his conversion (Acts 7:58; 8:1; 9:1–2; 22:3–5). After Christ confronted him, he gave glory to God, as when he wrote to the Ephesians, "To me, the very least of all saints, this grace was given, to preach to the Gentiles the unfathomable riches of Christ" (Eph. 3:8).

Beginning in verse 25, Paul returns to the question of the Jews by recalling the words of Hosea and Isaiah. These two Old Testament prophets tell a tale of two vessels: Israel, a "vessel of wrath," and Judah, "a vessel of mercy." Two stories of divine election that ended very differently.

Hosea lived and wrote long after the realm ruled by David and Solomon had been divided into the northern kingdom of Israel and the southern kingdom of Judah. Israel had a long history of idolatry and unfaithfulness, and despite generations of warning, never repented. Not long after rejecting Hosea's oracle, the Assyrian Empire began a series of invasions, finally wiping out the last of Israel in 722 BC. The invaders deported most of the inhabitants and transplanted people from other nations into Israel, encouraged intermarriage, and within a generation had successfully bred the remaining citizens out of existence. Except for a faithful remnant, the southern kingdom of Judah was all that remained of the Hebrew people.

Isaiah, a contemporary of Hosea, prophesied in the southern kingdom of Judah, which could claim a handful of faithful kings throughout their history. They heeded Isaiah's warning for a time and survived the Assyrian siege of Jerusalem. But after one generation, they too fell headlong into rebellion against the Lord. In 586 BC, Nebuchadnezzar defeated Judah and carried the best and brightest Jews away to serve him in Babylon.

After decades of captivity, the Promised Land had been purged of faithless Hebrew kings. Then the Lord gathered a remnant of His covenant people and returned them to start again, just as Hosea and Isaiah had foretold. The rebellious Hebrews God had called "not-my-people" were redeemed from captivity and renamed "my people."

As we examine this tale of two vessels, we see God repeatedly warning both Israel and Judah over a period of centuries. Both failed to heed His warnings and then suffered grave consequences. He was fair to both in that He pursued them with equal passion. The offer of salvation in response to repentance was the same for both. And the consequences for continued disobedience was identical, deportation and exile, just as He had warned (Deut. 28:15–68). However, He exercised His prerogative as the sovereign ruler over all creation and extended mercy to one: Judah. He preserved a remnant in order to fulfill His unconditional promises to both Abraham and David.

Paul extended the application of these Old Testament prophecies. The small percentage of Hosea's "not-my-people" who again became "my people" were Hebrews. And Isaiah's "remnant" were Jews who returned with Ezra and Nehemiah to rebuild the nation. Nevertheless, Paul saw the redemption of Gentiles as deeper fulfillment of those prophecies.

I love how God always exceeds expectations!

## Application

### *Going to Extremes*

In Romans 8:28–39, Paul assures his readers that despite our feelings to the contrary, the salvation of believers is secure—not because we are faithful, but because God is faithful. This, of course, begs the question: "So if God is faithful to preserve His elect, what about nonbelieving Jews? God's unconditional covenant with Abraham's descendants appears to be in jeopardy." Paul's response (9:1–11:36) begins with a defense of God's character. He does this by explaining the doctrine of predestination, which establishes four truths:

- Predestination begins with the sovereign choice of God (9:6–13).
- Predestination upholds the perfect character of God (9:14–18).
- Predestination shows us the mercy of God (9:19–22).
- Predestination defends the fairness of God (9:23–33).

Paul's teaching can be boiled down to the following couplet:

> God is faithful to save His chosen remnant;
> the condemned have condemned themselves.

We are wise to allow the couplet to stand on its own without succumbing to the temptation to resolve any perceived contradictions. Unfortunately, some cannot leave well enough alone and have taken the doctrine of predestination to one of two extremes.

The first, and most common, is to say that salvation is *entirely* a "freewill choice" made by an individual. While this sounds reasonable on the surface, the implications are clearly unbiblical. This extreme:

- places the burden of salvation squarely on the shoulders of the individual
- denies or minimizes the depravity of the human heart
- suggests that one can lose his or her salvation, either by choice or by sinning
- invariably leads to legalism (overemphasis on keeping laws to retain salvation)

The second extreme is to say that humanity plays no part at all in salvation or condemnation. Many go to this extreme to uphold the sovereignty of God and to avoid giving any glory to an individual for his or her salvation. While this is a noble end — one I appreciate — it nevertheless leads to equally unbiblical conclusions. This extreme:

- places the liability for an individual's condemnation entirely on God
- leads to the conclusion that God is culpable for evil
- suggests that humanity has no stake at all in God's plan to redeem the world
- invariably leads to fatalism and paralysis (an underemphasis on human responsibility)

History is replete with examples of people who have taken this issue to one extreme or another, and evangelism has suffered as a result. Those who emphasize God's sovereignty and neglect human responsibility conclude that those predestined to believe will come to Christ whether Christians proclaim the good news or not. Foreign evangelism remained idle for decades until William Carey, a Calvinist, took his brothers by the theological lapels and shook some sense into them.

Those who emphasize the responsibility of humanity and ignore God's sovereign choosing adopt every means of manipulation imaginable to coerce individuals into trusting Christ. Now we have entire denominations unwittingly proclaiming, "God helps those who help themselves." They add deeds to grace and saddle members with the responsibility to preserve their justification.

As an intern under the tutelage of Ray Stedman at Peninsula Bible Church, I served alongside a fellow intern. If the man cleared his throat, it was because God led him to clear his throat. If he spit, God led him to spit. If he belched, God led him to belch. And if he sinned, somehow God was even in that!

I, by contrast, was more Wesleyan. Living honorably and obediently was all about what I do. So I ran on the spiritual treadmill like a dutiful Christian, certain that

I could become more and more Spirit-minded by my efforts. And since that other intern lived with us the entire summer, oh, how we argued. Cynthia finally asked, "Can we please have supper rather than solve the mysteries of the universe?"

Eventually my dear friend balanced out and Ray helped me dig deeper into the Scriptures to find the right perspective. He got my attention by asking a surprising question. "Chuck, what are you so afraid of? Why are you so afraid of the doctrine of God's sovereignty?"

I blinked, looked out the window, down at my feet, and then back into Ray's eyes. "I'm afraid I'll lose my zeal for the lost. I'm afraid that if I really do believe this, I'll become passive as a minister; I'm afraid I will leave everything to God to sort out the elect and will do nothing."

Ray said, "You need to remember Spurgeon, the sovereign grace Baptist, who said, 'If God had painted a stripe down the back of the elect, I'd spend my days walking up and down the streets of London lifting up shirttails. But because He said, "Whosoever wills may come," I preach the gospel to everyone, and I rely on Him to lead those to faith who are His.'"

That was a great help. The longer I serve God in ministry, the more comfort I find in the doctrine of God's sovereign choosing. Rather than making me passive, confidence in God's complete control has freed me to proclaim the good news with even more zeal and greater freedom. And I am less burdened with whether I am "successful" or not. My responsibility is to be faithful; He is responsible for the results.

To *God* be the glory!

## Straight Talk about Responsibility (Romans 10:1–21)

---

¹Brethren, my heart's desire and my prayer to God for them is for *their* salvation. ²For I testify about them that they have a zeal for God, but not in accordance with knowledge. ³For not knowing about God's righteousness and seeking to establish their own, they did not subject themselves to the righteousness of God. ⁴For Christ is the end of the law for righteousness to everyone who believes.

⁵For Moses writes that the man who practices the righteousness which is based on law shall live by that righteousness. ⁶But the righteousness based on faith speaks as follows: "Do not say in your heart, 'Who will ascend into heaven?' (that is, to bring Christ down), ⁷or 'Who will descend into the abyss?' (that is, to bring Christ up from the dead)." ⁸But what does it say? "The word is near you, in your mouth and in your heart" — that is,

the word of faith which we are preaching, ⁹that if you confess with your mouth Jesus *as* Lord, and believe in your heart that God raised Him from the dead, you will be saved; ¹⁰for with the heart a person believes, resulting in righteousness, and with the mouth he confesses, resulting in salvation. ¹¹For the Scripture says, "Whoever believes in Him will not be disappointed." ¹²For there is no distinction between Jew and Greek; for the same *Lord* is Lord of all, abounding in riches for all who call on Him; ¹³for "Whoever will call on the name of the Lord will be saved."

¹⁴How then will they call on Him in whom they have not believed? How will they believe in Him whom they have not heard? And how will they hear without a preacher? ¹⁵How will they preach unless they are sent? Just as it is written, "How beautiful are the feet of those who bring good news of good things!"

¹⁶However, they did not all heed the good news; for Isaiah says, "Lord, who has believed our report?" ¹⁷So faith comes from hearing, and hearing by the word of Christ.

¹⁸But I say, surely they have never heard, have they? Indeed they have;

> "Their voice has gone out into all the earth,
> And their words to the ends of the world."

¹⁹But I say, surely Israel did not know, did they? First Moses says,

> "I will make you jealous by that which is not a nation,
> By a nation without understanding will I anger you."

²⁰And Isaiah is very bold and says,

> "I was found by those who did not seek Me,
> I became manifest to those who did not ask for Me."

²¹But as for Israel He says, "All the day long I have stretched out My hands to a disobedient and obstinate people."

---

For centuries, philosophers and scientists argued over the nature of light. Some claimed that light behaves like a wave traveling through space, much like sound. Others disagreed, stating that light is a stream of tiny particles emanating from its source. Unfortunately, experimentation didn't help. When tested as a wave, light proves to be a wave. When tested as a particle, light proves to be a particle. And as people who understand such things explain it to me, one experiment should disprove the other. Yet, experiments don't lie.

The debate divided the world's most brilliant minds into opposing camps, each experimenting, calculating, theorizing, and writing to prove the other wrong. Then, in 1905, a scholastic undesirable—a relative unknown man who worked as a patent examiner during the day and spent his nights unraveling great mysteries—published an article in Germany's leading physics journal that would change everything. Albert Einstein put forward the idea that light is both, a wave *and* a particle. His theory made no sense at all, yet his calculations satisfactorily answered every objection.

As scientific laymen, we can barely appreciate the effect his idea had on the world. His theory, which eventually won him a Nobel Prize, defies the laws of physics as we understand them. This "dual nature of light" should not be possible. Yet, somehow, in a dimension beyond our intellectual capacity, the mystery of light is as simple as 2 + 2.

The world of theology has its unsolvable puzzles as well. How can God be one and three, yet One? We really cannot comprehend it. Nevertheless, the Bible clearly presents Him as a tri-unity. It is a paradox that threatened to divide the Christian world soon after the apostles died simply because many teachers preferred a deity they could comprehend. Many of those early heresies exist now as cults, which cleverly disguise themselves to appear authentically Christian.

Another paradox has been described as "the sovereignty of God versus the free will of humanity." Theologians past and present have been guilty of bending one to serve the other, which inevitably leads to nonbiblical belief and practice. For example, the Calvinist Baptists of eighteenth-century England believed that evangelism presumed to interfere with God's sovereign predestination. When a young William Carey suggested that missionaries be sent to foreign lands in obedience to the command of Christ in Matthew 28:16–20, an older minister scolded, "Sit down, young man. You are an enthusiast! When God pleases to convert the heathen, He will do it without consulting you or me!"[2]

On the other extreme, teachers of "free will" believe that salvation is entirely in the hands of each person—hands that may grow weary clinging to Christ, lose their grip, and allow the believer to fall away into unbelief. A person may or may not be declared righteous by faith at any given moment and may either plunge into hell or fly up to heaven, depending, of course, upon his or her mental and spiritual state at the time of death. People in these sects continually struggle with fear and doubt, which inevitably lead to works-based religion—the very opposite of salvation *by grace alone, through faith alone, in Christ alone!*

So how do we reconcile these great truths—the sovereignty of God and the free will of humanity? According to J. I. Packer, someone put that question to the great Calvinist preacher C. H. Spurgeon. "I wouldn't try," he replied; "I never reconcile friends."[3] What a sensible approach! Neither position ceases to be true simply because we cannot accept the paradox.

In Romans 9, Paul has confirmed that salvation is the work of God. He has elected some and He has "hardened" others. Naturally, this doctrine of election or predestination prompted a reasonable question, "How can God justly condemn those who did not choose to believe if their choosing was not the will of God?" (my paraphrase of 9:19). After defending the Lord's absolute sovereignty, upholding His perfect righteousness, showing us His mercy, and defending His fairness, Paul appropriately turns his attention to the responsibility of humanity.

Putting chapters 9 and 10 together, we see two sides of this issue. Truth be told, we must uphold each without diminishing the other.

Side A: God rejects rebellious people because they have rejected Him (Matt. 10:33; 21:42–44; John 15:22–24; Rom. 1:28–32).

Side B: We love God because God first loved us (Rom. 5:8; 8:28–30; 1 John 4:10).

As the apostle confronts humanity with the truth of the gospel, he closes off four possible routes of escape.

The gospel is available; therefore, those who hear are accountable (10:8–10).

The gospel is universal; therefore, no one is exempt (10:11–15).

The gospel is plain; therefore, the unsaved are responsible (10:16–20).

God is faithful and immutable; therefore, the crisis of responsibility remains (10:21).

## —10:1–4—

As Paul continues his explanation of the Jews' relationship with the Lord, he again expresses his passionate desire for his kindred nation to embrace the gospel. Far from condemning or criticizing his fellow Jews, Paul weeps for them. He is heartbroken. He remembers the fellow students with whom he traveled and studied when he left Tarsus to learn under the tutelage of Gamaliel and other rabbis. He remembers former friends and fellow Pharisees, all pursuing the wrong objective with zeal, determination, and sincerity. Instead of embracing their Messiah, they passionately and sincerely pursued a righteousness of their own making, supposing it would be enough to please God.

Paul knows from his own experience the futility of sincere zeal without correct knowledge (Acts 22:3; Gal. 1:14). In the case of Paul's kindred Jews, they have failed to understand both the character of their God and the manner in which to please Him. Rather than submit themselves to the righteousness of God and allow it to rule them from within, they try to bend it to achieve their own ends.

How often I have discovered the same tendency in Christian churches! And, from what I have observed, there are two primary reasons churches lose their way. First, ignorance. They don't know the Scriptures and they don't know how to form their basic beliefs around the Bible. Consequently, they pursue what most would consider good goals—food, clothing, and shelter for the poor; peace for the world; the end of disease—supposing that God will be pleased by their earnest effort.

Second, churches can become stubborn, so set in their ways they unconsciously serve their own traditions and fail to heed the commands of Scripture. When a church cannot break out of the mold of its own customs, it has begun to serve itself rather than the Lord. Preserving itself becomes the top priority instead of advancing God's kingdom.

The tradition of the Hebrews had long ago turned from its original purpose and had become a tragic perversion. The Law of Moses was never intended to become the means by which people obtain the righteousness of God. On the contrary, "Christ is the *telos* of the law." *Telos* has a wide range of meanings, including "achievement; fulfillment, completion, perfection; execution, termination." Most scholars have settled on "termination." Indeed, Jesus brought an end to the Law.

While I see their point—Jesus ended the old system and brought about the new covenant—I am not satisfied. *All* of those English terms are correct in their own right, but they are best taken together. Jesus did not abolish the Law; He fulfilled it. People no longer pursue the Law as an expression of the faith they place in God; they come directly to God in and through the person of His Son, Jesus Christ.

—**10:5**—

Paul clarifies, again, the role of the Law in God's plan to bring His righteousness to the world. God revealed His Law through Moses as an expression of His righteous character. It was to confront humankind, saying in effect, "Here is the standard of righteousness I require; for you to be declared righteous enough to escape the consequences of sin, eternal torment, you must keep every letter." Thus, salvation by works is a *theoretical* possibility. However, like leaping high enough to enter heaven, it's a *practical* impossibility. No fallen human can achieve it. The only proper response to the Law is to cry out in humility, "Who can possibly be declared righteous this way? Certainly not me!" Jesus, then, becomes the "end of the law" for those who place their faith in Him.

- Jesus achieved the demands of the Law, in that He kept it perfectly.
- Jesus fulfilled the intent of the Law, in that He pleased the Father with His obedience.
- Jesus completed the purpose of the Law, in that He fulfilled all of its requirements.

- Jesus executed the covenant of the Law, in that He claimed the rewards of obedience.
- Jesus perfected the requirements of the Law, in that He exceeded its expectations.
- Jesus terminated the need for the Law, in that He became the Word of God to humanity.

## —10:6-7—

The only response to these truths can be humble submission. To illustrate that righteousness through faith is not a new concept, Paul draws on the words of Moses in Deuteronomy 30:9–14. As the Israelites were about to enter the Promised Land, God explained again the great rewards of obedience and the dire consequences of rebellion, reminding them that He did not expect moral perfection from them. Rather, he wanted their devotion. He called them to "turn to the LORD your God with all your heart and soul" (30:10).

Perfection is not a reasonable expectation. Devotion, however, is a faith response that is very much within the reach of humanity. The Israelites during the time of Moses were given access to the righteousness of God through faith in God, and the same is true of us today. We are not expected to ascend to heaven to obtain anything; Christ has descended to bring us everything we need. Nor do we have to pay our penalty for sin; Christ paid that penalty for us and has risen again to give us life. The righteousness of God is received through faith, not our own merit. What each person chooses to do with these truths determines his or her destiny, which leads to Paul's fourfold defense of human responsibility.

## —10:8-10—

*The gospel is available; therefore, those who hear are accountable.* Ironically, Paul quotes a passage in Deuteronomy in which the Lord put two choices before His covenant people just as they were about to enter the Promised Land. He had set before them life and good, death and evil, and then challenged them to choose. The choice for obedience would bring blessing; the choice for disobedience would bring curses (Deut. 30:15–20). More than two thousand years later, Jesus confronted Israel with a similar choice: receive Him by faith and be declared righteous, or pursue righteousness by works and be condemned. Grace or guilt. Furthermore, through the testimony and preaching of believers like Paul, Israel was again confronted with a choice in the form of the gospel message: believe and "you will be saved."

Some have disparagingly called this truth "easy believism." They cannot accept a gospel of faith because it appears to let humanity off God's hook too easily. But there it is in ink on papyrus, preserved through the centuries by the faithfulness of Spirit-led martyrs and now available in a multitude of languages. "With the heart a person believes, resulting in righteousness, and with the mouth he [or she] confesses, resulting in salvation." As any who have believed will tell you, that kind of belief is uncomplicated, but it's anything but "easy."

It wasn't easy for Christ, who paid for our salvation with His death and resurrection. It wasn't easy for the apostles, who preserved this message and subsequently died preaching it. It wasn't easy for thousands of martyrs, who bore witness to this message through humiliation and torture before dying. It wasn't easy for the Reformers, who gave up everything to reclaim it from the apostate church in Rome. And it wasn't easy for the men and women who sacrificed their own comfort and safety to carry it to hostile places around the globe. Moreover, it isn't easy for naturally sinful people to believe this supernatural truth.

Nevertheless, the gospel message is available to all, it is free, and there are no restrictions. Availability results in accountability.

— 10:11–15 —

*The gospel is universal; therefore, no one is exempt.* Paul again quotes the Old Testament (10:11, 13), this time drawing on an illustration of Isaiah familiar to any mason worker (Isa. 28:16). The chief mason lays the first stone at the exact location of the building's corner, at exactly the right elevation. This cornerstone becomes the standard reference point. The correct position of every other stone will be judged accordingly. It's a picture of obligation and responsibility. The standard of righteousness is belief in Jesus Christ. Whoever believes in Him will be square, plumb, and level with the cornerstone. The standard applies to every stone in God's building, Jew and Gentile alike.

Furthermore, everyone is responsible to meet the standard of the gospel — belief — because the good news is intended for everyone. Some theologians object to this because responding in faith to the gospel appears too much like a good deed. By their reasoning, if people have the ability to believe in Christ of their own free will, then they can claim credit for their own salvation. Because we know that no one can be declared righteous except by the gracious act of God, it follows that his belief in Christ must not be freely and independently chosen, but compelled by the Holy Spirit. This doctrine (called "irresistible grace" by theologians) is the result of reasoning that sounds logical, but finds *no* direct support in the Bible.

If we continue this line of reasoning, you must conclude that only those who are compelled by the Holy Spirit have the ability to accept the gift of Christ's atonement. Therefore (these same theologians conclude), Christ died only for those who were predestined to believe … and no one else. This is known as the "doctrine of limited atonement." And this is nothing less than contrary to Scripture.

The riches of His grace abound to all who "call upon Him."

- "Whoever will call on the name of the Lord will be saved" (Rom. 10:13).
- "For God so loved the world, that He gave His only begotten Son, that whoever believes in Him shall not perish, but have eternal life" (John 3:16).
- "He Himself is the propitiation for our sins; and not for ours only, but also for those of the whole world" (1 John 2:2).
- "Jesus, because of the suffering of death [is] crowned with glory and honor, so that by the grace of God He might taste death for everyone" (Heb. 2:9).

Unquestionably, Christ died for *all*. The gift of His atonement is offered to *all*. It is available to *the whole world*.

I am especially intrigued by the apostle Peter's statement concerning false teachers in the church, people he equated with false prophets in the Old Testament. Note what he said of them:

> But false prophets also arose among the people, just as there will also be false teachers among you, who will secretly introduce destructive heresies, *even denying the Master who bought them*, bringing swift destruction upon themselves (2 Peter 2:1, emphasis mine).

I can personally contrive a dozen different ways to spin that passage to fit any theological system anyone cares to name. I've seen that passage turned in every conceivable direction. But the plain sense meaning remains the same: Some people who were guilty of teaching error in the church were destined for eternal torment because they were denying Jesus Christ, who had paid the price to redeem them. He paid for the sins of the whole world, including these lost teachers of false religion.

The truth is inescapable; all are accountable for their response to the good news.

### —10:16–20—

*The gospel is plain; therefore, the unsaved are responsible.* Paul is writing specifically of the Jews, who were in a unique position to hear the truth of God's Word. But hearing doesn't automatically result in believing. He returns again to the Old Testament and the prophet Isaiah, who asked the rhetorical question, "Who has believed our message? And to whom has the [power] of the LORD been revealed?"

(Isa. 53:1). The answer implied by the question is "Israel! So they have no excuse for not believing."

The apostle directs his readers' attention to Psalm 19:4, which celebrates the Lord's revelation of Himself in the splendor of creation. Theologians call this "general revelation." The psalm goes on to celebrate the Lord's supernatural revelation of Himself to the Hebrew people in the form of Scripture. This is called "special revelation." Both of these leave the Jews without excuse — even less than the Gentiles (Rom. 1:18–20).

If the Lord's revelation of the truth through creation and His giving of truth through the Scriptures weren't enough, He also made salvation available to Gentiles to shock His people out of their stupor. He played upon the selfishness of human nature to entice them to pursue what had been given to them first. Nevertheless, many who heard the good news rejected it.

## —10:21—

*God is faithful and immutable; therefore, the crisis of responsibility remains.* Our sovereign Creator does not change. His nature and His character are the same today as always, and nothing in the future will make Him become anything different. However, He has dealt with humanity differently in various stages of history. For instance, He no longer calls us to bring animal sacrifices to His priests at the door of a sanctuary. Instead, Christ became "the mediator of a new covenant" (Heb. 9:15), in which He became the sacrifice "once for all" (9:12) and remains our High Priest.

This is not to say that God changed the way of salvation — as some slanderously charge me with saying. Salvation is now as it has always been: by grace alone, through faith alone, in response to God. Jesus is the perfect revelation of God, His eternal Word in human flesh. Faith in Jesus Christ alone is the only way to be declared righteous and thereby receive the gift of eternal life.

So, while God never changes His nature or character, He does relate with humanity differently through time. The crisis of responsibility that confronted the Jews in Paul's day remains until now. The Lord continues to hold open the invitation to receive His grace through faith in Jesus Christ. To remind everyone, including his Jewish brothers and sisters, Paul quotes Isaiah 65:1–2, God's response to the repentance of the Jews after suffering in exile:

> "I permitted Myself to be sought by those who did not ask *for Me*;
> I permitted Myself to be found by those who did not seek Me.
> I said, 'Here am I, here am I,'
> To a nation which did not call on My name.

"I have spread out My hands all day long to a rebellious people,
Who walk *in* the way which is not good, following their own thoughts."

Paul freely quotes Isaiah for the same reason I might include the following line in a sermon on Galatians 2:3–5: "Give me liberty or give me death." Many Americans in the audience would immediately recognize Patrick Henry's call to arms in the American Revolution and the long struggle the colonists had to endure to achieve independence. But that brief allusion would be lost on those who aren't familiar with American history. Similarly, Jews would have quickly understood Paul's point in quoting Isaiah; Gentiles, however, living more than two millennia after these events, will need some historical context.

Having endured the awful consequences of their sin, a broken and humbled Israel lamented:

> But now, O LORD, You are our Father,
> We are the clay, and You our potter;
> And all of us are the work of Your hand.
> Do not be angry beyond measure, O LORD,
> Nor remember iniquity forever;
> Behold, look now, all of us are Your people.
> Your holy cities have become a wilderness,
> Zion has become a wilderness,
> Jerusalem a desolation.
> Our holy and beautiful house,
> Where our fathers praised You,
> Has been burned *by* fire;
> And all our precious things have become a ruin.
> Will You restrain Yourself at these things, O LORD?
> Will You keep silent and afflict us beyond measure? (Isa. 64:8–12)

The Lord responded to their plea with a guarantee to fulfill His promises to the Hebrew descendants of Abraham. However, the fulfillment would be only to a remnant. To make his case for responsibility and to explain the response of the Jews, Paul alludes to the text of Isaiah, whose oracle predicted that the majority would remain in their rebellion while a minority would claim the covenant blessings. Isaiah's message then called for the people of Israel to choose wisely because their destiny would remain their responsibility.

> Thus says the LORD,
> "As the new wine is found in the cluster,
> And one says, 'Do not destroy it, for there is benefit in it,'
> So I will act on behalf of My servants

In order not to destroy all of them.
"I will bring forth offspring from Jacob,
And an heir of My mountains from Judah;
Even My chosen ones shall inherit it,
And My servants will dwell there.
"Sharon will be a pasture land for flocks,
And the valley of Achor a resting place for herds,
For My people who seek Me.
"But you who forsake the LORD,
Who forget My holy mountain,
Who set a table for Fortune,
And who fill *cups* with mixed wine for Destiny,
I will destine you for the sword,
And all of you will bow down to the slaughter.
Because I called, but you did not answer;
I spoke, but you did not hear.
And you did evil in My sight
And chose that in which I did not delight." (Isa. 65:8–12)

As you examine both passages in Isaiah, take note of two facts. First, God's sovereignty and human responsibility exist in effortless harmony with one another. No reconciliation necessary! Neither Isaiah nor Paul tries to explain how both can be true despite the apparent logical conflict. Second, while God's nature and character do not change, He will not "spread out [His] hands all day long to a rebellious people" (Isa. 65:2) forever. The time for choosing will come to an end. It could be any moment.

When the Lord turns the page on this chapter in history, the time for final judgment will begin and the time for choosing will have ended. Should that occur at sunset today, would you be ready?

## Application

### *Finding Freedom in the Sovereign Will of God*

God is sovereign in the choosing of His people: Abraham out of all the Chaldeans; Isaac, not Ishmael; Jacob over Esau; a believing remnant out of a nonbelieving majority. Nevertheless, each person is responsible to respond to God's offer of grace and is blameworthy for refusing it. Those who suffer the penalty of eternal torment for sin will do so without excuse. The gospel is within reach of all people (10:8–10); no one is exempt from the offer of eternal life (10:11–15); receiving the gift requires no human effort (10:16–20), and this free gift of eternal life remains available (10:21).

God is sovereign; people are responsible. These two truths must be held simultaneously or evangelism suffers. The Lord's sovereignty gives me great comfort in two respects. First, I rest secure in the fact that my relationship with Him cannot be severed by my unfaithfulness. Inhibited? Yes. Grievous to both of us? Undoubtedly. But dissolved? Not a chance! That's because He has chosen me and will faithfully equip me to enjoy eternal life with Him.

Second, I rest secure in the fact that the salvation of others is His accomplishment, not mine. I can only imagine the unbearable pressure of holding the eternal destiny of another in my feeble hands. I would continually worry that a slip of the tongue, a poorly chosen word, a zig instead of a zag in my approach would push someone closer to the edge of damnation. I think I would be paralyzed by the awesome consequences of failure on my part and then fail to speak a word.

Because the sovereign control of God determines the destiny of another, I can boldly proclaim the truth without fear. I am not responsible for the salvation of people; however, my responsibilities are considerable—as are yours, if you are a believer. And those responsibilities are vital to the success of God's plan. While He does not need us, He has given us a genuine stake in His redeeming the world. He is omnipotent, but we have three fundamental tasks:

1. We must *care* enough for the souls of another to go out of our way, to leave our comfort zones, to lay aside our desires in order to proclaim the gospel where it would not otherwise be heard.
2. We must *share* the good news faithfully, freely, and often—preferably with competence, even better within the context of an obedient life.
3. We must *pray* that the gospel will penetrate guarded minds and then resonate in the hollows of empty souls. As we faithfully and competently offer the free gift of justification by grace alone, through faith alone, in Christ alone, we must submit their destinies to the loving care of their Creator. Pray that blind minds will see and deaf souls will hear.

I am frequently reminded of how our responsibility and God's sovereignty work together to accomplish this great enterprise called evangelism. A man once approached me, stuck out his hand, and said, "Chuck, I want you to know that I started listening to you on the radio years ago."

He shook my hand firmly, held his grip, and put another hand on my shoulder as he continued. "I had no idea what you looked like. I had no idea where you were. I didn't know you from Adam. I listened to your message and I thought, *Well, that sort of makes sense.* And it was completely different from what I'd ever believed. I listened a little further, tuned you in the next day, listened some more, and tuned you in again. And you know what?"

He released my hand and threw both arms out. "Come here! You're my spiritual father." Then he wrapped me in a crushing bear hug that nearly squeezed the life out me.

Why was he so happy? Because I cared, shared, and prayed. I didn't even know him. Now, he's a genuine son of God.

Thanks to the vision of a few people many years ago and the labors of many more today, I have the rare privilege of addressing unknown multitudes through the medium of radio and through other technological media. I never know from day to day who will hear the good news and then respond in faith. And, believe it or not, the same is true for you, even if you never stand behind a microphone or a pulpit a day in your life. Megawatts and local congregations will never compare to the measureless, supernatural power of the Holy Spirit to carry your faithful proclamation of the good news to ears that need to hear it.

By the sovereign will of God, let me urge you to care, share, and pray. Stay faithful. Be diligent. And may the rewards of your faithful diligence return to hug you too.

## The Jews: Forgotten or Set Aside? (Romans 11:1–14)

---

¹I say then, God has not rejected His people, has He? May it never be! For I too am an Israelite, a descendant of Abraham, of the tribe of Benjamin. ²God has not rejected His people whom He foreknew. Or do you not know what the Scripture says *in the passage* about Elijah, how he pleads with God against Israel? ³"Lord, they have killed Your prophets, they have torn down Your altars, and I alone am left, and they are seeking my life." ⁴But what is the divine response to him? "I have kept for Myself seven thousand men who have not bowed the knee to Baal." ⁵In the same way then, there has also come to be at the present time a remnant according to *God's* gracious choice. ⁶But if it is by grace, it is no longer on the basis of works, otherwise grace is no longer grace.

⁷What then? What Israel is seeking, it has not obtained, but those who were chosen obtained it, and the rest were hardened; ⁸just as it is written,

"God gave them a spirit of stupor,
Eyes to see not and ears to hear not,
Down to this very day."

⁹And David says,

> "Let their table become a snare and a trap,
> And a stumbling block and a retribution to them.
> ¹⁰ "Let their eyes be darkened to see not,
> And bend their backs forever."

¹¹I say then, they did not stumble so as to fall, did they? May it never be! But by their transgression salvation *has come* to the Gentiles, to make them jealous. ¹²Now if their transgression is riches for the world and their failure is riches for the Gentiles, how much more will their fulfillment be! ¹³But I am speaking to you who are Gentiles. Inasmuch then as I am an apostle of Gentiles, I magnify my ministry, ¹⁴if somehow I might move to jealousy my fellow countrymen and save some of them.

---

After forty-five years in pastoral ministry (and counting), two problems continue to challenge my confidence in the gospel: the moral pagan and the immoral Christian. The first, I admit, doesn't try my theology all that much. It makes sense to me that humanity, though lost, continues to bear God's image; so I should not be surprised to see glimmers of His glory peaking through the crusted layers of sin clinging to nonbelievers.

Christians, however, frequently tip my confidence in the gospel out of balance. More than once, I have built great confidence in someone I thought to be a rock-solid believer in Jesus Christ only to discover later that it was all an act. And, frankly, I find churches their favorite places to hide out. These people say the right things, quote the Bible expertly, lead others effectively, and some even preach and teach with conviction, but beneath this impressive Christian veneer there is *nothing*.

Glittering examples of hypocrisy. Morally hollow moralists. Living monuments to the attractiveness of sin — and its deceptive, deadly consequences. These moral train wrecks would be enough to send me sulking into retirement were it not for a precious few who return to Christ, broken, utterly empty of pride, finally at peace with their need for the Savior. Thank God I am not God! I would have lost my patience, crumpled them up like scrap paper, and tossed them into the flame. In such impatient moments, I call to mind one of the great psalms of grace. In it I read:

> The LORD is compassionate and gracious,
> Slow to anger and abounding in lovingkindness.
> He will not always strive *with us*,

# The Remnant

Throughout history, God has used various means of dividing the faithful from the unfaithful, the elect from non-elect. While theologians struggle to understand the interaction between God's sovereign choosing and humankind's self-determination, one truth remains clear:
God keeps His promises despite human failing.

In the end, only Jesus is 100% faithful; therefore, only those "in Christ" will persevere.

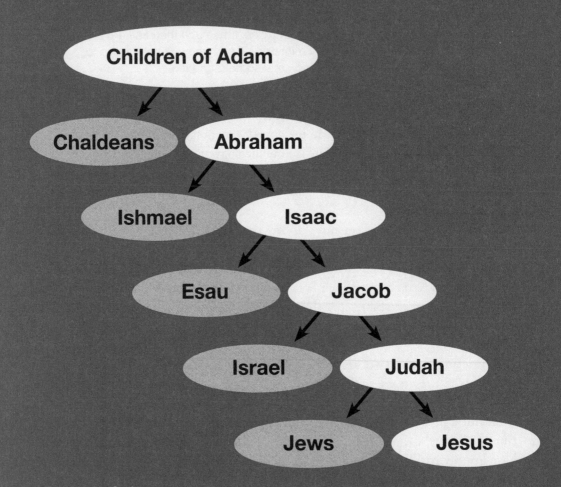

### The Remnant in Scripture

Gen. 45:7;  2 Kings 19:30–31; 21:14; 2 Chron. 34:9, 21; 36:20; Ezra 9:8–15; Neh. 1:1–2; Isa. 10:20–22; 11:11–16; 28:5; 37:31–32;  Jer. 6:9; 23:3; 31:7; 40:11–15; 42:2, 15, 19; 43:5; 44:7–14, 28; 50:20–26; Ezek. 9:8; 11:13; Amos 5:15; Mic. 2:12; 4:7; 5:7–8; 7:18; Zeph. 2:7, 9; 3:13; Hag. 1:12–14; 2:2;  Zech. 8:6–12

Nor will He keep *His anger* forever.
He has not dealt with us according to our sins,
Nor rewarded us according to our iniquities.
For as high as the heavens are above the earth,
So great is His lovingkindness toward those who fear Him.
As far as the east is from the west,
So far has He removed our transgressions from us.
Just as a father has compassion on *his* children,
So the LORD has compassion on those who fear Him.
For He Himself knows our frame;
He is mindful that we are *but* dust. (Ps. 103:8–14)

When I begin to lose confidence in the gospel because of the unpredictable nature of humanity, I do my best to remember that the remedy is obvious. Or it should be. I must turn my eyes from the horizontal and gaze vertically into the rock-solid faithfulness of my sovereign God, for whom there are no surprises and who assures me at such times that everything is under control. What wonderful reassurance!

When confronted with the problem of Jewish unbelief, Paul's readers need that same reassurance. The idea that God's chosen people would reject God and doom themselves to eternal punishment simply boggles the mind—not unlike the morally corrupt Christian—and it creates a crisis of assurance. "God has not rejected His people, has He?" (11:1). "[The Jews] did not stumble so as to fall, did they?" (11:11). The issue of Jewish unbelief has particular relevance for Gentile Christians. After all, Paul has assured us that victory for the believer is inevitable (8:28–39). But if God crumpled up the old covenant and tossed it into the flame, who's to say He won't do the same with His new covenant when it comes to us?

Paul answers both questions the same way: "May it never be!" He then points to the sky and offers us privileged, behind-the-scenes access to the Lord's grand plan for the Hebrew children of Abraham. But to appreciate it, we must first adjust our perspective to align with God's, which makes two distinctions:

Remnant versus majority (11:1–6)
Discipline versus punishment (11:7–14)

— **11:1** —

The concept of a remnant has always been a part of God's redemptive plan, so it should be no surprise to see it in effect today. Paul explains and illustrates the concept beginning with his own experience, which is the remarkable story of a man moving away from the plan of God. In another letter, he describes himself as "circumcised the eighth day, of the nation of Israel, of the tribe of Benjamin, a Hebrew of Hebrews; as to the Law, a Pharisee; as to zeal, a persecutor of the church; as to the righteousness which is in the Law, found blameless" (Phil. 3:5 – 6). His belief in the old covenant was so strong, he dedicated himself to the destruction of any who appeared to undermine it. His prime target? Christians. He once recalled his former zeal in a speech to a crowd of kindred Jews.

> "I am a Jew, born in Tarsus of Cilicia, but brought up in this city, educated under Gamaliel, strictly according to the law of our fathers, being zealous for God just as you all are today. I persecuted this Way to the death, binding and putting both men and women into prisons, as also the high priest and all the Council of the elders can testify. From them I also received letters to the brethren, and started off for Damascus in order to bring even those who were there to Jerusalem as prisoners to be punished." (Acts 22:3 – 5)

While on his way to Damascus, the risen Christ confronted the apostle, struck him blind with a laser-like light, knocked him from the beast on which he was riding, and there, on the side of the road, redeemed His wayward son of the covenant. Before long, Paul returned to the very people who funded his campaign of death against the new covenant and proclaimed the good news. He was a living example that God has not rejected His people. Paul is one man among a remnant, proof that God is faithful to preserve those He foreknew (Rom. 8:28 – 39).

## — 11:2 – 4 —

Paul undoubtedly felt like the Old Testament prophet Elijah, who stood against the godless king Ahab and his viciously scheming wife, Jezebel, and the apostle draws on that story. The Israelites had "exchanged the glory of the incorruptible God" (1:23) for an image of rain, the Canaanite storm god, Baal, and his consort, Asherah, the sea goddess. And they aggressively persecuted anyone who didn't follow their idolatrous lead. So the faithful prophet cursed the land to receive no rain for three and a half years, which humiliated Ahab, Jezebel, and the prophets of their imaginary gods.

Finally, Elijah called for a showdown. He challenged Ahab to summon "all Israel" and 850 prophets of Baal and Asherah to Mount Carmel for a demonstration of divine power. The prophets were challenged to build an altar to Baal and then summon him to supernaturally consume the sacrifice. But after a full day of gyrating, writhing, bloodletting, and wailing ... nothing. Meanwhile, the lone prophet mocked, "Hey, maybe he's busy relieving himself or out-of-town on vacation, or perhaps he's just napping. Scream a little louder!" (cf. 1 Kings 18:27). (This didn't win him any friends in the palace.)

Once it became clear the prophets of Baal had failed, Elijah prepared his altar. He placed the sacrifice on the wood and ordered men to douse the entire stack in water until everything was soaked and the water filled a trench surrounding the stones. At the time of the evening sacrifice, Elijah offered a short prayer in the hearing of everyone and then stood back. "Then the fire of the LORD fell and consumed the burnt offering and the wood and the stones and the dust, and licked up the water that was in the trench" (1 Kings 18:38). The prophet then ordered the citizens of Israel who had witnessed the challenge to put the minions of Baal to death. Finally, he prayed for rain, which came in a torrential downpour.

Ahab and Jezebel were humiliated. And when megalomaniacs are humiliated, they become more dangerous than ever. Before long, a messenger appeared on Elijah's threshold with a threat from Jezebel, promising to end his life. So he did what any reasonable person would do: he ran and hid.

In the solitude of his hideout, Elijah lamented, "I have been very zealous for the LORD, the God of hosts; for the sons of Israel have forsaken Your covenant, torn down Your altars and killed Your prophets with the sword. And I alone am left; and they seek my life, to take it away" (1 Kings 19:14). The Lord then promised to execute justice on the guilty. He announced that a series of events would thin the ranks of Israel but, after the dust settled, a remnant of seven thousand faithful Hebrews would remain (19:18).

This is a vivid example of God's bringing justice on the rebellious majority of Israelites while preserving a faithful minority. In the mind of God, the majority does not speak for the nation. The faithful remnant is what may be termed "the true Israel." These—not the idolatrous leadership or the majority of the people—will inherit the promises God made to Abraham.

—11:5–7—

Paul could have chosen any one of a dozen different anecdotes from Israel's history to illustrate God's preserving a remnant. So, how was Elijah's particular experience the same as Paul's and ours? Just like in Elijah's day, outward appearance would suggest that all of Israel has rejected God and is forever lost. The situation looks so desperate, we might be tempted to follow the example of Elijah, who asked the Lord to end his life since there was nothing left to hope for. Instead of bringing Elijah home and closing the book on Israel's future, God encouraged the dejected prophet in three ways.

First, the Lord assured Elijah that the majority opinion doesn't dictate Israel's future; God will see to that. Furthermore, the majority opinion doesn't represent the true Israel; God recognizes only the faithful, whether their number is great or small.

Second, the Lord gave Elijah work to do. He would use the prophet to set a series of events in motion that would eventually punish the apostate leaders and wipe the rebellious majority off the map of the Promised Land (1 Kings 19:15–17).

Third, the Lord announced that during the coming scourge, He would preserve no less than seven thousand Israelites who had silently refused to follow the majority into apostasy. They would become His remnant and reap the covenant promises.

Paul recalls the experience of Elijah because it is another potent story for Jewish readers; it perfectly illustrates God's choosing a remnant to carry His plan forward. The same reassurances the Lord gave Elijah can be applied today. Israel is not lost; a faithful minority of Jews has embraced their Messiah, and there is still hope for them because the Lord has empowered believers to proclaim the good news. But our greatest hope for Israel rests in the character of God. We know the Lord always fulfills His promises, so we know there will be an Israel to receive them. "In the same way" that God chose a remnant to preserve Israel in Elijah's day, He will choose a remnant of Jews to become the true Israel. Moreover, His sovereign choice will be motivated solely by grace, not by any merit on behalf of the chosen.

## —11:7–14—

Having identified the true Israel as a faithful remnant instead of the rebellious majority, Paul establishes a second helpful distinction: discipline versus punishment. The difference is subtle, yet profound. In the Bible, punishment is a matter of justice in which a person must suffer the consequences of sin: eternal separation from God in torment. It is permanent, punitive, and retributive. Discipline, on the other hand, is a matter of sanctification, in which all things—both good and bad—are utilized by God to develop a person's character. It is usually temporary and always constructive.

On one hand, there is no distinction between Jews and Gentiles. Some individuals are sovereignly chosen by God's grace; others are hardened in their sin. The blessings of salvation are the same for both, as are the curses of damnation. Ethnicity has nothing to do with the eternal destiny of an individual, for God is impartial. On the other hand, the Lord has special plans for the collective identity of the Jews. They play a crucial role in the final chapters of Earth's history; therefore, they receive unique attention from the Lord as a people.

At the present time, the whole Hebrew race is under discipline, including elect and lost Jews. Again, Paul draws upon Old Testament history to show that this era of discipline is consistent with God's relationship with Israel throughout history. The first quotation in verse 8 is part of Deuteronomy 29:4, from a speech given to Israel as they stood again on the border of the Promised Land after forty years of wandering in the wilderness.

> "Yet to this day the LORD has not given you a heart to know, nor eyes to see, nor ears to hear. I have led you forty years in the wilderness; your clothes have not worn out on you, and your sandal has not worn out on your foot. You have not eaten bread, nor have you drunk wine or strong drink, in order that you might know that I am the LORD your God." (Deut. 29:4–6)

You may remember that when Israel stood on this spot the first time, they sent twelve men as spies to check things out. They returned with a divided report. Two men encouraged Israel to trust God while the other ten urged an immediate retreat. When the Lord chastised Israel for its lack of faith, His discipline affected the entire group, including the remnant. Unfair as it seems, the period of discipline accomplished two great objectives. To the elect, it demonstrated God's faithful provision and continued care over His people, despite their failure to trust Him. To the lost, it provided ample opportunity to repent of their sin.

This forty-year period of discipline was a season of grace in which God put His plans on hold—at least from a human perspective. (The failure of the Israelites and the resulting "delay" in giving them the Promised Land was in His plan from the beginning.) He allowed this season of grace for the benefit of everyone, Jew and Gentile alike. We must not forget that during this forty-year intermission, while the Hebrew children of Abraham loitered on the outskirts of the Promised Land, the Gentiles living in Canaan had ample opportunity to learn of God's plan and get on board.

Imagine how differently history would have unfolded if the Canaanite kings had sent a delegation to greet the Hebrews. "We have heard how your God decimated the armies of Egypt with a flick of His fingernail and He obviously wants to give you this land. We will give it to you, free and clear, for the opportunity to learn of your God and serve Him. On behalf of the United Counsel of Canaanite Kings, 'Welcome home!'" In fact, one major city of Gentiles did exactly this (see Josh. 9)![4]

Paul's second Old Testament reference in verse 9 is part of a messianic psalm of lament.

> Reproach has broken my heart and I am so sick.
> And I looked for sympathy, but there was none,
> And for comforters, but I found none.

They also gave me gall for my food
And for my thirst they gave me vinegar to drink.
May their table before them become a snare;
And when they are in peace, *may it become* a trap.
May their eyes grow dim so that they cannot see,
And make their loins shake continually.
Pour out Your indignation on them,
And may Your burning anger overtake them. (Ps 69:20–24)

This was David's call for eternal punishment to fall on those who had rejected the Lord's anointed king. Paul alludes to David's poem to remind his readers that each period of discipline for the nation eventually came to an end, at which time faithful individuals were rewarded while faithless individuals received eternal punishment. Unfortunately, the lost Hebrews usually outnumbered the elect.

The same appears to be true today, which prompts a rhetorical question in verse 11: "[The Jews] did not stumble so as to fall, did they?" To which Paul answers, saying in effect: "May such a thing never occur!"

The Jews have not been permanently cast out; rather, they have been temporarily set aside. Just as the Lord did during the days of Moses and Joshua, He has suspended His plan for Israel to allow a season of grace. He did this for the benefit of everyone: the Israelites wandering and waiting to receive their covenant blessings and the Gentiles who presently enjoy what belongs to the Jews. In fact, Paul sees a double benefit in this arrangement.

First, this pause in God's plan allows the Gentiles ample opportunity to hear the good news and submit to His master plan (11:12). Israel's current wilderness wandering will eventually come to an end and God will resume His plan for the Hebrew children of Abraham. (Naturally, "pause" and "resume" is how we see it from our limited perspective. From the eternal perspective, nothing has been paused. All of this was God's plan from the beginning.)

The second benefit is ingenious. One of the great roles Gentiles have to play in life is to fully enjoy the new covenant, which is so enriching, life-changing, transforming, exciting, and fulfilling, that the Jew will become zealous to regain what he's missing (11:11, 14).

Imagine the best restaurant in the world opened in your town. They have everything you can think of, from gourmet creations, prime rib, and seafood all the way down to grilled cheese sandwiches and hamburgers. So you get a table for your party of six or seven and, because you're short on money, all you can afford is a hotdog and a basket of fries to share among you. At the table next to you, a party of fourteen has ordered the best, most expensive food on the menu. A team of servers emerges from the kitchen and begins covering the table with the most delectable dishes you can imagine. But as soon as the culinary parade has concluded, the host suddenly stands up and says to the owner, "Look, I'll pay for the meal, but nobody wants to eat this. This isn't really what we wanted," and they all walk out.

So, with a feast all prepared and paid for with no one to enjoy it, the owner glances your way and motions toward the abandoned table. He smiles as he announces, "There's nobody else in the restaurant and we're virtually closed. If you don't mind eating with some of the busboys, the waiter staff, and me, you can have what the other party rejected." Before he's finished the last sentence, your feet are under that other table and everyone is digging in.

Now, imagine in the meantime, the other party is halfway home when they say to one another, "Wait! What were we thinking? We're hungry … so, let's go back!" But by the time they arrive, the doors are locked and you're just enjoying the first course of that five-course meal. So, there they stand, noses pressed against the window, watching you, your friends, and the hired help enjoy what could have been *their* feast.

"Jealous" is not the best rendering of Paul's Greek. The verb he chose means "to provoke zeal." The party outside the restaurant would certainly envy you and your friends, but jealousy will not fill their stomachs. Zeal for food (being *really* hungry) will prompt them to do something about their situation.

That is Paul's greatest desire. While he has dedicated his life to proclaiming the gospel to Gentiles, he longs for his Jewish brothers and sisters to become zealous for the righteousness that comes by grace through faith in Jesus Christ. At present, they are zealous without knowledge (10:2), but it will not always be so. When this blindness is lifted, when this temporary time of being set aside ends, the Hebrew children of Abraham will be in their land under their own flag, exalting the Messiah, who will reign as King of kings and Lord of lords. Jesus Christ will be crowned as the supreme leader of the world in the city of Jerusalem, where He will guide the affairs of every country. Knowledge of the Lord will flood the earth. The righteousness of God will overshadow all other influences. The curses will be lifted. Crime, poverty, pollution, disease, and war will become a distant memory; ecological and sociological problems a thing of the past. Satan and his demons will be bound and gagged.

This is Israel's future. This is the fulfillment of their covenant promises, not a thin strip of land deeded to them by a bunch of diplomats. This is what they have to look forward to as a people. Victory! Abundance! Blessing beyond our comprehension! "God has not rejected His people, has He?" (11:1). "[The Jews] did not stumble so as to fall, did they?" (11:11).

May such a thing never occur!

## Application

### *The God of Hopeless Causes and Impossible Odds*

The Lord chose the Hebrew descendants of Abraham to be His covenant people. He made an unconditional promise to give them a vast stretch of land between the Mediterranean Sea and the Euphrates River, bordered on the south by Egypt and stretching as far north as Assyria (Gen. 13:14–15; 15:18; Deut. 1:7–8; Josh. 1:4). He promised to bless the Hebrew people and then bless the whole world through them.

But they rebelled. The Jews rejected His covenant in favor of manmade religion. Consequently, the rejection of the Jews would appear to place God's covenant in jeopardy. After all, how can a righteous God reward sin by blessing unrighteous people? Yet if God does not fulfill His promises, He can no longer be called righteous.

Some have tried to resolve this apparent conundrum by suggesting that the body of believers (also known as "the church") has replaced the nation of Israel and stands to inherit the blessings of Abraham's covenant. In other words, the "spiritual descendants of Abraham" will receive the covenant blessings instead of Abraham's physical descendants. To support this claim, one must no longer interpret the Bible in a straightforward manner. At the very least, the reader must mentally replace "Israel" with "church." Then, interpreting the book of Revelation (not to mention other sections of Scripture) becomes almost impossible.

Paul offers another, more sensible approach. First, he rejects the notion that the majority of rebellious Jews represent the true Israel (11:1–6). Unlike a democracy in which a majority vote defines the nation, a theocracy is defined by the will of God. Those who rebel—even if they can claim superior numbers—are not the true Israel. God calls the faithful few a "remnant."

Second, God has neither forgotten nor forsaken His covenant people. They have merely been set aside for a time. The Jews have not been punished; they are under discipline (11:7–14). And at some future date, the remnant will arise and claim all that God has promised the nation of Israel.

Paul's explanation highlights two principles that apply to everyone, not just to Abraham's descendants:

1. *Unlike humanity, God does His best work through a remnant, a faithful minority.* The Bible is filled with examples of how God deliberately stacked the odds against Himself in order to reassure His people. He led the Israelites out of Egypt and into a wilderness where no water could be found, only to

provide water miraculously (Ex. 17:1–7). He instructed Gideon to whittle his army down to a three-hundred-man strike force, only to route a massive enemy army on their behalf (Judg. 7:19–25). In Elijah's standoff with the 450 prophets of Baal, God instructed the prophet to douse the altar until the sacrifice was soaked, water ran down the stones, and stood in the trench. While Baal, the fictitious god of lightning and thunder, couldn't generate so much as a spark, fire from heaven consumed Elijah's sacrifice, the water, the altar, and a good portion of the ground (1 Kings 18:25–38)!

You may find yourself facing an impossible situation, a hopeless cause. The odds against you may be humanly overwhelming. Moreover, you may be asking yourself, "Where did I go wrong? What did I do to bring this upon myself?" The answer could quite possibly be "Nothing!" The world may have conspired against you — as Jesus forewarned (John 15:18–19) — only to give God an opportunity to demonstrate His desire to bless you.

You may be in a holding pattern right now, enduring an unproductive season, unable to accomplish anything. You may feel as if you have been benched in the game of life, set aside, forsaken. Or you may find yourself standing alone against an unjust majority. God still delights to accomplish good through a faithful remnant. Remain steadfast in what you know to be right.

2. *Unlike humanity, God always keeps His promises.* Ours is a dishonest generation. Precious few can be trusted. Wedding vows are broken. Contracts mean little. The courts are overloaded with endless broken promises to settle. Counseling offices struggle to mend broken hearts because of broken promises. Men and women of integrity are increasingly hard to find. Nevertheless, God will never fail to keep His promises. He will keep His promises to the Jews and He will keep His promises to us.

My mother had a wonderful habit of putting together handwritten "Promise Books" for people who were enduring difficult circumstances. When she encountered someone grieving the loss of a family member, or struggling to survive a broken marriage, or battling poverty, or fighting through depression, she would prepare a little notebook with carefully printed verses of Scripture containing God's promises. What a wonderful gift to give someone who needs encouragement. What a wonderful gift to give yourself if you are facing a hopeless cause or overrun by impossible odds.

Let me also encourage you to be careful with the word "promise," especially with your children. Make "promise" a precious and rare term in your vocabulary around the house, uttered only as a sacred pledge to bring your deeds into line with your words. Resolve to teach your own children that God can be relied upon to fulfill His promises by faithfully honoring your own.

## Horticultural Ethics (Romans 11:15–29)

[15]For if their rejection is the reconciliation of the world, what will *their* acceptance be but life from the dead? [16]If the first piece *of dough* is holy, the lump is also; and if the root is holy, the branches are too.

[17]But if some of the branches were broken off, and you, being a wild olive, were grafted in among them and became partaker with them of the rich root of the olive tree, [18]do not be arrogant toward the branches; but if you are arrogant, *remember that* it is not you who supports the root, but the root *supports* you. [19]You will say then, "Branches were broken off so that I might be grafted in." [20]Quite right, they were broken off for their unbelief, but you stand by your faith. Do not be conceited, but fear; [21]for if God did not spare the natural branches, He will not spare you, either. [22]Behold then the kindness and severity of God; to those who fell, severity, but to you, God's kindness, if you continue in His kindness; otherwise you also will be cut off. [23]And they also, if they do not continue in their unbelief, will be grafted in, for God is able to graft them in again. [24]For if you were cut off from what is by nature a wild olive tree, and were grafted contrary to nature into a cultivated olive tree, how much more will these who are the natural *branches* be grafted into their own olive tree?

[25]For I do not want you, brethren, to be uninformed of this mystery — so that you will not be wise in your own estimation — that a partial hardening has happened to Israel until the fullness of the Gentiles has come in; [26]and so all Israel will be saved; just as it is written,

> "The Deliverer will come from Zion,
> He will remove ungodliness from Jacob."
> [27] "This is My covenant with them,
> When I take away their sins."

[28]From the standpoint of the gospel they are enemies for your sake, but from the standpoint of *God's* choice they are beloved for the sake of the fathers; [29]for the gifts and the calling of God are irrevocable.

I have known a few privileged people who remain humble despite their power, beauty, wealth, position, or popularity. A precious few. Most are insufferably conceited. Quietly smug behind the gracious façade they wear for polite company. And — if you can believe it — many profess to be Christians. The humble few who somehow remain unaffected by their privileged status appear to have two things in common: a painful past and a close connection to that history.

I have had the privilege of getting to know some of the most powerful men in the United States military, and I notice that their humility exists in direct proportion to the number of scars in their minds and on their bodies. One man who commands hundreds of fellow warriors can barely hold his own spoon; torture as a POW left his fingers looking like twisted pipe cleaners. Yet, now that he's no longer in uniform, you might mistake him for a shoe salesman or an accountant.

I have known a few incredibly wealthy people whose feet remain firmly on the ground. They make it a point to surround themselves with reminders of life in the real world. Not only do they live far beneath their means, they regularly detach themselves from the realm of the rich to rub shoulders with ordinary souls—helping people in need.

I have noticed a similar trend among spiritually mature Christians. Where pain has purged them of pride, a keen memory of where they came from keeps them sweetly self-effacing and genuinely gracious. By contrast, a lack of trials and a short memory almost always produce a spirit of entitlement and a judgmental attitude. Candidly, I find few things more repulsive than an arrogant Christian.

Having assured Gentile believers of their place in God's family as adopted sons and daughters, and having described the temporary setting aside of the Jews, Paul recognizes the potential for a new kind of danger. Gentiles now enjoy a place of honor in the Lord's grand plan to redeem His creation, a privilege the Jews once enjoyed. Therefore, Paul needs to give his Gentile readers a good dose of humility lest they become smug and arrogant.

After nearly two decades of preaching to Jews and Gentiles in cities throughout the eastern empire, the apostle has mastered the art of illustration. To help Gentile believers understand their place in God's plan, he draws on an image that everyone in the Mediterranean world would appreciate: the cultivation of olives. Unfortunately, most people today have never been on a farm, much less one with an olive grove. So, let me state Paul's primary point at the beginning and then list three supporting statements based on this horticultural lesson in ethics.

*What the Gentile Christians now enjoy was once reserved for the Jews, and it will be the Jews' honored place again in the future.*

*The Jew is now being disciplined, but it's temporary.* Paul has already explained this in detail; his illustration merely reaffirms the fact as the basis for this lesson.

*The Gentile now enjoys a place of honor, but he must not become smug.* This honor cannot be earned through merit, only received as a gift of grace. Moreover, the arrangement is temporary.

*The Lord is currently working with both the Jew and the Gentile, but His plan is inscrutable.* While we can observe the Lord's plan unfolding, we cannot possibly understand how or why God does what He does.

— **11:15** —

Paul has acknowledged that the temporary setting aside of the Jews in God's redemptive plan was beneficial for the Gentiles. But that's not to say it's ideal. If God can use their disobedience to His advantage, how much greater benefit will their obedience be for the world? The Jews are like a member of the family who has been tragically killed in an accident. The surviving members can survive and even grow spiritually from the loss, but how wonderful if the deceased could be resurrected and return to the household! Can you imagine the party that family would throw?

This is Paul's way of finding the good in the midst of his own heartache. He would trade his own salvation to see his kindred Jews saved. So we can only imag-

Magnus Manske/Wikimedia Commons

Long ago, farmers learned how to graft feeble fruit-bearing branches into the hardy stock of wild olive plants. However, Paul turned the image around to illustrate the wonders of grace. Wild branches—which cannot bear fruit and are therefore useless to the farmer—are nonetheless given the gift of life as they are grafted into the cultivated stock of God's redemptive plan.

ine how painful it must have been for the apostle to hear Gentile Christians revile the Jews for rejecting Christ. While we have no direct evidence of Jew-Gentile strife within Christian churches, Scripture implies that it was a problem (Acts 15:1–5; Gal. 2:11–14; Eph. 2:11–22). Furthermore, persecution by the Jews in local synagogues against Christians could only have inspired resentment toward Jews, both saved and hardened. So, Paul seeks to give our current observations an eternal perspective.

### —11:16—

Before introducing his primary image for illustration, Paul quickly alludes to a Jewish custom based on Numbers 15:17–21. When Israel first entered the Promised Land, the Lord instructed them to observe a ritual involving "first fruits." After laboring all season, a Hebrew farmer eagerly awaited the first sign of produce because it indicated the quality he could expect from the rest of the crop. By offering a "first fruits" sample of a good harvest, he said to God, "This is because of Your provision; therefore, I thank You and I dedicate it to Your use and for Your glory." Everything that followed, as it grew from the ground, was equally dedicated to God.

This same principle applied to every other provision as a continual reminder that God is the source of all good things. So, when a woman mixed a batch of dough, she would set aside a small sample to be given to the priests. Like the first of the harvest, this "first fruit" sample represented the whole batch. Similarly, Abraham was the first fruit of a people set apart for the use and glory of God; therefore, his descendants are no less set apart. The relationship between Jews today and their God is no less special than the relationship enjoyed by Abraham.

### —11:17–18—

Paul quickly turns to his primary illustration involving the cultivation of olives and the mysterious practice of grafting. Ancient growers discovered that the roots and stock of wild olive trees could tolerate harsh conditions, such as wind and drought, while cultivated trees were not as successful. So, they combined the best elements of both, the hearty root system of the wild tree and the delicious fruit of the cultivated tree. Paul's illustration, however, gives the image a surprising twist. In his example, wild olive branches draw nourishment from the sap and roots of a cultivated stock.

This is a dramatic picture of grace. Wild olive branches can produce only small, hard, nubs of fruit containing very little oil. In other words, wild branches are useless! Nevertheless, in a bizarre turn of horticultural good sense, some cultivated branches were pruned away because they *did not* bear fruit to make room for wild branches which *cannot* bear anything useful. The wild branches now receive life-giving nourishment from the cultivated stock; however, the graft does not change the nature of the branch.

It is actually possible to graft a branch from a pear tree into the stock of an apple tree; however, this doesn't change the nature of the pear branch. It doesn't begin producing apples just because it receives nourishment from the stock of an apple tree. In keeping with its nature, it produces pears. Similarly, wild olive branches cannot produce better fruit simply because they have been grafted to a cultivated tree. In fact, the wild branches receive nourishing sap but have no ability to contribute anything in return. How foolish it would be for them to feel superior to anyone, especially the branches that were removed.

We must be careful not to take Paul's illustration too far. Or, as one of my mentors used to say, "Let's not make this walk on all fours." This is not talking about salvation. Nor is the "fruit" referring to the fruit of the Spirit or the fruit of good works. Paul is simply saying that God did not set aside the Jew and then include the Gentile in His redemptive plan because one is better or more useful than the other. God grafted Gentiles into His plan to show them grace. And because grace is always unmerited, no one can look down on another.

— **11:19–24** —

Paul anticipates a reasonable conclusion on the part of Gentiles. "Branches were broken off so that I might be grafted in," infers the attitude that says, "I am more desirable than they. Isn't that the nature of biblical choice—preference?" Yes, but not on the basis of merit, but by grace through faith. Moreover, the choice is by no means permanent! He can just as easily reverse the process and gain branches that produce fruit (11:20–24).

On the surface, this can appear to undermine everything Paul has written about eternal security. He has said that nothing can separate believers from the love of God and that victory for them is assured (8:28–39). Furthermore, he wrote this entire section to affirm the faithfulness of God to care for His chosen people—Jew *and* Gentile. Therefore, we must be clear about the image and what it represents.

The "rich root of the olive tree" (11:17) is a metaphorical image of Abraham's *privileged position* in God's redemptive plan for the world, not the patriarch's salvation. The Jews inherit covenant promises from father Abraham, not righteousness. Paul painstakingly argues against the notion that anyone can be saved by virtue of their DNA or the rite of circumcision or obedience to the Law or any means other than grace, which is received through faith. Furthermore, this privileged position is given to a people as a whole. We may enjoy God's favor as individuals by our participation, but the grafting is of an entire race (11:20–23).

Paul is careful to maintain a distinction between the church and Israel in this illustration. (He has not forgotten his illustration of the grafts and branches broken off). In other Scripture, he stressed the unity of Jew and Gentile Christians, declaring them to be a new, single species of humanity unlike any before (Eph. 2:14–16). Some have concluded that God set aside the literal nation of Israel and superseded it by establishing a "spiritual Israel" called the church, which is made up of this new race of humankind. Furthermore, they claim that the church will inherit the promises of Abraham's covenant, not literally, but "spiritually"—which can mean just about anything you care to read into it.

Again, we have a paradox on our hands. Paul stresses Jew and Gentile unity, but he also stresses their distinction in terms of how God will carry out His redemptive plan for the world (11:22–24). I cannot fully explain how both can be true, but I take the evidence at face value and affirm each truth without slighting the other. God promised the Jews land—literal real estate, and lots of it. He promised them a conquering Messiah-King, who will reign over a literal worldwide government for no less than a thousand years. Gentiles may share those blessings and enjoy that privilege alongside Israel, but Gentiles have not been promised this as a people. Jews have.

Nevertheless, Paul's purpose here is not to unveil the future but to speak prophetically against the non-Christian, sinful attitude of anti-Semitism.

## —11:25–29—

Again, Paul's stated purpose in this passage is to prevent Gentiles from becoming "wise in yourselves," which is an idiom for "conceited" (11:25). To preclude their conceit, he reveals a "mystery," a previously unknown spiritual fact; in this case, a glimpse of the future from God's perspective. What has occurred is a "partial hardening" of Israel, meaning that some, but not all Jewish individuals have been hardened. However, the current era of temporary discipline will end when "the fullness of the Gentiles has come in."

During His earthly ministry, Jesus revealed that God's plan included bringing elect Gentiles into the fold (Luke 21:24; John 10:16). The word "fullness" is extremely important to note. God knows the number and the identities of the Gentile individuals and has orchestrated world events around the time of their belief. How long is that? Only the Father knows (Matt. 24:36). All we know is that since the days of Israel's exile, the Jew has lived under the heel of the Gentile world, which is part of God's severe mercy on His people (11:22). But, when the time is right, when all of the elect Gentiles have entered the fold, the gate will close and the partial hardening of Israel will end.

When the era of the Gentiles has ended, "all Israel will be saved" (11:26). This may or may not include the majority of Jewish individuals. Remember, "all Israel" or the true Israel is not determined by numbers, but by belief. Therefore, "all Israel" and "the fullness of the Gentiles" represent the sum total of God's elect. When all of God's chosen individuals have believed, the next age will begin. Paul alludes to this coming era by quoting from Isaiah 59.

In this prophetic song, Isaiah laments the sorrowful condition of Israel, in which there is no justice or righteousness. And because Israel is supposed to be God's example of righteousness for the rest of the world, all of creation is corrupt. Moreover, "there was no one to intercede" (Isa. 59:16), no one to make things right. So, God Himself dons His armor to invade and conquer this hostile territory, to bring evildoers to justice and to redeem "those who turn from transgression in [Israel]." At this future time, Jesus Christ will come to this earth, claim the throne of Israel, and establish a nation that is obedient to Him. He will come to earth like a mighty, rushing river and flood the whole world with His righteousness (Isa. 59:19). Furthermore, He will put into effect the full provisions of the new covenant (Jer. 31:31–34).

That new era will be glorious! At that time, the Hebrew children of Israel will finally receive *all* of their covenant blessings. They will have their Promised Land—all of it! They will have their king—not a mostly good, sometimes unjust king, but a perfectly righteous, obedient king. They will become the earthly means of God's righteous rule over the whole earth.

Unfortunately, at the present time, the great majority of Jews are "enemies of the gospel" in that, as a people, they have rejected grace (11:28). But rather than judge them by their present condition, we Gentiles should first be thankful for the blessings we currently enjoy at their expense. In fact, we should honor them for their future role in God's plan to redeem His creation.

Finally, take special note of Paul's concluding statement on the matter: "the gifts and the calling of God are irrevocable" (11:29). This is a general principle that applies to all people throughout all time. It is true of believing individuals, whether Jew or Gentile (8:28–39), and it is true of His chosen people, the Hebrew children of Abraham.

To summarize, let me list two facts we can glean from Paul's horticultural lesson in ethics:

*The Jew is currently hardened, but ultimately beloved.* When you meet an individual Jew who is presently hardened, recall the time you were still hardened in your sin. Like you, whom God loved even while you were rebellious (5:8), He loves this covenant son or daughter. Remember also that this individual remains a member of a beloved people. As they used to tell us in the Marines, "Salute the rank, not the man."

*We are spiritually honored, but morally undeserving.* As a people, Gentiles don't have much of an honored heritage to claim with pride. We don't deserve this place of honor, but it's ours. That's why Paul wrote to the Christians in Ephesus, "But now in Christ Jesus you who formerly were far off have been brought near by the blood of Christ" (Eph. 2:13). When you encounter a Jew, remember Paul's illustration. You are grafted into your place of honor "contrary to nature" (Rom. 11:24) by grace. The privileged position in God's redemptive plan for the world rightfully belongs to the Jews.

If there is anyone in the world who should not be smug or arrogant, it is the Gentile Christian. We have no superiority to claim. Our heritage is barbarous and heathen. Our ancestors didn't merely stray from God's righteousness, they never knew it. Spiritually speaking, our roots are rotten to the core. So, to those who claim superiority over the Jew or boast in their privileged position in God's plan, I say with the prophet Isaiah, "Look to the rock from which you were hewn and to the quarry from which you were dug" (Isa. 51:1). That's a humbling exercise for the Gentile … and just what we need from time to time.

## Application

### *To Whom Much Is Given…*

As Paul upheld God's right to rule over humanity and defended God's character, the apostle addressed an obvious question, "Have the Jews been forsaken?" His reply rested on two points of fact:

1. The true children of Abraham are the faithful few, not the rebellious majority.
2. The true children of Abraham are subject to God's discipline, but it is temporary.

So, how does God's present dealing with Israel affect Gentile believers? Several implications quickly come to mind.

1. *We must reject a smug attitude.* My wife, Cynthia, and I had the privilege of rearing four children. When one child required discipline, we carefully monitored the attitudes of the other three to be certain they didn't add humiliation to an already humbling event. Paul's lesson from the olive grove (11:15–29) has a similar purpose. God's disciplining Jews does not suggest that His love for them has diminished. On the contrary, His chastening demonstrates His fatherly love for them. Therefore, Paul encourages Gentiles to recognize their provisional place in the forefront of God's plan and to avoid any hint of arrogance.

2. *We must esteem Jews—believing and nonbelieving—as honored sons.* I love the game of football and have enjoyed watching high school, college, and professional games for as long as I can remember. And I can recall several times when a star professional player was placed on the sidelines as the result of a suspension. A serious ethical violation required discipline, so the league required him to miss several games. Although he had been specifically drafted for the position and he possessed the ability to play well, the team had no other alternative than to give his position to another man. Even when the replacement performs well, he is wise to respect the player whose position he occupies, for he fulfills the role temporarily.

   I don't mean for my illustration to suggest that any one race is superior to another, or that God values anyone more than another. The Lord is impartial. Nevertheless, He gave the Hebrew descendants of Abraham an honored place in His plan to redeem humanity. It is a role that deserves respect. At present, the body of believers, the "church," occupies this esteemed position, but we are wise to continue honoring those who have been temporarily set aside.

3. *We must respect the place of honor we occupy and steward it well.* A place of honor in God's redemptive plan comes with great privilege and considerable responsibility. For example, the Hebrew descendants of Abraham were given land with astounding strategic importance. Anyone traveling between the three major empires—Egypt, Assyria, or Babylon—had to pass through the Promised Land. Imagine the impact on pagan travelers, merchants, and armies passing through the land inhabited by people obedient to God, who in turn blessed and protected them. Imagine how that testimony would have changed the world.

As children of the new covenant, we possess a privilege of far greater worth than land or wealth. We have the very presence and power of almighty God living within, a privilege the Old Covenant believers would have found staggering! We have God's unconditional promise to use every circumstance—even our own ethical and moral failures—to transform us from within and train us to be obedient. And we have been guaranteed victory over sin and death.

Jesus said, "From everyone who has been given much, much will be required; and to whom they entrusted much, of him they will ask all the more" (Luke 12:48). We have a responsibility to steward the privileges we have been given, not to lord it over others but to be living invitations to receive God's grace.

Someday yet future, with Christ as its king, Israel will return to the forefront of God's redemptive plan, will receive all of the covenant blessings God has promised, and will become the means by which God blesses the whole world.

## Unsearchable, Unfathomable, and Unmatched! (Romans 11:30–36)

---

[30]For just as you once were disobedient to God, but now have been shown mercy because of their disobedience, [31]so these also now have been disobedient, that because of the mercy shown to you they also may now be shown mercy. [32]For God has shut up all in disobedience so that He may show mercy to all.

[33]Oh, the depth of the riches both of the wisdom and knowledge of God! How unsearchable are His judgments and unfathomable His ways! [34]For who has known the mind of the Lord, or who became His counselor? [35]Or who has first given to Him that it might be paid back to him again? [36]For from Him and through Him and to Him are all things. To Him *be* the glory forever. Amen.

---

The Himalayan Mountains rise four to five-and-one-half miles above sea level. Because of this, they have been the climber's dream since humankind first thought to climb mountains. However, no one attempted to scale them until 1920. Then, between 1920 and 1953, eleven expeditions attempted to reach the summit of the highest mountain peak in the world, Mount Everest. The first ten ended in failure and claimed the lives of George Mallory and Andrew Irvine, who were last sighted at a thousand feet below the peak and never seen alive again.

Twenty-nine years later, Sir Edmond Hillary and his Sherpa guide, Tenzing Norgay, answered the challenge of Everest with the ninth British expedition and reached the summit on May 29, 1953. For the first time in history, a human foot set down on top of the world, 29,028 feet above sea level. To my knowledge, neither man recorded what he saw. Hillary explained how he climbed and why, but never described what he saw or how he felt as he surveyed the world from its pinnacle. I suspect he had no words to report. Who would?

Nineteen hundred years earlier, the apostle Paul sat in the city of ancient Corinth and, with stylus in hand, scaled the Himalayan heights of theology. As we look down the slope, we see our three base camps. First we came to Camp Sovereignty (9:1–33), where we discovered that "the plan of salvation" isn't about the individual at all. God's plan of salvation is His intention to reclaim His creation, purge it of evil, and restore its original order and purpose. Furthermore, He invites us to join His plan.

Let me be clear. According to Paul's teaching, God chose who would be saved. He didn't choose merely by virtue of His foreknowledge; He chose based on His sovereign right as the Creator of everything and His righteous character as its Judge. But He did.

We continued our ascent toward the next waypoint, Camp Responsibility. It was here we learned that God's sovereignty does not nullify any person's accountability for his or her free will choice to believe or reject God's invitation. The air was noticeably thinner there. Many people turned back at this point, unable to tolerate the paradox:

God rejects rebellious people because they have rejected Him (Matt. 10:33; 21:42–44; John 15:22–24; Rom. 1:28–32).
We love God because God first loved us (Rom. 5:8; 8:28–30; 1 John 4:10).

Brave souls that you are, you continued on to our third waypoint, Camp Humility. There we discovered that neither Jews nor Gentiles can boast in their privileged position in God's redemptive plan. Jews have been temporarily broken off—an ignoble consequence of divine discipline. Grafted-in Gentiles now receive blessings but cannot produce anything to justify their presence.

Now, having been stripped of all the nonessentials, we head for the glorious summit. Unfortunately, our numbers have become less. The fainthearted have already dropped out and begun their descent.

— **11:30–32** —

Paul summarizes his teaching on the current disposition of the Jews in God's plan using words for "mercy" four times in three verses (11:30–32). The apostle rarely repeats himself, so this is remarkable. The Greek term *eleos* was used in the Greek translation of the Old Testament to express the Hebrew term *chesed*. And *chesed* describes the unrelenting, inexplicable, overwhelming grace of God for His covenant people. The Greek term, as well as the Hebrew, is filled with emotion, referring to God's inclination to relieve our misery.

The apostle uses another word group four times in the same space: *apeitheia*, which many translations render "disobedience." The literal meaning is "the condition of being un-persuadable"[5] or "obstinate." He then uses these two terms in a playful interchange to show how God uses the disobedience of one group as a means of showing mercy to the other.

| | |
|---|---|
| [30] For just as you once were *disobedient* to God, | [31] so these also now have been *disobedient*, |
| but now have been shown **mercy** | that because of the **mercy** shown to you |
| because of their *disobedience*, | they also may now be shown **mercy**. |

The Lord, through a grave act of tough love, said to the Jews, in effect, "That's enough. You have rejected the Messiah even though I warned that I would turn to the Gentiles. Therefore, you are set aside." He then called the most hardened Jew in Jerusalem, a zealous persecutor of the church named Saul, to proclaim the good news among the Gentiles. The mercy shown to the Gentiles will now become His means of stimulating the zeal of the Jews to claim His promised grace.

God, in His unsearchable mercy, has used the disobedience of all humankind to "shut up" or capture us (11:32). The Greek term is a compound word, joining "with/together" and "to enclose." It's the same word used in Luke 5:6 to describe a fishing net "enclosing together" a great quantity of fish. The idea is that God is surrounding us with our own sin and drawing the net closed to cut off any means of escape. Why? To give us grace.

Frankly, I don't understand His motivation. Why would a holy God go to such great lengths to show such unmerited kindness to creatures who have not only rebelled, but are resistant to grace? That's as nonsensical as grafting fruitless branches into a perfectly good olive tree. But such is the nature of grace. It cannot be explained, only received with gratitude as one in great need.

— **11:33–35** —

Reflecting on the unsearchable mercy of God prompts Paul to break forth in a doxology. Such inexplicable grace can only come from a God of infinitely deep goodness. To praise his Creator, Paul searches his extensive vocabulary to find the right words. It's as if he is stringing verbal pearls onto a magnificent necklace of praise, selecting each one ever so carefully: "Oh, the depth of the riches both of the wisdom and knowledge of God! How unsearchable are His judgments and unfathomable His ways!" (Romans 11:33).

*Bathos* means "depth." For the first-century traveler, nothing was more powerful and profound than the sea. Its depths were dark and mysterious, defying any to know its secrets.

*Ploutos* means "wealth." Loosely based on the verb "to flow," the basic sense is "spilling over with goodness." The wealth can be physical, spiritual, or moral. Of course, in reference to God, it is all three.

*Sophia* and *gnōsis* ("wisdom" and "knowledge") represent the sum total of all there is to think. They speak of God's knowledge of all things and His ability to perfectly order all events.

*Anexeraunētos* means "unsearchable." The root word is a verb meaning "to track," in the sense of hunting down an animal by following its trail. The Lord's judgment cannot be traced through human logic. It is beyond our ability to comprehend.

*Anexichniastos* is virtually identical in meaning to the previous term, but is found nowhere outside the Bible and Bible-related literature. Many translations render the term "unfathomable," both for style and to reflect Paul's original "depth" theme.

Paul reinforces his worship by alluding to two passages from the Old Testament. The first comes from Isaiah 40:13, a curiously appropriate selection. In the words of one commentator, "In chapters 1–39 [of Isaiah] judgment on sin is stressed; in chapters 40–66 atonement for that sin *and* the resulting change in people and the world system are discussed."[6] Isaiah marked the shift of emphasis from humanity's sin to God's inexplicable grace by celebrating His sovereignty and wisdom, which Paul paraphrased, "Who has known the mind of the Lord, or who became His counselor?"

The second passage is an allusion to Job 41:11, in which the Lord challenges the bewildered and suffering patriarch, "Who has given to Me that I should repay him? Whatever is under the whole heaven is Mine." This divine challenge comes at the end of a long quest for answers by Job and his friends, a journey that called into question God's integrity, wisdom, and goodness. Then, just like now, they faced tragedy with a singular question on their lips: *Why?* And for months, the man's so-called friends speculated about His nature and spun a tangled web of vain theologies. Job's wife counseled him to forsake life and end his own misery. Eventually, the man was brought to his end and strongly demanded his day in court, where he felt sure he would be vindicated and the Lord caught short.

After a long time — we don't know how long — the Lord broke the silence as He confronted the man who was "blameless, upright, fearing God and turning away from evil" (Job 1:1). However, He didn't come with answers. Job never learns of Satan's challenge in heaven. Job never receives an explanation. He is never presented with a logical list of reasons that his tragedy was ultimately a part of God's good plan for him and everyone affected. Instead, he encounters God Himself — and this meets his need. Seeing God's unsearchable mercy and gazing into His unfathomable ways end the man's desperate quest for answers. He puts his hand over his mouth and repents of his foolish outbursts. And, at that point, he worships.

Paul can identify with Job. The apostle has done his best to reveal the plans of God and to explain His methods as the Holy Spirit supernaturally directed him. Eventually, however, his efforts to explain things that exceed the limitations of human ability dissolve into silence. And he stands silent before the magnificence of God and marvels at the sophistication of His ways.

As I reflect on Paul's doxology, it occurs to me that the only words even remotely suitable to describe God are "un-" words. Unsearchable. Unfathomable. Words that highlight His utter "otherness." A.W. Tozer's thoughts are especially helpful here:

> To say that God is infinite is to say that He is measureless. Measurement is the way created things have of accounting for themselves. It describes limitations, imperfections, and cannot apply to God. Weight describes the gravitational pull of the earth upon material bodies; distance describes intervals between bodies in space; length means extension in space, and there are other familiar measurements such as those for liquid, and energy, and sound, and light, and numbers for pluralities. We also try to measure abstract qualities, and speak of great or little faith, high or low intelligence, large or meager talents.
>
> Is it not plain that all this does not and cannot apply to God? It is the way we see the works of His hands, but not the way we see Him. He is above all this, outside of it, beyond it. Our concepts of measurement embrace mountains and men, atoms and stars, gravity, energy, numbers, speed, but never God ... Nothing in God is less or more, or large or small. He is what He is in Himself, without qualifying thought or word. He is simply God.7

## —11:36—

Having exhausted all thought and having considered all rational explanations on the topic of God's plan for the Jews, Paul's journey ends with the beginning:

- from Him—God is the source of all that exists.
- through Him—God sustains all things and gives everything purpose and movement.
- to Him—God is the purpose for which all things exist.

All things. Think of it! That includes your current situation. That includes what you cannot figure out. That includes your loss of employment. That includes your promotion. That includes the blessing of your family. That includes the loss of your precious loved one. That includes the bewildering test you're enduring. That includes *whatever* situation you happen to be in right now, regardless of how painful or how pleasant it might be. All things.

God does not conceal Himself. Nor does He hide His will. If we do not see, it is because we are looking for something He is not. If we do not understand, it is because we have expectations He chooses not to fulfill. But those limitations are ours, not His.

Paul reveals to us everything God has revealed to him. We have no reason to suspect he has held anything back. Nevertheless, many questions go unanswered. How is God's kingdom already here, but not yet fully? Why does He allow evil to continue while His elect suffer dreadful and cruel persecution? At what point in the future will He fulfill all of His covenant promises to Israel? How does someone rejoice in his or her affliction? On and on … Like you, I have a list of questions I would like to ask the Lord when I get to heaven. But then, like Job and Paul, I suspect it won't mean very much when I see Him. At that time, it will all make sense.

So why worry over my list of unanswerable questions? Why not worship Him here and now, on this side of eternity, and let His unsearchable mercy, His unfathomable wisdom, and His unmatched character be enough? Is this not a reasonable sacrifice considering that He is God and I am not?

---

NOTES: The Majesty of God (Romans 9:1–11:36)

1. Walter Chalmers Smith, "Immortal, Invisible," 1867 (public domain).
2. H. Leon McBeth, *The Baptist Heritage* (Nashville: Broadman, 1987), 185.
3. J. I. Packer, *Evangelism and the Sovereignty of God* (Downers Grove, IL: InterVarsity Press, 1991), 35.
4. The city of Gibeon made this offer under false pretenses and Joshua failed to consult the Lord. Nevertheless, Israel upheld its end of the bargain. Perhaps if Gibeon had approached Israel before God pronounced judgment on Canaan, He might have agreed to their offer. My purpose here is to show what could have been.

5. W. E. Vine, Merrill F. Unger, and William White, *Vine's Complete Expository Dictionary of Old and New Testament Words* (Nashville: Nelson, 1996), 2:173.

6. John F. Walvoord, Roy B. Zuck, and Dallas Theological Seminary, *The Bible Knowledge Commentary: An Exposition of the Scriptures* (Wheaton: Victor, 1983), 1:1032.

7. A. W. Tozer, *The Knowledge of the Holy* (San Francisco: HarperSanFrancisco, 1961), 45–46.

# THE RIGHTEOUSNESS OF GOD (ROMANS 12:1–15:13)

God's plan of salvation isn't merely an invitation to escape the eternal consequences of sin; it's a divine invasion of planet Earth, which will remove Satan from his seat of power and replace his world system with the "righteousness of God." It would be appropriate to call this takeover "hostile," not because the Lord is malicious, but because Satan hates God, his world system opposes the Lord's original created order, and most people on earth remain hardened in their rebellion against their Creator. Evil considers His goodness hostile. Furthermore, Daniel, Ezekiel, John, and even Jesus described that future "day of the Lord" in startlingly violent terms. Suddenly, and at any moment, Christ will tear the veil between the heavenly realm and His fallen creation. At that time, the entire universe will be purged of all evil and then transformed. Everything from atoms to galaxies will be made good again.

While "the day of the Lord" is yet future, in some respects it is already here in the hearts of His followers. Therefore, the good news of salvation is more than a personal fire escape. The gospel is God's invitation to all of humanity to join Him in this transformation of creation, to become His first examples of regenerated creatures. We are invited to become agents of His power and ambassadors of His will, to labor under His direction in support of this inevitable end.

Earlier, Paul described the gospel as the means by which "the righteousness of God is revealed from faith to faith" (1:17). I envision this as grace coming down vertically from heaven. Paul then quoted the prophet Habakkuk: "But the righteous man shall live by faith." That's grace flowing out horizontally to others on earth. If we were discerning enough to notice, we might have recognized that Paul was there outlining the structure of his letter, which follows the purpose of the gospel. Grace flows down from heaven and then outward to others. The first eleven chapters reveal God and His righteous plan, vertical grace:

> We were confronted by the fearsome wrath of God. (1:18–3:20)
> We learned of salvation by grace alone, through faith alone, in Christ alone. (3:21–5:21)
> We encountered God's faithfulness. (6:1–8:39)
> We gazed into His unsearchable, sovereign ways. (9:1–11:36)

Then with the words, "Therefore, I urge you...," Paul turns from this vertical orientation to the horizontal. Believers—both as a body and as individuals—stand

## KEY TERMS

συσχηματίζω [*syschēmatizō*] (*4964*) "model after, conform to the pattern of"

This verb combines the Greek preposition *syn* ("with") and *schēma* ("pattern"). The resulting definition is "to be conformed according to the pattern of." The most common use of the word in secular literature is in reference to molding clay around a form or casting metal. In both instances in the Bible (Rom. 12:2 and 1 Peter 1:14), the verb is passive.

μεταμορφόω [*metamorphoō*] (*3339*) "to transform, to change into another form"

The English term *metamorphosis* is of course a transliteration from the Greek and best illustrated in nature when a caterpillar is transformed into a butterfly. Whereas *syschēmatizō* stresses external change, *metamorphoō* describes a fundamental transformation in the nature of something without altering its identity. For example, an acorn and the tree it produces are the same individual; however, the nature of the acorn has been radically altered. (See also Matt. 17:2; Mark 9:2.)

δοκιμάζω [*dokimazō*] (*1381*) "to prove by testing, to assay, to discern through observation"

Based on the root word *dokeō*, "to watch," this was a term commonly used in the trade and crafting of metals. The most reliable means of determining the worth of a coin or ingot is to heat it to the point of melting and observe its behavior. Both secular and religious writers used the term figuratively of warriors in battle and leaders in adversity. (The English word "mettle" is an alteration of the word "metal.") Earlier in Paul's letter to the Romans, the apostle used the negative, *adokimos*, to describe sinful humanity as "depraved"; that is, "proven to be worthless."

προσλαμβάνω [*proslambanō*] (*4355*) "accept, to receive, to take to oneself"

This verb redoubles the emphasis of the Greek verb *lambanō*, "to receive" with the preposition, *pros*, "unto" or "toward." The supreme example of this is Christ's "receiving to Himself" or "accepting" sinful people as they are.

---

at the intersection of God's grace from heaven and God's grace to the world. And it puts the believer in a kind of crisis. What will he or she do with the grace that has been freely given from heaven? Will he hoard it for personal gain? Will she become a miser of living water? Hopefully not. In my experience grace turns stagnant unless it flows freely.

The grace the Lord pours into each life is intended for everyone, the whole world. Once it fills His chosen vessel, it should overflow and then flood everything around him or her. That is why He leaves His beloved sons and daughters in the world, to give His grace a horizontal dimension. However, believers cannot perform this vital function on their own or in their old manner of life. Something must change.

## A Compelling Commitment (Romans 12:1-8)

¹Therefore I urge you, brethren, by the mercies of God, to present your bodies a living and holy sacrifice, acceptable to God, *which is* your spiritual service of worship. ²And do not be conformed to this world, but be transformed by the renewing of your mind, so that you may prove what the will of God is, that which is good and acceptable and perfect.

³For through the grace given to me I say to everyone among you not to think more highly of himself than he ought to think; but to think so as to have sound judgment, as God has allotted to each a measure of faith. ⁴For just as we have many members in one body and all the members do not have the same function, ⁵so we, who are many, are one body in Christ, and individually members one of another. ⁶Since we have gifts that differ according to the grace given to us, *each of us is to exercise them accordingly*: if prophecy, according to the proportion of his faith; ⁷if service, in his serving; or he who teaches, in his teaching; ⁸or he who exhorts, in his exhortation; he who gives, with liberality; he who leads, with diligence; he who shows mercy, with cheerfulness.

Pivotal moments in human history are often punctuated by epochal statements, words that seem ordinary at the time but become more profound as we understand their full significance. In Genesis 22, an elderly man with a knife in his hand and his teenage son—his "only son"—climbed Mount Moriah with some wood and a torch to prepare a sacrifice to God. The son innocently asked, "But where is the lamb for the burnt offering?" (Gen. 22:7). Abraham replied with this statement: "God will provide for Himself the lamb for the burnt offering, my son" (22:8).

And provide, He did! (John 1:14).

A few centuries later, an eighty-year-old shepherd kept watch over his father-in-law's sheep when a voice called to him from a flaming bush. The Lord ordered him to confront the most powerful king on earth and to demand the release of God's people from slavery. When the stammering has-been leader reminded the Lord of his own shortcomings, God's words must have stunned the old shepherd, "Now then go, and I, even I, will be with your mouth, and teach you what you are to say" (Ex. 4:12).

Moses had no idea the Lord would make him a divine instrument by which He would deliver the Hebrews from bondage and later give them the Law.

Centuries later still, another young shepherd was faithfully tending flocks when a summons came from the main house. He came in from the fields to find an elderly prophet waiting for him. A few words and a trickle of oil, and his life changed forever—as did the life of Israel. After decades of victory and defeat, obedience and shame, the Lord reassured David with another statement that was difficult to completely grasp: "Your house and your kingdom shall endure before Me forever; your throne shall be established forever" (2 Sam. 7:16).

David, despite his failures, remained a man after God's own heart, and his descendant will one day rule the world from the throne of Israel.

Then, many centuries after David, the promised Messiah, crowned with thorns and nailed to a criminal's cross, consummated God's grace to the world. Jesus punctuated this vertical stroke of the plan of salvation with, "It is finished" (John 19:30).

Epochal words for the entire world!

Paul's letter to the Romans contains no less than three statements epochal in character, each of which punctuates a pivotal moment in the life of each believer.

- First, there is the moment when a person receives God's gift of grace through faith: "Therefore, having been justified by faith, we have peace with God through our Lord Jesus Christ" (Rom. 5:1).
- Second, when that individual discovers that his or her eternal destiny is secure, comes this verse: "Therefore there is now no condemnation for those who are in Christ Jesus. For the law of the Spirit of life in Christ Jesus has set you free from the law of sin and of death" (Rom. 8:1–2).
- Finally, each believer stands at a pivotal moment in his or her own history, at the intersection of grace from heaven and grace to others. There we are confronted with a compelling call in Paul's incredible words: "Therefore I urge you, brethren, by the mercies of God, to present your bodies a living and holy sacrifice, acceptable to God, which is your spiritual service of worship. And do not be conformed to this world, but be transformed by the renewing of your mind, so that you may prove what the will of God is, that which is good and acceptable and perfect" (Rom. 12:1–2).

These last two verses represent God's all-important call to consecration and transformation. The first is about our bodies; the second is about our minds. The first verse concerns our surroundings and how we live in them; the second looks within to discover what goes on in our minds. Like the first notes of Beethoven's *Fifth Symphony*, we will hear these truths repeated in different forms throughout his call to extend the grace we have received to others.

## —12:1—

Paul begins this section of Romans with the Greek word *parakaleō*, "I urge you"—the verb form of the term used of the Holy Spirit, "the Paraclete" (John 16:7). It carries the idea of standing alongside someone in order to provide counsel, courage, comfort, hope, and positive perspective. A good encourager challenges without condemnation, instructs without lecturing, inspires without condescending, and helps another toward excellence. Like a coach who encourages and challenges an athlete to reach a particular goal, Paul urges believers to consecrate themselves.

Consecration in this particular context is a radical separation from a secular worldview to adopt instead a Christlike purpose and way of life. This doesn't automatically happen when someone becomes a believer in Christ. This is what I would call a "cooperative command." God gives a command that we are then to obey with full cooperation. However, even in this, He has not left us alone. Note the phrase "by the mercies of God." We learned in Paul's description of God's unsearchable character that He is merciful above all. Moved by His ready inclination to relieve the misery of fallen humanity, He stands ready to help us when we respond to His call.

Paul's primary focus in the first verse is the use of our physical bodies, which we are to "present." He used this verb earlier to steer believers away from sin.

> Therefore do not let sin reign in your mortal body so that you obey its lusts, and do not go on *presenting* the members of your body to sin as instruments of unrighteousness; but *present* yourselves to God as those alive from the dead, and your members as instruments of righteousness to God ... Do you not know that when you *present* yourselves to someone as slaves for obedience, you are slaves of the one whom you obey, either of sin resulting in death, or of obedience resulting in righteousness? (Rom. 6:12–13, 16, emphasis mine)

The idea is to give over the use of something for a specific purpose. In the Old Testament, it was not uncommon for people to present gold, silver, building supplies, and even food to the priests, who then used the donations to construct a place of worship as well as to survive physically (Ex 25:1–8; 1 Chron. 22:14; Ezra 1:4–6). However, anything presented to the temple had to be first rate. Sacrifices had to be without blemish or defect. Materials had to be of the best quality. And nothing offered could have been previously used in the service of another god.

Similarly, our consecrated bodies are to be:

• *living*—a deliberate, ongoing sacrifice given again and again over a lifetime
• *holy*—an undefiled offering dedicated exclusively to the Lord and His purposes
• *acceptable*—a well-pleasing sacrifice in that it honors God's character

Paul calls this consecration of our bodies a "spiritual service of worship." The Greek word translated "spiritual" is *logikos*, an adjective meaning "in keeping with the nature of a thing." Because Paul is obviously calling for a nonliteral, but very real sacrifice of our bodies, translators choose to render the term "spiritual," in keeping with godly conduct.

However, there is another way of rendering *logikos*. Earlier, the apostle stated that believers presenting their bodies to sin didn't make logical sense (6:1–3, 15–16). Why would freed slaves continue to serve their old master? Presenting our bodies to serve the interests of our new Master, on the other hand, is completely logical—very much in keeping with good sense. Therefore, some translations render the last phrase "reasonable service" (KJV, NET).

## —12:2—

The second part of Paul's epochal statement penetrates the physical, external world to confront the internal world of the mind. Jews focused all of their attention on the ethical behavior of a person, which is good in many ways. It's a very bottom-line approach to good and evil. However, Jesus was not satisfied with mere external, physical obedience. He called for His followers to have clean hearts first, then clean hands (Matt. 15:17–20; Mark 7:14–15). That's because both sin and righteousness begin in the mind.

We have a choice between two alternatives:

- *syschēmatizō*— "to be molded according to a pattern." The Greek word is a compound of the preposition "with" and the term from which we get our English word "schematic."
- *metamorphoō*— "to be changed from one thing into another." This Greek word is transliterated to render the English word "metamorphosis," which is commonly used to describe the transformation of a caterpillar into a butterfly.

*"Do not be conformed to this world ..."* The pattern we are to reject is a grotesquely twisted version of God's original creation, which He repeatedly called "good" in Genesis 1. Paul does not use the Greek word for "world" or "universe" here, but a term meaning "eon, era, or age." The world was not originally evil; it has been corrupted. Paul's use of the term "age" stresses the fact that the present condition of creation is temporary. Before this age, the universe moved in perfect harmony with God's nature, which is righteousness and love. And when Christ returns, the world will be refashioned to reflect God's character.

Unfortunately, we—in our natural-born state—are part and parcel of this fallen creation and its system, which is ruled by evil, selfishness, greed, deceit, and violence. God's economy is exactly the opposite, finding pleasure in good, selflessness, trust, gentleness, and truth. There is no middle ground between them. The apostle John describes the two systems as "darkness" and "light" (1 John 1:5–6); Paul called them "flesh" and "Spirit" (Rom. 7:14–8:11). This age and the age to come answer the following questions very differently:

> What is the meaning of life?
> What makes a man or woman great?
> Who or what determines right and wrong?
> How should one respond to an offense?
> What determines a person's worth?
> Why do kind people suffer while cruel people prosper?

"… *but be transformed by the renewing of your mind.*" If we are to behave differently from the fallen world system—into which we were born and of which we are made—we must change. Unfortunately, we cannot change ourselves, so we must "be transformed." This will be accomplished through "the renewing of our minds." Centuries before the Messiah came to bring the new covenant, the Lord promised through the prophet Jeremiah, " 'But this is the covenant which I will make with the house of Israel after those days,' declares the LORD, 'I will put My law within them and on their heart I will write it; and I will be their God, and they shall be My people' " (Jer. 31:33).

The exhortation to be transformed is another "cooperative command." As we respond to the call through submission, the Lord does the transforming. We learn to view the world through the grid of Scripture and we learn to respond as Scripture prescribes. The Holy Spirit, promised by Jesus on the eve of His crucifixion, uses Scripture, our experiences, trials and hardship, as well as fellowship with other believers to renovate us from the inside out. Gradually and supernaturally, our mind begins to think as God thinks, desire what God desires, love as God loves, and see things with the same perspective as He sees them. As this becomes a reality, we are able to discern the will of God and to cooperate with Him in accomplishing it (Eph. 4:17–24; Col. 3:1–11).

—**12:3**—

This program of renovating the world through the gradual transformation of believers must begin with how they view themselves. Paul wants his readers to guard against the subtle development of arrogance. Arrogant people love to tell you how well educated they are, they focus on how much they have accomplished or acquired, and they can't hear a story without having to top it. They know more, travel farther, work harder, and play better, and they are never, ever wrong. But, as a good friend once reminded me, cemeteries are full of indispensable people.

Note how Paul softens his confrontation with the phrase, "through the grace given to me." This is likely Paul standing on his apostolic authority to avoid any accusation of hypocrisy, but there is more here. I see in this a hint of transparency, suggesting that he considered himself arrogant at one time in his life. He is saying, in effect, "As one who once nurtured an exalted view of myself, let me give you some humble advice."

In this single verse, Paul uses a form of the Greek word *phroneō*, "to think," no less than four times. We are to avoid "over-thinking" ourselves and, instead, "have sound judgment," which is how the NASB renders the word *sōphroneō*. The root term, which is loosely based on a combination of *sōs* ("safe") and *phrēn* ("mind"), rarely appears in the Bible but was ranked high among secular Greeks as a civic virtue. A society was said to be "of sound mind" when the competing classes all agreed on direction or leadership.

In warning his readers to avoid thinking too highly of themselves, Paul didn't suggest they should think too little. While humanity is depraved, we are nevertheless God's great treasure. We are to become servants in the world, not doormats or worms. Too often the great Puritan theologians and artists pushed the doctrine of human depravity to extremes. While I affirm their desire to remain humble before God and grateful for His salvation, we were given adoption papers that provide us the honor of being called children of God (8:14 – 17). This is cause for celebration, not self-condemnation.

We are to have a balanced, sensible, realistic view of ourselves. In other words, we are to see ourselves as God sees us, not in comparison to others. Our relationship—our "peace with God"—is not secure because of anything we provide; we brought nothing into the relationship at the beginning and we do not have anything to give that we didn't first receive from Him. Neither does God love us more or less because of our relative value to Him in comparison to other believers. That describes how love and relationship work in this age, not before our God.

In terms of worth or value before God, we all stand on the same high platform. All believers are chosen by the sovereign will of God; the choice is the result of unmerited favor; and this grace is received through faith in Jesus Christ. Any notion that any one believer is better than another is folly.

## —12:4–5—

The human body as an illustration of unity in Christ is a favorite of Paul's (see 1 Cor. 6:15; 12:14–25; Eph. 4:16), and he returns to it again to demonstrate that equality is not sameness and difference is not inequality. Each human body is put together with many parts. We have vital organs—none of them visible—that keep us alive. We have various limbs that perform different, yet crucial functions, such as walking or grasping. We have sensory organs that allow us to perceive the world in different ways. And when everything is working in harmony, life is good. But when one part is injured or paralyzed, the whole body suffers.

What is true of the human body is true of the body of Christ. There is no such thing as an unimportant or worthless believer, even though some functions are more public than others.

Paul's illustration highlights three important truths about the body of Christ:

- *unity*—We derive our life from the same Source; none of us can exist outside the body. And we have one head, Christ, who controls and coordinates each member for the good of the whole.
- *diversity*—God *loves* variety! A careful study of plant and animal life reveals a marvelous creative spirit in the Creator; we can even go so far as to call it playful. I have little doubt that God smiled when He created the duckbilled platypus.
- *mutuality*—We need one another. When one person is injured or grieving, the whole body feels that pain. When one part cannot keep up, the others compensate. When disease attacks, the whole body reacts.

The concept of body-life is almost foreign to our secular world. While many business books teach and encourage teamwork, the motivation almost always comes back to the fulfillment of the individual. In other words, "You should think in terms of teams because that's the best way to achieve your own personal success." Even in Eastern cultures, where supposedly the emphasis is on the collective good of society over the individual, there sits at the top a few privileged leaders who like the system very much!

But in God's organizational chart, our motivation is mutual service prompted by love and compassion within the body in obedience to the Head, Jesus Christ.

## —12:6–8—

Now that we have a sensible view of ourselves in relation to God and fellow believers, we must consider our respective roles within the body, specifically, "spiritual gifts." These are supernatural abilities given by God to individuals that enable them to perform a function with ease and effectiveness.

Here Paul lists seven spiritual gifts:

*Prophecy.* Strictly speaking, prophets before the Bible was complete spoke when prompted by God and by the authority of God, and their words were to be taken as though heard directly from Him. They were literally God's "mouthpiece." They spoke without error and if even the slightest mistake was detected, they were to be hauled to the edge of town and stoned to death immediately. When the last letter of the Bible was penned and the last apostle died, there was no more need for a divinely inspired prophet. We now have the inspired and completed Scripture.

However, in a broader sense, there remains in the body those "prophets" today whose primary role is forth-telling. These individuals are gifted by the Holy Spirit with the supernatural ability to proclaim God's written Word in penetrating and convicting ways. They speak as God's "mouthpiece" insofar as they remain faithful to the message of Scripture. Evangelists, preachers, and writers are good modern-day examples.

*Serving.* Some call this the gift of helping. The Greek verb *diakoneō* is the origin of our word "deacon." I find it interesting that in Paul's list, serving is placed right next to the most public and most acclaimed gift, prophecy. It's as though he wants to highlight the fact that serving, the least desired, least public, and least honored gift in this "age" is an exalted position in God's system. Jesus said, "Whoever wishes to become great among you shall be your servant [**diakon**os]; and

### SPIRITUAL GIFTS LISTED IN SCRIPTURE

Paul lists seven spiritual gifts in his letter to the believers in Rome, but his list is not exhaustive. At least three other partial lists can be found in 1 Corinthians, Ephesians, and 1 Peter.

| | |
|---|---|
| Romans 12:6–8 | Prophecy |
| | Service |
| | Teaching |
| | Exhorting |
| | Giving |
| | Leading |
| | Mercy |
| 1 Corinthians 12:4–11 | Word of Wisdom |
| | Word of Knowledge |
| | Faith |
| | Healing |
| | Miracles |
| | Prophecy |
| | Distinguishing spirits |
| | Speaking in languages |
| | Interpreting languages |
| Ephesians 4:11 | Apostles |
| | Prophets |
| | Evangelists |
| | Pastors |
| | Teachers |
| 1 Peter 4:10–11 | Speaking |
| | Serving |

whoever wishes to be first among you shall be slave of all. For even the Son of Man did not come to be served [*diakonēthēnai*], but to serve [*diakonēsai*]" (Mark 10:43–45).

Those with this gift rarely have to be told what is needed; they simply discern needs, know how to help, and then do so without any need for notice or expectation of applause.

*Teaching.* Teachers have the ability to communicate revealed truth with knowledge, ease, and clarity. They are gifted in bringing the printed Word into flesh-and-bone life. They help others learn accurate facts, discover principles, see the practical relevance, and apply them.

*Exhortation.* This is the gift that mimics the Holy Spirit. The term is derived from the same Greek word translated "urge" in 12:1, *parakaleō*. Exhorters have the ability to drive truth home passionately, confront wrong constructively, turn Scripture reading into an action plan, unite believers behind a common endeavor—and they usually do this without offence. Their tough talk is laced with encouragement.

*Giving.* While all believers are instructed to be generous, these people look for opportunities to give, offering what they have beyond normal measure. Sometimes they are wealthy; more often, they are people of average means who generally give their time, energy, and expertise.

Gifted givers don't want bronze plaques or buildings named after them. There's nothing particularly wrong with either, but supernatural givers don't want all that attention. They much prefer anonymity. They see a need and then seek to meet it.

*Leading.* The Greek term can be translated either "to lead" or "to care for," which are identical in Christian ministry! Paul uses the term to describe those who possess unusual ability to provide guidance and administration to a group.

*Mercy.* Those with the gift of mercy exercise an extraordinary ability to sense the need of those who are hurting—to know what to say and how to say it, and when to remain silent. These people are invaluable to hospitals, where patients and families face serious illness and death.

Paul's epochal words are not only truth in which to rest; like 5:1 and 8:1–2, they are a call to respond. While God has promised to transform us and His Holy Spirit will not fail in His mission, we have a choice. We can choose to remain stubbornly aloof and resist His work, or we can tune into what He's doing and participate in His transforming process. And this choice begins with how we decide to regard ourselves, what priority we give fellow believers, and how we can turn our spiritual gifts into gifts that benefit others.

## Application

### *Consecrate and Transform*

The words "Therefore, I urge you" (12:1) indicate a critical transition in Paul's letter. God's grace to us must now take on a horizontal dimension. But we are not able to do this ourselves—not in our present state. We were born as part of this fallen creation, and we bear its twisted manner of thinking and living all the way down to the marrow of our bones and the motive of our hearts. We must be changed, remolded from within according to a new pattern. The Holy Spirit will be faithful to do the supernatural work of inner transformation; however, the apostle urges us to participate in the work. He calls us to two great endeavors: consecrating our bodies and transforming our minds.

"Present your bodies a living and holy sacrifice." This is *consecration*. This is a radical separation from a secular worldview, which begins with a decision to give our bodies over to a divine purpose. This has tangible, practical implications we must not ignore. It affects where we go, what we choose to feed our minds, how we treat our bodies, what influences we receive or reject, how we spend our time, how we spend our money, and what we choose to accomplish day in and day out (to name only a few specifics).

"Be transformed by the renewing of your mind." This is *transformation*. The ultimate objective is a transformed heart, a fundamentally different nature from the inside out. However, we cannot transform our own heart; only God can do that. We *can* gain new knowledge and change our perspectives. This transformation of the mind merely represents the believer's participation in God's renovation program.

Let me turn from the theoretical to the practical by asking a penetrating question. To what are you devoting your body? You have two excellent, yet painful tools of analysis at your disposal: your schedule and your financial records. Devote a couple of hours to reviewing both.

First, take a blank sheet of paper and create a chart of your typical week. (Use the example below as a guide.) Label the blocks of time based on your routine, which includes formal commitments and your typical habits.
Recognizing that most of us must devote no less than forty hours each week to earning a living, to what is the balance of your time (128 hours) devoted? Marriage and family? Excellent! Serving others? Wonderful! Personal enrichment? Great! Relaxing, resting, sleeping? Highly recommended!

Or (be honest, now) do you see time devoted to activities that contribute nothing to your life as a consecrated instrument of God's grace? Such soul-searching can be convicting.

| | Mon | Tues | Wed | Thur | Fri | Sat | Sun |
|---|---|---|---|---|---|---|---|
| 5 am—6 am | | | | | | | |
| 6 am—7 am | | | | | | | |
| 7 am—8 am | | | | | | | |
| 8 am—5 pm | | | | | | | |
| 6 pm—7 pm | | | | | | | |
| 7 pm—8 pm | | | | | | | |
| 8 pm—9 pm | | | | | | | |
| 9 pm—10 pm | | | | | | | |
| 10 pm—11 pm | | | | | | | |
| 11 pm—12 pm | | | | | | | |

Next, review your finances. A good place to start would be your bank and credit card statements. Use a set of colored highlighter pens to mark each line item according to a set of categories, such as:

*Necessities*: housing, groceries, utilities, and other expenditures that cannot be eliminated

*Debt*: auto loans, consumer loans, credit card payments, late fees, and bank charges

*Discretionary*: entertainment, vacations, dining out, upscale clothing, or other treats

*Giving*: donations to your local church, missions, charities, or needy family and friends

*Waste*: expenditures that add little or nothing to life, or worse, cause additional sorrow

Your categories may be different. The point of the exercise is to be brutally honest and to become intentional about where we spend our money. Again, such self-analysis can cut deeply.

Once you have analyzed your schedule and your financial records, *consecrate* them. Here's how: Present them to the Lord in a prayer of dedication and ask Him to begin the work of heart transformation on your behalf. Then, start making necessary adjustments. Rather than allowing your schedule to unfold haphazardly, become strategic in how you direct your time and energy. Rather than allowing your finances to flow unregulated based on impulse, let your values take over.

Block out time to pursue what you *say* you treasure—spiritual growth, marriage, children, charitable work, rest—and *protect those blocks of time.* Prepare a budget, devoting money to sustain and build what you *say* you value—*starting with giving*—and then discipline yourself to *follow your budget.*

Make no mistake; consecration and transformation are anything but theoretical concepts. They have tangible expression for the believer. I'm not suggesting that the exercises I have outlined—or any other human activity—are sufficient for spiritual growth or that they can substitute for the supernatural work of the Holy Spirit. However, they are a good place to begin participating in His program of soul renovation. As you consecrate your time and money, you have taken a giant step forward in consecrating your body. As this occurs, I guarantee your mind will begin a process of transformation as well.

## Christianity 101 (Romans 12:9–16)

---

⁹*Let* love *be* without hypocrisy. Abhor what is evil; cling to what is good. ¹⁰*Be* devoted to one another in brotherly love; give preference to one another in honor; ¹¹not lagging behind in diligence, fervent in spirit, serving the Lord; ¹²rejoicing in hope, persevering in tribulation, devoted to prayer, ¹³contributing to the needs of the saints, practicing hospitality.

¹⁴Bless those who persecute you; bless and do not curse. ¹⁵Rejoice with those who rejoice, and weep with those who weep. ¹⁶Be of the same mind toward one another; do not be haughty in mind, but associate with the lowly. Do not be wise in your own estimation.

---

What legacy are you creating for the next generation? What are you leaving in the minds of those who will outlive you so that their lives are deeper, richer, better than yours has been? In 1999, the popular American novelist Stephen King faced this question head-on as he lay in a ditch after being struck by a drunk driver. Although wealthy and successful by any standard, he recognized the fleeting value of temporal things and concluded, "All that lasts is what you pass on."

Take a few moments now and imagine yourself standing beside your own casket, invisibly attending your own funeral. Your life on earth has ended. Your family is sitting nearby staring blankly, blinking through tears. Your friends are there, recalling your life and sharing stories. What are your family and friends remembering? It's fairly certain they aren't talking about your financial portfolio. They aren't taking an inventory of your possessions—unless, of course, that is all you have left them to remember.

If you leave the next generation with anything of inestimable value, it won't be tangible. The treasures you leave are the memories your loved ones take with them as the lid of the casket is closed and your body is lowered six feet and covered with soil. Your most valuable legacy will be your example of a life well lived, the love you have steadily and faithfully given away each day, your model of grace. These will enable those who knew you to enjoy life more fully than you did.

Wouldn't it be helpful if someone could put together a straightforward guide to help us live well and leave a truly valuable legacy? A simple daily checklist of attitudes and actions would be so helpful. I'm happy to say that such a list has been preserved, and it's not simply the writing of a brilliant man who made a major impact on the first century. It's an inspired list preserved for us by God Himself, bearing His stamp of approval.

While 1 Corinthians 13 is the most beautiful and most eloquent treatise on love, Romans 12:9–16 is the most succinct. In less than eighty Greek words, Paul teaches us how to love others in practical, tangible ways that will fill the memories of those we love and teach them how to live well.

## —12:9: Unhypocritical Love—

Genuine love has two primary qualities: sincerity, the opposite of hypocrisy, and discernment, the opposite of gullibility.

A literal rendering of the first Greek words in this verse is, "Love, un-hypocritical!" English translations must add something to produce a smooth, readable style, such as:

Let love be without hypocrisy. (NASB)
Love must be without hypocrisy. (NET)
Love must be sincere. (NIV)

I prefer to keep it simple: "Love is un-hypocritical." The Greek word is *anypokritos*, which is the compound of *an*, "no," and *hypokritos*, "pretense" or "pretext." This word illustrates better than any other the difference between the world system and God's order. The verb *hypokrinomai* means simply "to answer back," usually in the context of debate or acting. Therefore, secular Greek writers used the term both positively and negatively, depending on the situation. So, "the noble person can play any part assigned with no loss of inner stability."[1] If we were to apply this Greek mindset to a modern example, we would expect the White House Press Secretary to present and defend the President's policy on a given matter, even if he or she disagrees with it personally. His or her job is to provide information and answer questions on behalf of the President. In a positive sense, this individual is dutifully placing his or her private opinion in the background in order to fulfill a public role.

When used negatively, "the stage is a sham world and actors are deceivers."[2] Greeks and Romans despised deception as much as anyone.

The Jews used the term almost always negatively, which is not surprising considering their unwillingness to see motivation and deeds as separate things. (In the Hebrew mind, knowledge was not enough. One could not be considered wise unless he or she translated knowledge into behavior.) The New Testament writers followed Jesus, who used *hypokritos* to describe people who had fallen away from truth received from God, but acted otherwise. Therefore, to be a hypocrite was to lie through behavior instead of speech.

If hypocrisy creeps in, love ceases to be love and becomes something grotesque — manipulation, quid pro quo, competition, pretense. There's no place for a mask; there's no playacting; there's no room to think one way and act another. That's because love and truth go hand-in-hand.

Love must also be discerning. Paul commands, "Abhor what is evil," using a Greek verb meaning "to shrink back, detest." When love encounters what is evil, it refuses to participate. Love doesn't embrace evil, nor does it merely look the other way. Love dares to confront someone doing evil, not to judge or browbeat but to inspire righteousness.

By contrast, love "clings to what is good." Jesus used this word in reference to marriage, in which "a man shall leave his father and mother and be *joined* to his wife, and the two shall become one flesh" (Matt. 19:5, emphasis mine). In order to repel evil and cling to good, love must know the difference.

In a class I attended in seminary, Charles Ryrie likened love to a river that is bounded on either side by truth and discernment. If either boundary breaks down, the river spills over its banks and causes horrific damage.

## —12:10–15: Eight More Facets of Love—

Having declared that love is guided by truth and discernment, Paul highlights eight additional qualities to help us express love in ways others can experience it.

*Devoted affection* (12:10). Paul's terms are drenched with tenderness and kindness. Our love is to be characterized by the warm affection shared between members of a family. But, truth be told, family members can be especially difficult to love! Nevertheless, we make every effort simply because we have a family bond that cannot be broken.

*Honor.* The word used here means "respect" or "value." Honoring someone begins with a willingness to let another have his or her preference in nonessential matters. We are to listen when someone speaks and give his or her words careful consideration. We must allow others to disagree, respecting their opinions even though we disagree. We are to treat another person's feelings with care and respect, demonstrating gratitude for one another.

Interestingly, Paul encourages his readers to outdo one another in this area. The Greek phrase "give preference to one another in honor" can also be translated, "outdo one another in showing honor." In other words, if you insist on competing, see who can genuinely value the other more.

*Enthusiasm/passion* (12:11). The Greek phrases have in mind the idea of boiling over or boiling up, as if water were boiling in a pot. A quality of love is passion for doing well by others, boiling up in the Spirit, serving the Lord. This enthusiasm is characterized by active optimism and energetic zeal that cannot be contained; it's the very opposite of lethargy and indifference. Everyone wants to be loved enthusiastically and passionately, not passively or out of obligation.

*Patience* (12:12). The three phrases that comprise 12:12 are all about patience. And if you look closely, you'll see a progression that cannot be anything but deliberate.

### Hope ▸ Tribulation ▸ Prayer

How do we remain patient through tribulation? We continue to hope, anticipating that which has not yet happened and celebrating as though it has. We continue to fulfill our obligations and enjoy our blessings even when we're discouraged and want to quit. And all the while, we devote ourselves to prayer.

These qualities of love are indispensable. When people can hope together, remain relentlessly devoted to one another and to Christ, and talk to the Father on one another's behalf, nothing can tear their community apart.

*Generosity* (12:13). Love isn't stingy; love freely shares whatever it has. Paul's phrase "contributing to the needs of the saints" uses the Greek word *koinōneō*, which is the quintessential term of the church. It means "to share in, be in fellowship or to participate in." I believe this has more in mind than sharing one's abundance with someone in need. This has shared suffering in mind. Love gives even when it hurts. It shares money freely even when money is tight. And when the contributions have run out, love continues to share in the need of another.

*Hospitality.* Love is also hospitable. The original meaning of the term is "love of strangers." It carries the idea of extending love to those who are different—sojourners from another culture, another race, or a different belief. Furthermore, the term

## From My Journal

## Be a One-Buttock Christian!

Benjamin Zander wrote a great book that he titled *The Art of Possibility*. At the time, Zander was conductor of the Boston Philharmonic and a professor at New England Conservatory of Music. He wrote as a musician, not surprisingly, but in doing so, he also masterfully blended the world of music with everyday life. In a chapter on passion, he included the story of a particular student who played Chopin perfectly, but without an essential quality that makes a performance great.

A young pianist was playing a Chopin prelude in my master's class and although we had worked right up to the edge of realizing an overarching concept of the piece, his performance remained earthbound. He understood it intellectually, he could have explained it to someone else, but he was unable to convey the emotional energy that is the true language of music. Then I noticed something that proved to be the key: His body was firmly centered in the upright position. I blurted out, "The trouble is you're a two-buttock player!" I encouraged him to allow his whole body to flow sideways, urging him to catch the wave of the music with the shape of his own body, and suddenly the music took fight. Several in the audience gasped, feeling the emotional dart hit home, as a new distinction was born: a one-buttock player. The president of a corporation in Ohio, who was present as a witness, wrote to me: "I was so moved that I went home and transformed my whole company into a one-buttock company."[3]

What a great goal for believers, to become *one-buttock Christians*! People would come from everywhere to know the God we serve if we lived the truth we carry in our hearts with vibrant, enthusiastic passion. It's time we started living out the truth of the gospel with the kind of boiling-over passion and zeal described in the words, "Not lagging behind in diligence, fervent in spirit." If enough of us started doing that, we could watch as the world around us is transformed.

translated "practicing" is better rendered "pursuing." Love takes the initiative, actively looking for opportunities to benefit another, especially those who are different.

*Graciousness* (12:14). Of all the qualities of love, this is undoubtedly the most difficult to carry out. The others may fall by the wayside because we are busy or tired or self-absorbed, but we typically don't resist them. Returning good for evil, however, goes against every natural instinct we possess, especially when the offender is a fellow Christian. Grace in response to sin is a quality unique to God, and this ability can only come from Him and be enabled by Him. Paul extends his teaching on the subject in 12:17–21.

*Sympathy* (12:15). True love never stands aloof. When love knows that a brother or a sister is rejoicing, it cannot contain excitement. Instead, it celebrates his or her joy. And, with just as much empathy and passion, it grieves the loss of another as if it were its own.

An old Swedish proverb that hung in my childhood home frequently comes to mind: "Shared joy is a double joy; shared sorrow is half a sorrow."

## —12:16: Humility and Love—

Paul concludes his list of love qualities by returning to where he began, with the quality of humility. Four phrases frame the picture of humility and, if you look closely, you'll detect the image of Jesus.

"Be of the same mind toward one another" doesn't encourage "group-think." Paul is not suggesting that thinking differently on one topic or another is necessarily bad. The Greek word rendered "mind" means "understanding" or "mindset." We are to be *for* the same things, even if our perspectives or approaches differ. That means we agree on the essentials and allow latitude wherever possible. Furthermore, humility seeks to understand before being understood. Humility prefers to communicate rather than do battle with words. Humility tries to find common ground with others without sacrificing truth. And humility regards the thoughts of others with high regard.

"Do not be haughty in mind" counsels against thinking of oneself as highborn, high-ranking, high-class, or high-minded, distinctions that expect corresponding treatment. In his letter to the Philippian believers, Paul reminded them of how Jesus climbed down from His heavenly place to suffer the humiliating death of a criminal ... for us.

"Associate with the lowly" in the Greek means, literally, "Allow yourself to be carried away by people of low rank." In secular Greek and Roman culture, to be seen with people of much lower rank could be fatal to one's ambitions. Not only were they socially undesirable, they were thought to corrupt the morals of upright citizens. To the contrary, Paul taught that humility seeks out people on the fringes and risks embracing them.

"Do not be wise in your own estimation" repeats the apostle's thought in 12:3. People who think they are wise and attempt to let others in on the secret are usually the most laughable characters of all. If someone is wise, others notice.

It's fair to say that most people aspire to the kind of love described by Paul. I don't know of anyone who wouldn't want to create an enduring legacy of loving memories for family and friends. So why is Christian love so rare? Why do people hide behind masks or become so undiscerning? Two reasons: pride and fear.

Pride poisons love. Some men and women possess incredible talent and impressive intellect, but fail to love because they are too proud to stoop, too proud to reach out, too proud to ask for help, too proud to be vulnerable. So, they cover their faces with something pretty, put on a good show, pretend to care, and keep all of their relationships superficial. That way there's no risk of being truly known . . . or hurt.

Fear is no less deadly to love. Some fear giving genuine love because it comes with the terrifying risk of loss or perhaps rejection. So, they settle for pleasing people no matter what the cost to their personal integrity. Too timid to confront and too fragile to seek good, they accept whatever comes their way and comfort themselves with the words, "I love unconditionally." But really, their love is a cheap trinket.

The irony is that people know when love is hypocritical or undiscerning. Sooner or later, they know when pride is putting on a show or when fear is bargaining for security. Love motivated by pride or fear is self-centered and nothing substitutes for real love, which is above all selfless. Love, in its simplest terms, is seeking the highest good of the other person.

Sometimes, love is tough, stern, strong-hearted, unwilling to look the other way when evil is present. It's not making someone comfortable by telling them what they want to hear. Sadly, love occasionally has to be tough, firm, and unbending. More often, however, love must be tender, marked by compassion, understanding, tolerance, grace, and forgiveness. In every case, whether tough or tender, authentic love seeks the highest, greatest good of the other.

## Application

### *Authentic Love and the Body of Christ*

Paul continues his appeal for grace in the horizontal dimension by calling for "un-hypocritical" love. Whereas hypocritical love is nothing more than impulsive urges and idle feelings, genuine love takes action to do what is in the best interest of the other person. However, genuine love is also discerning, not gullible (12:9). Call me unromantic, but I don't believe in unbounded love or love without limits. Genuine love never spills over the boundaries of truth on one side and discernment on the other. For example, a child may say to his or her parent, "If you love me, you'll give me what I want." A wise parent will respond, "Because I love you, I'll give you what is best for you."

Paul goes on to describe love as affectionate, honoring, enthusiastic, patient, generous, gracious, sympathetic, and ultimately fueled by humility, seeking the highest, greatest good of another before our own (12:10–16). Interestingly, Paul's exhortation on authentic love immediately follows his description of spiritual gifts and the body of Christ. He did the same in his letter to the Corinthians. His famous "love chapter" (1 Cor. 13) follows his lengthy description of body-life (1 Cor. 12).

Most of us have little trouble understanding how these truths apply to love within a household or between members of our extended family. While we frequently fail to apply what we know, we nevertheless know what we *should* do. But how does one demonstrate "love without hypocrisy" within the local church body, especially one serving hundreds of believers we cannot possibly know personally?

The answer is "by serving." God has given you a supernatural ability to function within the body of Christ as a vital member. You have within you a gift that may or may not be influenced by your personality type or your training or your vocation. It is supernaturally provided by the Holy Spirit because He loves you and—just as important—He loves your church. He has specifically arranged for you and the body to need one another. In other words, your church is incomplete without you, like a body missing a vital organ, and when you fail to supply what God has placed within you, the whole church suffers.

Let me offer a few practical suggestions for those who may not have served in church and perhaps don't know where to begin.

1. *Know yourself.* I am not a big fan of spiritual gift inventories. The only way to discover one's spiritual gift is to get busy serving! However, a well-designed spiritual gift test or a church-specific personality profile can be a good place to start if you don't already know how you would like to help. Your church staff may have a survey they favor, or you can find them online. Don't ignore the results. At the same time, pay close attention to the desires of your heart. Both are important. Do you find yourself drawn to a particular ministry or role?

2. *Ask for help.* Call your church office and ask who would be the appropriate person to help you find a place to serve, then set an appointment. At

the meeting, explain your desire to serve and ask for help finding the best match between your desire and the church's need. Be prepared to revive the poor soul! This will be a delightful shock. I can count on both hands (with fingers left over) the times I've had parishioners follow through in that manner.

3. *Faithfully serve.* Most churches will ask you to commit to a minimum term of service. You will undoubtedly face challenges by the demands of the role and you will be tempted either to shy away . . . or to quit. But stick with it. Share your struggles with your leader, ask for help, and faithfully serve to the best of your ability. Then, at the end of your term, use your experience to find a more suitable role. Eventually—and sooner than you think—you will have found your place. One reminder: It will call for sacrifice. But as the years pass, the words of the great preacher John Henry Jowett ring true: "Ministry that costs nothing, accomplishes nothing."

4. *Discover your gift.* As you faithfully and sacrificially offer un-hypocritical love within your congregation, you will discover where and how you best serve. When the work becomes a labor of love, when you feel energized by the tiredness, you will have discovered your place in the body. That's when the joy really begins! Strange as it may seem, the ministry is run by tired people!

Like most things in life, authentic love is neither quick nor easy. But when you make serving the body of Christ a priority, you won't be able to imagine life without it. Furthermore, the rewards that come your way will be remarkable.

## Doing Right When You've Been Done Wrong (Romans 12:17–21)

---

[17]Never pay back evil for evil to anyone. Respect what is right in the sight of all men. [18]If possible, so far as it depends on you, be at peace with all men. [19]Never take your own revenge, beloved, but leave room for the wrath *of God,* for it is written, "Vengeance is Mine, I will repay," says the Lord. [20]"But if your enemy is hungry, feed him, and if he is thirsty, give him a drink; for in so doing you will heap burning coals on his head." [21]Do not be overcome by evil, but overcome evil with good.

---

Will Rogers, the late actor, author, and humorist, once said, "I never met a man I didn't like." Obviously Will Rogers never met my Marine Corps drill instructor. He was three-fourths gristle and the rest backbone, and I can't be certain that his own mother liked him. Will Rogers didn't know the church elder who once began a private meeting with me by brandishing his gun and proving that it was loaded! And you're fairly certain Will didn't know the person who made life unbearably difficult for you.

Let's be honest, we all have people we don't like and there are probably more who don't like us. We want to believe they're absent from our thoughts, but like a phantom they haunt us when we're fatigued or lonely or discouraged. It's frustrating because we've presented ourselves as living sacrifices, yet the sinful actions of another person tempt us to crawl off the altar and get some much-deserved justice.

To remain sacrificed, to remain submitted to God's way instead of the world's system requires something greater than natural strength. Fortunately, the Lord has promised to provide supernatural ability to rise above the malicious deeds of another. But, like grace, it comes through faith. And faith is a choice to obey God when the age in which we live urges us not to.

## —12:17—

Paul's counsel is straightforward enough: "To no one give back evil against evil" (my literal translation). While explaining the qualities of genuine love, Paul echoed the words of Christ, "Bless those who persecute you; bless and do not curse" (12:14; Matt. 5:44; Luke 6:28). Isn't it interesting that both Jesus and Paul instruct us to watch our speech? The heart is a well and the tongue is a bucket. The lips can only draw from what's in the heart, and an untransformed heart contains an insatiable desire to protect its own rights.

Plans for revenge begin with cursing. *The Theological Dictionary of the New Testament* notes: "Curses, found in almost all religious history, are utterances that are designed to bring harm by supernatural operation."[4] Today we don't traffic in black magic and malicious incantations, but we do curse, we do wish harm to come on the person who has injured or offended us. How we choose to respond verbally prepares us for our next decision. If we want to obey the command to avoid returning evil for evil, we must bring our tongues under control. We must first obey the command to "bless and not curse."

The Greek word for "bless" means "to speak well of." It's the same term from which we get the English word "eulogy." We are to eulogize the person who has offended us ... *before his or her life has ended.* However, we cannot wait until we feel like it; we must choose deliberately, contrary to our nature. Otherwise, the desire for retaliation will fester.

Note the alternative to returning evil with evil: "Respect what is right." The Greek for "respect" means "to foresee, take thought of, have regard for." It relies heavily on the concept of seeing or vision. This makes a great deal of sense. We are to look past the offense to see what good we can do, so that our actions aren't mere reactions. Our behavior should be guided by godly character, not pulled here and there by this insult or that offense.

## —12:18–20—

Paul is realist, however. He—perhaps better than most men—understands that some people are determined to be our enemy regardless of how we choose to behave. Some folks simply live to fight and wouldn't know what to do without someone to harass. Insofar as it depends on us, we are to live at peace with everyone. How? Paul suggests two responses, one passive and one active.

First, when an enemy deliberately causes harm, we are to let it go unanswered. Now, allow me to clarify. This is not a situation in which one person in a relationship causes harm to another and must be confronted in order to restore the bond. In that case, we must follow the procedure outlined by Jesus in Matthew 18:15–17. Here, Paul is referring to the deeds of an enemy—presumably someone outside the body of Christ, though not necessarily!—in which he or she clearly intends to harm another. Confrontation would be pointless. Paul's advice: let it go.

Note the reason we are to set aside our revenge. It is to "leave room for the wrath of God." At first, I took that to mean something like this: "Don't seek to harm your enemy in return for an offense. Let God do it for you because He can hurt 'em a whole lot worse than you can!" And chances are good you've heard that kind of teaching before. However, the wrath of God is always redemptive, never retaliatory or spiteful. The wrath of God during this age of grace pursues the sinner, cuts off his escape, confronts her with the consequences of sin, chastises him, and makes her continued sin miserable. Why? To bring the individual to repentance. To give him or her grace. To redeem our enemy as He has redeemed all believers.

When we take our own revenge, we dare to stand between God and His beloved, whom He may choose to pursue. Furthermore, we presume to take the Creator's place on the seat of judgment in the life of another creature. Eventually, the age of grace will end and the time of judgment will begin. If that person is ultimately doomed to suffer God's eternal wrath, they are those we pity, not those with whom we dream of settling scores.

Paul's second suggested response is more active: extend him or her the same hospitality you would a friendly stranger. The reference to food and drink draws inspiration from the Near Eastern duty to provide travelers a meal and a safe place to sleep. However, let me clarify a few misconceptions.

This is not a proof text for pacifism. Paul wasn't writing about the foreign policy of a nation. These are instructions for individuals who find themselves the target of another's evil deeds. Furthermore, Paul does not intend to condemn the good sense to defend oneself or one's family against a physical attack. If someone tries to break into your house in the middle of the night, you don't say, "Hey, don't forget to look in the media room, there a lot of electronics you might enjoy." No! Fight! Call the police, have the intruder arrested, and press charges.

Paul does not intend this to prohibit protecting one's homeland or preserving one's wife and/or family from an intruder. Rather, this is about heated arguments, malicious lawsuits, deliberate slander, and dirty politics at work or school or neighborhood or even church. It's okay to protect yourself and your family. However, there's a fine line between protection and retaliation. It can be difficult to see, especially in the heat of the moment. Our best policy is to look for ways to be kind to an enemy and fight only to survive an immediate danger to life and health.

The purpose of returning good for evil is to "heap burning coals on his head." No one knows for certain the origin of this odd centuries-old metaphor. Some suggest it points to an ancient Egyptian practice of carrying a pan of coals on one's head as a sign of contrition. I believe the phrase is merely an idiom describing humility, not unlike our expression, "He came to me with his hat in his hand." During the Great Depression in America, a cash-strapped man might have no other choice than to approach a group of friends for a donation. It was a humiliating experience for him to hold out his hat in the desperate hope they would drop a few precious coins into it. In ancient times, allowing one's household fire to go out was seen as the epitome of irresponsibility. The humiliating experience of walking home from a neighbor's house with a pan of coals probably gave rise to this word-picture for humility.

Whatever the exact origin of the phrase, the meaning is clear. The purpose of kindness is to allow the conscience of the enemy to do its job. Hopefully our good conduct, our humility, will bring about humility and repentance in return.

### —12:21—

Paul's summary statement on the issue of retaliation could be a mission statement for what we might call "the master plan of salvation." God's ultimate purpose is to reclaim His creation from the control of evil, supernaturally transform it, and bring it back under the control of His righteousness. In other words, He will overcome the world's evil with His good. In following the command of Christ to "bless and not curse" (12:14; Matt. 5:44; Luke 6:28) and by returning good for evil, we do as God does and we become active participants in His great plan for the world.

As I look back over Paul's teaching on how to respond to enemies, I see a great deal of seasoned wisdom and practical sensibility. His counsel is concise without becoming trite. It is ruggedly realistic. Note, however, that he never uses the word "easy." Returning good for evil is not a complicated concept; it's very simple. However, it's also one of the most difficult tasks we undertake throughout life.

Let's be honest. Forgiving an offense is much easier when the guilty person is contrite and has sincerely apologized. When we see our pain reflected in their remorse, curses easily dissolve into blessings. But when the offender takes delight in our suffering or personally benefits from our injury, choosing to treat him or her kindly defies everything we know about justice and fair play. Kindness is a response beyond our natural capability. It will require supernatural strength. Fortunately, that is precisely what God has promised.

Here is where Paul's reassurance in 8:28–39 finds practical application. When beaten down by an enemy, when reeling from his or her last evil deed, it's easy to wonder, *If I'm not looking out for my welfare, then who is?*

Sadly, it's rare to find other believers jumping to our aid when enemy arrows fly. Many prefer to treat our wounds after the attack rather than risk standing beside or in front of us when we need help the most. Advocates are rare! And, to make matters worse, God often seems distracted or disinterested if not cruelly distant while enemies have their way. (Ask Job.) At times like these, Paul's earlier question demands an answer. "If God is for us, who is against us?" (8:31). It's a faith question. Do we really believe that God is in control and that He will preserve us through danger—including enemy attacks? How we answer will determine whether cursing or blessing falls from our lips, which in turn leads either to kindness or retaliation.

I said earlier that the heart is a well and the lips can only draw from what the heart contains. Long before an enemy creates a crisis, the answer to Paul's faith question must fill our hearts. If we wait until we're dodging missiles, our answer will be grim. So, let's prepare now. Let's settle the issue before the crisis and let our hearts be fully convinced. Read the answer to Paul's faith question in 8:32–39 and make believing it your current spiritual objective. Reread it … aloud. Pray over it. Ask the Holy Spirit to transform your mind (cf. 12:2) so that you accept its truth as naturally as you live with the law of gravity. Then, when fired upon by an enemy, you'll have the supernatural ability to respond with calm, resolved, composed, God-assured kindness.

## From My Journal

### "Honey . . . Let It Go."

Ministry doesn't get any easier after forty-six years. Even after all that experience, I still have the occasional ulcer-generating church member determined to run me out of the pulpit. I've learned to shred anonymous letters before reading them and to ignore anyone who claims to speak for a silent, yet powerful faction—oldest tricks in the church—but this one sought to hurt me through my family. *That* boiled my blood, and I was on the verge of saying too much and going too far with my response.

One day my wife, Cynthia, heard me unloading the verbal truck about the situation over the phone to a close friend. When the conversation ended, I hung up and slumped back in my chair. Cynthia had been down in our bedroom when she heard me and came to the bottom of the stairs. I heard her ask rather quietly, "Can I say something to you?"

I got up from my desk, walked to the stairway, sat down on the top stair, and said, "Yeah."

"Let it go." She stood there, looking up, staring. "Let it go!" she repeated.

Her words flew up the stairs and pierced me through the heart.

"I heard your voice, I heard your tone, and I heard your volume way down here from the bedroom. Come on, Honey . . . Let it go."

Wise words from a concerned wife. She wasn't worried about my doing anything wrong, or offending anyone, or even my taking any particular action. None of that mattered. She was concerned about what my resentment was doing to *me* down deep inside.

I needed to let it go. I did.

Neil Anderson wrote, "Forgiveness is agreeing to live with the consequences of another person's sin. You're going to live with those consequences whether you want to or not; your only choice is whether you will do so in the bitterness of unforgiveness or the freedom of forgiveness."[5]

As long as you hold onto a wrong done to you, you will be overcome by evil and you will be victimized by the very thing you are trying to get rid of. So, you have only one choice. It's uncomplicated, yet anything but easy. Learn from my experience. Let it go.

## Application

### What to Do When You've Been Done Wrong

If anyone understood the pain of personal offense, it was Paul. In addition to the perils of nature, he survived numerous and brutal assaults while crisscrossing the empire between Jerusalem and Rome. He endured multiple lashings and even stonings by men who wanted to silence the gospel. He withstood withering verbal attacks from religious rivals, including pagans, Jews, and even fellow Christians. No leader in the first-century church suffered more at the hands of other people than Paul. So his command in 12:17, "Never pay back evil for evil to anyone," came at great personal sacrifice.

The apostle's teaching on personal attacks can be reduced to three principles, each suggesting a godly response.

1. *Evil stirs up more evil; refuse to obey your natural reaction.* All of us have natural instincts that reside deep within. Every cell of our bodies is programmed for survival. When something comes too close to our face, we flinch. When we're about to fall, we throw out our hands. We're in our car and another car starts backing up quickly, we honk, honk, HONK! Those are natural, instinctive responses. When someone causes us harm, our natural instinct is to seek justice by getting even. Paul calls us to respond supernaturally, which means we must arrest our natural response.

2. *Our desire for justice is corrupt; refuse to seek your own.* Justice honors God. That's why the Lord gave us governments, which He empowers for the common good. As bearers of our Creator's image, we desire justice when wronged by another; however, unlike our Creator, our desire for justice is fueled by pride, fear, hatred, and selfishness. Therefore, we are unqualified. Paul calls us to surrender our desire for justice and to seek blessing for the offender instead.

3. *Our vengeance leaves no room for grace; surrender the matter to God.* Each person has an unavoidable appointment with death, at which point each one will stand before his or her Maker to be judged. If punishment is due, then—and not a moment sooner—will God mete out vengeance according to his or her deeds. In the meantime, the Lord extends the offer of grace to all who do wrong. Even the justice dispensed by governments is an instrument of chastening in His hand, which He uses to bring nonbelievers to repentance. Dare we interfere? Paul calls us to allow God to be the judge of souls, to dispense justice or bestow mercy according to His infinite wisdom.

After suffering the sinful deed of another, we need healing, and vengeance whispers a tantalizing promise, doesn't it? "Getting even will heal that emotional wound and make you feel warm all over." But that's a lie. Vengeance cannot heal wounds. Only grace can do that. Grace in the form of heartfelt repentance and a sincere apology will go a long way, but offenders almost never risk that kind of humility. Fortunately, God's grace is available in abundant supply, just for the asking. So, instead of seeking retribution, ask for grace. Then stifle the persistent lies of vengeance by taking another step toward healing: "Bless those who persecute you; bless and do not curse.... Do not be overcome by evil, but overcome evil with good" (12:14, 21).

## How to Be a Godly Rebel (Romans 13:1–7)

¹Every person is to be in subjection to the governing authorities. For there is no authority except from God, and those which exist are established by God. ²Therefore whoever resists authority has opposed the ordinance of God; and they who have opposed will receive condemnation upon themselves. ³For rulers are not a cause of fear for good behavior, but for evil. Do you want to have no fear of authority? Do what is good and you will have praise from the same; ⁴for it is a minister of God to you for good. But if you do what is evil, be afraid; for it does not bear the sword for nothing; for it is a minister of God, an avenger who brings wrath on the one who practices evil.

⁵Therefore it is necessary to be in subjection, not only because of wrath, but also for conscience' sake. ⁶For because of this you also pay taxes, for *rulers* are servants of God, devoting themselves to this very thing. ⁷Render to all what is due them: tax to whom tax *is due*; custom to whom custom; fear to whom fear; honor to whom honor.

For the next few moments, travel back in time with me and imagine yourself wrestling with a particular moral dilemma. You must either follow your Christian conscience or obey your government.

We begin in 1760. You're an English man or woman. You were reared and educated in London, where your family has lived for generations. You are loyal to the crown, even though you don't always agree with King George's policies. England has been good to you; your family's business has prospered. In time, your father senses your need for adventure and proposes that you establish a presence in the colonies across the Atlantic. You're attracted to the risk and the possibilities of life in New England. So you plan the voyage, sail to America, purchase property, and begin building your business.

When you arrive, there is talk of revolution, but nothing you feel compelled to heed. However, as the years pass, you understand why the colonists are upset. Taxes appear everywhere and threaten to drain your fledgling business. And the money doesn't appear to be returned in the form of government services. You have shared the injustices your American friends have endured, yet you are still a loyal subject of the crown.

Time passes quickly. The question of revolution cannot be avoided much longer. You must choose your loyalty. What do you do? Your heart is in your homeland but your conscience has taken root in American soil. Do you stay? Do you side with the English or do you oppose the people of your birth? Soon a coalition of revolutionaries invites you to join them in arms. Do you become a Minuteman or do you distance yourself and pray for Red Coats to appear?

Travel forward in time one hundred years to 1860. You own a plantation in southern Alabama, twelve thousand acres of cotton, corn, peaches ... and many slaves to do the work. The system has allowed you to increase your wealth year after year, and things couldn't be better for you and your estate. But you've recently placed your faith in Jesus Christ, and now you struggle because your pastor, an uncommon man of courage, is preaching against slavery. Your peers tell you slavery is moral and even justified by Scripture, but deep down in the quiet of your soul, you know better.

Then, the issue confronts you in flesh and bone when a new president is elected to office in November of 1860, your state secedes from the Union in February of 1861, and all-out war begins in April. What do you do? Do you release your slaves, abandon your family homestead, move north, and fight for the Union army? Or do you ignore your conscience, keep the slaves, and remain in the South?

Fast-forward again to the year 1936. You're a German Christian living in Berlin. A dictator, mad with prejudice, has been given immense power by growing numbers of undiscerning and sometimes violent fellow citizens. But the future is bright for Germany. Prosperity has returned, people are working again, your business is finally turning a profit, and the Berlin summer Olympics will allow Germany to feel proud again.

Meanwhile, some of your Jewish friends and neighbors have been forced to wear an ominous Star of David and have been disappearing without explanation. With each passing day, you are pressured to choose your loyalty: support Der Führer and the majority of your peers or advocate for the fair treatment of Jews and other "undesirables." Do you openly stand against your government, or do you recognize its sovereignty and obey its commands?

The believers in Rome undoubtedly found it easier to remain safely cloistered in their own communities than to engage their pagan magistrates. By keeping their distance from anything involving government, they would have encountered fewer moral dilemmas. Unfortunately, I see a lot of this going on today. Christians can become defiantly independent, nurturing a resentful animosity and even an antigovernment attitude. They almost see it as their duty to tweak the State's nose whenever they can. My own mentor, Ray Stedman, admitted to developing this attitude when he first had to pay income tax.

> My income had been so low for a long time that I didn't have to pay any taxes. But gradually it caught up and I finally had to pay. I remember how I resented it. In fact, when I sent my tax form in I addressed it to "The Infernal Revenue Service." They never answered, although they did accept the money. The next year I had improved my attitude a bit. I addressed it to "The Eternal Revenue Service." But I have repented from all those sins, and I now hope to pay my taxes cheerfully.[6]

I also encounter an attitude of uninvolved indifference, which is equally unhealthy. People with this backward-leaning posture think, *We're citizens of God's kingdom, so any and all participation in civil affairs is a waste of time at best, and potentially sinful at worst. Why bother?*

The apostle Paul thinks differently and explains why Christians should avoid either of these two extremes.

---

### —13:1—

An important aspect of what I have been calling "horizontal grace" is responsible citizenship. Paul commands the residents of Rome—and all who will later read the letter—to subject themselves to governing authorities. The term is *hypotassō*, which is a military term describing voluntary deference to the wishes of another.

If that were all we had to go on, this requirement would be confusing. Temporal authorities are destined to fall when Jesus returns to rule the earth as king. Furthermore, these authorities are part and parcel of a world system that rewards evil and opposes the righteousness of God. So, isn't obeying them tantamount to opposing God's order?

Not necessarily. Paul explains further that while the world has rebelled and an evil world system reigns over us, God remains in control. All earthly authorities are given a limited amount of autonomy, and while they frequently behave poorly, the Lord uses them to accomplish His purposes nonetheless (Isa. 45:1; Jer. 25:9; Dan. 4:32). Therefore, as a general rule, we should not subvert them. Paul then gives three reasons:

Earthly authorities are agents of law and order (13:1).
Civil obedience allows us to fear God, not people (13:2–4).
Civil obedience allows us to live above reproach (13:5–6).

*Earthly authorities are agents of law and order.* After God created the world, He filled it, organized it, and gave purpose to each created thing. When governments establish laws and prosecute justice, they honor His created order, even when they don't do it perfectly. Anarchy, however, is bad for everyone. Therefore, governments serve the purposes of God, whether they mean to or not. They form and thrive with His permission, and they cease to exist when they no longer serve His plan.

—13:2–4—

*Civil obedience allows us to fear God, not people.* To put ourselves at odds with a government is to oppose God's instrument of justice—generally speaking. (There are rare exceptions to this rule.) All governments, even cruel, totalitarian regimes, want their citizens to live peacefully, remain productive, and cause no trouble. The only people who really need to fear are those who are doing something wrong. If you want to live without fear, then do what is good. Obey the laws, pay your taxes, stop at red lights, don't take advantage of your neighbor's property, don't invade their privacy, don't rob banks. In addition, if we do what is right, we will gain a good reputation with those in authority.

The benefit of living without fear of the government is twofold. First, it frees us to fear God—that is, to respect His authority and to do right because it pleases Him. Second, it frees us to serve God more freely than if we are stuck in prison unnecessarily.

—13:5–6—

*Civil obedience allows us to live above reproach.* The motivation for Christians to behave well and obey laws is not merely to avoid being caught and punished, but to satisfy their own consciences. Presumably, the Christian conscience is the product of the Holy Spirit's transformation. So, again, to obey civil law is to submit to God.

Jewish Christians would have struggled with the issue of paying taxes to a pagan government, not because of greed but from a desire to remain holy. Jews commonly understood taxes paid to Caesar as money taken from God (Matt. 22:17–22; Mark 12:14–17; Luke 20:22–26). Paul merely regarded paying taxes to be a contribution to the common good, which God encouraged even during the exile: "Seek the welfare of the city where I have sent you into exile, and pray to the LORD on its behalf; for in its welfare you will have welfare" (Jer. 29:7). Furthermore, because the magistrates serve with God's permission, paying their salaries serves His interests.

—13:7—

Paul's summary statement encourages Christians to live respectfully and honorably in the eyes of the government, fulfilling all requirements and meeting all obligations. Note that our debt to government includes more than mere taxes and tolls (money); we also owe respect, which Paul describes as "fear" and "honor."

The apostle is simply applying an earlier principle to our relationship with government: "So far as it depends on you, be at peace with all men" (12:18). As we fulfill all the requirements of good citizenship, we cast Jesus Christ in a positive light and, perhaps, create opportunities to share the good news with greater freedom.

Paul knows that the question of obedience to worldly authorities can be thorny for the Christian. After all, he is writing the believers in Rome near the middle of Nero's reign, which will turn horrifically brutal within a few years. He sympathizes with the fact that we obey a heavenly King—which most governments do not recognize and frequently oppose—yet we must "be at peace with all men" (12:18), including those in authority. It's a delicate balance that can be difficult to maintain. We must remain meaningfully engaged with worldly authorities without losing our moral distinctiveness. We must cooperate with the demands of government while peacefully trying to infiltrate it with the good news. Put simply, we must learn how to become godly rebels!

However, on rare occasions, we are left with no choice but to disobey the commands of government and, on even rarer occasions, must seek to remove it from power. All governments do things that are immoral, but usually our best response is to remain meaningfully engaged so that our influence can change things for the better. However, when a government authority commands us to do something immoral, it's a different matter entirely. We have a duty to *disobey* that command (cf. Acts 5:29). Peacefully and respectfully, we must do as God commands. This may result in our having to accept the consequences of our choice, which may include punishment, persecution, or having to take refuge elsewhere.

Very rarely, we may be called to take up arms and fight to protect the innocent from especially cruel regimes. But when that does occur, it is only right to fight.

## Application

### *Knowing When It's Right to Fight*

Paul was concerned for the Christians in Rome. The political climate was quickly turning hostile toward both Jews and Christians, who had gained a reputation for "their hate and enmity to human kind," according to one Roman writing during that time.[7] The apostle knew better, of course, but reputations—even unfair ones—can be powerful things. The absence of Christians from public life created a vacuum, which inevitably filled with fear and slander. Therefore, in a radical departure from first-century Jewish policy, which encouraged Jews to remain separate and distinct, Paul urged believers to be meaningfully engaged in public life and to support their pagan government as God's unwitting instrument.

The United States government is following close behind other nations in becoming hostile—not merely indifferent—toward Christianity, even seeing theism as a threat to the common good. Consequently, Christians around the world are increasingly finding greater affinity with the Christians in first-century Rome. Our response now should be no different from that of Paul's original audience. We must remain meaningfully engaged in public affairs and let our positive influence create opportunities for the spread of the gospel.

Unfortunately, on some occasions we must oppose our governments. Most democracies provide a means of "civil disobedience," whereby dissention from public policy can be expressed peacefully from within the system. In stable governments that are relatively free of corruption, this is the most effective means of correcting official wrongs. Courtrooms can be useful tools for change.

On rare occasions, government policies must be confronted more dramatically. When laws are passed that require one to violate the clear commands of Scripture, we have a duty to peacefully disobey. When government policy begins to abuse or victimize those who are helpless, we must take peaceful action to oppose such persecution. A good example of this kind of action is the campaign of civil disobedience conducted against the racist laws of the American South during the 1960s. The demonstrators, though often mistreated, never fired a shot.

In extremely rare circumstances, when all other means of change have been exhausted, the injustices have become matters of life and death, and urgency leaves no alternative, good men must take up arms and confront evil by force. This is not to condone terrorism or other savage acts of violence, but to acknowledge that sometimes war is a grave necessity.

When governments behave badly, disobedience and opposition should not leap to mind before every effort to obey has been exhausted. Paul commanded this, not merely to teach believers how to exist in awkward tension with nonbelieving governments, but to encourage a love relationship between Christians and their civil authorities. Yes, you read that correctly. A love relationship. A growing rapport in which government officials feel affirmed, supported, encouraged, even appreciated. How wonderful it would be for a beleaguered bureaucrat to heave a great sigh of relief when he or she discovers you are a Christian.

## Wake Up and Get Dressed! (Romans 13:8–14)

> [8]Owe nothing to anyone except to love one another; for he who loves his neighbor has fulfilled *the* law. [9]For this, "You shall not commit adultery, You shall not murder, You shall not steal, You shall not covet," and if there is any other commandment, it is summed up in this saying, "You shall love your neighbor as yourself." [10]Love does no wrong to a neighbor; therefore love is the fulfillment of *the* law.
>
> [11]*Do* this, knowing the time, that it is already the hour for you to awaken from sleep; for now salvation is nearer to us than when we believed. [12]The night is almost gone, and the day is near. Therefore let us lay aside the deeds of darkness and put on the armor of light. [13]Let us behave properly as in the day, not in carousing and drunkenness, not in sexual promiscuity and sensuality, not in strife and jealousy. [14]But put on the Lord Jesus Christ, and make no provision for the flesh in regard to *its* lusts.

I am amazed by the ability of modern men and women to tune out much of what goes on around them, especially when living in large, over-crowded cities. With all the noise and activity and rapid movement of our times, the ability to remain undistracted is a matter of survival. But it comes with a price. We can too easily overlook the obvious, miss what's important, and thereby fail to get involved where we should.

Paul's readers undoubtedly felt the same pressure in first-century Rome, the center of Western civilization. Their great temptation must have been to withdraw from involvement with politics; after all, why waste time with a government doomed to fall when Christ returns? I'm sure they saw little need to interact with their neighbors, whose anti-Jewish and anti-Christian sentiments were just beginning to germinate under the insane rule of Nero. Furthermore, they probably felt their time on earth was short, as Christ had promised to return at any moment and establish His kingdom. So, Paul tackles their mistaken notions head-on.

Having examined the believer's relationship with others in the body of Christ (12:2–16) and having taught them how to respond to destructive enemies (12:17–21), the apostle addresses other pressing issues for the Christian: our interaction with government (13:1–7), our relationship with unsaved neighbors (13:8–10), and our responsibility as ambassadors of God's righteousness in the world (13:11–14).

## —13:8—

The command to "owe nothing to anyone" is surprising for two reasons. First, it would appear to be a direct contradiction to what he commanded in 13:7: "Render [or return] to all what is due [or owed] them." Words for "owed" (*opheilō* word group) occur in both verses. So Paul seemingly writes contradictory statements:

> Repay to all what you owe them (13:7).
> Don't owe anyone anything (13:8).

Second, this would appear to be a prohibition against ever borrowing money or carrying any debt, which some expositors use to discourage credit cards, auto loans, mortgages, and even church building loans.

It would be magnificent if all of us could live debt-free. Some do and everyone applauds that. People have asked, "Is our church in debt?" "Yes," I reply, "and it's a debt we can manage." Some have adopted a superior tone and asked, "Well, why are we in debt?" to which I reply with tongue in cheek, "Because we preferred not to meet in the rain!"

Back when we rented space, we could have continued to pay that monthly fee to others (money down the drain), or we could turn that same payment into a mortgage and pay that money toward something permanent. Sometimes a mortgage is the best way to steward the money God entrusts to us. Furthermore, paying money over time allows us to have adequate facilities while serving the needs of the people God sends our way.

Nevertheless, we must be disciplined and wise with debt. The verb in 13:8 is present tense, suggesting that we are to avoid habitual, repeated, or ongoing debt. In other words, don't allow debt to continue indefinitely. Pay it off. Don't let it remain outstanding. Don't add debt on top of debt. Don't allow debt to become a comfortable addition (I'm trying hard not to write "addiction") to your lifestyle. And by no means default on a loan.

Credit is nothing more than a tool, which can be properly used or habitually abused. Unfortunately, most people today abuse credit. So, I can appreciate the intent of those who see debt as a great evil to be defeated.

Having established my position on debt, let me direct you to the rest of Paul's sentence. Note that the context is broader than money. In 13:7, we owe government officials money (taxes and tolls) and respect (fear and honor). The command to avoid owing anything extends beyond money to include intangible things. The only exception is love.

Paul's point is simple. Be a person of honor. Fulfill your obligations. Don't make creditors track you down; seek them out, be completely honest and forthright, pursue arrangements to pay off what you owe. If someone holds a particular position that is due respect, give it freely and with enthusiasm. If you have committed your time or given your promise, be all *there*. The reward for living this way is freedom. The less we must do out of obligation, the more we are able to give freely. Keeping our list of obligations short allows us more room to give grace.

The command to "love one another" goes beyond merely loving fellow believers. The Greek term translated "neighbor" is *heteros*, "one of a different kind." The first is another like you; the other is someone very different from you. Different in beliefs and theology. Different in personality. Different in politics. Different in mannerisms. Different in tastes and race and values and history. In other words, with love, difference should make no difference. This is a perpetual debt that can never be zeroed out.

— **13:9–10** —

Paul called love the fulfillment of the Law, which recalls the teaching of Jesus (Matt. 22:35 – 40; Mark 12:28 – 31). The Law is not only an expression of God's character, it points to His original created order, His vision for how the universe should work. However, sin always distorts what God created to be good; it always causes harm. Therefore, sin and love cannot coexist. Love doesn't commit or condone adultery. Love cannot murder. Love cannot deprive another person of his or her possessions. And love cannot hunger after the blessings of another. Those are all actions that serve self at the expense of a victim. And rest assured, there is no such thing as a victimless sin.

For Paul, love embodies the highest ideals of the new kingdom that Jesus will establish and enforce upon His return to Earth. At that time, God's original created order will be restored. In the meantime, the apostle desires that all believers become living examples of this new kingdom. Just like in the beginning, before the fall, people are to be righteous because He is righteous. They are to love one another because God is love. They are to live according to the truth because God is truth. As we are transformed to fulfill God's original vision for creation, the world should also be transformed — even if only a little — because of our influence.

## —13:11—

Note the urgency in Paul's words. It's as though he were sounding reveille to rouse soldiers out of their racks and onto their feet in the morning. We are to rise and get busy because of the time.

The apostle could have used either of two words for "time." The first is *chronos*, from which we get our word chronology. It refers to time on a sundial or days on a calendar. The other is *kairos*, which is a fixed or appointed season. It also refers to the quality of a certain period, so that Charles Dickens might have opened his book *A Tale of Two Cities* with the words, "It was the best of *kairos*, it was the worst of *kairos*."

Paul writes, in effect, "Do this knowing the kind of time in which we live." Do what? Love. We are to love those around us in the following ways:

Maintain a balanced view of ourselves (12:3).
Utilize our gifts for the good of the body (12:4–8).
Outdo other Christians in showing honor to one another (12:9–14).
Return good for evil and leave room for God to convict and redeem others
   (12:17–21).
Meet all of our obligations to government officials and give them the respect
   they are due (13:1–7).

These create a foundation of love on which we can build relationships and hopefully extend the new kingdom.

Paul describes our "time" as one in which "salvation" is closer to arriving than ever before. Of course, this is not our personal salvation. That has already been accomplished. Paul is referring to the return of Jesus Christ and the restoration of God's righteousness, the master plan of salvation. Because it is closer than before and could occur at any moment, we cannot afford to be sleeping right now. We need to be alert, living in eager anticipation of that day.

## —13:12–13—

Paul then gives his illustration of night and morning a dramatic turn. As the long, dark night continues before the dawning of Christ's return, some believers are sleeping, while others engage in deeds of darkness. The apostle lists these sins in three pairs:

*Carousing and drunkenness.* These words refer specifically to wild, nighttime festivals in honor of Bacchus, the Greek god of wine, which began with a drunken parade through the streets and ended with sexual immorality. This is not a prohibition against having fun or even against alcohol in moderation. This has to do with turning alcohol into recreation, even an addiction, allowing a substance to control the person instead of the Holy Spirit.

*Sexual promiscuity and sensuality.* The literal translation of the first term is "beds," which is a euphemism for sexual excess. "Sensuality" in the context of marriage is, of course, perfectly fine. Paul's intent is not to restrict spontaneous and creative intimacy between married partners. A better rendering would be "licentiousness" or "wanton excess." The sense is to treat sexual norms with contempt.

*Strife and jealousy.* Literally, these terms mean "infighting" and "zeal." Earlier, Paul praised zeal for God (10:2), but when zeal is misdirected, it tears the community apart.

— **13:14** —

The Greek language offers a choice of two contrasting conjunctions that can be translated "but." One is routine and common. The other, *alla*, is reserved for drawing stark and emphatic contrasts. And this is Paul's choice here. In absolute, unequivocal contrast to deeds of darkness we have been given armor of light (1 Thess. 5:8). We are to put on or clothe ourselves with the Lord Jesus Christ (Gal. 3:27; Eph. 4:24).

The idea of "putting on" something, such as Christ (Gal. 3:27), "the new self" (Eph. 4:24; Col. 3:10), or "the armor of God" (Eph. 6:10–17) reminds me of the old adage, "Clothes make the man." In the East—even today—clothes are very much a part of one's identity, signifying where he or she fits in society. In the West, a dramatic upgrade in our wardrobe can become a source of confidence. It's not merely vanity that makes us feel good in a new outfit.

To "put on" something is to believe a certain way and then behave accordingly. "Putting on Christ" sounds a little artificial, like "putting on airs." However, we aren't putting on something to hide what's inside but to display our true identity in Christ. What we "put on" reminds us of who we are, which allows us to behave properly with greater ease. Police officers, for example, put on a bulletproof vest, which reminds them to be careful. They put on a uniform, which reminds them to be aware of their identity and the example they set. They put on a badge, which reminds them of their responsibility to represent the city and its citizens. And they strap on a weapon, which reminds them to steward the lives they encounter with great care and restraint.

The other side of Paul's command is to "make no provision for the flesh." As we learned earlier, "flesh" is a technical word used by the apostle. It refers not to our material aspect, but to our old enslavement to sin and the corrupt world system. Although we are new creatures, our transformation is not yet complete. We have not entirely sloughed off the old self, so it is there to drag us back into sin if we heed its pleading for satisfaction.

The word "provision" literally means "forethought" or "planning." In other words, "make no [forethought or planning] for the flesh" is a warning that sin often begins with a plan, or at least a decision to leave the option open for sin. Instead, we must be proactive. Plan ahead to make sin inconvenient because the flesh is impulsive.

We often hear the word "love" in Christian circles. Whereas secular culture restricts the term to romance between couples and perhaps affection within families, Christians prefer a broader application. We are taught to care deeply for others within our congregations and to show kindness to strangers. This is good; however, Paul's application is broader still.

We don't think of paying our taxes as demonstrating love, but according to Paul, it is. When we obey the speed limit, get our automobiles inspected on time, serve on jury duty, and let our voices be heard in the voting booth, we express love. When we treat other drivers respectfully on the road and allow someone else to take the better parking spot, we express love. Even when we leave a generous tip in a restaurant, we express love in tangible, meaningful ways that others can appreciate. And believe me, they notice.

Let me leave you with a letter we received at Stonebriar Community Church.

I'm sending this message to let you know how much members of your church have touched my life. Four years ago, my husband and I lived in a small two bedroom apartment with our two small children when we were suddenly stunned, blessed, and challenged by the birth of identical triplet boys.

All of our family lived 1,000 miles away and we had no help. Three weeks after they were born and the day after they came home from the hospital, I had to get a job. To pay for diapers and formula, I got a job waitressing at a restaurant near your church. I was still in immense pain and was truly frightened that this was more than my family could handle.

On that first day at work I waited on a group of people from your church. They were single adults. I had been a waitress in college and knew that Christians or people coming from church were not only horrible tippers, but also very difficult and rude. But I was pleasantly surprised. They noticed I was a little slow and instead of complaining, they were forgiving. They even asked about my life and learned about my situation with the triplets.

This group continued to come in on Sundays and I felt honored to serve them. They'd ask me about my children and encouraged me in ways I needed. They lifted my spirits in ways I can't describe. It made me look at waitressing as a way of serving people for God. I'd say a prayer when I dropped off a plate of food or thought of a blessing to give them. I had been feeling so confused about God and His plans, and then out of nowhere this group of Christians entered my life in such a strange way. And they gave me comfort.

Our first Christmas with the triplets was financially devastating. We were barely paying our bills. The group didn't come in to eat (to my disappointment), but they came in and left an envelope with A LOT of money for me. I went shopping at Toys-R-Us that night on my way home from work and cried the entire time. I know I was getting a lot of strange looks, but I didn't care.

It has been years now since I've seen the singles group from Stonebriar. My husband was transferred back to Chicago and now makes enough money where I can stay at home with our children 7 days a week. Things are much, much better now. That whole experience recently came to mind and I wanted to let you know that something very special happened in my life to make me a Christian. I thank God for having served this group.

Wake up! Put on Christ! And find someone to love ... including those who serve us at restaurants!

## Application

### *Plan Your Trip to Avoid a Tumble*

As I read Paul's exhortation to pursue love and avoid evil, I am impressed with the urgency of his writing and his insistence that we take deliberate action. He calls this intentional manner of living "putting on Christ." We are to love others by avoiding sin (13:8–10) because there is no sin without a victim. And we are to look for opportunities to accomplish good (13:11–14). The world will make godly living (13:13) neither easy nor automatic. On the contrary, temptations and traps lie just outside the threshold of each home. Therefore, we should not be surprised when we encounter them. Rather than bemoan every occasion of stumbling, let's turn each into an opportunity to honor Christ. That means leaving nothing to chance.

For example, if you find certain television channels even the slightest bit tempting, call your service provider and ask to have them blocked at the source. When you travel, call the hotel in advance and have any adult-oriented content blocked from your room. If you struggle with other temptations while out-of-town, arrange to travel with a suitable companion, such as a friend or coworker of the same gender, your spouse, or another family member.

If the Internet presents even the slightest temptation to go where no mind should go, place your computer where anyone passing by can see your screen. Allow anyone in your household to have free access to your computer. Best of all, install accountability software on your computer and have the reports sent automatically to someone who will hold you accountable. Because embarrassment is a potent negative motivation, agree to have any violation reported to someone whose respect or admiration you want to maintain.

In addition to proactively avoiding temptation, Paul encourages us to seek out ways to strengthen our Christian walk. If you are reading this volume, it's safe to assume you have decided to become a student of the Scriptures. *Well done!* Let me encourage you to continue studying. Continue to fill your spiritual reservoir with divine truth. You will need it when the bottom drops out of your life. A time of great disappointment or personal failure or deep grief is *not* the right time to seek wisdom; that is when you must draw upon the wisdom you have faithfully stored up.

Build on the wisdom you gain through Scripture by accomplishing something of practical value. Join with others in doing something good for your community. Discover what the people you respect and admire are doing to improve the world and join them. Not only will you give the gospel practical relevance to a world that desperately needs divine truth, you will benefit greatly from the influence of other godly men and women.

As you gain wisdom and maturity, pass it on! Find a willing learner and invite him or her to join your Christian walk. This doesn't have to be a planned curriculum, although some have been published. Mentoring is really nothing more than allowing others to observe your life as you do what is right. They learn from your errors, they find wisdom as you recover, and they gain strength in your victories.

"Putting on the Lord Jesus Christ" is a purposeful decision, not something that will happen automatically. Putting on Christ is like placing an emblem on our chest that reminds everyone—ourselves and those who observe us—that we belong to Him. Putting on Christ establishes a standard of conduct, to which all of life must conform. In this way, putting on Christ "makes no provision for the flesh" (13:14).

## Putting Grace into Action (Romans 14:1–12)

¹Now accept the one who is weak in faith, *but* not for *the purpose of* passing judgment on his opinions. ²One person has faith that he may eat all things, but he who is weak eats vegetables *only.* ³The one who eats is not to regard with contempt the one who does not eat, and the one who does not eat is not to judge the one who eats, for God has accepted him.

⁴Who are you to judge the servant of another? To his own master he stands or falls; and he will stand, for the Lord is able to make him stand.

⁵One person regards one day above another, another regards every day *alike*. Each person must be fully convinced in his own mind. ⁶He who observes the day, observes it for the Lord, and he who eats, does so for the Lord, for he gives thanks to God; and he who eats not, for the Lord he does not eat, and gives thanks to God. ⁷For not one of us lives for himself, and not one dies for himself; ⁸for if we live, we live for the Lord, or if we die, we die for the Lord; therefore whether we live or die, we are the Lord's. ⁹For to this end Christ died and lived again, that He might be Lord both of the dead and of the living.

¹⁰But you, why do you judge your brother? Or you again, why do you regard your brother with contempt? For we will all stand before the judgment seat of God. ¹¹For it is written,

> "As I live, says the Lord, every knee shall bow to Me,
> And every tongue shall give praise to God."

¹²So then each one of us will give an account of himself to God.

---

Rome prized Corinth because it controlled a strategic intersection of trade. Rather than brave the treacherous journey around the Cape of Malea, ship owners preferred to drag their ships, cargo and all, across the narrow isthmus. Moreover, this natural land bridge governed traffic to and from Achaia (southern Greece today).

On the eve of His crucifixion, Jesus bowed His head and prayed for His followers. He prayed for the Twelve, He prayed for the new disciples they would train, and He prayed for the generations of followers yet to be born. After praying for our safety from evil and for our preservation through suffering, He added a final request:

> The glory which You have given Me I have given to them, that they may be one, just as We are one; I in them and You in Me, that they may be perfected in unity, so that the world may know that You sent Me, and loved them, even as You have loved Me. (John 17:22–23)

Clearly, our unity was on Christ's mind as He offered up His prayer. However, "unity" does not mean "uniformity." People often confuse them. While we are called to be one, to work together, to serve together, we cannot ignore the fact that we are all different. Each one of us bears unique DNA. Furthermore, each one of us has been shaped by unique circumstances. We have different viewpoints, different opinions, different preferences, different ways of solving problems. We each come to the community of believers with our own set of convictions and prejudices, some of which we are willing to defend to the death. Nevertheless, God expects us to coexist in unity and harmony. But that has rarely occurred.

Turn to any page in the chronicles of the church and you will find conflict. Those who wish for "the good, old days," back in the first century when everyone got along, will be disappointed to hear the facts. The truth of the matter is first-century Christians struggled to maintain unity the same as we do today. Paul wrote to the believers in Corinth because the congregation was on the verge of imploding. Open sin scandalized the church, while in other gatherings legalism put a stranglehold on the body of believers. False accusations from the outside the congregation fueled false teaching from within. Some factions favored Paul, while others favored Peter or Apollos (1 Cor. 1:12), and theological debates between the groups kept the church in continual turmoil.

In other churches, Alexander the coppersmith relentlessly opposed Paul (2 Tim. 4:14), Diotrophes usurped John's apostolic authority (3 John 9–10), and Hymenaeus and Philetus undermined the faith of believers in scores of churches (1 Tim. 1:20; 2 Tim. 2:17). Paul had to oppose Peter for his hypocritical treatment of Gentile Christians in the presence of other Jews (Gal. 2:11–14). The apostle even found himself in angry disagreement with Barnabas, of all people, so that the two had to part ways, never to work together again (Acts 15:39)!

If the apostles struggled with conflict, certainly we will too. That's not to say that all disagreement is necessarily evil. In fact, differences of opinion can become a great advantage to the body. The same can be said of most differences. It's all a matter of how they are handled. With patience, the right perspective, good communication, and plenty of grace to keep all the moving parts well oiled, unity isn't difficult to achieve.

— **14:1** —

Paul recognizes that differences can lead to disunity and disharmony if not addressed. So, he chooses to focus on two hot-button issues in the Roman church: diet and days. Initially, he notes that some issues have the capacity to divide people into two groups. Some he calls "weak in faith." The idea behind the term "weak" is feeble or frail. Think of someone whose legs are badly injured and, after a long recovery, he or she attempts to walk again. Weakness takes its toll.

The "strong" (cf. 15:1) are to accept (or, literally, "receive to oneself") those who struggle to walk on wobbly legs of faith. The purpose for receiving them, however, is to make them welcome, to accept them without changing them or their opinions. The phrase translated "passing judgment" is a particularly strong form of the verb "to judge." It means "to distinguish between persons" or "to discern the relative value of someone" (Acts 15:8–9). In other words, the weak in faith must be accepted unconditionally, just as they are, without any expectation of change.

## CORINTH

Corinth (see map, p.284) presided over the isthmus between the Gulf of Corinth and the Saronic Gulf, which gave this ancient Greek city incredible strategic importance. Rather than brave the dangerous journey around Cape Malea, ship owners preferred to have their vessels dragged across this narrow strip of land. Whoever controlled Corinth controlled the flow of trade in the region. Eventually, a Roman general destroyed the city, exterminated the males, and sold the women and children into slavery, after which it lay in ruins for nearly a century. In 46 B.C. Julius Caesar resurrected Corinth as a colony for Roman freedmen and as a means of preserving the isthmus for Roman interests.

By the time of Paul, this Roman colony of approximately 80,000 beat with the heart of Rome and strongly resembled the capital city. Corinth worshiped the emperor, upheld Roman law, pulsated with international trade, hosted athletic games, beckoned pagan worshipers, thrived on slavery, tolerated a strong Jewish presence, and struggled to understand a fledgling new sect of people calling themselves "little Christs." The lessons Paul learned in Corinth would become the instruction he gave to Rome: "Be on the alert, stand firm in the faith, act like men, be strong. Let all that you do be done in love" (1 Cor. 16:13–14).

## —14:2-3—

Many Christians in Rome had been converted out of paganism after many years in idolatry, which typically involved animal sacrifice in honor of the god. Leftover meat that was not consumed by the fire or was cooked to be eaten during the ritual might be sold in the public market. Believers with idolatry in their unsaved backgrounds were repulsed by the idea of eating meat offered to idols. Typically, they avoided eating meat they had not personally prepared.

Paul, however, taught that idols were not real; therefore, any significance attached to the meat is imaginary. Meat from an idol's altar is no better or worse than any other (1 Cor. 8:1–13). The apostle considers this the perspective of "strong faith."

I can appreciate the perspective of the so-called "weak faith" people. Let me illustrate their difficulty in today's terms. Think of a man who wasted his youth chasing the folly of Haight-Ashbury and the false teaching of Timothy Leary. More than a decade of LSD, marijuana, "free love," and homelessness eventually left him nothing to show for his years than a frail, pockmarked, diseased body. Then, like the prodigal, he came to his senses, repented, and found complete redemption in Christ. A community of genuine believers helped him cope with the damage done by the past and helped him find steady work. Meanwhile, he studied the Word and grew strong in his faith.

That was ancient history for the man. Today, his old hippie friends would barely know him. His eyes sparkle with hope. He bounces when he walks. He positively beams with the love of Christ. And he's a strong leader in his church, well-liked and deeply respected.

One day, the young pastor in charge of the teen ministry at church decides to have a little fun with the kids. (I so admire youth pastors. They come up with the most creative ways to teach teens in the process of having fun.) He organizes a sixties party. Tie-dyed tee-shirts, beads, wigs, black light posters, smoke machines ... the works.

I don't need to go any further, do I? I suspect you see trouble brewing for that unsuspecting youth pastor. To him, the CDs contain nothing more than "oldies," antiquated "soft rock." Nothing compared to the vulgarities that blare from thumping hotrods on urban streets today. The costumes are nothing more than an excuse to laugh at one another. And the decorations? Harmless fun.

To the ex-hippie, however, the sixties were anything but harmless. To him, the songs are anthems to sin of the most degrading and destructive kind. The costumes reflect the misguided philosophies of people long dead from overdose. And can you imagine the sickening sorrow in the pit of his stomach upon seeing his church decorated to resemble his life before Christ?

Paul describes those who avoided meat as "weak in faith"; however, we would be wrong to see the term as derogatory. We are all "weak"—feeble and frail—in one way or another. The ex-hippie's weakness does not make him inferior. In some ways, he may be more mature and stronger than his peers. However, his faith will always be weak in the area of his deepest wounds.

The same was true for those who hated the idea of Christians eating meat that had been offered to idols. Therefore, Paul commands each side of the issue to treat the other with understanding, compassion, and tenderness. The "weak" need to be strengthened and the "strong" need to be considerate in the exercise of their freedom. The same is true today.

— **14:4** —

Paul quickly points to the core issue: accountability. To put his question in a modern business-world context: "Who are you to review the performance of someone else's employee?"

It's important to note that Paul's question is asked in the context of nonessential matters. Paul expressed his outrage with the believers in Corinth because they tolerated the outright sin of a man who had been sleeping with his father's wife. He commanded them, "Remove the wicked man from among yourselves" (1 Cor. 5:13). Matters about which there is no clear scriptural teaching are morally neutral. They might be unwise, but they are not sin.

The apostle's use of the verb "stand" is one of his favorite expressions. It means to be in good standing, confidently and resolutely doing as one should and receiving favor as a reward (1 Cor. 16:13; Phil. 1:27, 4:1; 1 Thess. 3:8; 2 Thess. 2:15). Obviously, to "fall" is to do the opposite. This has nothing to do with the final judgment; it has everything to do with God's favor and whether one deserves chastisement.

When it comes to morally neutral matters, only God has the right to evaluate the soul and judge the deeds of another believer. If He is not pleased with the conduct of His servant, He will address the issue in such a way as to continue the believer's transformation.

— **14:5** —

Another hot-button issue in the first century church was the observation of holidays, pagan or otherwise. Whereas Jewish and Gentile believers most likely regarded the eating of meat offered to idols as repulsive, the veneration of certain days would have divided them.

Jewish identity rested on three pillars: Father Abraham, the Promised Land, and the Sabbath. The Gentile can barely appreciate the significance of the Sabbath in the life of godly Jews. The Sabbath isn't limited to the seventh day of the week; the spirit of the Sabbath rest runs through Israel's many festivals. Most were instituted by God Himself and were established to help the Hebrews maintain a sharp focus on their identity as His priestly race, their responsibility as His agent of evangelism, their future role in governing the world, and their continual need of grace.

Gentiles, by contrast, also had a calendar full of pagan holidays and festivals. Not all were celebrated with drunken revelry and sexual immorality. But they honored fictitious gods and treated the earth as though it were a person. These holidays "exchanged the truth of God for a lie, and worshiped and served the creature rather than the Creator" (1:25). To the converted Gentile, observing specific days as holy smacked of idolatry.

So, the time of Passover rolls around. Imagine the tension mounting in the church as Jews joyfully sweep their houses clean of yeast and dust. The Passover celebration was instituted to be a perpetual custom for them (Ex.12:24), and there is no indication that the new covenant should necessarily end it. Though released from the burden of obedience to the Law, why wouldn't Christian Jews want to continue celebrating God's freeing them from slavery and bringing them into the Promised Land?

According to Paul, the veneration of certain days, like eating meat potentially offered to idols, is a matter of conscience. It is a morally neutral issue. Is there benefit in observing holidays? If done in the right spirit and for the right motives, absolutely! Should we continue to set aside one day per week for spiritual refreshment and physical rest? Clearly, this is wise. God established the Sabbath for our good. However, we have been released from the command to do so. Under the new covenant, observing Saturday or Sunday or whatever day is a matter of conscience.

Matters of conscience are those issues that involve no clear command of Scripture and therefore result in no sin. We are encouraged to hold one another accountable and to encourage one another to be morally pure. However, we are to be guided by our own conscience for other decisions. That's what it means to be "fully convinced in his own mind."

—**14:6**—

Now, let me clarify that this does not in any way suggest that truth is relative or that morality is now defined by whatever each person's conscience can tolerate.

Paul takes two things for granted as he loosens up the restrictions believers place on one another.

First, some matters are absolutely and categorically wrong and must be corrected through mutual accountability. However, the morality of some matters is relative to the individual. For matters of conscience, the individual's motivation determines its morality. Paul highlights this fact with the repeated phrases "for the Lord" and "thanks to God."

Second, the Christian's conscience is gradually being transformed by the Holy Spirit to reflect the mind of Christ. Before the Holy Spirit took up residence in the heart of the believer, the conscience was like a broken compass, pulled this way and that by popular opinion, personal lusts, upside-down morality, and ignorance. Now, however, that compass is able to find true north with increasing accuracy as the Holy Spirit retrains and guides the needle.

— **14:7–9** —

We belong to God, not to one another. We are *His* prized possessions. *He* is responsible for the renewing of a mind, not us. Therefore, we must allow Him opportunity to do His transforming work without distracting one another with attempts to control or coerce behavior based on what pleases us. He's the one who died and rose again to accomplish this transformation. We are His "workmanship" (Eph. 2:10).

In our eagerness to see them grow, mature believers frequently rob their new brothers and sisters of their joy by laying burdens on them right away. "Stop smoking." "Start reading your Bible." "Get out of debt and give more money to the needy." "Dress more appropriately." "Eat less fat." And on, and on, and on …

All of those life changes are good. I have dedicated my life to helping people see the wisdom of applying the principles of Scripture and encouraging them to follow the example of Christ. However, it's foolish to expect a new believer to behave like a mature Christian overnight. Furthermore, the motivation for doing so must come from a transformed conscience, a renovated spirit that wants to please God as an expression of love, not a misguided need to meet the expectations of one's peers.

— **14:10–12** —

Paul brings the issue back around to its origin—that of accountability—by asking two rhetorical questions. By placing them in parallel, we are able to discern exactly what the apostle meant by "judging." This is important because the precise meaning of the verb "to judge" depends heavily on the context in which it is used (emphasis added below).

"Why do you *judge* your brother?"
"Why do you *regard with contempt* your brother?"

The Greek word in the second sentence means "to despise someone or something on the basis that it is worthless or of no value."[8] Clearly, we are to have standards of conduct and we have been commanded to hold one another accountable. Remember, Paul counseled the Corinthian believers to put a sinning man out of their congregation until he repented of his evil (1 Cor. 5:1–5, 13). This was not "judging" as Paul defines it here. His purpose was to protect the integrity of the congregation until the man repented and could be restored. This act of tough love was also for the benefit of the man.

"Judging," in this sense of the word, has no positive element. It can only be negative and cruel. This kind of judging presumes to appraise the value of another person based on a flawed, human standard. Our ability to judge has several shortcomings:

We are not omniscient, so our judgment doesn't have all the facts.
We are not objective, so our judgment is tainted by self-interest.
We are not perfect, so our judgment is hypocritical.
We are not God, so our judgment has no jurisdiction.

Only God has the right to assess the value of people because He alone owns them. He made people, He redeemed them, He knows them, and He cares for them.

Paul opens his argument by describing the issues that sharply divided believers in his day, and he closes his argument by reminding them of what they share in common. Despite whatever differences keep believers from uniting, we will all stand before the same Judge and will be measured against the same standard. To prove that this has always been the plan, Paul paraphrases a verse from the pen of the Old Testament prophet Isaiah (Isa. 45:23), who describes the day when the Lord will visibly rule over His creation. When we see the true Judge, we will all assume the same posture and will bow before Him in humble submission.

Paul's teaching on how to put grace into action can be summed up this way: Just let one another be! Christians don't need others to lecture them or to become their self-appointed life coaches. Most believers already have a long list of changes they would like to see in their own behavior. So, having someone add a few more doesn't help. In fact, it hurts. Most new believers already feel overwhelmed as it is.

If we genuinely desire to help fellow believers along in their transformation, we must set them free from demands—ours or anybody else's. Instead of providing what they already have—obligations, chastisement, doubt, and negativity—we need to supply what they lack. We can allow them room to breathe, room to try new things (and fail!), room to discover for themselves what God would like to change. Without frowns and demands and expectations and the chatter of other believers to distract them, they will be freed to feel the tug of the Holy Spirit and then experience genuine, lasting growth. Perhaps by trusting the goodness that is prompted by the Spirit who lives within fellow believers, even during setbacks, we will see entire congregations flourish and become havens of grace.

If we can just let one another be.

## Application

### *Three Grace-Related Principles*

Paul reflected the desire of Jesus that congregations become havens of grace, places where people have the freedom to be who they are and to become what God desires—according to His plan and along His timetable. I find in Romans 14:1–12 at least three principles of grace that would transform every church if the members took them to heart.

1. *A life of grace begins with mutual acceptance.* Accepting another person doesn't require us to agree with him or her. We can respectfully disagree with ideas or opinions without rejecting the person who holds them. Acceptance takes the other person seriously and gives his or her perspective the benefit of consideration. Acceptance leaves lots of room for differing preferences. One person's taste in music, food, art, and other matters of personal liking might be vastly different from yours or others'. Acceptance delights in the delight of another. Acceptance allows another person the opportunity to be different without judgment, takes the time to understand him or her, and extends the benefit of doubt.

Acceptance allows others to feel safe in being who they are, even when their poor behavior must be reproved or their opinions challenged. There are times that we must confront error; the Bible commands it. And sometimes godly confrontation leads to separation. It isn't pleasant, but it's right. When certain convictions are clearly established in Scripture and maintaining a relationship requires those convictions to be compromised, something has to give. In this difficult circumstance, Scripture must stand and the relationship must give.

Acceptance does not require truth to be set aside or sin to be ignored. Acceptance merely calls for truth and love to guide our relationships.

2. *An attitude of grace requires releasing others to be who God wants them to be.* This is simply releasing someone who has harmed me to answer to God for his or her actions, leaving matters of justice and mercy in the Lord's hands, and trusting that He will do with them what is best for all concerned. In other words, an attitude of grace refuses to become someone else's Holy Spirit! We can confront with loving firmness (Matt. 18:15 – 17), but we must release the offender to be directed by God.

Each of us must stand before God to answer for our own choices. We will not be asked to comment on the behavior of another. An attitude of grace allows this truth to become the foundation of our relationships with others, especially those who cause us harm.

3. *A commitment to grace forbids one to become the judge of another.* I cannot become someone else's judge because I do not possess the qualifications required for the position. Three reasons come to mind.

First, I am not omniscient, so I cannot know all the facts. I must have *all* the facts if I am to judge correctly, but I barely know enough to make wise decisions concerning my own life, to say nothing of someone else's.

Second, I cannot be completely objective. I am biased. I am selfish. I am finite. I am unable to see the big picture. When God makes decisions, each choice takes every factor in the universe into account. I cannot do that because of my own sinfulness and limited mind.

Third, I can condemn, but I cannot redeem. When God confronts sin, He always offers a means of redemption. Christ died on the cross and rose from the dead to make redemption possible. The Holy Spirit can convict sin and then transform a soul. The Father offers hope after someone has failed. My condemnation, however, offers nothing but rejection.

Imagine the spiritual oasis these three principles could create if we allowed them to guide our relationships. How delightfully refreshing would our homes and churches become if people were freely accepted, allowed to live beyond the exacting expectations of others, and judged only by God, whose judgment is always wrapped in understanding and love! How much more productive would the office become if the boss maintained high standards of excellence, yet managed according to the principles of grace.

There's only one way to know: Begin applying grace-related principles wherever you live and work.

## Liberty on a Tightrope (Romans 14:13–23)

[13]Therefore let us not judge one another anymore, but rather determine this — not to put an obstacle or a stumbling block in a brother's way. [14]I know and am convinced in the Lord Jesus that nothing is unclean in itself; but to him who thinks anything to be unclean, to him it is unclean. [15]For if because of food your brother is hurt, you are no longer walking according to love. Do not destroy with your food him for whom Christ died. [16]Therefore do not let what is for you a good thing be spoken of as evil; [17]for the kingdom of God is not eating and drinking, but righteousness and peace and joy in the Holy Spirit. [18]For he who in this *way* serves Christ is acceptable to God and approved by men. [19]So then we pursue the things which make for peace and the building up of one another. [20]Do not tear down the work of God for the sake of food. All things indeed are clean, but they are evil for the man who eats and gives offense. [21]It is good not to eat meat or to drink wine, or *to do anything* by which your brother stumbles. [22]The faith which you have, have as your own conviction before God. Happy is he who does not condemn himself in what he approves. [23]But he who doubts is condemned if he eats, because *his eating is* not from faith; and whatever is not from faith is sin.

On August 7, 1974, the citizens of New York noticed something strange 110 stories above the streets. As the sun peeked above the horizon, they saw a man casually walking between the twin towers of the World Trade Center, balanced on a taut steel cable he had stretched between them the night before. Philippe Petit, then a mere twenty-five-year-old French tightrope artist, walked, danced, hopped, and ran across the 140-foot span no less than eight times. At one point he even dropped to one knee for the traditional salute of the tightrope walker. After forty-five minutes, the daredevil stepped off the wire into the waiting grip of exasperated New York police officers.

Friends warned him that winds could cause the towers to sway and snap the cable, or perhaps toss him from the wire, but he insisted on doing the stunt without a harness. He didn't want anything to restrict his feeling of complete freedom or diminish "the rapture of the heights." The only apparatus he used was a fifty-five pound balancing pole. Philippe Petit believed that feeling of freedom was worth all the risks.

Romans 14:1–12 describe an analogy to an acrobat on a wire, experiencing the rapture of the heights and enjoying complete freedom. The next eleven verses explain the balance he or she must maintain while traveling along the tightrope of liberty. To stabilize that delicate walk, the believer must hold in his or her hands a balance pole. On one end, self-control. On the other, love for others. Neither should tip much higher than the other.

## —14:13—

Paul addresses both the "weak in faith," whose excessive caution might make them fearful and legalistic, and the "strong," whose love of liberty might make them callous and careless. He exhorts believers of both persuasions to avoid "judging," that is, "despising one another as worthless" based on how we conduct ourselves in matters of conscience.

The legalist might question the genuine faith of someone who doesn't share his or her convictions on a certain matter. The libertine might question the genuine faith of someone who cannot stop quoting the Law. Put them together in the same congregation and the environment can become toxic for everyone.

Paul's primary concern is to avoid two specific dangers. First, the legalist might cause the free-flying strong Christian to crash to the ground. Second, the libertine might cause the careful, weak Christian to fall into sin. He gives these two dangers names: *skandalon* ("obstacle") and *proskomma* ("stumbling block"). Many writers used the two terms interchangeably, but I believe Paul wants to play on the subtle difference in their meanings.

A *proskomma* can be the result of a tumble, such as a bruised knee or a knot on the forehead, or it can refer to the trip hazard itself, such as a stumbling stone. Picture a Christian running with his head thrown back and wearing a giant smile, enjoying his freedom in Christ without a worry in the world. Then imagine a legalist sticking his foot out.

A *skandalon* is a trap. In the literal sense, a *skandalon* is a baited cage with a spring-loaded door, not unlike a rabbit trap. Figuratively, it was used to describe any means by which a person is brought to his or her end. Picture a brand-new Christian carefully trying to discern what is appropriate for a believer and what is not, perhaps taking her cues from the example of mature Christians. Now picture a reckless believer who frequently drinks to the point of intoxication and defends his choices as "his freedom in Christ." The reckless example has set a trap for her new sister in Christ.

The balance between enjoying one's liberty and exercising self-control is not mastered overnight. To help everyone find that balance and keep it, Paul offers three principles to live by:

Nothing is clean or unclean by itself (14:14–16).
The essence of Christianity is not found in external matters (14:17–19).
When liberty hinders the work of God, it must yield (14:20–23).

— **14:14–15** —

*Nothing is clean or unclean by itself.* Inanimate objects can be neither good nor evil because they do not have a mind or a will. Furthermore, they lack the capacity to do anything on their own. Idols are nothing until someone ascribes significance to them. The pieces of polished wood or stone are not evil; the worship of them is evil. Meat offered to a fictitious god is no different than any other meat, except for the meaning attached to it by people.

However, perception can be a powerful thing, especially to an untransformed mind. The sights, sounds, and symbols associated with someone's sinful past can pose a genuine threat to spiritual progress. For example, alcohol is not evil and bars are not evil places. Alcohol *abuse* is evil and evil *people* may frequent bars. But neither of these should concern a mature Christian whose conduct isn't easily influenced. A recovering alcoholic, just days after his or her fresh start in rehabilitation, however, has good reason to fear. Only a callous Christian would chastise him or her for wanting to avoid temptation. To that person, alcohol and bars are evil.

When someone who stands on feeble legs of faith recoils from a perceived danger, the mature believer has a choice: love for pleasure or love for the other. Paul's admonition "Do not destroy with your food him for whom Christ died" appears at first glance to be overly dramatic and has been interpreted in various ways.

"Destroy him" could refer to destroying the faith of the other person. However, the object of the Greek verb is "him," that is, the person. Furthermore, the faith of a genuine believer cannot be destroyed; therefore, he or she is eternally safe regardless of what other people do.

"Destroy him" can mean enabling someone's physical destruction by setting a poor example. This is possible, but unlikely. The first part of verse 15 refers to the brother being "hurt," which is how the NASB has rendered the Greek verb *lypeō*, "to distress" or "to grieve." The injury is emotional, not physical; relational, not spiritual. Furthermore, the general context of this passage is unity in the body of Christ and bearing one another's differences.

A less common definition of the Greek term translated "destroy" is "lose" or "suffer the loss of."[9] Fail to honor another believer's conscience and you will likely lose the individual by compromising your relationship. Furthermore, you run the risk of bringing disrepute upon the thing you enjoy, making it harder for other mature Christians to enjoy their freedom.

So, does this mean that the mature believer must continually exist in a prison constructed by the feeble sensibilities of weak Christians? No, that need not happen. Protect your privacy and choose your environment. No one says you have to surround yourself with weak-faith people. When you find yourself in their company, however, voluntarily set aside your liberty for a time. It's a mistake to think you can loosen them up by flaunting your freedom. Heed the Old Testament proverb: "A brother offended is harder to be won than a strong city" (Prov. 18:19). People find it difficult to learn when they are offended. Instead, create a teachable moment by deferring to the preference of the other. Ease the crisis; then, perhaps, a few well-placed questions might be in order.

—**14:17–19**—

*The essence of Christianity is not found in external matters.* Jesus said, "It is not what enters into the mouth that defiles the man, but what proceeds out of the mouth, this defiles the man" (Matt. 15:11). How easy to get hung up on tangible things, such as foods, habits, clothing, recreation, music, and even decorations. The organ of life's richest delights is not the stomach, it's the heart. At the end of day we will answer not for what we put into our stomachs, but what the attitudes we have nurtured in our hearts.

What is our focus? Are we more concerned with people's preferences than the true product of Christian growth: righteousness, peace, and joy? When the outside world peeks through the windows of our church, what do we want them to see? List-makers dashing about enforcing rules while others defiantly ignore them? What a chaotic scene! Who would want that?

Instead, let's serve Christ by giving one another space to breathe and respecting the sensibilities of others. Paul put it best when he wrote, "You were called to freedom, brethren; only do not turn your freedom into an opportunity for the flesh, but through love serve one another" (Gal. 5:13).

—**14:20**—

*When liberty hinders the work of God, it must yield.* Paul wrote to the believers in Corinth, "All things are lawful, but not all things are profitable. All things are lawful, but not all things edify. Let no one seek his own good, but that of his neighbor" (1 Cor. 10:23–24). Nothing should hinder "the work of God," which is nothing short of bringing salvation to the world, reclaiming His creation, and washing away evil in the flood of His righteousness. We must keep our focus on what's important. How silly to quibble about petty differences in nonessential matters.

— **14:21–23** —

We must remember that some Christians are stronger in their faith than others, but there is always someone stronger than us. While we are compassionately limiting our freedom for the sake of someone else's weakness, another Christian is doing the same for us! Or do you think you're the most mature person in your community? I hope not. That's a sure sign of spiritual weakness.

Everyone has room for growth. Everyone is still learning to maintain balance. It takes a mature wisdom to know the difference between essential matters of morality and nonessential matters of conscience. It takes mature love to put one's own preference behind the good of others. It takes uncommon foresight to look beyond the immediate sacrifice of freedom for the sake of God's great plan for the world. It takes supernatural grace to give others the freedom to be different without suffering

## YOU ARE WHAT YOU EAT

In 587 BC, Nebuchadnezzar sacked the ancient fortified city of Jerusalem and removed the citizens of Judah away from their temple. Living in a foreign land among foreign people, they were expected to assimilate, which put their covenant to the test. Earlier, the northern ten tribes of Israel had been overrun by the Assyrians, scattered across their empire, forcibly intermarried, and eventually bred out of existence. Now the Jews faced a similar threat to their existence. And if there are no descendants of Abraham, there is no covenant.

Fortunately, four brave young men — Daniel, Hananiah, Mishael, and Azariah — set a precedent for the Jews in captivity. While their temple lay hundreds of miles away, soon to be in ruins, the Law of God was hidden in their hearts. Obedience would preserve their identity and keep them distinct until God returned them to the land. When challenged to eat the king's meat, which had been almost certainly offered to idols, Daniel and his friends refused, choosing instead a diet of vegetables and water. The Lord blessed the four men and ultimately gave them honored positions in Nebuchadnezzar's government where they could protect their kinsmen and influence their captors (Dan. 1:11–21).

While surrounded by Gentiles, far from home, Jews had only their lineage and their Torah to keep them tethered to the promises of God. In the strict Jewish mind, to eat pagan meat offered to pagan gods was to become pagan.

our condemnation. It takes love to let others be. So if you find yourself thinking less of another believer because he or she enjoys something distasteful to you, you are the weak-faith person in that relationship!

Paul, ever practical in his teaching, offers three simple reminders to help us maintain our own balance on the tightrope of freedom and to help others gain theirs.

First, *be considerate* (14:21). What you enjoy in the privacy of your home is entirely between you and the Lord. All things are lawful; not all things are constructive. Know the difference and thank God for all the wonderful things He created for you to enjoy. When you are in public, don't restrict yourself unnecessarily, but be aware of the potential effect your actions have on others. Be sensitive to reactions and graciously adjust your behavior accordingly.

Second, *be convinced* (14:22). Truth be told, many Christians are not clear within themselves what they believe, so they live in perpetual frustration trying to please everyone around them. But, as we discovered earlier, everyone is different and their convictions are contradictory. Please one and you're likely to displease another.

Instead, carefully examine your matters of conscience to be certain they are not indeed a clear moral issue. Determine what Scripture has to say. Discuss them with trusted, mature believers. Consider the impact they have on others and yourself, both positively and negatively. Then, once you have settled the issue, you can enjoy your freedom with complete confidence. You won't need to react defensively, you won't have to convince anyone else, and you won't even second-guess yourself. Furthermore, that quiet confidence will allow you to let others be.

Third, *be consistent* (14:23). Consistently match your actions to your conscience. But don't be surprised to find that your conscience gradually changes over time. Some things that caused you no problem years ago irritate your conscience today. This is to be expected. Your conscience should never stop growing.

In my own experience, I have found that my list of universal standards has grown shorter as I have grown older. When I first graduated from seminary, I would die defending any one of a hundred different theological hills, and I had a long list of "absolutely essential" do's and don'ts. Today, my list is much shorter. Nevertheless, there are several matters of conscience in which I felt complete liberty to enjoy in the past that my conscience no longer allows. So — for me personally — those things are off-limits. Thankfully, I'm still growing up.

As our conscience is transformed by the Holy Spirit and becomes more mature, we are wise to heed it. However, that's not to say our developing conscience needs to become anyone else's.

Dancing along a high wire is dangerous business, a feat reserved for those who have learned to balance self-control with love for others. But the rapture of the heights, the exhilaration of freedom is not only worth the risk, it's what we were made to do. Never, ever forget that we were reborn to be free (Gal. 5:1, 13).

## Application

### *Life for All to See*

In an ideal world, Paul's instructions in 14:13–23 would not be necessary. Everyone would be fully enjoying his or her freedom in grace and would liberally give others the grace to enjoy theirs without condemnation. Unfortunately, nothing this side of heaven is ideal. Sin and selfishness grow like weeds among the flowers of grace in God's garden. Therefore, the Holy Spirit directs the apostle to urge balance. Otherwise, communities can be torn apart by—of all things—grace!

Paul reminded the Roman believers that nothing is unclean in and of itself (14:14–16). People give things purpose, good or bad, depending on their intentions. He also reminded them that the essence of Christianity is not found in external matters, but in matters of eternal consequence, issues involving the heart (14:17–19). Rather than focusing on what touches the hand or the mouth of a person, we should be more concerned with what we nurture in our hearts. And the apostle established a clear priority, saying that when liberty hinders the work of God, it must yield (14:20). How tragic it would be for a ministry to lose its effectiveness or grind to a halt because people placed their own desires ahead of the greater good.

Naturally, Paul's reminders place the Christian in a kind of tension that is not easily resolved. At what point are we limiting our freedom unnecessarily? We cannot be so concerned about living in a fishbowl that we fail to enjoy all that God intended. Conversely, at what point are we allowing our freedom to hinder the work of God? We never want some expendable pleasure to hinder the faith of a nonbeliever or alienate a brother or sister. So, where do we draw the line? Perhaps an illustration will help.

Many years ago, after a long week of travel and back-to-back speaking engagements, I sat down in a restaurant in Northern California to enjoy a nice meal—a great ending to a wonderful week of ministry. The food smelled delicious and a couple of the selections on the menu would have been perfect with a small glass of wine. I was all alone in a place where no one knew me—not by sight, anyway—and I thought, *Why not?*

After a few moments, my waiter approached the table and introduced himself. We exchanged pleasantries for a few moments and he said, "Your voice is familiar."

Immediately, I thought, *Rats!* and let it go without comment.

"Would you like something to drink?" he asked.

"Iced tea would be great," I replied.

When I finished the meal and gave him my credit card, he immediately responded, "Whoa! I *knew* I knew you!"

We talked for a short time and he eventually confessed, "You know, I didn't know who you were but I decided to watch you because I knew there was something familiar about you."

"Really?" I said without thinking. "Why is that?"

"Well, you see, I just completed a recovery program for alcoholism."

I said, "Boy, that's great, I admire you for doing that. That's wonderful."

He shared a few other details that I'll keep private, but he made it clear that my choice of beverages encouraged him. His feeble first steps in sobriety were made stronger by my limiting my own freedom.

Because I am privileged to have a public platform for the gospel, I consider this a small sacrifice. But if I took this too far, I would never order anything more than water and toothpicks in public. Someone might be offended because I ate two pieces of pie for dessert, or if I ordered red meat! Gotta keep this stuff in balance, don't we?

So, where is the line? I wish I could draw one for you ... or myself, for that matter! All I know is that my conscience told me to avoid a simple glass of wine that evening, and thankfully, I heeded the prompting. Not all decisions should be made this way. Sometimes we must choose between what is clearly right and clearly wrong. More often, however, we must wrestle with "matters of conscience" — that is, matters about which the Bible is silent and others are divided. Then, we must heed the voice of a mind that is being transformed by the Holy Spirit.

Sometimes, we'll get it wrong. We'll follow our conscience and someone is hurt or offended. Rather than justify ourselves, or mount a logical defense, or challenge the offended person to "get over it," we must empathize with the genuine hurt he or she feels and then respond with understanding. Afterward, we rest in grace, learn from the experience, and become wiser as a result.

I wish matters of conscience were less ambiguous. I wish it was easier to discern the safest path through the minefield of people's sensibilities. Perhaps that's why grace is best lived out by the mature. Remember this tip: The gift of freedom always comes in the plain wrapping of responsibility. Fortunately, we have an Advocate who never condemns, only instructs. He never gives up on a project; He'll never walk away in disgust. While others—grace-killers especially—hurl criticism and cast blame, the Holy Spirit whispers encouragement and trains us to see everything from His perspective.

The gift of freedom is sometimes burdensome, but when I consider the alternative, I wouldn't want it any other way. Besides, we're not in this alone. We have one another, and we have the Spirit of Christ within. No one ever said it better than Paul:

> It is absolutely clear that God has called you to a free life. Just make sure that you don't use this freedom as an excuse to do whatever you want to do and destroy your freedom. Rather, use your freedom to serve one another in love; that's how freedom grows. (Gal. 5:13, MSG)

## We Are One ... Or Are We? (Romans 15:1–13)

[1]Now we who are strong ought to bear the weaknesses of those without strength and not *just* please ourselves. [2]Each of us is to please his neighbor for his good, to his edification. [3]For even Christ did not please Himself; but as it is written, "The reproaches of those who reproached You fell on Me." [4]For whatever was written in earlier times was written for our instruction, so that through perseverance and the encouragement of the Scriptures we might have hope. [5]Now may the God who gives perseverance and encouragement grant you to be of the same mind with one another according to Christ Jesus, [6]so that with one accord you may with one voice glorify the God and Father of our Lord Jesus Christ.

[7]Therefore, accept one another, just as Christ also accepted us to the glory of God. [8]For I say that Christ has become a servant to the circumcision on behalf of the truth of God to confirm the promises given to the fathers, [9]and for the Gentiles to glorify God for His mercy; as it is written,

> "Therefore I will give praise to You among the Gentiles,
> And I will sing to Your name."

[10]Again he says,

> "Rejoice, O Gentiles, with His people."

[11]And again,

> "Praise the Lord all you Gentiles,
> And let all the peoples praise Him."

[12]Again Isaiah says,

> "There shall come the root of Jesse,

And He who arises to rule over the Gentiles,
In Him shall the Gentiles hope."

[13]Now may the God of hope fill you with all joy and peace in believing, so that you will abound in hope by the power of the Holy Spirit.

---

The airport terminal buzzed with the familiar sounds of travel. Random announcements squawked and reverberated off the high ceiling and then faded into the steady hum of mingled voices. Luggage wheels clacked by at random intervals and jet engines whined just outside the enormous plate-glass windows. It was all so ordinary until a sound I hadn't heard in more than four decades flicked me hard on the ear. It was the bulldog bark of a Marine Corps drill instructor.

I turned in the direction of the annoyance and quickly put the familiar sound with a familiar sight. A V-shaped man in a crisp, tan uniform and wide-brimmed hat nudged fresh recruits into neat, close-ranked rows using his most effective tool: intimidation.

I couldn't suppress a chuckle when I saw how different they all looked. Short hair, curly hair, shaggy hair, neatly trimmed hair, red, blonde, brown, and black. Jeans and slacks, tee-shirts and oxfords, sneakers and penny loafers. Even their expressions were different. Some trembled with anxiety, some stood ramrod straight, others barely contained their giggling. Black, white, Asian, Latino, and Native American all squeezed uncomfortably close until the nose of one touched the back of another's head.

They had no idea what the next twelve weeks would hold for them, but I remembered all too well. The first priority of recruit training is to strip each man of his individuality, starting with a haircut. Fatigue and pressure grind away all distinguishing marks, physically and emotionally, and the unrelenting pace of training leaves no energy for defiance. Eventually, the shared ordeal reduces the men to their most basic elements, crushes them together, and remolds them after the pattern of the ideal warrior.

The military is all about creating unity by purging individuality and compelling uniformity. The process isn't pretty, but after more than two hundred years, it's a proven method for turning undisciplined, uncooperative individuals into a single, cohesive fighting machine. Such is the imperative of war, which is governed by only one rule: kill or be killed.

Some would like to see the transformation of Christian minds follow a similar pattern, although they dare not say so out loud. Uniformity is indeed an effective way to create unity. Churches would be a lot less likely to split or experience internal strife if everyone would simply think alike, behave alike, worship alike, dress alike, and even like the same likes. However, war—the art of killing and destroying—is not our mission as soldiers of Christ. We work instead to accomplish the righteousness of God, which is anything but oppressive. The righteousness of God produces love, peace, joy, and freedom.

Unity in the new kingdom is the very opposite of unity in the corrupt world system. In the new kingdom, unity and individuality are friends, not enemies. For now, however, before the return of Christ, we must accept that differences continue to cause friction and sometimes spark conflict. Therefore, until the righteousness of God floods the world, we must learn to manage our differences by applying the principles of the new kingdom, regardless of how unnatural they feel to untransformed minds.

— **15:1–2** —

Except for a brief comment or two, Paul has directed all of his teaching to the "strong," among whom he counts himself. The "strong" include those who are not "weak in faith" (14:1) and have "faith that he may eat all things" (14:2). In other words, the strong are people who have risen above the drag of lists, people-pleasing, and performance-based righteousness. The strong know deep down they are righteous because of the Father's grace, the Son's gift of eternal life, and the Spirit's indwelling presence. They rest confidently in their eternal security, knowing they have nothing to prove and everything to give.

Here he exhorts these mature believers—the *dynatoi*, the "powerful"—in Rome "to bear the weaknesses" of the weak. The verb he chose is *bastazō*, which means "to carry, take on oneself." The idea is to lighten the load of another by carrying some of it for him or her. Think of a team of backpackers heading up a mountain. All of the equipment and provisions need to be carried to the top; however, some can carry more weight than others. The strong are to lighten the burden in the packs of the weak and add it to their own.

So, what exactly are the strong supposed to bear? The "weaknesses" of less mature believers, which Paul has defined as the inability (or unwillingness) to live without unnecessary restrictions or to tolerate the liberty of others. Rather than please themselves, mature believers must encourage unity by accepting the burden of legalism. Paul illustrated "accepting the burden of legalism" by giving it specific application in 14:14–15 and again in 14:21. If eating meat compromises unity with another believer, get a "to-go" box or stick to the salad bar. It is a sad and difficult gift to give, but nothing more than what Jesus Christ gave each of us. Paul earlier stated, in effect, "If Christ considered a fellow believer worth dying for, certainly you can forego eating meat" (14:15).

Paul's phrase "please his neighbor" does not encourage pleasing others at the expense of doing what is right. Neither does it suggest that our motive is to gain the favor of others. Paul did not encourage "people-pleasing" as we understand it. The apostle merely wants believers to value the welfare and comfort of others above their own.

### —15:3–4—

Whenever Paul wants to illustrate the quality of selflessness, he points to the example of Jesus Christ:

> Have this attitude in yourselves which was also in Christ Jesus, who, although He existed in the form of God, did not regard equality with God a thing to be grasped, but emptied Himself, taking the form of a bond-servant, and being made in the likeness of men. Being found in appearance as a man, He humbled Himself by becoming obedient to the point of death, even death on a cross. (Phil. 2:5–8)

What a perfect example of someone voluntarily climbing down from a place of high honor to bear the weakness of weak people. He condescended from the highest place of glory in the universe to suffer the most humiliating of deaths in order to lift us up.

To highlight Christ's setting aside His own comfort for the sake of the weak, Paul quotes from Psalm 69:9: "The reproaches of those who reproached You fell on Me," which is the lament of a righteous sufferer. This in turn reminds him of Scripture's enduring value as a source of hope. Note three benefits he stresses:

- *The comprehensive value of Scripture*: All of God's Word from cover to cover is equally beneficial for instruction.
- *The contemporary relevance of Scripture*: Although written long ago to cultures long extinct, God's Word teaches timeless principles that apply to all of humanity throughout all time.
- *The practical application of Scripture*: Diligence to apply the principles taught in the Bible helps us to overcome challenges and to cultivate a spirit of confident assurance.

### —15:5–6—

Paul's benediction summons the power of God to unite believers in a common cause. However it is not "to be of the same mind with one another." That's the kind of group-think Jesus came to break. We are already overly influenced by one another. Furthermore, an entire congregation can "be of the same mind with one another" and be completely wrong!

We are to be of the same mind "according to Christ Jesus"; that is, "in the manner of" God's Son. This is not the same as trying to imitate one another, which is futile. A symphony orchestra is a perfect illustration of the difference.

Imagine how boring Beethoven's *Ninth Symphony* would be if performed by one hundred violins. Don't misunderstand. I love the violin. But that's not the sound the composer imagined when he put quill to parchment nearly two centuries ago. He called for a variety of instruments, each producing a sound unique to its design. He called for strings, woodwinds, brass, percussion, and even the human voice to perform his masterpiece. He carefully crafted a specific part for each instrument. They start and stop at different times, and they play different notes in different patterns. Nevertheless, they play in one accord.

The church is an orchestra. We are instruments crafted by the Artist. We play a score written for us by the Composer, which allows our individual notes to create harmonies. Having tuned ourselves to the Perfect Pitch living within, we play as one, interpreting the Composer's masterpiece with passion and precision. And the result is stunning; we display the glory of God.

## — 15:7–12 —

Paul again turns to Christ as our example and, again, encourages "acceptance" (cf. 14:1, 3, 18). The Greek term for "accept" means "to take to oneself," which of course the Son did for the sake of the Father's glory. His ministry of acceptance took two forms, one to the Jews and another to the Gentiles.

Jesus was born a Jew and followed the rites and customs of the Jews. He was circumcised to identify with God's covenant with Abraham (Gen. 12:1–3; 15:17–21), and then He fulfilled the requirements of God's covenant with Israel (Deut. 28) by living as they should have lived. He claimed the blessings of that covenant as a sinless representative. And He fulfilled the covenant of David (2 Sam. 7:16) by claiming the throne of Israel as his descendant.

Paul then quotes four Old Testament passages (in sequence: Ps. 18:49; Deut. 32:43; Ps. 117:1; and Isa. 11:10) to show that Gentiles were part of God's redemptive plan from the beginning. The Lord originally planned for His blessing to Abraham to become the means of His extending grace to the whole world. The Israelites were to settle in the Promised Land and become a living example of God's government, one so steeped in grace that sojourners would never want to leave.

And the kings of Israel were to remain perfectly obedient to God, leading all of their followers in worship and eventually bringing Gentiles under His worldwide theocracy.

Where the descendants of Abraham failed, the Israelites disappointed, and the kings disobeyed, Jesus Christ succeeded.

The righteousness of God was ultimately revealed in the person of His Son, Jesus Christ. When He returns, the world will be recreated all the way down to the atom to reflect that righteousness. So, if we want to know what the new kingdom will look like, we need only look to its King. And during His earthly ministry, the King was a servant.

## — 15:13 —

Paul concludes the final section of his teaching with a benediction. "Hope" is, again, not a tentative wish that may or may not come true. Christian hope is an assured expectation based on a promise of God (4:18; 5:1–5; 8:24–25; 15:4). Because God always keeps His promises, we have a guaranteed future that awaits us. Therefore, we can endure trials with joy and peace. Our believing will keep us moving when we might otherwise become discouraged and quit.

"So that" is a conjunction that indicates a cause-effect relationship. Note that God does the filling with joy and hope; our only responsibility is to believe. Paul desires that this process of believing and receiving will result in believers overflowing with hope—perhaps enough to flood the world and produce change, if only a little.

This benediction marks the end of Paul's teaching to the Romans. The balance of his letter addresses several personal matters and outlines his future plans.

Paul has packed a lot of practical wisdom into this final section of teaching. If you retrace his thoughts, you will notice a pattern. Every lesson involves a particular kind of relationship—grace within oneself (12:1–2), grace within the body of Christ (12:3–16; 14:1–15:13), grace to the outside world (12:17–13:14)—and specifically how those relationships are to be impacted by believers. These are lessons on horizontal grace, the first trickles of the coming flood. Soon the righteousness of God will split the barrier between heaven and earth like a mighty river breaches a dam, but for now, that righteousness comes through us—or at least it's supposed to.

So, good believer, what are you doing with the grace you have been given? Are you allowing it to change you from within? Are you allowing God's grace to fill you with joy and peace so that others can share in your confident assurance? Are you a foreshadowing of God's coming righteousness? Let me leave you with Paul's challenging exhortation and reassuring benediction:

> I urge you, brethren, by the mercies of God, to present your bodies a living and holy sacrifice, acceptable to God, which is your spiritual service of worship. And do not be conformed to this world, but be transformed by the renewing of your mind, so that you may prove what the will of God is, that which is good and acceptable and perfect. (12:1–2)
>
> Now may the God of hope fill you with all joy and peace in believing, so that you will abound in hope by the power of the Holy Spirit. (15:13)

---

NOTES: The Righteousness of God (Romans 12:1–15:13)

1. Gerhard Kittel and Friedrich, *Theological Dictionary of the New Testament: Abridged in One Volume,* trans. Geoffrey W. Bromiley (Grand Rapids: Eerdmans, 1985), 1236.
2. Ibid.
3. Rosamund Stone Zander and Benjamin Zander, *The Art of Possibility* (Boston: Harvard Business Press, 2000), 118–19.
4. Kittel and Gerhard Friedrich, eds., *Theological Dictionary of the New Testament: Abridged in One Volume,* 75.
5. Neil T. Anderson, *The Bondage Breaker* (Eugene, Ore.: Harvest House, 1990), 194–96.
6. Ray Stedman, *From Guilt to Glory* (Waco, Tex.: Word, 1979), 126–27.
7. Tacitus, *The Works of Tacitus,* 2nd ed. (London: Woodward and Peele, 1737), 2:698.
8. Johannes P. Louw and Eugene Albert Nida, *Greek-English Lexicon of the New Testament: Based on Semantic Domains,* electronic ed. of the 2nd ed. (New York: United Bible Societies, 1996 [orig. 1989]), 1:762.
9. Of the 92 occurrences of this Greek term, the King James Version opts for "lose" 22 times.

# THE COMMUNITY OF GOD (ROMANS 15:14 – 16:27)

As a baby camel dipped his head to drink from a pool of water, he studied his reflection. After a few moments he asked his mother, "Why do we have such long eyelashes, Mama?"

His mother said with great dignity, "Because we have to be able see our way through sandstorms. We can keep going when others can no longer find their way."

The baby camel looked at his feet, compared them to his mother's, and after another sip of water, asked, "Why do we have such wide feet?"

His mother replied, "So we can traverse the shifting sands of the desert without sinking down."

The young camel then asked, "Why do we have such large humps on our backs?"

His mother responded patiently, "So we can travel for days through barren wilderness without a drop of water to drink. No other animal can see as clearly, walk as far, or live as long in the desert as the majestic camel."

After a long silence, the young camel asked, "But mother, since all of that is true, why do we live in a zoo?"

People don't generally do well in isolation. Prisoners, hospital patients, people too sick to leave home, fulltime mothers of small children, and lonely retirees often struggle against the deadly effects of isolation. Prolonged seclusion from others and the outside world eventually begins to undermine one's sense of identity. Isolated people frequently forget that the world is much larger than their immediate environments. They suffer a lack of motivation because their vision is limited. They commonly spiral into a depression fueled by self-pity and hypochondria because their minds have nothing on which to focus beyond themselves.

People need problems to solve and challenges to overcome. We thrive on opportunities to participate in something greater than ourselves. Furthermore, we were created to enjoy relationships with one another, to grow in greater intimacy with our Creator, and to rule as His vice-regents over creation, so that all things exist in perfect harmony with His purposes and reflect His glory (Gen. 1:26–28). But all of that can become lost or confused when we spend too much time alone.

The debilitating and sometimes deadly effects of isolation can also bring Christian communities to their ruin. They are preoccupied with their own problems. They begin to suspect, doubt, blame, and control one another. They become overly concerned with preserving their own identity and soon forget the desperate needs of people in surrounding communities. Isolation muzzles motivation, extinguishes enthusiasm, and ultimately reduces the entire community to a self-induced, self-sustained amnesia. They forget who they are, why God gave them certain gifts, and what their purpose is in the world.

This was a particular danger for the church in Rome. Nero's brutal persecution of Christians did not occur overnight. Several years before the burning of Rome in AD 64, Christians had become the objects of a growing disdain. Romans considered Judaism the religion of a barbaric, atheistic race and Christianity a particularly sinister mutation that perverted the morals of otherwise upright citizens. Consequently, believers huddled closer together for mutual support and encouragement. They often gathered together in secret, regarded newcomers with suspicion, avoided drawing attention to themselves, and in the process of self-preservation, became increasingly isolated.

Having explained God's master plan of salvation—highlighting both the vertical and horizontal dimensions of grace—and having encouraged the believers in Rome to fulfill their responsibilities as ambassadors of that grace, Paul turns his attention to the future. The apostle saw himself as a part of God's grand plan and the Roman

## ROMANS, RELIGIONS, RITUALS, AND RELATIONS

In most ancient cultures, religion was the glue that held tribes together and religious rituals solidified tribal identity. And in the first century, Rome was the largest tribe of all. To belong was to enjoy a powerful camaraderie; to opt out was to invite loathing. To be Roman was to reach the pinnacle of sophistication; those who did not aspire to be Roman were obviously subhuman and deserved to be treated as such. Therefore, "separation of church and state" would have been a ghastly thought to any loyal citizen of the empire.

Romans were remarkably inclusive when it came to religion. They not only tolerated the religious beliefs of the cultures they conquered, they added these gods to their own pantheon, believing it was safer to worship a false deity than to risk offending one that potentially existed. Furthermore, they recognized the value of shared ritual as a means of expanding the tribe.

Jews and Christians posed a difficult problem for the Romans. They worshiped a God who could not be seen and whose name could not be uttered. To make matters worse, this God demanded *exclusive* devotion, something utterly unthinkable to a culture founded on expanding religious beliefs. How narrow-minded! How arrogant! How absurdly aloof! Such people could never be trusted to become members of the tribe. They rejected Roman deities — including the emperor — and they despised Roman rituals; therefore, they must be completely devoid of all virtue.

Ironically, Jews and Christians were not hated because they worshiped another God; Romans despised Jews and Christians as "atheists."

## KEY TERMS

ὑπακοή [*hypakoē*] (*5218*) "obedience, compliance, heeding"

As the opposite of *hamartia*, "sin" (Rom. 6:16), *hypakoē* is the behavior of someone who hears and then heeds the voice of divine authority. The supreme example is Christ (Rom. 5:19), who set the standard of true belief. Therefore, Paul frequently uses the term to describe genuine Christianity (Rom. 1:5; 15:18; 16:19; 2 Cor. 7:15; 10:6; see also 1 Peter 1:2, 22).

συνίστημι [*synistēmi*] (*4921*) "to commend, to place together, to associate"

This compound Greek verb has a broad range of uses, but Paul almost exclusively draws on the classical sense of "to commend, recommend for acceptance, present for consideration." For example, God "commends" His love toward us through the death of His Son (Rom. 5:8). The word does not convey a passive, laissez-faire suggestion, but an urging to heed the wishes of the speaker.

διχοστασία [*dichostasia*] (*1370*) "dissention, discord, disunity"

The emphasis of this term is not opposition to the established authority as much as discord among peers. "Dissention" is the dichotomy of a group such that one faction stands apart from another while holding an "us-versus-them" attitude. People can disagree without dissention.

σκάνδαλον [*skandalon*] (*4625*) "hindrance, occasion of stumbling, trap"

The original and most literal meaning is "springing back and forth" or "slamming closed," as with a spring-loaded animal trap. Therefore, the noun generally stands for "the means of closing something in." The figurative use of this word is rare outside of Jewish and Christian writings, but not absent. One Greek playwright describes an unjust accuser dragging innocent men into court and "laying traps" with his questions.[1] In the New Testament, Jesus Christ is an intellectual and moral trap for those who oppose God and think themselves righteous (Rom. 9:33; 11:9; Gal. 5:11; 1 Cor. 1:23). In relation to the church, a *skandalon* is any doctrine that is contrary to the truth taught by Jesus and the people He personally trained.

believers as a vital part of its success. He very much thought a partnership with the Roman church would extend the reach of the gospel even farther than before.

Paul's conclusion to this letter is by no means a haphazard collection of thoughts and personal greetings. It is carefully crafted to draw the Roman believers out of their isolation, to remind them of their identity in Christ, to commend them for their faithfulness thus far, and to call them to specific action in advancing God's plan of salvation. And the apostle has his eye on Spain—Rome's frontier province—and its desperate need for the righteousness of God.

## Partners, Plans, and Prayer (Romans 15:14–33)

[14]And concerning you, my brethren, I myself also am convinced that you yourselves are full of goodness, filled with all knowledge and able also to admonish one another. [15]But I have written very boldly to you on some points so as to remind you again, because of the grace that was given me from God, [16]to be a minister of Christ Jesus to the Gentiles, ministering as a priest the gospel of God, so that *my* offering of the Gentiles may become acceptable, sanctified by the Holy Spirit. [17]Therefore in Christ Jesus I have found reason for boasting in things pertaining to God. [18]For I will not presume to speak of anything except what Christ has accomplished through me, resulting in the obedience of the Gentiles by word and deed, [19]in the power of signs and wonders, in the power of the Spirit; so that from Jerusalem and round about as far as Illyricum I have fully preached the gospel of Christ. [20]And thus I aspired to preach the gospel, not where Christ was *already* named, so that I would not build on another man's foundation; [21]but as it is written,

> "They who had no news of Him shall see,
> And they who have not heard shall understand."

[22]For this reason I have often been prevented from coming to you; [23]but now, with no further place for me in these regions, and since I have had for many years a longing to come to you [24]whenever I go to Spain — for I hope to see you in passing, and to be helped on my way there by you, when I have first enjoyed your company for a while — [25]but now, I am going to Jerusalem serving the saints. [26]For Macedonia and Achaia have been pleased to make a contribution for the poor among the saints in Jerusalem. [27]Yes, they were pleased *to do so*, and they are indebted to them. For if the Gentiles have shared in their spiritual things, they are indebted to minister to them also in material things. [28]Therefore, when I have finished this, and have put my seal on this fruit of theirs, I will go on by way of you to Spain. [29]I know that when I come to you, I will come in the fullness of the blessing of Christ.

[30]Now I urge you, brethren, by our Lord Jesus Christ and by the love of the Spirit, to strive together with me in your prayers to God for me, [31]that I may be rescued from those who are disobedient in Judea, and that my service for Jerusalem may prove acceptable to the saints; [32]so that I may come to you in joy by the will of God and find *refreshing* rest in your company. [33]Now the God of peace be with you all. Amen.

Ben and Jerry. Wozniak and Jobs. Crick and Watson. Wilbur and Orville. Stanley and Livingstone. Lewis and Clark. Moody and Sankey. Luther and Melanchthon. Graham and Barrows. Great partnerships are rare because they depend on a delicate blend of least three qualities that are tricky to match and then difficult to maintain:

- *Corresponding competence.* Potential partners must first recognize their need for someone else to supply what they do not possess in themselves. This doesn't come naturally to highly competent people. Furthermore, it is incredibly rare to find two humble achievers who naturally complement one another.
- *Mutual trust.* The individuals must be trustworthy because partnerships—like all good relationships—grow strong when each person can wholeheartedly rely on the integrity and ability of the other.
- *Shared vision.* The two competent, trustworthy people must want to achieve common goals; otherwise, they will continually frustrate one another.

Because the alignment of these essential qualities—competence, trust, and vision—is so rare to find and so difficult to maintain, partnerships usually fall apart soon after they begin. But when a great partnership forms and then manages to thrive, the results are always extraordinary.

Paul understood the perils and power of collaboration. He and Barnabas accomplished much together. They were both competent and trustworthy, but they no longer shared the same vision of ministry—specifically, how it should be carried out. Barnabas wanted to give John Mark another chance after the young man deserted their first missionary journey; Paul did not. Consequently, their partnership ended after a heated disagreement (Acts 15:36–40). Although they repaired their friendship and ultimately supported one another theologically, they never chose to collaborate again.

Paul labored with other partners. At various times, he teamed with Silas, Timothy, Titus, and Luke. And near the end of his life, the apostle called for John Mark to join him "for he is useful to me for service" (2 Tim. 4:11).

Paul's pioneering work demanded partnership. As the apostle ministered in Corinth, his third missionary journey was more than half complete. New churches had been founded and existing churches strengthened. He had trained local leaders to nurture the gospel where they lived and equipped his apprentices to continue his itinerant ministry throughout the empire east of Rome. To conclude the journey, he would travel back around the Aegean Sea to Miletus and then sail for Jerusalem to deliver the famine-relief funds he had collected along the way.

Most would consider three circuits around the Roman Empire a full life of ministry and a great time to retire. Not Paul! With the work in the "civilized world" resting in capable hands, the opportunity to take the gospel to where it had never been proclaimed proved too irresistible for the pioneering apostle. He began to chart a course from Jerusalem to the Roman frontier of Spain. However, he knew his greatest challenge yet would demand more than he could provide himself. This would require a partnership with the trustworthy and resourceful church in Rome.

The outline of his proposal is simple: you … me … together. To enlist their help, Paul identifies the strengths of the Roman believers and reminds them of their calling (15:14−16), he confirms his own calling and reveals his plans (15:17−29), and then he invites them to join him in a partnership, starting with prayer (15:30−33).

## —15:14—

Throughout the letter, Paul has been writing "to" the church in Rome. At this point, he begins to write "about" them. He affirms his brothers and sisters in Rome by using three phrases of commendation, each one pointing to a specific character trait he has observed among the few members he had encountered or identified as a result of their reputation.

*"Full of goodness."* The word "full" means "filled to overflowing" and the word for "goodness" describes moral and ethical purity. It includes kindness and thoughtfulness and even charity toward those in need.

Everett F. Harrison writes, "[Goodness] is not a native disposition but the moral excellence wrought into the texture of life by the Spirit's indwelling."[2] Remember, these are the same Romans who were earlier told that all are depraved. Believers remain depraved individuals in our old nature, but we receive a new nature with the regeneration and subsequent filling of the Holy Spirit. This new nature evidences acts of goodness.

*"Filled with all knowledge."* Literally, they are "filled to overflowing" with such knowledge as to be completely informed and adequately aware. Obviously, only God is omniscient, but the men and women in Rome have demonstrated a mature command of Christian truth and understood the issues that impacted their corner of the world. When believers are fully and completely informed, when they have become adequately aware, they understand their times and realize what they must do. They don't typically lack for zeal or vision.

*"Able to admonish one another."* The word rendered "able" comes from the Greek term *dynamis*, which means "power." They are empowered from within to apply

their knowledge in a constructive way. The word "admonish" comes from a compound of the two Greek words, *nous* ("mind") and *tithēmi* ("to place"). The idea of placing something in the mind of another was how the Greeks understood the process of education. The Roman Christians are able "to impart understanding," "to set right," "to lay on the heart" in such a way as to influence not merely the intellect, but the will and disposition as well. "The word thus acquires such senses as 'to admonish,' 'to warn,' 'to remind,' and 'to correct.'"[3]

These three qualities essentially describe a mature Christian. Imagine the impact churches would have on the world if they were composed of people who are morally clean and ethically pure, filled with such knowledge as to be completely informed and adequately aware — able to educate one another and hold each other accountable. Pastors devote their lives to seeing their churches transformed, one person at a time, to be full of goodness, filled with all knowledge, and able to admonish.

### — 15:15–16 —

After Paul's long discourse on the basics of the gospel, one might think the Roman believers are not mature in their faith or in dire need of instruction. So the apostle clarifies that he has not written this bold Christian manifesto to provide new information, but to help them retrace the steps of their own spiritual journey, to help them appreciate again the inestimable value of the grace they have received, to confirm them in the security of their salvation, and to prompt them to action. Moreover, he sees this as his apostolic duty — his debt (1:14; 1 Cor. 9:16) — to teach and strengthen all churches, including the one in Rome.

Paul is not merely justifying his letter by restating his duty as an apostle and reiterating his particular mission among the Gentiles. He stated at the beginning of this letter that his intention was to visit the capital city in order to "obtain some fruit among you also, even as among the rest of the Gentiles" (1:13). He hoped to join them in evangelizing Rome. Here, at the end of the letter, however, he takes these intentions a step further. As he surveys the potential for ministry in Rome, he sees even more lying beyond their western horizon. Having identified the Roman believers as worthy partners, he shares his vision and plan for the next phase of his ministry.

### — 15:17–21 —

In addition to the timeless principles contained in this section of Scripture, we can enjoy a great side benefit. We have a rare opportunity to learn something about the apostle I have described as a man of grace and grit. Despite his impressive resume of qualifications and accomplishments, he thinks of himself as merely a bond-slave of Jesus Christ. He remains unwilling to take any credit for the deeds of his Master. The miracles he has performed are genuine because the power of the Holy Spirit within him is real. Gentiles have been won and their obedience is seen in what they said and did because God has chosen to preach through him. The gospel thrives in cosmopolitan cities because Paul has obeyed and persevered. No one can argue that his ministry was ineffective.

Note the word "fully" in 15:19. The apostle declares that he has "fully preached the gospel" in the expanse between Jerusalem and Illyricum, which comprised most of the territory Rome fully controlled. He says, in so many words, "My job in this part of the world is complete and I leave it in very capable hands." He then quotes Isaiah 52:15 to underscore his primary motivation: to go where the gospel has not yet been heard.

Isaiah's vision of the Messiah ruling over all the earth and Gentiles from every nation falling prostrate before Him became Paul's mandate. His first three missionary journeys have barely begun to fulfill the prophet's oracle. Therefore, the apostle's vision always exceeds his horizon, compelling him to go wherever the gospel is unknown. And—I love this about Paul—*his dreams are always greater than his memories*. Memories can either anchor you to the past or thrust you toward new challenges. Paul's memories of past success don't slow him down; on the contrary, they inspire him to achieve more for the sake of Christ.

Paul recalls his former success and abiding vision, not to boast or to garner admiration for himself but to lay the foundation for his proposal. He says, in effect, "My vision has always been to proclaim the gospel where it has never been heard; by the grace of God, this ministry has been successful; and I have done all I can to the east of Rome, so ..."

## —15:22–25—

Paul quickly turns his perspective from the past to the future. In the past, his ministry kept him occupied with necessary work in the east, "but now" new plans lie to the west, in Rome and far beyond. Having affirmed the church in Rome as a valuable partner and having presented himself as someone trustworthy to represent them in ministry, Paul graciously suggests a joint venture. He plans to complete his current mission, deliver the famine-relief collection to the church in Jerusalem, and then set out for Spain.

## From My Journal

### Why I Will Never Retire

Several years ago, a woman called and said, "You don't know me, but I listen to your radio program. In fact," she continued, "that's how things turned around for me."

She then began to cry. "I had made a complete mess of my life and was at the end of my rope. I had gone through two abortions and I had abandoned my family, my husband and three children. I had destroyed everything that was important to me and when I had nothing left to lose, I bought a gun and checked into a cheap motel."

My stomach tightened. I could hear the despairing anguish in her voice as she tearfully recalled that awful night.

"Sitting on the side of the bed, I shoved the gun in my mouth ... and, all of a sudden, the radio alarm clicked on. It was your broadcast. For all I know, some religious fanatic had set that radio alarm to start playing that religious program. I heard music, and then I heard your voice."

By now, I had to sit down.

"I slowly pulled the gun out of my mouth as I listened ... and I realized that I had nothing in front of me but sorrow, whether I lived or died. I laid the gun aside, dropped to my knees by the bed, and asked Jesus Christ to save me. There are times I can still recall the taste of that gun in my mouth."

I am frequently asked if or when I will retire.

Never. I may have to slow down or curtail my activities as my physical abilities diminish, but I will never stop proclaiming the good news. Never!

How can I?

Paul's typical strategy for evangelizing a region began by establishing a base of operations in a large city along major trade routes. For example, Ephesus allowed him access to supplies by sea, the safety and stability of government, and well-kept roads throughout the Roman province of Asia. The same was true of Corinth, from which he saturated Macedonia with the gospel, and Mysia, which would have given him access to Bithynia.

Using Rome as a launching point, Paul plans one of two potential missions. He could board a ship in Rome and sail directly for the region we now call Spain. This territory had been conquered by Rome but was much like the American West in

A large Roman city gave Paul three crucial advantages when evangelizing a region: abundant provisions, efficient transportation (ships and roads), and almost limitless networking opportunities. He likely planned to use Rome as a base of operations, much like he did Ephesus and Corinth.

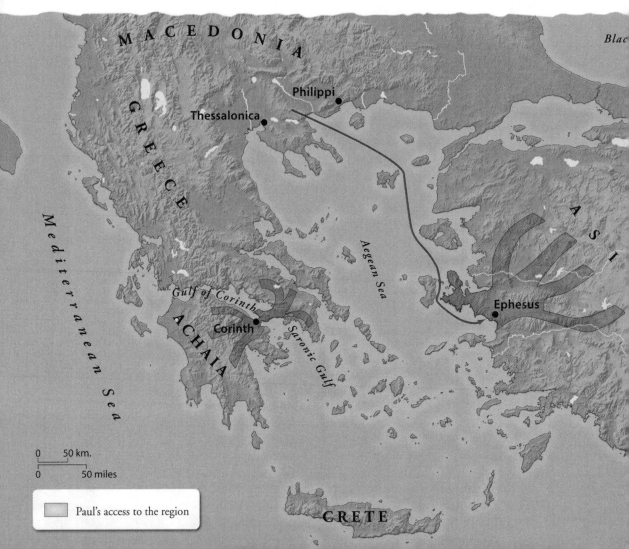

1840—filled with potential, yet largely untamed. However, it is more in keeping with Paul's history to see "Spain" as symbolic of his desire to evangelize the West, working his way through northern Italia and present-day France and ultimately crossing the Pyrenees to claim "Hispania" for Christ.

Paul doesn't dream on a small scale! The land mass he plans to evangelize exceeds the territory covered by his first three missionary journeys. And the extent of the hardship on those journeys alone is a good comparison as to what might lie ahead of him on the fourth journey:

> Five times I received from the Jews thirty-nine *lashes*. Three times I was beaten with rods, once I was stoned, three times I was shipwrecked, a night and a day I have spent in the deep. *I have been* on frequent journeys, in dangers from rivers, dangers from robbers, dangers from *my* countrymen, dangers from the Gentiles, dangers in the city, dangers in the wilderness, dangers on the sea, dangers among false brethren; *I have been* in labor and hardship, through many sleepless nights, in hunger and thirst, often without food, in cold and exposure. Apart from *such* external things, there is the daily pressure on me *of* concern for all the churches. (2 Cor. 11:24–28)

Think of it! This is his experience in the "civilized" part of the empire! His plans will take him to the fringes of the *Pax Romana* (the "Roman peace") and beyond, where he will be at the mercy of "barbarians"—people who answered to no one.

## —15:26–29—

Paul uses the generous example of the churches in Macedonia and Achaia—present-day Greece—to inspire the church in Rome. The Gentile believers in Greece viewed their sharing of material wealth as a mere token of the debt they owed Jerusalem for the gift of the gospel, an immeasurable spiritual treasure. Clearly, Paul implies that Rome also owes a debt of gratitude, which can be honored by helping his mission to rescue other Gentiles.

The apostle is certain of his visit to Rome; however, he could not have imagined the circumstances that will take him there. After delivering the famine relief funds he collected on the third journey, the apostle is falsely accused by Jewish leaders in the temple—the very men he formerly served when persecuting Christians—and arrested. After several hearings, a foiled assassination plot, months in protective custody, and a lengthy trial, Paul exercises his right as a Roman citizen to have his case heard in Rome (Acts 21–26). So, the apostle does reach his intended destination, only later than he planned and under the protection of Roman guards.

## —15:30–33—

Paul pleads with the church in Rome to begin their partnership with him by praying "by [*dia*] our Lord Jesus Christ and by [*dia*] the love of the Spirit." The Greek preposition *dia* has a wide range of uses, always depending on the context. In this case, the complete sense of the word is "by the agency of" or "through." They are to approach the Father through the Son and the Spirit. Furthermore, Paul urges his brothers and sisters to "strive together" with him, using a term commonly used in athletics that picture a team strenuously working together to achieve victory.

Paul is not overstating his desire for their earnest prayer. While he feels duty-bound to deliver the famine-relief funds to Jerusalem, he has serious misgivings about his safety upon returning there. Later, during his voyage from Corinth to Jerusalem, he calls the church leaders in Ephesus to meet him before his ship put back out to sea. He stated flatly:

> "And now, behold, bound by the Spirit, I am on my way to Jerusalem, not knowing what will happen to me there, except that the Holy Spirit solemnly testifies to me in every city, saying that bonds and afflictions await me. But I do not consider my life of any account as dear to myself, so that I may finish my course and the ministry which I received from the Lord Jesus, to testify solemnly of the gospel of the grace of God." (Acts 20:22–24)

This real danger prompts Paul to ask for three specific answers to prayer. First, he prays his enemies will be unsuccessful in their attempts to keep him from continuing his ministry. Second, he prays that the Jewish Christians in Jerusalem will accept the monetary gifts offered by their Gentile brothers and sisters in Greece. And, third, he prays that his plans for continued ministry beyond Rome will not only escape delays but also find help in the Roman church.

Paul is undoubtedly the most pioneering of all the apostles. The biblical record shows that he logged more miles, planted more churches, trained more leaders, and wrote more Scripture than any other person in his generation. Nevertheless, we rarely if ever find him alone. He surrounds himself with gifted, driven people who share his obligation to preach the gospel and to strengthen churches. He seeks partners he can wholeheartedly trust, those who will not settle for anything less than complete devotion. And when he finds trustworthy coworkers, he is quick to place them where they will have the greatest impact.

Although seasoned by struggle and hardship, although undeterred by danger, Paul knows his vision to blaze new trails through the Roman frontier can only be realized with the help of dependable partners. We can only speculate as to how his plans might have unfolded. The book of Acts ends with Paul under house arrest in

Rome. However, I personally believe he realized at least part of his vision before a second imprisonment in Rome and eventual martyrdom there.

If Paul's dreams did carry him westward toward Spain, I have no doubt the help of his Roman brothers and sisters filled his sails.

## Application

### *How to Turn Big Dreams into Even Bigger Realities*

Great men and women become great because they dream on a grand scale and then set out to turn their vision into reality. Paul's vision for the gospel stretched farther than any of his contemporaries dared to imagine. After three circuits around the eastern part of the Roman Empire, every major city had a relatively stable church with fairly capable leadership to guide them. It was then that Paul set his sights on the western part of the empire. He would build on past success by employing the same principles that had guided him thus far. I find four in Romans 15:14–33.

1. *Life's greatest achievements are accomplished through joint effort (15:17–18).* We often imagine Paul trudging from town to town all alone, except for a faithful companion or two. In reality, he often traveled with a relatively large entourage, which is why he frequently received help from churches to continue his mission. He understood the power of collaboration, recognizing that the involvement of others would compound his own effectiveness. He was ever on the lookout for capable people he could energize by sharing his vision.

2. *Great accomplishments are never achieved without hindrances (15:22).* One wise author wrote, "If I'm told that the road to my glorious destination is marred by loose rocks and potholes, every jolt along the way reminds me that I'm on the right road." Evangelizing the eastern half of the empire did not occur quickly or easily. Paul faced exposure, hunger, shipwreck, robbers, imprisonment, floggings, stonings, slander, and even opposition from his closest friends (see 2 Cor. 11:23–33). Any one of these might have discouraged the apostle. Many might have taken this opposition to be a sign of God's disapproval. But Paul remained determined.

3. *Hindrances are overcome by sustained hope (15:23–25).* As Paul languished in prison, deterred from his planned objective, he trusted that the Lord would use the evil deeds of evil people to advance the good news of Christ (Phil. 1:12–14). If you run with people who dash your hopes and dreams, you're running with the wrong crowd. Get new friends. Genuine friends give wise,

realistic counsel, but they also encourage us. They remind us that nothing is impossible with God. Hope is sustained by trusting the Lord as we remain focused on a God-honoring vision.

4. *The essential ingredient of sustained hope is enthusiasm (15:29).* Ralph Waldo Emerson wrote, "Nothing great was ever achieved without enthusiasm." He was right. However, don't confuse enthusiasm with excitement. They often go together, but excitement fades quickly, usually after the first couple of setbacks. Enthusiasm is a sustained positive attitude fueled by the steadfast conviction that one's vision *must* become reality.

By the way, Paul did go to Rome … and the government paid his way! While fighting false charges leveled against him by his former colleagues and dodging assassination attempts, he was transported to Rome under Roman guard to have his case heard by Emperor Nero. He remained under house arrest in Rome with a Roman soldier to guard him, which he viewed as another grand opportunity. He turned his circumstance into an opportunity to evangelize the palace guard!

If you have a great vision, you are a leader. You also have been given a responsibility to turn that worthy dream into reality. Share your vision with others and don't hesitate to enlist help. Expect hindrances and remain focused on fulfilling your vision. Smother your dreams in prayer, asking that the God-honoring vision you hold will be accomplished through God's power, and choose companions who remind you of His faithfulness. And when you inevitably face setbacks, refuse discouragement—remain enthusiastic. Allow your convictions to carry you forward and discover ways to turn each difficulty into an advantage.

If your vision is something that honors God and brings the righteousness of God to the world, you can be certain He will turn your grandest dream into an even grander reality. Trust Him!

## Love, and a Holy Kiss (Romans 16:1–16)

¹I commend to you our sister Phoebe, who is a servant of the church which is at Cenchrea; ²that you receive her in the Lord in a manner worthy of the saints, and that you help her in whatever matter she may have need of you; for she herself has also been a helper of many, and of myself as well.

³Greet Prisca and Aquila, my fellow workers in Christ Jesus, ⁴who for my life risked their own necks, to whom not only do I give thanks, but also all the churches of the Gentiles; ⁵also *greet* the church that is in their house. Greet Epaenetus, my beloved, who is the first convert to Christ from Asia. ⁶Greet Mary, who has worked hard for you.

⁷Greet Andronicus and Junias, my kinsmen and my fellow prisoners, who are outstanding among the apostles, who also were in Christ before me. ⁸Greet Ampliatus, my beloved in the Lord. ⁹Greet Urbanus, our fellow worker in Christ, and Stachys my beloved. ¹⁰Greet Apelles, the approved in Christ. Greet those who are of the *household* of Aristobulus. ¹¹Greet Herodion, my kinsman. Greet those of the *household* of Narcissus, who are in the Lord. ¹²Greet Tryphaena and Tryphosa, workers in the Lord. Greet Persis the beloved, who has worked hard in the Lord. ¹³Greet Rufus, a choice man in the Lord, also his mother and mine. ¹⁴Greet Asyncritus, Phlegon, Hermes, Patrobas, Hermas and the brethren with them. ¹⁵Greet Philologus and Julia, Nereus and his sister, and Olympas, and all the saints who are with them. ¹⁶Greet one another with a holy kiss. All the churches of Christ greet you.

---

Of all the words used to describe our finest organizations, several are inappropriate when attached to a local body of believers. A church may be large, but "mega" is not a compliment. A church should always hold open its arms to welcome any who wish to learn about Christ for the first time, but it should never exchange its identity for a "seeker-friendly" persona. A church should always stress the "good-story" of Jesus Christ ("gospel" in the Old English) and should always engage people on the cutting edge of society and culture, but no church should deny its apostolic heritage or shun theology in order to "emerge."

Furthermore, a church should be organized and would be wise to apply the best tools of management and to employ the latest technology, but the local church must never become an efficient corporation with a cross stuck on the roof. The first words that come to mind must not be "efficient," "driven," "focused," or even "expanding"—at least not for the people crossing the threshold. A church is supposed to be like a family, in which older people train and encourage the younger, where everyone is accountable and finds security, acceptance, hope, and help. The church must be a place where words are reliable, worship is meaningful, faith is invincible, grace is noticeable, and love is tangible.

The church must be a warm, welcoming body, not a well-oiled, slick machine.

Several years ago, I traveled with a group of pastors and pastoral interns, visiting a number of churches to learn about how they started, what guided their activities in the community, and how they intended to meet the needs of a growing and ever-changing culture. We stood in the foyer of a fairly well-known, larger church, waiting for our appointment—we had arrived early and the church's staff was still preparing for our visit. During our wait, one of the custodians walked up and started chatting with us. (I love talking to custodians. While others see the church how they *hope* it will be or how it's *reported* to be, custodians usually see the church as it really is.) Before long, the conversation turned to size, and he was quick to tell us about how large they had become. I asked, "How large are you?" He said, "Well, we process about 2,500 people every Sunday."

Process? I took his choice of words to be reflective of his church's culture, but I withheld judgment at the time. I didn't hear the word again that day, but it became obvious the methods and attitudes of the staff had shaped the custodian's vocabulary. What happens to a church that begins to "process" people? Processing is something you do in a meat-packing plant, not in a church!

Paul's obvious intellect and theological acumen have been celebrated for centuries, largely because of his letter to the believers in Rome. But he was also deeply concerned about people; relationships were immensely important to the apostle. Weaving itself through the black, white, and grey theological issues, we can trace a scarlet thread of love.

God "poured out" and "demonstrated" His love for us (5:5, 8). Nothing can separate us from the love of God (8:28–39). Love must be unhypocritical as we devote ourselves to loving one another (12:9–10). We must continually love those outside the church by honoring them and returning blessing for evil treatment (13:8–10). We are to love other believers more than we do our own comfort or pleasure (14:15). Then Paul called upon the love of his brothers and sisters in Rome to join him in continued ministry (15:30).

Paul considers love crucial because he values people above all else. So it is no surprise to see a long list of names—some Latin, some Greek, and all personally cherished by the apostle—appear at the end of his letter. Paul could have told a story about each person he greets, but he has just room enough to briefly acknowledge them, which he does for two reasons. First, he wants to greet them and to assure them that neither time nor distance has diminished his love for each individual; second, he wants to assure the church in Rome that his interest in them is personal, not utilitarian. Although he has not met the majority of those in the congregation, he loves these brothers and sisters.

## —16:1–2—

Phoebe means "pure, bright, radiant." Paul referred to her as "our sister" and called her a *diakonos* ("deacon"; NASB "servant"). There is no feminine form of that term in Greek; therefore, I take this to mean she was a deaconess in the city of Cenchrea, which lay seven miles east of Corinth. Moreover, he "commends" her, which means that he is sending her with his personal endorsement. This was a common courtesy given to someone delivering a letter, so it's likely that Paul has selected Phoebe for this very important mission.

He asks that the congregation "help" or, more literally, "stand beside" Phoebe, just as she has done for Paul and other people in ministry. He appears to ask for something more than routine hospitality. Perhaps she plans to relocate to Rome or needs help with delicate matters involving the government. Regardless, the apostle thinks highly of her.

— 16:3–4 —

To "greet" someone has no complex meaning. The ancient greeting is much like we think of it today. In Western Europe and the Americas, we shake hands. In Eastern Europe and the Middle East, they kiss one another on each cheek. In the Far East, greeting is accompanied with a bow. In ancient times, a greeting was no less diverse, especially in the cosmopolitan capital of the empire. Nevertheless, all greetings express the same sentiments: well-wishing, appreciation, and camaraderie.

Paul first greets the couple Prisca (also known as Priscilla) and Aquila, whom he first met in Corinth during his second missionary journey. They fled their home in the capital city during the persecution of the Jews under Emperor Claudius. The Lord providentially used this event to put them in contact with Paul, who shared their tent-making trade and may have led them to Christ (Acts 18:1–3). Obviously, his influence on them was profound. When it came time for the apostle to move on from Corinth, they accompanied him as far as Ephesus, where they remained for a number of years (Acts 18:18–19). He undoubtedly encouraged them to settle there.

The church in Ephesus was his base of operations in Asia Minor and continued to serve as a major stabilizing influence for the region. However, the church was itself unstable and needed mature, knowledgeable Christians (1 Tim. 1:3). The couple's home became a meeting place for worship and instruction (1 Cor. 16:19), and the couple faithfully instructed those who needed guidance, including a dynamic Jewish evangelist named Apollos (Acts 18:24–28).

Paul owed his life to the couple, who set aside their own safety for the sake of their friend. The apostle doesn't elaborate here, but they doubtless "risked their own necks" more than once. Both Corinth and Ephesus were major pagan worship centers, which suffered financially as a result of the growth of Christianity. Therefore, Gentile officials in both cities saw Christianity as a monster ready to devour everything they valued most and Paul as the head to cut off. Were it not for influential friends like Priscilla and Aquila, they might have succeeded.

Eventually, after Claudius was apparently murdered by his wife to ensure succession by Nero, the couple moved back to Rome. There, as in Corinth and Ephesus, they provided mature leadership for the growing body of believers and made their home a safe place for Christians to gather, fellowship, learn, and grow.

When pastors pray, couples like Priscilla and Aquila top their list!

## —16:5—

Apparently, Epaenetus joined Priscilla and Aquila when they returned to Rome. Paul calls him (literally) "the first fruits of Asia." It is possible that Paul came to the region and was delighted to find a small band of loosely connected believers struggling to survive. Epaenetus, as the first convert among them, would have been particularly appreciated by Paul. However, it is just as likely that Epaenetus was the first convert to Christ to whom Paul personally witnessed.

## —16:6–7—

Mary (an anglicized version of the Hebrew name Mariam) was a Jewish woman who "toiled much" on behalf of the church. We can only speculate as to what that means, but Paul apparently expects the believers in Rome to know the details of her service.

Paul greets Andronicus and Junias, whom he describes using four significant titles:

- "Kinsmen" most likely means Jewish (9:3).
- "Fellow prisoners" apparently refers to an unrecorded time the apostle was in imprisoned with these two believers.
- "Notable among the apostles" (literally) could mean they were considered apostles by the early church, or simply that they were highly regarded by the apostles. Some use this phrase to suggest that the two were considered "apostles" in a broader sense of the term. There were, of course, only twelve apostles designated by Christ Himself, but the early church also used the term "apostle" to designate anyone officially sent on official church business, such as Paul and Barnabas (Acts 13:1–3). Therefore, "apostle" in a wider sense of the term meant "evangelist" or "leading authority." Ultimately, we cannot use Paul's phrase to determine what official roles they fulfilled, if any, in the early church.

- "Had become in Christ before me" (literally) is self-explanatory. They were Christians before Paul.

Andronicus and Junias may have been two male ministry partners, like Paul and Barnabas or Paul and Silas. But it's also possible they were married believers, like Priscilla and Aquila. "Andronicus" is a male name, but the Greek form of "Junias" used by Paul can be either masculine or feminine. This is important to some, who use this verse to establish female leadership in the early church. If the two were apostles and Junias was female, then the implications are obvious. However, the debate is moot if Junias was male.

Unfortunately the passage is not clear enough to be helpful in theology. Junias could have been either male or female, and there is compelling evidence pointing in both directions. Furthermore, "notable among the apostles" is equally ambiguous. We are much better to read this as it was intended, as a heartfelt greeting from Paul to two people who shared some of his most difficult ordeals and most joyous victories in ministry.

## —16:8–15—

The next twenty names offer little information. Each of the apostle's comments is like the tip of a narrative iceberg. Beloved. Fellow worker. Approved in Christ. Kinsmen. Workers in the Lord. A choice man. Brethren. "Holy ones." We can only imagine what stories each remark could introduce. All we know for certain is that each name brings to mind a relationship the apostle cherishes and shares in common with the church in Rome.

## —16:16—

After commending Phoebe and greeting his many friends in Rome, Paul encourages them to greet one another with a "holy kiss." This is not an uncommon request of Paul; he places high value on this particular form of greeting (1 Cor. 16:20; 2 Cor. 13:12; 1 Thess. 5:26). However, it seems he stressed the importance of this custom in places where other forms of greeting—specifically the Roman handshake—were more common. We can only speculate as to why, but I believe the reason is threefold.

Paul encouraged the believers to fully engage the culture around them. They are to respect government authority, honor their neighbors, and enjoy their Christian liberty as they impact their communities. However, they must not become so absorbed by their societies as to lose their distinctiveness. The kiss was quintessentially an Eastern custom, especially among the Jews. I believe Paul wants to preserve this simple act of intimate greeting—a brief peck on the cheek—as a public symbol of unity and acceptance. As two men or two women bumped into one another in a public place, others would witness their kiss and eventually identify them as members of a curious and close bond, which they shared in the name of a man named "Jesus, the Christ."

Second, I believe Paul wants the Eastern kiss to remind believers living in the West of their origins. The "holy kiss," like the handshakes of secret societies, would reinforce their shared identity.

More than anything, this particular greeting is difficult to do with people who are at odds or whose intimacy is strained. I can shake hands with almost anyone, but there is no way I can kiss the cheek of a man I barely know. And I'm even less likely to kiss someone I do not respect. Paul's command would be powerful motivation for me to keep my relationships clear and close.

Unfortunately, advancements in technology have allowed us to stay in contact with one another like never before. With a free email account and access to a public terminal, almost anyone can send an instant letter to virtually anyone living anywhere on the planet. Most in North America and Europe can afford to carry a personal telephone, which can be used to call or text-message others around the clock and around the world. Yet, more and more people in these technologically advanced societies complain of loneliness.

Vance Packard wrote in 1972 that the United States had become "a nation of strangers." We still are—more than ever. The Gallup Poll continues to report an increasing trend of isolation and depression among people living in densely populated areas. Imagine that! People surrounded by people, yet feeling utterly alone.

People crave meaningful connection with others as much today as two thousand years ago. This is not to suggest we revive an antiquated custom or contrive a new one. However, we must find ways to accomplish the purpose of the "holy kiss."

Verse 16 is all about connection. Individuals are united meaningfully "in Christ," and congregations share that same bond.

As I reflect on these verses—which are too easily dismissed as we near the end of Paul's letter—I find several truths concerning the body of Christ illustrated.

*The body of Christ has variety within its unity.* Paul's close associates include singles, married couples, widows, and widowers. He greets men and women, slaves and social elites, new Christians and mature believers, Greeks, Romans, and Jews. He has met some in prisons, many in synagogues, several in marketplaces, a few in churches—yet all of them in the course of proclaiming Christ. They came from all over the empire from multiple backgrounds and traditions, but they all share one thing in common: salvation by grace alone, through faith alone, in Jesus Christ alone.

*The body of Christ is held together by those who serve in obscurity.* Phoebe was a unifying force in the church near Corinth and someone whom the Lord called to carry this monumentally important letter to Rome. Yet we know nothing more about her. Mary, Urbanus, Tryphaena and Tryphosa (twins perhaps?), and Persis are noted for their faithful labors. Nothing more is known of them, neither from Scripture nor any reliable historical documents. Priscilla and Aquila served with Paul in Corinth, stabilized the church in Ephesus, and undoubtedly did the same in Rome. Yet, again, we know nothing of them beyond these brief acknowledgments in Scripture. The twenty-seven names in this list represent countless others who quietly and profoundly enrich the body of Christ.

*The body of Christ is characterized by simple, down-to-earth love.* Paul's greetings are relatively unadorned considering the bond he shares with many of the individuals. Phoebe was crucial to the church in Cenchrea. He shared his vocation of tent-making and his ministry of disciple-making with Priscilla and Aquila in Corinth, Ephesus, and now Rome. He shared a dungeon with Andronicus and Junias, and labor with Mary, Urbanus, Tryphaena, Tryphosa, and Persis. He has shared history with these twenty-seven men and women, and his love for them transcends the need for flowery words. Instead, Paul uses words to *demonstrate* the value he holds for them rather than merely to *tell* of his feelings.

Paul's list of greetings reflects his vision for the local church. A congregation should be no less diverse than the community surrounding it, yet unified by singular devotion to their Savior. A congregation should be filled with people who desire to work, serve, share, and suffer without accolades. A congregation should be eager to express appreciation for one another for specific reasons that can be called to mind quickly. And a congregation should be so united in love that a kiss on the cheek would feel as natural as a hug or a handshake.

But don't kiss me if you don't love me.

## Application

### *The A, B, Cs of Authentic Affection*

Paul and his companions in Rome did not share a lukewarm love. The hardships and victories of ministry had bound their hearts together in a deep, abiding affection that neither time nor distance could diminish. He hoped this same kind of affection would bind the believers in Rome into an indivisible, tight-knit community. As a matter of fact, he would want the same for us today.

As I review the list of twenty-seven persons greeted or commended and then reflect on Paul's personal connection with each individual, I find that he had diligently applied the lessons he taught in 12:1 – 15:13. To help make these lessons easier to remember—and therefore apply—I have reduced them to four simple commands. Think of them as the A, B, Cs of love within the body of Christ.

**A.** *Accept one another.* Accept variety. Not only did God create people with diverse appearances, He gave us a broad range of opinions, values, interests, gifts, and abilities. Some think, eat, breathe, and dream missions. Many pursue opportunities to teach. Others cannot imagine devoting themselves to anyone other than special needs children. Still others are wonderful conduits of music. We need them all.

Moreover, we are a community of Christians at varying stages of growth and growing at different rates. We have brand-new Christians who still cuss (and some older Christians who cuss and try to hide it). We have people who've been in the church all their lives and many who are still discovering what life in the body is all about. We're a diverse family, not a collection of clones. Rejoice in variety, and accept—"receive unto yourself"—those who are unlike yourself.

**B.** *Become a servant.* Communities work best when we serve one another. Find something that needs doing or someone who needs help and don't hold back! If you aren't sure where to begin, find someone who's been around awhile and ask, "What can I do to help around here?" If you want to see a pastor faint, walk up and ask him. Most people want to find only the best fit for their gifts or the precise place to exercise their gifts without regard for the most pressing needs. Servants aren't picky.

**C.** *Cultivate esteem for others.* I use the word "esteem" in the archaic sense, meaning "to show value or worth." The best way to appreciate the worth of another is to treat him or her as you would a VIP.

Think of someone you greatly admire. For me, that might be Abraham Lincoln. If this great president were to enter my home, I would behave in a certain manner to express my immense respect for him. Because our attitudes tend to follow our actions, I can cultivate esteem for someone I don't even know by giving him or her the same VIP treatment I would offer Lincoln.

Cultivating esteem for some people will be easier than for others. Let me encourage you to concentrate on giving VIP treatment to those you might ordinarily avoid.

**D.** *Demonstrate your love.* Love without deeds is no better than cold indifference. It feels the same. Therefore, find ways to demonstrate love through acts of kindness. And if you're really up for a challenge, try expressing your love in a more tangible way. Men find this difficult, but we have to get over it.

Once, I was teaching a mid-week service at a church when the back door blew open and two rough looking guys walked in. One wore a sleeveless shirt, revealing a network of tattoos running down one arm. The other wore a leather Harley jacket and held a Nazi helmet under his arm. They walked heavily to the back seats and sat down with a loud thump. The guy with the sleeveless shirt never took off his sunglasses, and they both sat like statues with their arms folded.

After the service, the crowd mingled and talked. The pair of heavies made a beeline for me. The guy with the helmet said, "Your name Swindle?"

"Sure, that's me," I gulped.

"You the guy on the radio?"

"Yes, I'm probably the one you've heard."

At that point, he dropped his helmet and gave me a bone-crushing hug, lifting me straight off the ground. My feet dangled helplessly as I struggled to breathe. "Chuck, don't ever quit. You told me about Jesus and I want to thank you. I also want you to know *I love you, man!*"

After he put me down, his buddy walked up and gave me another painful hug. And I loved every minute with those two crusty guys. Their authentic demonstrations of unguarded love are exactly what we should be expressing each time we meet one another.

Take a few moments to review the A, B, Cs of authentic affection. Then close your eyes and imagine the people in your church faithfully carrying out these four commands—accepting one another without judgment, serving one another without pride, treating one another like VIPs, and freely expressing heartfelt fondness for one another. You'd have to shut off the lights and lock the doors to make them go home! Who wouldn't want to be a part of something that contagious?

If this is the kind of church you want to call home, take the lead; be the first. Become an example of authentic affection and praise those who join you. Ignore the frowning critics and genuinely smile down every sourpuss. Then see what effect it has on attendance.

## Boars in God's Vineyard (Romans 16:17–20)

> [17]Now I urge you, brethren, keep your eye on those who cause dissensions and hindrances contrary to the teaching which you learned, and turn away from them. [18]For such men are slaves, not of our Lord Christ but of their own appetites; and by their smooth and flattering speech they

deceive the hearts of the unsuspecting. [19]For the report of your obedience has reached to all; therefore I am rejoicing over you, but I want you to be wise in what is good and innocent in what is evil. [20]The God of peace will soon crush Satan under your feet.

The grace of our Lord Jesus be with you.

---

On June 15, 1520, Pope Leo X issued an official decree excommunicating Martin Luther. In it, he likened Christendom to a vineyard, planted by God and entrusted to Peter and his successors. He also likened Luther to a wild boar from the forest seeking to destroy and devour the vineyard. This is ironic, coming from a man who consumed the papal treasury within two years—not to support works of charity, as some pretend, but to surround himself with lavish abundance and to stage extravagant festivals. After Pope Leo X had swallowed the last morsel of worshipers' penance, he sold church positions off to the highest bidder. When every vacancy had been filled, he created more positions and sold them as well. Still, as the treasury shrank, the pontiff's appetite grew. Eventually, he reduced the Catholic Church's assumed role of dispensing grace to little more than a business transaction, most notably by selling indulgences as fast as they could be printed.

The corruption of Leo X was not new. There have always been boars who ravage God's vineyard. Jesus stood alone in opposition to hypocritical Pharisees and proud Sadducees. Paul warned the elders in Ephesus of wolves in their midst (Acts 20:29) and routinely confronted false teachers and deceivers throughout his ministry (Acts 13:6–11; 2 Cor. 11:11–15, 26; Gal. 2:4–5; Phil. 3:2; 1 Tim. 6:20; 2 Tim. 1:14–15; 2:16–18; 4:14). Much of John's writings were an answer to one kind of heresy or another, and near the end of his life he wrote letters to encourage churches to reject false teachers (1 John 4:1; 2 John 7–8; 3 John 9–11). Peter and Jude faced the same difficulties (2 Peter 2:1–3; Jude 4). So it should come as no surprise that the church in Rome was susceptible to boar-like intruders.

To prepare the Roman believers, Paul teaches them how to detect the presence of "boars" (16:17) and reveals their quintessential character traits (16:18). Fortunately, the congregation is strong, so his instruction on how to defend God's vineyard is brief and mostly takes the form of affirmation (16:19–20). His advice is succinct, which makes it especially valuable.

## —16:17—

Paul "urges" (*parakaleō*) the Romans only two other times in his letter. He urges them to present themselves as living sacrifices (12:1) and he urges them to pray that his plans for Spain will not be hindered (15:30). In this case, the apostle urges the congregation to examine itself for certain behavior. The term is *skopeō*, as in micro*scope* or tele*scope*. One uses these instruments to observe details. The whole congregation — not just its leaders — is to "scope" themselves for two deadly dangers: "dissensions" and "hindrances."

Some people have the uncanny ability to split a group into two factions and have them arguing in no time. It has been my experience to observe that divisive people are difficult to identify because they are masters of stealth. Whispering and private, one-on-one meetings are the tools of their trade. And worst of all, they don't even recognize themselves as dividers of people. They're just "trying to help" by offering advice wherever they can.

The best way to identify a creator of dissension is to take note of drama and then listen to the conversations that surround it. Before long, a name will surface in one incident that's common to the others. (Dividers are rarely satisfied with only one schism.)

Another indication of a "boar in the vineyard" is the development of "hindrances." The Greek word is *skandalon*, which we learned in the exposition of 14:13 is a trap. These people set theological traps that bait unwary Christians. Their teaching is attractive, yet contrary to the truth taught by Jesus and the people He personally trained. Today we have this truth inerrantly preserved for us in Scripture. Therefore, a "hindrance" is any doctrine or practice that Scripture does not support.

## —16:18—

Having identified the telltale signs that an intruder has entered the church, Paul exposes his or her true nature. Such people do not serve Christ because they are slaves to their own "appetites" ("bellies"). Their teaching — along with every other activity — benefits them personally. The payoff may be money, power, prestige, control, sympathy — anything that depravity craves. And to conceal their true intentions, they project a remarkably admirable image. They have mastered church vocabulary — a dialect I call "Christianese" — and have perfected the demeanor of a mature believer.

Divisive people and false teachers keep their people skills polished to a high gloss. They instinctively find trusting people in positions of influence and then play to their weaknesses. If it's pride, they flatter. If it's fear, they reinforce their sense of control. If it's insecurity, they make them feel important. If it's despair, they promise the impossible. Because the truth is often uncomfortable to hear, they avoid saying anything resembling the truth. And so the unwary are led away. By the time the lies are finally exposed, the loss is incalculable.

## —16:19–20—

Paul's letters to church leaders Timothy and Titus contain specific advice on how a pastor should deal with destructive people and false teachers. He emphasizes a pro-active stance in protecting the church. The guilty person must be confronted with his or her error and then, if repentance doesn't follow, he or she must be disciplined and, if necessary, separated from the congregation.

In this case, Paul is not addressing the leaders of a church but the congregation at large. Therefore his counsel is different. The primary responsibility of any congregation is obedience to the truths of Scripture. And in this regard, the Romans have earned an exemplary reputation among other churches.

Take note of his specific advice. They are to be "wise in what is good," meaning that knowledge and behavior are to be congruent. If you really believe something is true, your choices should adjust accordingly. In fact, Paul notes to his colleague Titus that the invariable characteristic of a false teacher is his or her failure to obey the truths of Scripture (Tit. 1:15 – 16).

Additionally, the congregation is to be "innocent in what is evil." The Greek word for "innocent" originally described city walls that had survived a siege. "Intact" or "unscathed" would be accurate synonyms. Evil will certainly attack and its assault will be intense; however, the walls of the congregation's integrity must hold.

While the leaders have a responsibility to confront divisive people and false teachers, the congregation does not. Wisdom and vigilance are all the church needs. A wise and wary congregation knows when the people have been divided and quickly recognizes the tactics of those who thrive on dissension. Then, the members can simply refuse to be divided or misled. Destructive people tend to move on when they lose their audience.

Because the church in Rome has always been strong in this regard, Paul assures his readers that God will soon defeat Satan, and His means will be the feet of His faithful followers.

God's vineyard will always attract boars. This has been true throughout the history of the church and will continue today. Therefore don't be surprised to discover a divisive person or false teacher in your midst. This doesn't necessarily reflect poorly on your congregation. What matters is how the members respond. Are they equipped to recognize the telltale signs of a divider? Have they learned to spot the error of a deceiver?

Here are four questions every member of a church should be trained to ask. Think of them as truth filters. Everything we hear should easily pass through all four.

"Does what I am hearing agree with Scripture?"

"Does what I am hearing honor my Lord and Savior, Jesus Christ?"

"Does what I am hearing help me become more godly?"

"Does what I am hearing cause me to think more highly of my fellow believers?"

Imagine how ineffective a divider or deceiver would become if everyone they encountered subjected everything they hear to those four tests. If every congregation were this wise and wary, boars would never devour God's vineyard.

## Application

### *How to Deal with Boars in God's Vineyard*

Anything worth protecting will eventually come under attack. But don't expect the assault to come from barbarians at the gate. More often, churches are subtly taken apart from within by those who divide people and spread false teaching, usually in hushed conversations, one person at a time. Ironically, these destroyers think they are accomplishing something good. French mathematician and Christian philosopher Blaise Pascal wrote, "Men never do evil so completely and cheerfully as when they do it from a religious conviction."

When boars invade God's vineyard, leaders must not remain passive. They must act swiftly, firmly, and decisively. Three words describe the best means of preserving a congregation from the destruction of divisive people and false teachers: observation, confrontation, and separation.

1. *Observation* (16:17). Like a shepherd who constantly scans the flock for predators, leaders must remain alert, watching for schisms, looking for deceivers, and listening for error. I'm not counseling a totalitarian approach to leadership, and paranoia would be counterproductive. Nevertheless, don't be surprised to discover a divisive person whispering in the shadows of your congregation. Every church has them . . . even healthy, growing churches.

2. *Confrontation* (3 John 10). Confrontation has become an unpleasant term in our vocabulary, perhaps because it is rarely done well. Confrontation is nothing more than bringing the truth of a situation out of the shadows and into the light by choosing to discuss it openly. This can be done tactfully by avoiding accusations, choosing to ask the responsible person some honest

questions instead. As facts are discussed and explanations are sought, truth will inevitably rise to the surface. And, thankfully, that's often enough. Divisive people and false teachers thrive on secrecy, so once their cover is blown, they usually back off. On occasion, they move on.

3. *Separation* (Titus 3:9–11). Sometimes divisive people and false teachers retreat for a time and then resume their destructive activity later. There are those who openly defy spiritual leaders, feeling they have enough support to usurp authority. Unfortunately, leaders must remove such destructive people from the congregation in order to preserve the integrity of the body. Boars, if allowed to run loose, bring disorder, promote distrust, and create serious messes.

Leaders rarely confront divisive people and false teachers, and even more rarely follow through by removing them. Sometimes they fear criticism; usually they unwisely hope the problem will resolve itself if ignored. They also fear that confrontation and separation will lead to the loss of some church members. In reality, leaders cannot prevent the loss of members either way. However, by acting swiftly and decisively, they can limit the damage. The longer they wait, the larger the rift will become and the larger the destruction will be.

If you are a leader in your church, someone appointed to shepherd the flock, don't hesitate when you spot a destructive person sowing discord or teaching error. Don't wait for problems to solve themselves. They won't. Confront swiftly and firmly, yet wisely. And then press on, doing what must be done to preserve unity.

If you are a member of a congregation, do whatever you can to support your leaders when they must accomplish this unpleasant task, even if you aren't aware of all the details. They need advocates — faithful and true friends in their corner. This is not something they enjoy, and they have undoubtedly exhausted every other option. Trust them to lead with integrity and then praise their courage. Leadership in any ministry is a lonely task filled with misunderstanding. Those who lead well deserve your loyal support.

## Lifting Up Friends and Glorifying God (Romans 16:21-27)

---

21Timothy my fellow worker greets you, and *so do* Lucius and Jason and Sosipater, my kinsmen.

22I, Tertius, who write this letter, greet you in the Lord.

23Gaius, host to me and to the whole church, greets you. Erastus, the city treasurer greets you, and Quartus, the brother.

24[The grace of our Lord Jesus Christ be with you all. Amen.]

---

²⁵Now to Him who is able to establish you according to my gospel and the preaching of Jesus Christ, according to the revelation of the mystery which has been kept secret for long ages past, ²⁶but now is manifested, and by the Scriptures of the prophets, according to the commandment of the eternal God, has been made known to all the nations, *leading* to obedience of faith; ²⁷to the only wise God, through Jesus Christ, be the glory forever. Amen.

---

When people describe the apostle Paul as they imagine him, adjectives usually include fearless, rugged, determined, passionate, prolific, and independent. My own childhood imagination had Paul tramping from town to town along the dotted line in the back of my Bible, traveling with nothing but a staff and a knapsack. I imagined a companion tagging along for the sake of company; first Barnabas, then Silas, then perhaps Dr. Luke and Timothy. But for the most part, I usually thought of Paul alone on the ministry trail.

A quick survey of Paul's letters paints a different picture. The apostle frequently stood alone on theological issues, but he was anything but independent or aloof. He usually traveled with an entourage that grew over time. By the time he wrote Romans toward the end of his third journey, Paul had no less than five serious ministers-in-training with him in Corinth and several others out on assignment (Silas, Luke, and Titus to name a few). When forced to travel ahead, he always waited for his group (e.g. Acts 17:16; 18:5), and when left alone during his second Roman imprisonment, he longed for companionship to the point of urgency (2 Tim. 4:9–11). Paul loved the people who labored alongside him. In fact, he depended on them. Having grown emotionally attached to his friends, his joy was diminished when they were not near.

This is as it should be. God did not create us to be alone or aloof. That's not to say we should be incapable of solitude; when left alone, Paul made good use of his time (Acts 17:10; 16–17; 18:1–4; 20:1–2). But collaboration fueled his enthusiasm and enlarged his ministry. He clearly preferred the company of others.

## —16:21–22—

After greeting a list of people in Rome Paul anticipated seeing (16:1–16) and after commending their internal strength (16:17–20), the apostle sends greetings from some of his top aides and closest friends.

Paul first met Timothy on his first missionary journey when visiting the towns of Lystra and Derbe (Acts 16:1–2), about one hundred miles from his own hometown of Tarsus. The young man impressed Paul so much that the apostle invited him to join the mission. By the time he completes this letter to Roman believers, Timothy has become one of his closest friends and among his most capable assistants.

Paul also names three other men who have joined the growing band of ministers. Lucius is probably one of the "prophets and teachers" ministering in Antioch who heard God's instructions to send out Paul and Barnabas (Acts 13:1). Paul first met Jason in Thessalonica, where he witnessed the man's bravery firsthand (Acts 17:5–9). And Sosipater joined the group when Paul ministered in Berea (Acts 20:4). Appropriately, Paul calls them "kinsmen," a term he reserves for Jews (9:3; 16:7, 11).

Paul permits his amanuensis, Tertius, to include his own greeting. It was common practice for Paul to have one of his assistants write out his thoughts for him. They have heard their mentor speak on a given subject dozens of times (perhaps hundreds in the case of Timothy) and could prepare a faithful draft with a little direction. Then, after a thorough edit by the apostle himself, his amanuensis would prepare the final draft using his best penmanship. Nevertheless, Paul frequently adds his own personal touch near the bottom of the Spirit-inspired documents (1 Cor. 16:21; Gal. 6:11; Col. 4:18; 2 Thess. 3:17; Philem. 19).

It would be wrong to say that his assistant "ghost wrote" a letter. The thoughts are 100 percent Paul's. He supervised, reviewed, and approved the actual wording, and he signed the document as his own. In time-honored tradition, he charged a trusted assistant with the actual task of drafting the document and penning the final product. In this case, the amanuensis is named Tertius, which means "third." Primus, Secundus, Tertius. His was a common name for a slave.

We can imagine the freed slave, "Third," feeling the thrill of writing Paul's theological magnum opus. We can imagine Tertius personally identifying with Paul's illustration of emancipated slaves receiving adoption papers from their Creator. Pause and picture in your mind this trusted assistant turning from the scroll to ask Paul, "May I add my greeting as well?" and the apostle responding, "Of course!"

*I, the freed slave, "Third," who pen this letter, greet you in the Lord.*
For my part, I *love* this personal touch!

—**16:23**—

During Paul's three months in Greece (Acts 20:2–3), he most likely used Corinth as his base of operations. His host is none other than a wealthy convert named Gaius, whom he personally baptized (1 Cor. 1:14). As Priscilla and Aquila did in

## Daddy Knows the Way

In 1944, I was ten years old and enjoying a summer vacation with my family on the gulf shore of Texas. Every year, my granddaddy allowed us to stay in his little bay cottage, a place that still holds wonderful memories for me. And one of the activities I enjoyed most was floundering with my dad.

If you've never floundered, let me describe the process. As night falls, flounder like to come close to the shore and lie still on the soft, sandy bottom, waiting for shrimp and mullet to swim by. So, you wade into the water up to your knees, carrying a Coleman lantern and a two-pronged spear, called a "gig." When you spot a flounder, you pause and "gig" it before it can swim off. Often, you walk a mile or more in the dark.

One particular moonless night, Dad and I walked slowly through the mud and sand away from the cottage, toward the point of the bay. I could hear my mom, brother, and sister laughing and playing games in the bay cottage a mile or so behind me as we walked deeper into the darkness. After we rounded the point, I could no longer hear their laughter or see the light of the cottage, and I was getting nervous.

"Daddy?"

"What son? Are you looking for flounder?"

"Yeah ... yeah Daddy, but you ... you know we can't see the cottage."

"I know, son, but we're going to be fine. Keep looking for flounder, okay? Sometimes when you gig a flounder, they flop and splash as you pull them up with the spear, and sometimes that cold water hits the hot lantern and the mantle goes out.

"We're going to get a big one here in a minute," he said. (Always the hopeful fisherman!)

"Daddy, when it throws its tail up, it's going to put the mantle out ... and we won't have any light."

He said, "Son, I've got a flashlight here."

"Daddy, are the batteries good in the flashlight?"

He's staring into the water, searching for flounder; I'm looking back around the point, hoping to catch a glimpse of the cottage.

"The batteries are good, son."

"Could we try them?"

That did it! My normally very-patient father reached the end of his tether. "NO, WE'RE NOT GOING TO TRY THEM, WE'RE *LOOKING FOR FLOUNDER!*"

After a long silence, I sheepishly asked, "Daddy, do you know where you are?"

"Yeah, I know where I am."

I believed him. I slipped my little ten-year-old fingers into his big hand. Once I did that, I never again looked back to see the lights of the cottage. He knew where he was and that was all that mattered; I felt safe with my hand in his.

Rome (16:3 – 5), Gaius allows his home to be the place where Christians met for worship, instruction, and fellowship.

Erastus is "the city treasurer," most likely of Corinth. City managers were often freed slaves who had attained a fair measure of wealth. His name means "beloved" and was a common choice of freed slaves who no longer wanted to be identified as merely a number. Most likely neither Erastus nor Gaius are the same people as those who traveled with Paul when he ministered in Ephesus (Acts 19:22, 29). Nevertheless, they are close friends and faithful advocates of Paul.

"Quartus" means "fourth." Like Tertius, he is probably a slave. Because he is grouped with Gaius and Erastus, we can assume he lives in Corinth and may have even served in the household of Paul's host. He must have brimmed with joy when Paul calls him "brother."

### —16:24—

While a majority of later manuscripts include this verse, it is relocated to 16:27 in some and is missing entirely from the oldest copies of the letter to the Romans. Therefore, it is likely a later addition. Nevertheless, the short benediction is in keeping with Paul's spontaneous style.

### —16:25–27—

The final chapter of Paul's letter can be divided into four sections. The first (16:1 – 16) personally greets people living in Rome. The second (16:17 – 20) encourages them to guard their vineyard from ravenous boars. The third (16:21 – 24) sent greetings from believers in Corinth. The final section (16:25 – 27) offers a benediction that praises the majesty of God.

As the apostle prepares to close his letter to the Romans, he sets aside his arguments, pushes doctrine to the background, turns his thoughts away from people, and gives full attention to the glory of God. These three verses form one long sentence, composed of several compound phrases, much like his opening line (1:1 – 7). The basic sense is, "Now to Him who is able to establish you ... be the glory forever." The words and phrases in between are anything but haphazard. Paul has carefully chosen each one to reflect the message of his letter and to ascribe them to the authorship of God.

"Now to Him who is able to establish you ..." identifies God as the sole source of stability and strength for the believer. While we are encouraged to engage in the

Holy Spirit's transforming work, we cannot transform ourselves. The Lord alone is able.

"… according to my gospel and the preaching of Jesus Christ …" The Lord establishes us in keeping with the promises of the gospel. Paul calls the good news "my gospel," not to claim authorship but to claim ownership. The gospel belongs to him because he has staked his own soul upon its truth. And the gospel is his to steward in keeping with God's calling (Rom. 2:16; 1 Tim. 1:11; 2 Tim. 2:8). Moreover, the good news of God's grace and His salvation through faith is centered on the person of Jesus Christ, and no one else.

"… according to the revelation of the mystery which has been kept secret for long ages past …" A *mysterion* is a divine truth not previously revealed. The "mystery" has nothing to do with secret information or mystical knowledge. The complete truth of Jesus Christ was not fully known until He rose from the dead and ascended to heaven. Now, it has been revealed in full, as summarized below:

> Christ died for our sins according to the Scriptures and He was buried. He paid the complete penalty for our sins on the cross and nothing else is needed to satisfy God's requirement for justice. Christ was miraculously and bodily raised from the dead to new life. He now offers that same eternal life to all who would receive it by grace through faith in Him. Those who receive God's free gift of eternal life will be raised to new life after death to be with Him forever. Those who reject this gift will spend eternity in torment.

"… but now is manifested …" What is so simple, clear, and available now was a mystery for many centuries before Christ revealed it. Paul counts it his privilege to proclaim this mystery now unveiled.

"… and by the Scriptures of the prophets, according to the commandment of the eternal God, has been made known to all the nations …" The gospel has always been a part of God's plan and can be traced through the Scriptures all the way back to the writings of Moses. Now, the partial message entrusted to the Jews has been revealed in full and made available to every race, culture, creed, nation, language, and generation. How gracious of our God!

"… leading to obedience of faith …" With this phrase, the apostle brings his letter—and the gospel—full circle. Both have the "righteousness of God" as their ultimate end. When Paul first mentioned the gospel, he declared, "For in it the righteousness of God is revealed from faith to faith; as it is written, 'But the righteous man shall live by faith'" (Rom. 1:17). The gospel has not achieved its complete purpose until those who believe and all of creation again, as it did in the beginning, exists in harmony with the goodness of God.

" … to the only wise God, through Jesus Christ, be the glory forever." The Lord created the world, filled it, organized it, and gave everything purpose. He then created humanity—male and female—in His own image and placed them in the world to live and enjoy its abundance. And He gave them a singular purpose, which the Larger Westminster Catechism states correctly: "to glorify God, and fully to enjoy him forever."[4] Jesus Christ made this possible, and He will consummate the restoration of all things to again reflect the glory of God.

And to this, I join Paul in declaring a passionate "Amen"!

---

NOTES: The Community of God (Romans 15:14–16:27)

1. Aristophanes, *Acharnenses*, 687.
2. Everett F. Harrison, "Romans," *Expositor's Bible Commentary*, ed. Frank E. Gaebelein (Grand Rapids: Zondervan, 1976), 10:155.
3. Gerhard Kittel and Gerhard Friedrich, eds., *Theological Dictionary of the New Testament: Abridged in One Volume*, trans. Geoffrey W. Bromiley (Grand Rapids: Eerdmans, 1985), 645.
4. *The Westminster Standards* (Philadelphia: Great Commission Publications, 1986), 35.

## Share Your Thoughts

**With the Author:** Your comments will be forwarded to the author when you send them to *zauthor@zondervan.com*.

**With Zondervan:** Submit your review of this book by writing to *zreview@zondervan.com*.

## Free Online Resources at
## www.zondervan.com

**Zondervan AuthorTracker:** Be notified whenever your favorite authors publish new books, go on tour, or post an update about what's happening in their lives at www.zondervan.com/authortracker.

**Daily Bible Verses and Devotions:** Enrich your life with daily Bible verses or devotions that help you start every morning focused on God. Visit www.zondervan.com/newsletters.

**Free Email Publications:** Sign up for newsletters on Christian living, academic resources, church ministry, fiction, children's resources, and more. Visit www.zondervan.com/newsletters.

**Zondervan Bible Search:** Find and compare Bible passages in a variety of translations at www.zondervanbiblesearch.com.

**Other Benefits:** Register yourself to receive online benefits like coupons and special offers, or to participate in research.

**ZONDERVAN**®

**ZONDERVAN**.com/
**AUTHORTRACKER**
*follow your favorite authors*